IN MIXED COMPANY

Small Group Communication

FOURTH EDITION

J. Dan Rothwell

Cabrillo College

WADSWORTH

THOMSON LEARNING ™

Australia • Canada • Mexico • Singapore • Spain
United Kingdom • United States

WADSWORTH

THOMSON LEARNING

Publisher: Earl McPeek
Acquisitions Editor: Steve Dalphin
Market Strategist: Laura Brennan
Developmental Editor: Laurie Runion
Project Editor: G. Parrish Glover
Art Director: Burl Sloan

Production Manager: Christopher A. Wilkins
Cover Photo: Charles Krebs, The Stock Market
Cover Printer: Lehigh Press, Inc.
Compositor: UG / GGS Information Services, Inc.
Printer: R.R. Donnelley, Crawfordsville

For more information about our products,
contact us at:
**Thomson Learning Academic
Resource Center
1-800-423-0563**
For permission to use material from this text,
contact us by:
Phone: 1-800-730-2214
Fax: 1-800-730-2215
Web: http://www.thomsonrights.com

Library of Congress Catalog Card Number:
00-102052

ISBN: 0-15-507000-2

Asia
Thomson Learning
60 Albert Street, #15-01
Albert Complex
Singapore 189969

Australia
Nelson Thomson Learning
102 Dodds Street
South Melbourne, Victoria 3205
Australia

Canada
Nelson Thomson Learning
1120 Birchmount Road
Toronto, Ontario M1K 5G4
Canada

Europe/Middle East/Africa
Thomson Learning
Berkshire House
168-173 High Holborn
London WC1 V7AA
United Kingdom

Latin America
Thomson Learning
Seneca, 53
Colonia Polanco
11560 Mexico D.F.
Mexico

Spain
Paraninfo Thomson Learning
Calle/Magallanes, 25
28015 Madrid, Spain

Preface

In Mixed Company has shown a substantial increase in popularity and acclaim with each successive edition. It has been used by more than 75,000 students at hundreds of colleges and universities. Consequently, for the fourth edition, I have preserved the essence of previous versions.

The central unifying theme, that cooperation in small groups is usually superior to competition, remains and has been expanded somewhat. Many textbooks on small group communication mention the need for and desirability of human cooperation and teamwork. They may even include a few pages on the subject. Such brief treatment, however, can provide no more than a superficial recipe for producing cooperation. Establishing cooperation and teamwork in small groups is a challenging, complex, sophisticated process that, I believe, requires more than a cursory treatment. The history of race relations in the United States, labor/management strife, and the so-called "gender war" make this point apparent. *In Mixed Company* thoroughly addresses the theme of *cooperation in small groups*. Specific instruction supported by extensive research is provided to help students build cooperation. You will not find a more thorough treatment of this essential theme in any small group textbook.

The *communication competence model* continues to guide discussions of key small group concepts and processes. The communication competence model is one of our discipline's unique contributions to understanding and improving human behavior. The model, as before, is thoroughly integrated throughout the text, not merely discussed in the first chapter and then dropped entirely or given only passing mention in later chapters.

Systems theory also remains as a key theoretical component of the text. The mere mention of "theory" can produce glazed looks and slumped posture from some students in introductory courses. Thus, I have made a special effort to explain systems theory in a way that will keep students' bodies upright and their eyelids from slamming shut. I have chosen to concentrate on this primary theory because it provides a framework for analysis and useful insights for students as they participate in group transactions. Offering a laundry list of theories that provide no central focus and may never be mentioned usefully in later chapters seems more burdensome than beneficial in a first small group course.

Finally, an extensive discussion and analysis of power in small groups continues to separate *In Mixed Company* from other textbooks. *Power* is inherent in all small group transactions. Power is a central underlying element in small group conflict, teamwork, decision making, problem solving, normative behavior, roles, and leadership. It is perplexing that most small group textbooks give scant attention to the integral role power plays in every group. It isn't that other textbooks never mention power. They just diminish its importance by providing little or no direct focus on the subject. Power thus becomes more an afterthought than an integral small group concept.

Although I have maintained the essence of previous versions of *In Mixed Company*, this fourth edition goes far beyond mere cosmetic changes. The key revisions made in this edition consist of the following:

1. All chapters have been thoroughly *updated.* One hundred and fifty-five references, all dated in the 1990s or the year 2000, have been added and numerous examples and many older references have been replaced with more current ones.
2. *"Closer Look"* segments, a critically acclaimed feature of the previous three editions, have been updated where warranted. A few have been deleted. I have also added five new Closer Looks. They discuss high school cliques, leadership and teambuilding, contrasting leadership styles, technology and the bias of speed, and Murphy's Law.
3. *Gender,* a subject that received considerable attention in the third edition, gains additional coverage with updated and expanded "Focus on Gender" segments. These segments are in addition to the numerous shorter, less-detailed references to gender already integrated throughout the text.
4. *Culture,* a subject that also received considerable focus in the third edition, is given even greater attention. I have organized extensive discussions of culture and ethnicity issues into nine "Focus on Culture" segments distributed across most chapters. Focus on Culture segments are in addition to the numerous shorter, less-detailed references to culture-related discussions integrated into all chapters.
5. *Ethics,* a subject given moderate emphasis in the third edition, has become a more central and important topic. Ethics has been incorporated directly into the communication competence model in Chapter One, with applications made in later chapters.
6. *Electronic technology* (e.g., the Internet, electronic brainstorming, electronic meetings, information overload, virtual groups, and technological bias and decision making) receives added emphasis. Integrating this material throughout the text seemed preferable to treating electronic technology in a final chapter where it might become expendable due to time constraints at the end of a term.
7. The treatment of *critical thinking,* previously covered extensively in Chapters Six and Seven and Appendix B, is expanded slightly to incorporate the Internet more completely.
8. A new section on intrinsic and extrinsic *motivation* has been added to the material on rewards as a power resource (Chapter Eight).
9. At the request of several reviewers, material on *listening* (Chapter Four), *anger management* (Chapter Ten), and *verbal and nonverbal communication* has been added or expanded. Some small group textbooks provide a separate chapter on one or more of these subjects. Such an approach is certainly defensible, but it is

not one that I prefer. I prefer instead to keep the focus of this textbook squarely on small group communication, not drift into more general communication discussions, so I have blended these subjects into the appropriate small group concepts and processes.

10. *Maintaining reader interest* has always been a paramount concern of mine. I continue to look for ways to boost the readability of *In Mixed Company*. With the impressive increase in research and knowledge on group communication, it would be easy to expand *In Mixed Company* into a bloated textbook the size of the New York City phone book. Since a small group text of such prodigious size, however, would probably read about as interestingly as a phone book, I have instead worked hard to streamline, not expand this text. Thus, I have removed redundant material, excised excessive detail, shortened chapters, and replaced commonplace examples with sharper, more student-relevant illustrations.

11. The size of the *glossary* has been increased significantly. Many terms appear in the glossary for the first time, and definitions for other terms have been made more concise and precise to assist students' comprehension.

For the third edition, the suggestion was made that I write a separate chapter on the influence of gender and culture/ethnicity on small groups. After careful consideration I decided not to follow the advice. I agree with Broome and Fulbright's (1995) viewpoint that a separate chapter does not fully integrate these subjects into discussions of small group process. Since gender and culture are relevant to issues discussed in *every* chapter of this text, integrating discussions of gender and culture into each chapter seems preferable to setting aside such discussions and reserving them for a later chapter. Such integration also reduces redundant references to material previously covered in earlier chapters. All reviewers of the third edition seemed satisfied with my decision, so I have continued integrating material on gender and culture into all ten chapters for this fourth edition.

OBJECTIVES FOR STUDENTS

I have three paramount objectives for students: that the material presented be clear and comprehensible, that the text be pragmatic, and that the text be highly readable. Regarding the first objective—*clarity and comprehension*—I have included an outline prior to each chapter. "Focus Questions" precede most major sections of each chapter to direct your attention to key points. I have integrated hundreds of examples—most of them actual occurrences rather than contrived instances—to illustrate concepts. A number of extended examples discussed in many Closer Look segments will aid your comprehension of the significant concepts discussed in each chapter. I also have included tables, each one called a "Second Look," that act as succinct summaries of complicated and/or detailed material. I am told by my students that these are very useful when studying for exams. Finally, a glossary of key terms for quick reference appears at the end of the text. Terms that are **boldfaced** in each chapter are included in the glossary.

I have attempted to realize my second objective—*pragmatism*—in a couple of ways. Recognizing that theory helps us understand how groups work but is limited unless it is made practical, I have chosen a wide range of examples and illustrations that show how the theory makes sense in real life. I have not simply described what competent communication is, but have also indicated, step-by-step, how you can become a competent communicator in groups.

My third objective—*readability*—has been no small challenge. There have been times when watching the weather channel seemed preferable to writing another word, phrase, sentence, or paragraph. Nevertheless, the advice of Samuel Johnson cannot be ignored: "What is written without effort is in general read without pleasure." My chief effort has been to write a different kind of textbook—one that might stir interest, not act as a sedative. The risk I run in telling you this, obviously, is that you may respond, "And that's the best you could do?" Alas, yes. Whatever the shortcomings of this work, I was ever mindful of my audience.

Textbooks are not meant to read like spy thrillers, but they certainly shouldn't read like instructions for filling out your income tax forms, either. Some textbooks should come with a warning: "Beware! Reading this text may induce a coma." Unlike calculus, which I have no idea how to make interesting, human communication should be a fascinating subject for most people. I have made a genuine attempt to excite interest in a subject—competent communication in groups—that plays such an integral part in our lives.

Toward this end, I have searched in obvious and not-so-obvious places for the precise example, the amusing illustration, the poignant instance, and the dramatic case to enhance reader enjoyment. I also have attempted to enliven the writing style by incorporating colorful language and lively metaphors that bring interesting images to mind. Finally, where applicable, I have related stories that I hope will invite the reader to turn the pages and become interested in the subject of this textbook. Easily half of the energy I expended on this project was spent on readability.

OBJECTIVES FOR INSTRUCTORS

My objectives for this text are somewhat different for instructors than they are for students. For instructors, <u>my principal objectives are that the text be theoretically and conceptually sound, current, innovative yet user-friendly, and logically organized.</u>

The first objective—*soundness of theory and concept*—has been achieved according to reviewers of all three editions. I appreciate their affirmation and guidance. I was spared a few embarrassments thanks to their conscientious critiques.

The second objective—*currency*—can be demonstrated less subjectively than the first. More than half of the almost 650 references are citations from the 1990s and beyond. I have incorporated many of the latest findings and conclusions from recent research in my discussion of group communication concepts and processes. In all subject areas I have searched energetically for the very latest research and insights. I have also referred to numerous recent events to illustrate key points.

The third objective—*innovative yet user-friendly*—was no small challenge. I have attempted to achieve this objective in several ways. One way is the use of the "perpendicular pronoun" **I**. I recognize that this is not standard academic practice, yet I feel that first-person singular speaks more directly and personably to students than the more bloodless and oblique style of writing commonly used in textbooks.

A second way is the use of a more *narrative or storytelling style* than is usual in textbook writing. Research (Fernald, 1987) confirms that students prefer the narrative style and benefit greatly from it in both comprehension and recall of information. The Closer Looks, vivid examples, and the personal experiences sewn into the fabric of the text are narrative in nature.

Several activities included in the Instructor's Manual provide a third way I have attempted to be innovative yet user-friendly. Having tired long ago of using excellent but shopworn group exercises such as "Lost on the Moon" and "Winter Survival," my colleagues and I have replaced the classic case studies, simulations, and structured experiences with original, and we think better, alternatives. We call your attention especially to the "Group Polarization and Pressure," "Group Synergy," "Group Size," "Abandon Ship," "Straw Bridge," and "Power Carnival" exercises as examples of enormously successful classroom-tested original group communication exercises that accompany this text.

One innovative testing feature highlighted in the Instructor's Manual is the *Cooperative Exam* in both objective and essay form. My colleagues and I have had great success incorporating cooperative learning strategies into the group communication course. A Cooperative Group Examination is one way simultaneously to test students and to apply the text material on building cooperation.

I have also produced a videotape entitled *Working Together*, shot in documentary style, which illustrates several key classroom activities (e.g., "Power Carnival," "Group Synergy"). This video can serve either as a substitute for having your students do the activities or as a visual guide showing how to conduct these very successful exercises in your class. The videotape is available as an ancillary to the text.

The final objective—*logical organization*—was also a challenge. Since students typically work in groups early in a term, all of the material in the entire textbook is almost immediately relevant to their needs, yet the material cannot be covered usefully in a few short weeks. Thus, some subjects must be covered sooner than others. Although there is no ideal organizational pattern, my schema for the chapter sequence is quite simple. I begin with a theoretical foundation (Chapters One and Two), progress to how groups form and develop (Chapter Three), then proceed to a discussion of how to establish the proper climate for the group to work effectively (Chapter Four). I then explain what roles group members are likely to play (Chapter Five) and discuss decision making/problem solving—the primary work to be performed by most groups, with special focus on critical thinking (Chapters Six and Seven). Finally, I explore in substantial detail the close connection between power and conflict

(Chapters Eight, Nine, and Ten). I can see other ways of organizing this same material, but the order I have chosen works well for me, students seem satisfied with the sequence of topics, and reviewers have praised the organization.

ACKNOWLEDGMENTS

My sincere thanks are extended to all those who reviewed this edition of *In Mixed Company*. A few reviewed it several times, proving that some of my colleagues haven't learned how to exercise their assertiveness and say no. I thank Robert Arundale, University of Alaska; Robert Burke, Bellevue Community College; Blanton Croft, Northern Virginia Community College; Risa Dickson, California State Univeristy—San Bernadino; Rebecca Johns, Weber State University; Derek Lane, University of Kentucky; Nancy Mahon, The Pennsylvania State University; Jan McKissick, Butte College; Ingrid Peternel, College of DuPage; and Gisele Tierney, Portland State University.

I offer a special belated thanks to Ellen Arden-Ogle of Cosumnes River College. It is a tribute to her humility that she continued to offer insightful comments for each edition of *In Mixed Company* even though, because of an oversight, she received no acknowledgment for her many contributions to the success of this project.

Those who deserve my gratitude for reviewing *In Mixed Company* in previous editions are: Debbie Analauren, Cabrillo College; Carole Barry, Cabrillo College; Sheryl Bowen, Villanova University; Judith Bunyi, Iowa State University; Sandy Robinson-Cadman, College of St. Rose; Lyall Crawford, Weber State University; Barbara Eakins, Wright State University; Betty Ensminger, Mission College; Barbara Gordon, Iowa State University; Joseph Hemmer, Carroll College; Michael Holmes, Purdue University; Larry Hugenberg, Youngstown State University; Pam Joraanstad, Glendale Community College; James Keaten, University of Northern Colorado; Sharon Kirk, La Salle University; Pamela McWherter, University of Alaska; Dan Millar, Indiana State University; Andrea Mitnick, Pennsylvania State University—Delaware City; Charlotte Morrison, Cabrillo College; Mark Murphy, Everett Community College; Michael Nicolai, University of Wisconsin—Stout; Ellen Arden-Ogle, Cosumnes River College; Gregg Phifer, Florida State University; Charlotte Tuckie Pillar, College of DuPage; Edwina Stoll, De Anza College; Claire Sullivan, University of Maine; Vic Wall, Cleveland State University; Marcy Wieland, Cabrillo College; and Mary Wiemann, Santa Barbara City College; Janet Yeddes, West Chester University. Many of the best features of this text resulted from suggestions of the reviewers.

Special thanks go to Topsy Smalley and Georg Romero, reference librarians at Cabrillo College, who located references and material that would have remained forever hidden from me if I hadn't the benefit of their herculean efforts. I continue to be amazed by their skills and unflagging energy, and I never cease appreciating their cheerful attitude when they assist faculty.

My gratitude is also extended to Steve Dalphin, Acquisitions Editor; Laurie Runion, Developmental Editor; Laura Brennan, Market Strategist; Laurie Bondaz and Parrish Glover, Project Editors; Burl Sloan, Art Director; Chris

Wilkins, Production Manager, and Cheri Throop, Permissions Editor. It is a pleasure to work with such capable and pleasant professionals.

Finally, I express my heartfelt gratitude to my colleagues in the Speech department at Cabrillo College. You are a continuing source of inspiration for me and you demonstrate daily that cooperation and teamwork can be practical realities, not merely wishful thinking.

ABOUT THE AUTHOR

J. Dan Rothwell is chair of the Speech Communication Department at Cabrillo College. He has a B.A. in American History from the University of Portland (Oregon), an M.A. in Rhetoric and Public Address, and a Ph.D. in Communication Theory. His M.A. and Ph.D. are both from the University of Oregon. He is the author of three other books: *In the Company of Others: An Introduction to Communication, Telling It Like It Isn't: Language Misuse and Malpractice,* and (with James Costigan) *Interpersonal Communication: Influences and Alternatives.*

Professor Rothwell encourages feedback and correspondence from both students and instructors regarding *In Mixed Company.* Anyone so inclined may communicate with him by e-mail at darothwe@cabrillo.cc.ca.us or by snail-mail care of the Speech Communication Department, Cabrillo College, Aptos, CA 95003. Dr. Rothwell may also be reached by phone at 1-831-479-6511.

Contents

Communication Competence

If you want to find out what people think about groups, ask them. I have. I've passed out a questionnaire in several of my small group communication classes. The results were quite revealing. The great majority of students had negative things to say. Comments included: "If God had ordered a committee to create the world, it would still be discussing proposals." "For every group I've enjoyed, there have been a dozen groups looking to make my life miserable—and succeeding." "Working in groups is like eating tofu. I'm told it's good for me, but it makes me gag." "I hate groups. I hate group assignments. I hate teachers who require group assignments. Take the hint."

Surveys in the business world duplicate the reactions of my students. A survey by Robert Half International, a consulting firm, (as cited in Alexander, 1989) found that executives spend approximately twenty-one weeks a year in group meetings and six of those weeks' worth of meetings were considered a total waste of time. That's equivalent to a year of fruitless effort in less than a decade. Stephen Winston, a time-management consultant and author, observes, "Most people I've talked to in the ranks see meetings as a species of event that's a drag" (Alexander, 1989, p. 1PC). Avid baseball fan and conservative columnist George Will, commenting on what he dislikes about football, remarks, "Football combines the two worst features of American life. It is violence punctuated by committee meetings" (Fitzhenry, 1993, p. 426).

Sorensen (1981) coined the term **grouphate** to describe how loathsome the group experience is for many people. Sorensen's research supports the view expressed by my students and business executives. She claims that most individuals do not like or enjoy working in groups.

Her most interesting result, however, <u>shows a direct relationship between the grouphate phenomenon and communication competence</u>. Those individuals least hostile to working in groups have the most instruction in effective group communication. Unfortunately, most people do not receive the requisite training in group communication, so grouphate flourishes. When we lack the training and thus the necessary knowledge and skills to function competently, we are inclined to avoid group membership (Leary, 1983), making any improvement in our attitudes about groups unlikely.

Groups are inescapable unless you plan to live your life alone in the cloistered confines of a cave like some out-of-touch survivalist. Most of you spend a substantial portion of your daily lives in groups of one sort or another. College students list as many as twenty-four groups that they belong to with eight as about average (Brilhart and Galanes, 1998). Even if you cared to try, you cannot escape groups. Your family is a group. So are athletic and debate teams; church and study groups; fraternities and sororities; clubs, boards, councils, and task forces; policy, executive, and ad hoc committees; discussion and class project groups; Internet chat groups; quality control circles and circles of friends; and personal growth, self-help, and therapy groups of almost infinite variety. This list could easily be doubled or tripled.

<u>Groups are inescapable because they are essential to our society</u>. As Frey (1994) observes, "The small group is clearly the tie that binds, the nucleus that holds society together" (p. ix). McCann and Margerison agree, "Today's business environment is so complex and in such a continual state of change that

success often depends on the outputs of teams or work groups rather than the efforts of a single person" (as cited in Cathcart & Samovar, 1996, p. 50).

Reliance on groups will increase, not diminish, in the future. As the first decade of the new millenium unfolds, it is predicted that nearly half of U.S. employees will participate in self-managed work teams (Freeman, 1996). The American Association for the Advancement of Science recommends that "the collaborative nature of science and technological work should be strongly reinforced by frequent group activity in the classroom" (as cited in Wooley, 1990, p. 32). The National Council of Teachers of English, the National Council of Teachers of Mathematics, and the National Communication Association also recommend frequent group activity in the college classroom.

Advances in computers and electronic technology will not slow the trend toward groups—quite the contrary. As Berge (1994) explains, "Electronic discussion groups will play an ever increasing role within the information culture. Netgroups often serve as powerful tools in the retrieval and exchange of information, bringing together persons with similar interests regardless of geographic distance or the time constraints dictated by face-to-face meetings" (p. 111). Lipnack and Stamps (1997) note, "In the coming decades, most people will work in virtual teams for at least some part of their jobs" (p. 1). A **virtual team** is a small group whose members interact by means of electronic technologies, not face-to-face, oftentimes across vast distances and time zones (Lipnack and Stamps, 1997).

Groups are here to stay. Competent communication probably won't transform grouphate into grouplove where dislike of group members is replaced with warm fuzzy feelings toward them. Since so much of your life revolves around groups, however, learning to communicate competently in this arena and thereby maximizing the benefits of group participation for yourself and others does seem like a worthwhile and practical goal.

The central purpose of this textbook, then, is to teach you how to be a competent, skillful communicator in groups. This purpose presupposes, of course, that there is much for you to learn. Because we all have been communicating for years, it may be tempting to conclude that there is relatively little for you to learn about communicating in groups. Experience, however, isn't always an effective teacher. Sometimes experience teaches us bad habits and misinformation (note the myths discussed in the next section). I will not presume to tell you what you do and don't know about small group communication. That is for you to assess, perhaps with the help of your instructor. When making this initial self-assessment, however, please consider two points.

First, we as Americans have a common tendency to overestimate our present knowledge and skills on a broad range of subjects. A survey by the Discovery Health Channel and *Newsweek* found that only 10% of respondents thought they were poorly informed about health-related matters ("How America," 1999). When given a test on basic health facts, however, only 10 of the 20 test questions were answered correctly by more than half of these same respondents. One study (Brownell, 1990) asked 144 business managers to rate their listening skills. Ninety-four percent saw themselves as "good" or "very good" listeners and no one chose "poor" or "very poor." Their employees disagreed. In another study, 25% of subjects ranked themselves in the top 1% of the population when asked about their ability to get along with others, and a scant 2% ranked their leadership abilities as below average. College instructors are not immune to these generous self-assessments. Ninety-four percent of university professors think they outperform their colleagues (as cited in Gilovich, 1991).

These figures are statistically nonsensical. Twenty-five percent can't logically be in the top 1% of anything, and 94% can't perform better than everyone else. Nevertheless, our cultural value of strong individualism, a subject for later exploration, encourages rosy self-assessments.

Second, consider the **hindsight bias** (Aronson, 1999). This is the "I-knew-it-all-the-time" effect. We tend to overestimate our prior knowledge once we have been told the correct answers. Thus, we may tend to view competent communication as "common sense" once we have received communication training. If, however, it is just common sense, why does miscommunication occur so often? Between half and three-quarters of teams in organizations, for example, fail to achieve their goals (Ju & Cushman, 1995), and between 80% and 90% of teams have significant difficulty performing effectively (Buzaglo & Wheelan, 1999). A principal reason that most teams struggle is lack of training in how to make teams work effectively (Goleman, 1998). The hindsight bias convinces us after receiving training that we knew everything already. The simple way to test this, of course, is to pose a question before training is received. For instance, consider the question, "How do you build a team so members will work together cooperatively and effectively?" Write down your answer for future reference, and be very specific. See if your answer written *now* makes as much sense *after* you have finished reading this text. Research shows that the answer to this question and its translation into actual practice is complicated and not well understood by most people.

Learning requires a degree of humility, a willingness to recognize and address our shortcomings. To paraphrase Alfred Korzybski, no one knows everything about anything. We all have more to learn. I invite you to approach this text, not with an attitude of contentment with your knowledge and skills (whatever their level), but with a strong desire to learn more and to improve your communication with others.

In this chapter, I will lay the theoretical groundwork for a communication competence approach to groups. My objectives are:

1. to correct some common misconceptions regarding the human communication process,
2. to explain what communication is, and
3. to identify broadly what constitutes competent communication.

MYTHS ABOUT COMMUNICATION

Before I tackle the question, "What is communication?" and then more specifically, "What is competent communication?" let me sweep out some of the musty misconceptions many people have stored in their intellectual attics regarding the communication process. As American humorist Will Rogers once remarked, "It isn't what we don't know that gives us trouble, it's what we know that ain't so" (Fitzhenry, 1993, p. 243). Foolishness springs from holding firmly to indefensible myths. Consider just three myths widely promulgated in recent years that merit the trash heap.

Myth 1: Communication Is a Panacea

Communication has been packaged as a panacea, a cure-all for almost anything that ails us. Communication has been sold as the magic elixir, hawked by con artists, gurus with gimmicks, pop psychologists practicing without licenses, and all sorts of profiteers looking to make a fast buck with fast talk.

Communication improvement is not the magical answer to all our woes. Sometimes more communication aggravates differences between people and exposes qualities in others we may find unappealing. Active listening may reveal truths that make it impossible for us to remain in a group. Sometimes groups dismantle, not because the communication is poor, but because members have personalities that severely clash or because they have contradictory visions for the group.

Communication is a tool that, in the possession of someone knowledgeable and skillful, can be used to help solve most problems that arise in groups. Communication, however, is not an end in itself but merely a means to an end. You will not solve every conceivable problem in groups by learning to communicate more effectively, because not all group problems are communication based.

Myth 2: Communication Can Break Down

Communication does not break down (Ruben 1978). Machines break down; they quit, and if they belong to me they do so with amazing regularity. Human beings continue to communicate even when they may wish not to do so. The view that communication breakdowns occur comes from a recognition that we do not always achieve our goals through communication. But failure to achieve our goals may occur even when communication between the parties in conflict is exemplary. So where's the breakdown?

We sometimes draw the mistaken conclusion that disagreement constitutes a communication breakdown. I may understand your message perfectly, however, but simply dislike what I'm hearing. In this case there is a difference of opinion, not a communication breakdown.

Myth 3: Communication Is Merely Skill Building

The skills orientation to communication assumes that if I learn a few magical communication skills, I will become a much better communicator. This skills-without-relevant-knowledge approach to communication, so prevalent in how-to guides filling the self-help section of local bookstores, calls to mind the story of a gorilla. This gorilla amazed everyone with his ability to drive a golf ball consistently more than 400 yards. When his trainer proposed that the gorilla be allowed to compete against professionals in a golf tournament, a chorus of objections arose, until one of the golfers happened to observe the gorilla play a practice round. Not only did the gorilla drive the ball more than 400 yards on his opening drive, landing on the edge of the first green about fifteen feet from the hole, but his next shot also traveled more than 400 yards. The gorilla did not know when to use his driving skill and when to give it a rest. He had been taught a skill separate from knowledge of the game.

Communication involves much more than learning a few isolated skills. Without understanding the complexities of the communication process, no amount of skills training will be meaningful, and may be harmful. Attention to skills development isolated from adequate knowledge of complex relationship patterns can jeopardize the physical well-being of a spouse or partner embroiled in a violent relationship (Whitchurch and Pace, 1993). Merely teaching the skill of assertiveness to a battered woman, for example, without addressing the volatile and often unpredictable circumstances of abusive relationships, could prove fatal for the abused woman and her children (O'Leary et al., 1985). Likewise, assertiveness with a mugger could put you in the hospital emergency room—or the morgue. Assertiveness with an autocratic boss may get you fired or demoted to a position equivalent to cleaning up after parading elephants. One skill doesn't fit all circumstances.

Teaching communication skills without knowledge, without a well-researched theoretical map guiding our behavior, is like constructing a house without a carefully developed set of blueprints. All the skills necessary to build a house won't be very useful without a thoughtful plan to guide the construction and prevent collapse of the structure. The blueprint I offer you as a guide to learning how to communicate and to function effectively in small groups is the communication competence model presented later in this chapter.

COMMUNICATION DEFINED

At this point I have indicated what communication is not. What it is can be seen clearly by first considering several fundamental principles.

Focus Questions

how what is said defines / Redefines group.

1. How are content and relationship dimensions of messages different from each other? *actually said*
2. "Communication is a process." What does this mean?

changes in events / relationships are part of continuous flow.

Communication Is Transactional

Wendall Johnson once defined human communication as a process with four legs. Merely sending a message does not constitute communication. There has to be a receiver, but communication is more than a mere transmission of information from sender to receiver and back again like ping-pong balls batted to and fro. Communication is a **transaction.** This means that each person communicating is both a sender and receiver simultaneously, not merely a sender or a receiver. As you speak, you receive mostly nonverbal feedback from listeners and this, in turn, influences the messages that you continue to send. Skillful communicators read feedback accurately and adjust their ensuing message appropriately.

Communication as transaction also means that all parties communicating have an impact on each other. We are mutually defined in relation to each other as we send and receive messages simultaneously. A leader of a group must have followers or she cannot claim such a role. The parent role requires at least one child. The teacher role assumes there are students to instruct. One doesn't exist without the other.

The messages we send and the feedback we receive from others influence our perceptions of who we are in relation to other group members and who they are in relation to us. This can be seen clearly by examining messages more closely. Every message has two dimensions—*content* and *relationship* (Watzlawick et al. 1967). The content dimension refers to what is actually said. The relationship dimension of a message refers to how that message defines or redefines the relationship between group members.

I knew a couple whose teenagers addressed them both by their first names. The teens made statements such as, "Bob! Give me your car keys" and "Beth! Do my laundry." Compare these statements to "Dad, may I please have the keys to the car?" or "Mom, will you do me a big favor and wash my clothes for me?" Both messages have the same essential content, but the relationship dimension is clearly different.

The first two messages exhibit disrespect and define the relationship as one where the teenager orders the parents, not the other way around, as we're more accustomed to experiencing. The second two messages, however, are requests, not orders. There is an outward display of respect for the parents and deference to their authority. The power relationship is a traditional one, where the parents are in control and the teenager asks for favors. Of course, nonverbal aspects of these messages must also be considered. The first set of messages could be said facetiously and the second set could be delivered in a condescending tone of voice. In such cases, the relationship dimension of each message is changed.

These examples illustrate the difference between content and relationship dimensions of messages, but they represent one-way communication devoid of feedback. They are not transactional. The following tongue-in-cheek example offered by humorist Dave Barry (1986) illustrates communication as transaction:

YOU: How is this wine that costs $12 a bottle?
WINE STEWARD: We use that primarily as a disinfectant.
YOU: I see. Then we'll have something much more expensive.
Wine Steward: Excellent choice. (p. 63)

In this transaction, the wine steward, whose job requires a certain deference to the customer's wishes, is actually shown deference by the customer who is influenced by the wine steward's initial sarcastic disapproval.

When we are in a group, every utterance, choice, and action continually defines and redefines who we are in relation to other group members and who they are in relation to us. This "definition-and-response-to-definition process," as Stewart (1986) puts it, is ongoing and unavoidable. Individuals affect the group and the group affects the individual. Communication in groups is a continuous series of transactions.

Communication Is a Process

Identifying communication as a process recognizes that nothing stands still, or as the bumper sticker proclaims, "Change is inevitable—except from a vending machine." Communication reveals the dynamic nature of relationships and events.

Communication is a process because changes in events and relationships are part of a continuous flow. You can't understand the ocean by freezing a single wave on film. The ocean is understood only in its dynamism—its tides, currents, waves in motion, plant and animal life interacting symbiotically, and so forth. Similarly, communication makes sense, not by isolating a word, sentence, gesture, facial expression, or exclamation, but by looking at currents of thought and feelings expressed verbally and nonverbally as a whole.

Students, for instance, affect their quality of instruction by their attitudes and degree of interest for the subject matter. Great lectures may fall flat with students who don't care or have an antagonistic relationship with the instructor. Conversely, mediocre presentations by instructors can be made more dynamic by the enthusiastic participation of students. Students may be bored one minute and attentive the next. Relationships between teacher and students may change in the short time of a single class period or in the flash of an ill-chosen phrase, especially when controversial material is presented.

We cannot freeze relationships in time. Every conversation is a point of departure for an ensuing conversation. Every communication experience is the result of the accumulation of experiences preceding the present one. Each new experience affects future transactions. Human communication is a process.

Communication Is Sharing Meaning

Life becomes intelligible to us when we assign form, shape, and structure to our experience with external "reality." In the absence of assigned order, shape, and structure, our world is chaotic, incomprehensible. Human needs cannot be satisfied adequately in such a disorganized environment.

Our world or our external reality becomes meaningful through communication with others. You do not establish meaning in social isolation. Sharing your ideas, feelings, ruminations, experiences, and even intuitions with others, and they in turn doing likewise is all part of the process of constructing meaning, of determining connections and patterns in our minds, of making sense of our world.

Every communication transaction has a **context,** or an environment where meaning emerges. Context consists of *who* (sender) communicates *what* (message) to *whom* (receiver), *why* (purpose) the communicator does it, *where* (setting), *when* (time), and *how* (way) it is done. The importance of context to sharing meaning with others can be seen when we consider the cross-cultural difficulties the British and Americans have understanding the English language. Our *private* school is Britain's *public* school. *Boot* to us is a type of shoe, but to the British it is also the *trunk* of a car. An American shopping in a London department store for *pants* and a *vest* will be surprised when shown *underwear* (boxers or briefs?) and *undershirts*. A Brit who asks for a *rubber* in a U.S. drugstore would be directed to the condom display, not to the school supplies section where the *erasers* are stacked. It is little wonder that George Bernard Shaw reputedly remarked, "Great Britain and America are two countries separated by the same language." The **referents**—the object, concept, or event referred to by a word—are different for more than 4,000 English words when used in one country or the other (Bryson, 1990).

Sharing meaning is a matter of translating verbal and nonverbal messages within a cultural context. For instance, what does the nonverbal act of hanging pears on barren trees in winter communicate to you? Without knowing the context, it probably means very little. Historians, however, may record this act as the precipitating event that led to the revolution against Nicolae Ceausescu, murderous dictator of Romania. In one of his final speeches, Ceausescu boasted that Soviet-style reform would infiltrate Romania when apple trees grow pears (in New rulers, 1989, p. 1A). A group of college students in Bucharest, in a taunting act of defiance, set about hanging any pears they could find on the trees, which were denuded by the bitter winter weather and were lining the capital's main street. This symbolic gesture of defiance so infuriated Ceausescu that he directed his secret police to identify the parties responsible. The police attacked the students in their dormitory, killing many. Angry students took to the university square to protest, where more than 100 were slaughtered. The country seized upon this massacre as a rallying point for outright rebellion. The government collapsed and Ceausescu was hastily tried and executed in December 1989.

I have thus far discussed what communication is not and conversely what communication is. To summarize by way of definition, **communication** *is a transactional process of sharing meaning with others*. The intricacies of sharing meaning with others in group situations will become more apparent when I discuss what constitutes competent communication, the next topic for consideration.

COMMUNICATION COMPETENCE

Knowing what constitutes human communication does not tell you how to engage in the process in a competent manner. In order to accomplish this goal it helps to understand what it means to communicate competently—the objective of this next section.

Focus Questions

1. How do you determine communication competence? *ability to comm in a personally effective + socially appro manner*

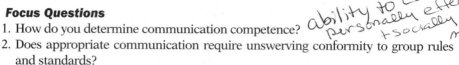

2. Does appropriate communication require unswerving conformity to group rules and standards?

3. Does being a competent communicator mean never engaging in poor communication practices?

Competence Defined

Trenholm and Jensen (1988) define **communication competence** as "the ability to communicate in a personally effective and socially appropriate manner" (p. 11). Littlejohn and Jabusch (1982) define it as "the ability and willingness of an individual to participate responsibly in a transaction in such a way as to maximize the outcomes of shared meanings" (p. 30). Adler and Towne (1996) define it as "the ability to get what you are seeking from others in a manner that maintains the relationship on terms that are acceptable to all parties" (p. 42). Although there is not one definition of communication competence that satisfies everyone, there are several points of agreement among most communication experts regarding this concept.

Matter of Degree Communication competence is a relative concept—a matter of degree (Spitzberg and Cupach, 1989). We speak of communicators along a continuum from highly competent or proficient to incompetent or deficient with designations such as minimally functional and average as gradations along the continuum. All of us have our communication strengths and weaknesses given certain situations and circumstances. Some individuals are at ease in social situations such as parties or gatherings of strangers, but they would rather be dipped in molasses and strapped to an ant hill than confront conflict in their own group. We can be highly proficient in one circumstance but minimally skillful or woefully inadequate in another situation. Therefore, the label "competent communicator" is a judgment of an individual's proficiency in a particular set of circumstances, not a designation of that person's identity as a human being.

We-not-Me Oriented Since communication is transactional, competence can only be ascertained in terms of our relationships with others. You can't be declared competent unless you're tested on the proving ground of human relations. In groups, our primary attention is on the group (we) not the individual (me), unless the individual has a direct bearing on the success or failure of the group. This, of course, is not the same as saying that groups should always supersede individual interests. Nevertheless, trying to achieve your individual goals at the expense of the group usually produces unsatisfactory outcomes for both you and the group. Zander (1982) even goes so far as to claim, "A body of people is not a group if the members are primarily interested in individual accomplishment" (p. 2).

There are potential dividends when group members assume a We-orientation. Usually, helping others satisfy their goals creates an environment conducive to the satisfaction of your own goals. Ridgeway (1982) found that one way for women and ethnic minorities to overcome bias that prevents them from achieving high status in a group is to act in a group-oriented, not a self-oriented, manner.

FOCUS on Culture

Individualism versus Collectivism: A Basic Cultural Difference

A poll of 131 businesspeople, scholars, government officials, and professionals in eight East Asian countries and the United States showed glaring differences in the value placed on order and personal rights and freedoms (as cited in Simons and Zielenziger, 1996, p. 22A). When asked the question *"Which of the following are critically important to your people?"* the results were as follows:

	Asians	Americans
1. An orderly society	70%	11%
2. Personal freedom	32%	82%
3. Individual rights	29%	73%

All cultures vary in the degree of emphasis they place on individuals exploring their uniqueness and independence versus maintaining their conformity and interdependence. This **individualism–collectivism dimension** is thought by some scholars to be the most important, deep-seated value that distinguishes one culture from another (Hui and Triandis, 1986). It is a values debate at the center of the communication competence model's We-orientation perspective.

The autonomy of the individual is of paramount importance in individualist cultures, hence, the emphasis placed on self-actualization and personal growth. Words such as *independence, self, privacy,* and *rights* imbue cultural conversations. Individualist cultures have an "I" consciousness. Competition, not cooperation, is encouraged. Decision-making is predicated on what benefits the individual even if this jeopardizes the group welfare. Private property, thoughts, and opinions are valued, and individual achievement and initiative are stressed (Samovar and Porter 1995). Self-promotion is expected, even encouraged.

In collectivist cultures, by contrast, commitment to the group is paramount. Words such as *loyalty, responsibility* (to the group welfare), and *community* imbue collectivist cultural conversations. Collectivist cultures have a "We" consciousness. Cooperation within valued groups (family, friends, coworkers) is strongly emphasized, although transactions with groups perceived as outsiders (foreigners, strangers) can become competitive (Yu, 1998). Individuals often downplay personal goals in favor of advancing the goals of a valued group, and privacy is sacrificed for the good of the group (Samovar and Porter, 1995). Self-promotion is discouraged.

All cultures have both individualist and collectivist influences, but one tends to predominate over the other (Gudykunst, 1991). A worldwide study of fifty countries and three geographic areas ranks the United States as the number one individualistic country followed by other Western countries such as Australia, Great Britain, Canada, New Zealand, Belgium, and the Netherlands. Latin American and Asian countries rank high on collectivism. Guatemala is the most collectivist. Ecuador, Panama, Venezuela, Colombia, Indonesia, Taiwan, and Singapore are also among the most collectivist (Hofstede, 1991). Approximately 70 percent of the world's population lives in collectivist cultures (Triandis, 1990).

In the United States, the preoccupation with individualism has drawn fire. Psychologist Carol Tavris (1989) argues that individualism in the United States has become excessive, producing what she terms the "Imperial I." The individual is king, regal in importance. Groups often are thought to exist to satisfy the needs of individual members, not to advance the greater social welfare. Sociologist Charles Derber (1996) claims, "As individualism intensifies, the balance of commitment can tilt so far toward the self that the family and other building blocks of society decompose. . . . Americans converted to the reigning ideology of 'looking out for number one' are proving ready to sacrifice not only outsiders but their kin on the altar of their own needs and pleasures" (p. 111).

Excessive individualism can be faulted, but excessive collectivism has its dangers too. The perils of group pressure, blind conformity to groups, and deindividuation, issues that will be discussed at length later in this book, remind us of the risks involved from excessive loyalty to any group.

Collectivist cultures require a level of conformity and sometimes authoritarian rule that would send shudders down the spines of most Americans. Singapore, for example, levies heavy fines on anyone littering, smoking in public places, or failing to flush public toilets, which are monitored by government employees (Bordewich, 1995). Requiring students to take drug tests is a routine practice and groups of five individuals or more cannot meet on the street without police permission. Importing chewing gum is outlawed, traffic laws are monitored by video cameras set up at busy intersections; heavy censorship of printed material, CDs, and motion pictures is widespread; only the police can own guns; and political opposition to the government is a risky undertaking, often resulting in fines and imprisonment for dissidents (Huckshorn, 1996).

Individualist and collectivist cultures exhibit glaring differences in their perceptions of the world and how people should behave. Individualist and collec-

tivist values, however, do not always conflict (Schwartz, 1990). When an individual learns conflict management skills or improves interpersonal communication skills, the group benefits as well as the group member. Nevertheless, <u>if groups are to succeed, individual goals and agendas should be of secondary, not primary importance</u>.

When individual goals are considered primary, groups often fail. Larson and LaFasto (1989), in a comprehensive study of seventy-five diverse teams, found that the "what's in it for me" orientation of team members was a primary impediment to effective teamwork and group success. Mountain climber George McLeod notes that the least effective mountaineering and exploration teams are those impeded by "skiving," whereby team members conserve energy and resources in order to achieve individual rather than team objectives. Sir Edmund Hillary, who, along with his climbing partner was the first to conquer Mount Everest, made this assessment of the May 1996 mountain climbing disaster, the worst ever on Everest: "There has been an erosion of mountaineering values. It used to be a team effort. Nowadays, it's much too everybody-for-himself. That can get you killed. Tenzing and I got to the top together, it wasn't first one then the other" (Hillary, 1996, p. 41). Lack of teamwork and ex-

The Tenerife air disaster, the worst in commercial aviation history, was caused in part by a lack of teamwork and excessive individualism.

cessive individualism were also blamed for safety-related incidents at Delta airlines, and for the catastrophic crash of two 747s at Tenerife airport in the Canary Islands in 1977 that killed 583 passengers and crew (Weick, 1990; Whitkin, 1987).

The We-orientation is a difficult perspective to accept in a Me-oriented culture. The We-perspective that is so necessary to group success, however, can be learned. Contrast the individualism of track sensation Carl Lewis with the collectivism of the U.S. women's basketball team at the 1996 Olympic Games in Atlanta.

When Lewis won the long jump for the fourth straight Olympics, he had tied for the most Olympic gold medals ever won by a single individual—nine total. Immediately he began lobbying for a place on the men's 4 x 100-meter relay team in order to get one last chance to earn another gold medal and go down in history as the most decorated Olympian ever. Interviewed on CNN, Lewis implored viewers to "call the Olympic people" and "make your voice heard" (as cited in Purdy, 1996, p. 1D). Lewis had not qualified for the relay team at the Olympic Trials because he finished last in the 100-meter final. The fact that placing Lewis on the relay team meant pulling off one of the U.S. sprinters who had qualified for the team, thus ending that runner's Olympic dream, seemed less important to Lewis than personal glory. Lewis had been invited to work out with the relay team as an alternate in case he was needed in the event of injury to a team member. Lewis declined. The U.S. relay team had the fastest qualifying time but lost to the Canadian team in the finals. The distraction of the Lewis controversy may or may not have contributed to the second-place finish; there is no way to determine this. Nevertheless, Carl Lewis clearly showed the individualist philosophy at work in a not-so-noble finish to his phenomenal Olympic career.

The U.S. women's basketball team, in stark contrast, worked together for a year developing teamwork and cohesiveness. All team members made significant sacrifices in order to take a year out of their lives, traveling more than 100,000 miles to put a winning team together. The women's team won all sixty games it played (fifty-two preparation games and eight Olympic contests). They defeated a very capable team from Brazil in the Olympic final, 111–87. A similar Brazilian team had defeated the United States by 37 points in the 1994 Pan Am Games. The 111 points scored by the Americans was an Olympic record. Tara VanDerveer, the gifted U.S. coach, noted after her team had won the gold medal, "There's a stereotype that women can't work together. What makes this special is that people had a team agenda. They weren't individuals. This team put the gold medal as their mission" (as cited in Killion, 1996, p. 3D).

More recently, the U.S. women's soccer team exhibited noteworthy We-not-Me orientation during their drive to win the 1999 World Cup. Mia Hamm, the internationally recognized star of the team refused to accept any individualistic notoriety. She appeared for clinics, autograph sessions, and promotions, but she steadfastly refused photo shoots for numerous high-profile publications

The 1999 U.S. Women's World Cup championship was a model of teamwork.

during the World Cup. "This isn't all about me," she noted. "Everything I am I owe to this team" (as cited in Starr & Brant, 1999, pp. 52–53). Self-lessness reigned supreme. Starters, even some players who were star performers on the 1996 gold medal Olympic team, accepted diminished roles without complaint. Shannon MacMillan came off the bench to score a goal and two assists in a game against North Korea. She could have cajoled team coach, Tony DiCicco, for a starting position. She didn't. "I'm going to do anything I'm asked for this team. My heart and soul is with it" (as cited in Starr & Brant, 1999, p. 53). Even a television ad taped by team members exhibited the We-orientation. A player comes out of the dentist's examination room and announces to fellow team members that she needs two fillings. Players sitting in the waiting room, one by one, stand up and announce, "Then I will have two fillings."

Carl Lewis demonstrated how difficult it is to put aside individualism even when collectivism is clearly required, and the women's basketball and soccer teams demonstrated that even in a highly individualist culture, collectivist behavior is possible and rewarding. Embracing the We-orientation and de-emphasizing the Me-orientation in the United States will not come quickly nor easily. The United States does not have to become a collectivist culture where the group is supreme, but teamwork and putting the group ahead of individual needs and goals is often appropriate and important. As Larson and LaFasto (1989) pointedly state:

> The potential for collective problem-solving is so often unrealized and the promise of collective achievement so often unfulfilled, that we exhibit what seems to be a developmental disability in the area of social competence. . . . Clearly, if we are to solve the enormous problems facing our society, we need to learn how to collaborate more effectively. We need to set aside individual agendas. (pp. 13–14)

Emphasizing team building and collaborative effort can prove beneficial to both individuals and society.

Questions for Thought

1. Do you agree that the United States has become excessively Me-oriented? Explain.
2. Singapore has low crime, safe cities, low unemployment, and few homeless citizens. The United States has the opposite. Should we strive to become collectivist and emulate the Singaporeans?
3. Could the United States ever become a collectivist nation given our individualist history?

Effectiveness   Communication competence is predicated on results. Consequently, **effectiveness** is defined as how well we have progressed toward the achievement of goals. Effectiveness is a litmus test of competence (Spitzberg and Cupach, 1989). Someone who knows what changes in communication behavior need to be made, and wants to make these changes, but never does, can hardly be deemed a competent communicator.

Individual effectiveness, however, may be deemed incompetent if such effectiveness precludes the possibility of others accomplishing their own goals (Spitzberg and Cupach, 1989, p. 20). A We-orientation requires concern for others as well as self. Consequently, communication competence in groups necessitates behavior that is both effective *and* appropriate.

Appropriateness   The appropriateness of one's communication is determined by examining the context. Thus, **appropriateness** means complying with rules, norms, and expectations that accompany a specific context. The difficulty determining appropriateness can be seen readily from the following intercultural example:

> An American college student, while having a dinner party with a group of foreigners, learns that her favorite cousin has just died. She bites her lip, pulls herself up, and politely excuses herself from the group. The interpretation given to this behavior will vary with the culture of the observer. The Italian student thinks, "How insincere; she doesn't even cry." The Russian student thinks, "How unfriendly; she didn't care enough to share her grief with her friends." The fellow American student thinks, "How brave; she wanted to bear her burden by herself." (DeVito, 1990, p.218)

The appropriateness of your communication cannot be determined by merely examining a message isolated from the rich complexity of context. For instance, you may self-disclose intimate information about yourself to members of some groups but not others. If you attend a therapy group on marriage, self-disclosing will be expected and encouraged because it is compatible with the group's purpose. If, however, you are talking to a meeting of the Student Senate or the Dormitory Advisory Committee, intimate self-disclosure will likely make members squirm in their chairs and wish for an earthquake. The purpose of these groups is not therapeutic, so the expectations regarding what constitutes appropriate communication in these contexts are different from expectations found at meetings of Alcoholics Anonymous or Marriage Encounter.

Meeting in a tavern or someone's dorm room suggests informality (some taverns and dorm rooms communicate greater informality than others). There will be less concern for propriety in language usage and behavior. Meeting in the plush surroundings of an upscale law firm, however, suggests formality. Great attention to proper communication etiquette will be encouraged by this setting.

Additionally, the time we choose to criticize, congratulate, or ignore group members can easily become an issue of appropriateness. If a group member criticizes you for poor performance on a project after others have similarly rebuked you, it may seem like piling on.

Although appropriateness of communication is determined on the basis of group rules and norms within a specific context, rules and norms are not untouchable. Some group rules should be changed. Most of the time, however, we merely need to adapt to the rules of the group, not tramp all over them. Communication becomes inappropriate if it violates rules and expectations of the group when such violations could have been avoided, without sacrificing a goal, by choosing different communication behaviors (Getter and Nowinski, 1981). In short, inappropriateness is usually the result of cluelessness or clumsiness.

When we need to change the rules in order to be appropriate, the change should be negotiated by group members. Professors who want to interact socially with their seminar students, for example, must work out a modification of the rules and expectations students have for professor–student relationships. As long as the students agree to the modification, appropriateness is maintained. If the professor persists in pushing the socializing when students are clearly uncomfortable, however, then such persistence becomes inappropriate. When such persistence takes place interpersonally, it is labeled harassment.

Elements of Competence

The definition of communication competence provides five elements that constitute the framework for analysis of small group communication. These elements are knowledge, skills, sensitivity, commitment, and ethics.

Knowledge   I have already noted the centrality of appropriateness and effectiveness to the definition of communication competence. Both require knowledge. **Knowledge** is understanding the rules, norms, and expectations required to be appropriate and effective.

Communication may be appropriate but not effective, and vice versa. Knowledge of the context tells you which is most likely. Consider this example:

> Brian Holtz is a U.S. businessperson assigned by his company to manage its office in Thailand. Mr. Thani, a valued assistant manager in the Bangkok office, has recently been arriving late for work. Holtz has to decide what to do about this problem. After carefully thinking about his options, he decides there are four possible strategies:
>
> 1. Go privately to Mr. Thani, ask him why he has been arriving late, and tell him that he needs to come to work on time.
> 2. Ignore the problem.
> 3. Publicly reprimand Mr. Thani the next time he is late.
> 4. In a private discussion, suggest seeking Mr. Thani's assistance in dealing with employees in the company who regularly arrive late for work, and solicit his suggestions about what should be done. (Lustig and Koester, 1999, pp. 67–68)

What choice would you make? The first option is a typical American way of handling this type of situation. It is direct and probably would be effective in getting Mr. Thani to arrive at work on time. Nevertheless, considering the Thai culture (context) where one person does not directly criticize another person, this choice would be very inappropriate, even disastrous. Conversely, the second choice would be appropriate but hardly effective since Mr. Thani would likely persist in his tardiness. The third choice would be neither appropriate nor effective. Public humiliation would likely induce Mr. Thani, a valuable employee, to resign in shame. Thus, the fourth choice is best because it is both appropriate and effective (Lustig and Koester, 1999). Mr. Thani would receive the message indirectly that he must arrive at work on time, yet he could save face. He can respond affirmatively to the indirect request that he change his behavior from tardiness to punctuality without suffering public humiliation.

Knowledge in any communication situation is critical, whether the context is our own or another culture. We cannot determine what is appropriate and effective without knowing the expectations, rules, and norms operating in a given situation.

We don't always make the wisest communication choices, but we are likely to make a fair number of foolish ones if our limited knowledge shields us from appropriate alternatives. You can exercise considerably more control over your life when your knowledge of what is required in a given communication situation is more than just superficial. In communicative matters, a little knowledge is like the dim flicker of a candle flame in a dark mine shaft. There's just enough illumination to see choices, but not enough light to provide effective direction. If you are uncertain what is expected or required in a given situation, you should seek knowledge from those who are likely to know and can enhance your understanding.

Skills   Communication competence encompasses the ability to apply your knowledge in actual situations. To be effective, you have to combine knowledge with skill. One study of undergraduate women (Christensen et al., 1980) found that even when subjects were told in advance the appropriate communication behavior in an interview situation, half still couldn't do it.

A **communication skill** is "the successful performance of a communication behavior . . . (and) the ability to repeat such a behavior" (Spitzberg and Hecht, 1984, p. 577). Practice, of course, is essential to the mastery of any communication skill. Members who are trained and practice together acquire skills and improve group performance (Hollingshead, 1998).

There is abundant evidence that links communication skills with success or failure in the workplace. Ninety-eight percent of 253 personnel interviewers at businesses large and small reported that oral communication skills significantly affect hiring decisions (Peterson, 1997). Communication ability was deemed the most desirable quality of college graduates by 480 companies and organizations looking to hire employees (as cited in Morreale, 1999). A survey of more than one thousand faculty members from a wide variety of disciplines and colleges identified problem solving, working in groups, and leading groups as *essential skills* for every college graduate (Diamond, 1997). Employers want to hire skillful communicators who can work in teams and make decisions in groups.

Communication competence, of course, is not simply a matter of learning a single skill or even a set of skills. As I indicated earlier, skills without knowledge of when and how to use them are mostly useless, even harmful. The key is learning many skills and using them flexibly given the proper knowledge of what's appropriate for a given context.

Sensitivity   The We-orientation requires a **sensitivity** to what is best for the group to achieve its goals. The definition of sensitivity has two elements. First, sensitivity means having your antennae extended to pick up any signals from the group that indicate disharmony, conflict, disenchantment, frustration, anger, and the like. Problems that lie just below the surface of consciousness go unattended by groups and magnify difficulties unless members are sensitive to the nuances and subtleties of communication transactions between members. Second, sensitivity also means showing concern for others, not just yourself. This means treating members with respect, dignity, and caring.

Some group training programs raise concerns regarding sensitivity. The Sterling Institute, for example, is a national organization that provides group-training workshops. Encouraged to disclose sexual escapades and traumatic experiences and to vent anger at the opposite sex during workshops, trainees who show reticence to do so or who question the trainer's methods risk being verbally accosted (Lubman 1996). Women have formally complained to the FBI about the abuse, and in 1996, the Better Business Bureau rated the Sterling Institute as "unsatisfactory" due to complaints of verbal abuse and physical threats (Lubman, 1996). Who wants to pay money to be treated with disrespect? The Sterling Institute is but one example of a training program that doesn't seem to appreciate the essential connection between communication competence and sensitivity.

Commitment   Effectiveness requires commitment. **Commitment** is the conscious decision to invest time, energy, thought, and feeling to improve oneself or one's relationships with others. Little that is worthwhile comes without commitment. You want to be a great athlete? You must commit yourself to the hard work necessary to achieve greatness. The U.S. women's basketball and soccer teams didn't achieve international glory by half-hearted commitment. They made big individual sacrifices, labored untold hours, and planned strategies carefully. You want to receive an academic scholarship, earn good grades, and a degree? It won't happen by listless attention in class and lackluster attendance. You have to want it, work for it, have a passion to achieve it—you must be committed.

The predominant motivation of the competent communicator is the desire to avoid previous mistakes and to find better ways of communicating with group members. Someone who makes the same mistakes repeatedly and shows little interest in altering his or her behavior is a nuisance, or worse, a dead weight that can sink a group. Such anemic commitment is a frequent source of frustration in groups that can fester into grouphate. It is easily the most frequent complaint I hear from my group communication students each term. Who wants to deal with a lethargic member who can't be counted on to produce and doesn't seem to care? In sports, they are booted off the team; in business, they are fired; in politics they are voted out of office; in college, they are invited to leave.

Commitment to improving your communication effectiveness requires self-monitoring. When you interact in groups you have to be a participant–observer. You assume a detached view of yourself. You analyze your communication behavior, looking for areas to improve while noting successes. Ultimately, the competent communicator considers it a personal responsibility to interact with group members as effectively and productively as possible.

Ethics   A 1997 survey of 1,324 workers by the Ethics Officer Association revealed that 48% of respondents admitted they had engaged in one or more unethical communication behaviors in the past year. Workers covered up unethical or illegal incidents; called in sick when they weren't ill; lied or deceived customers, coworkers, or supervisors; or took credit for a coworker's idea. Three-quarters of 747 companies surveyed by the Ethics Resource Center have ethics codes for all workers ("Cheating at work," 1997). American culture cares about ethics, but we don't always communicate ethically.

Why should anyone care about ethics in communication? The very definition of communication competence requires it. Appropriateness and the

We-orientation make ethics important. Competent communicators concern themselves with more than merely what works for them personally. Stealing someone's idea and taking credit raises the issue of right and wrong because another person is adversely affected. The theft of an idea is inappropriate and self-centered.

Ethics is a set of standards for judging the moral correctness of our behavior. Four essential values can serve as an ethical guide for our communication in groups.

1. *Honesty.* The American culture presumes that honesty is valued and dishonesty is wrong (Bok, 1978). Accuse a person of lying and immediately they become defensive. All ethical systems condemn lying (Jaksa & Pritchard, 1994). Imagine trying to keep a family together when everyone lies regularly and no one can be trusted.

2. *Respect.* Sensitivity requires respect, but from a practical not an ethical standpoint. Relationships in groups fall apart, and groups can't function effectively when members show disrespect for each other. From an ethical viewpoint, however, respect is right and disrespect is wrong even if showing respect to others works against a group goal (such as defeating a team). We aren't expected to show respect to group members only if it provides some tangible reward or advantage. "Some form of the Golden Rule is embraced by virtually all of the major religious and moral systems" (Jaksa & Pritchard, 1994, p. 101).

3. *Fairness.* Prejudice treats people unfairly. Bigots want different rules for themselves than those applied to a disfavored group. Bigotry should have no place in the communication arena. Students recognize immediately how unfair it would be if an instructor gave an advantage to some students in class and penalized others based on their sex, ethnicity, age, or lifestyle. Cheating on an exam gives an unfair advantage to the cheater. Although some students may cheat, few would be proud to announce it to others.

4. *Choice.* Freedom to choose for oneself without threat of force or intimidation is a basic ethical value (Jaksa & Pritchard, 1994). It is why most nations have outlawed torture. Coercion prevents choice. There is no real option presented. Choice goes hand in hand with honesty. If you fear reprisals for telling the truth, then your freedom to choose truthfulness instead of deceit is compromised.

When considered as general ethical guidelines, all four values are easy to justify. Group communication is so complex, however, that any list of standards used to judge members' communication ethics, applied absolutely, would immediately create problems. Ethical communication is a matter of context. A lie that accuses your roommate of stealing college property that a friend of yours actually stole is different than a lie that covers up an embarrassing family secret. Exceptions also will inevitably surface. Students don't have complete freedom to choose what they want to learn and how they want to learn it, nor should they. Few would freely take a public speaking course unless mandated by general education requirements because most people fear giving speeches. Honesty, respect, fairness, and choice, however, are strong values in most cultures, and they act as basic standards for our communication behavior.

second look

Communication Competence

Definition
Matter of Degree
We-not-Me Oriented
Effectiveness
Appropriateness (who, what, where, when, why, how)

Elements
Knowledge
Skills (flexibility)
Sensitivity
Commitment
Ethics

FOCUS *on gender*

Gender and Communication Competence

"Not all men are annoying. Some are dead." "Some women aren't at all irritating—those with their jaws wired shut;" "Why is it good that there are female astronauts? When the crew gets lost in space, at least the woman will ask for directions;" "What do you call a man with half a brain? Gifted!" "What do you call a woman with half a brain? Normal." Take a moment and consider these "jokes." Amusing? Offensive? (These are tame samples compared to the truly tasteless and mean-spirited jokes found on numerous Web sites.) These attempts at humor reflect an awareness that men and women communicate differently, which can be extremely frustrating to both sexes. The ridicule that men and women heap on each other as a result of these differences, however, is likely more a product of misunderstanding than maliciousness.

Deborah Tannen (1990), in her provocative book, *You Just Don't Understand* offers an even-handed analysis of conversational patterns of men and women. She explains that for most women talk is primarily a means to "establish connections and negotiate relationships," but for most men "talk is primarily a means to preserve independence and negotiate and maintain status in a hierarchical social order" (p. 77). According to Tannen, both men and women are concerned about the dual dimensions of status and connection during conversation, but status is usually given far more relative weight by men and connection is usually given far more relative weight by women (see also Coates, 1993; Wood, 1997). The

Despite the stereotype, men are more talkative in mixed-sex groups than are women. In this instance, we see that male talkativeness begins at an early age.

status dimension is very different from the connection dimension as indicated below, and therefore each produces very different communication expectations and patterns.

Status	Connection
Independence (separateness)	Interdependence (intimacy)
Competition (contest)	Cooperation (consensus)
Power (control)	Empowerment (choices)

In mixed-sex groups, men's speech consists mostly of task-oriented, instrumental communication such as giving information, opinions, and suggestions (James and Drakich, 1993). Men usually see talk as a contest, an opportunity to establish or increase status in the eyes of group members. Thus, men report their knowledge to the group. They tell more jokes than women typically do, impart more information and advice, and offer more solutions to problems. Why? Because this spotlights them as experts and raises their status in a group.

Conversely, women's speech consists more of supportive and facilitative communication such as agreeing, giving indications of interest in what others are saying, and encouraging others to participate in group discussions (James and Drakich, 1993). Women try to connect with other speakers, share feelings, and listen intently to establish rapport (Tannen, 1990). Displaying interest in other group members and offering encouragement to them establishes a connection.

The prevailing cultural belief that women are verbose and men are taciturn doesn't fit this explanation of gender differences in communication. This is not a problem since the belief is largely a myth. Fifty-four of fifty-six studies on talkativeness in mixed-sex groups found that men outtalk women (James and Drakich, 1993). Report talk (providing information, displaying expertise, solving problems) usually takes up more total talking time than rapport talk (encouraging others, agreeing, asking for more information). Speaking for longer periods of time is also a sign of power. Thus, men, focusing on status in group discussions as they have been socialized to do, must talk a great deal, while women, focusing on con-

nection as they have been socialized to do, talk but also listen intently.

Why is there a stereotype that women chatter nonstop and men talk little when the research indicates otherwise? Tannen (1990) argues that men talk more in public situations and women talk more in private situations. She contends that men talk more in groups because they feel the need to establish or maintain their status in the eyes of group members. In private situations, at home with his partner, a man feels less stress to impress. Private time is down time. When a woman wants to discuss the events of the day, this may be perceived by a man to be trivial chatter interfering with relaxation because it is talking when no talk is perceived to be necessary (James and Drakich, 1993). Women, however, see talk as essential to establishing and maintaining close relationships, so they talk more in private with their partners, yet often complain that they are living with silent partners who are also poor listeners.

The very act of listening has different meaning for men and women (Tannen, 1990). For men, listening, especially for a lengthy period of time without interruption, labels them as subordinate to the speaker. This places men in a seemingly one-down, low status position that is uncomfortable. For women, the act of listening is an opportunity to connect on a personal level with the speaker, to show interest, to confirm what is said, and to appreciate the information imparted. Listening inattentively or interrupting to seize conversational control would be insensitive to the feelings of the speaker.

One of the most widely reported claims about male–female communication patterns is that men interrupt more than women, especially in mixed-sex group discussions. An extensive review of the literature on this subject, however, shows no significant differences between the sexes in number of interruptions (James and Clarke, 1993). Women, however, interrupt to establish rapport or show interest and enthusiasm more than men do, and men interrupt more to seize the floor and make a point.

So are men jerks for seeing conversation as an opportunity to enhance status? Are women meek and emotional for seeing conversation as an opportunity to bond with others? Such interpretations are extremely limiting and simplistic. Consider the tendency of women to encourage members to participate in group discussions while men rarely show such a tendency. How should this be interpreted? From the connection perspective, women appear to be highly sensitive, caring group members and men seem to be insensitive clods. From the status perspective, however, women may appear to be the insensitive ones. Inviting a man into a conversation may diminish his status. It calls attention to his nonparticipation, making him appear unassertive. He may have little or no knowledge on the subject of conversation. Spotlighting his lack of knowledge in front of the group could be embarrassing. When men and women approach simple conversation from conflicting perspectives, it is not surprising that misunderstanding and ridicule result.

Not all men and women will follow the male and female patterns outlined by Tannen. Mostly, however, men and women exhibit recognizable, documented patterns of communication that manifest differences between the sexes when they engage in group discussion. As Tannen (1990) argues: "Pretending that women and men are the same hurts women, because the ways they are treated are based on the norms for men. It also hurts men who, with good intentions, speak to women as they would to men, and are nonplussed when their words don't work as they expected, or even spark resentment and anger" (p. 16).

Tannen's model of gender differences in communication has received two main criticisms. First, she has been accused of excusing male boorishness and expecting women to adjust to male communication patterns, not vice versa (Freed, 1992). Tannen (1990), however, clearly states that "women and men should both make adjustments" and male and female conversational styles are "equally valid" (p. 15). Second, Tannen is accused of seriously underemphasizing the role of unequal power that causes gender differences in communication. Women's style of communication is typical of relatively powerless people (Tavris, 1992; Freed, 1992). Tannen (1990) again clearly states, "No one could deny that men

as a class are dominant in our society, and that many individual men seek to dominate women" (p. 18). She adds, however, that "male dominance is not the whole story. It is not sufficient to account for everything that happens to women and men in conversation, especially in conversations in which both are genuinely trying to relate to each other with attention and respect" (p. 18).

Given their differences, how do men and women communicate competently with each other? First, knowledge of the different assumptions made by men and women regarding conversations has to be broadened. Applying the standards of one group to the behavior of the other can create misunderstanding (Tannen, 1990). Women will continue to misjudge men if they apply the single standard of connection to all conversations, and men will continue to misjudge women if they continue to apply the single standard of status to all conversations. Both status and connection are legitimate standards for assessing conversations, but we all can look silly, even half-brained, to the other sex when only one standard is applied.

Second, adaptation to each other's style of conversation would be beneficial. Men could make fewer interruptions that seize conversational control, be more attentive listeners, ask more questions to clarify points or seek information, and encourage women to join the conversation when appropriate. These adaptations show flexibility and a concern for connection without the appearance of subservience. Women who learn assertiveness skills expand their opportunities to be heard and taken seriously (status-enhancing) without losing their sensitivity to the importance of connection. Even if men and women don't exhibit the typical patterns outlined by Tannen, most individuals will favor one pattern over the other. Recognizing that they favor either status or connection allows you to adjust your communication appropriately as described above.

Questions for Thought

1. Can you think of additional ways men and women can adjust their conversational styles

in order to reduce misunderstandings and increase effectiveness?

2. Do the typical male–female patterns of conversation identified by Tannen correspond with your experience of communicating in mixed-sex groups?

3. Do you think the criticism of Tannen's model is justified? Apply your own experiences.

In summary, human communication is a transactional process of sharing meaning with others. Communication competence, a recurring theme throughout this book, is composed of knowledge, skills, sensitivity, commitment, and ethics. Learning to communicate competently in groups is of vital importance to all of us. With this as a backdrop, let's explore how groups function as systems.

Questions for Critical Thinkers

1. Are there any circumstances in which a Me-orientation becomes necessary when participating in a small group?
2. Does competent communication ever necessitate dishonesty? Explain.
3. When you are a member of a group should you always exhibit commitment to the group or are there exceptions? Explain.

man interrupt more

CHAPTER

2

Groups as Systems

On December 31, 1974, William O. Douglas, Supreme Court justice and energetic defender of liberal causes, suffered a serious stroke. The severity of the situation was increased by the fact that Justice Douglas was a determined man. He insisted on resuming his judicial duties even when he was clearly unable to function effectively due to his stroke. Bob Woodward and Scott Armstrong (1979) describe the effect on the entire group of one of its members struck down by illness:

> The other Justices had been waiting in the conference room for some time. . . . White seethed with impatience. He had expected Douglas to retire. Burger was polite and helpful. Brennan sat beside Douglas, assisting him with the files and papers. The conference ended at 3:45, earlier than usual.
>
> The rest of the week was torture for the other Justices. Douglas was in constant pain and barely had the energy to make his voice audible. He was wheeled in and out of conference, never staying the entire session, leaving his votes with Brennan to cast. Powell counted the number of times Douglas fell asleep. Brennan woke him gently when it came time to vote. . . . The tension grew. Get him out of here, White once told Datcher [Douglas's messenger], who had been summoned to wheel the sleeping Douglas from the conference room. (pp. 389–92)

Douglas, a once-towering legal figure, had become a nuisance to the Court, keeping the highest judicial body in the country from efficiently performing its duties.

One way to analyze a group such as the Supreme Court is to view it as a system. A **system** is a set of interconnected parts working together to form a whole in the context of a changing environment (Infante et al., 1997; Littlejohn, 1999). The Supreme Court is a system. It is composed of individual justices interrelating with each other. What happens to one justice affects the entire Court. What happened to Douglas couldn't be ignored by his colleagues, and all of the justices had to adapt to the changing circumstances caused by his failing health.

The operations, behaviors, and functions that occur within a group can be explained perceptively in terms of systems theory. Analyzing a group as a system clarifies how groups succeed and fail.

I have three chapter objectives. They are:

1. to explain the primary elements of a system and apply them to groups,
2. to define groups within a systems context, and
3. to set the boundaries of this book, specifying what size and types of groups will receive special emphasis.

INTERCONNECTEDNESS OF PARTS

Focus Questions
1. The ripple effect in a system means what?
2. What is synergy? How does it affect a group?

A group is a system composed of interconnected parts.

Every system is a collection of integrated parts that comprise a whole. All parts interconnect and work together. Thus, analyzing a single part without looking at its interconnectedness to the whole is relatively meaningless. This next section will discuss specific ways interconnected parts impact a group.

interconnect

Ripple Effect

In a system, one part can have a significant impact on the whole. This **ripple effect** or chain reaction spreads across the entire system much like a pebble tossed into a pond disturbs the water and forces adjustments.

can be positive

     The influenza pandemic of 1918–19 began in Europe but quickly rippled throughout the world. It sickened over *one billion* people, half the world's total population at the time, and left 21 million people dead worldwide (half a million in the United States). This was equivalent to the total deaths from both world wars of the twentieth century. So virulent was the virus that there was an instance reported of women boarding a New York subway in Coney Island feeling mild fatigue and being found dead when the subway train pulled into Columbus Circle some forty-five minutes later. Nearly 20 percent of Western Samoa died from the disease, and entire Inuit villages in isolated parts of Alaska were decimated (Garrett, 1994). This flu pandemic rippled through every part of society. Enormous stress was placed on health care systems that nursed the sick and on economic systems that struggled with a major portion of the workforce incapacitated. Even social relations were affected. People avoided contact with each other or, when forced to interact, commonly wore cloth masks across their faces in the mistaken belief that this would protect them from the virus.

A seemingly small part of a huge system can generate an enormous ripple effect. There was an immense ripple effect when 9,200 workers at two General Motors parts plants in Flint, Michigan, went out on strike in June 1998. By choking off the supply of critical car parts such as fenders, odometers, air filters, and hoods, 26 of GM's 29 assembly plants in the United States, Canada, and Mexico were shut down. More than 161,000 workers, most of whom were not on strike, were idled. GM lost more than $1 billion and workers suffered from lost wages (Sandoval, 1998). Both sides debated the justification for the strike, but there is no debate about the impact one seemingly small part can have on an entire system.

Even very small systems can experience the ripple effect. The family is a principal group in our society. It is also a system. If a parent dies, the family as a unit has to deal with the severe loss personally and financially. Coping with grief, selling the family house, moving to a new town or state, entering strange schools, feeling the pinch of tight finances, and watching the remaining parent scramble for employment are just some of the potentially unsettling effects of a death in the family. What happens to one member influences all members.

The ripple effect an individual has on an entire group, of course, does not have to be a negative experience. When a parent gets a job promotion or a significant raise in pay, all members stand to gain from the good fortune. If a child wins a scholarship to a major university, the entire family potentially benefits from the news. Accomplishments of individual family members may motivate others in the group to seek similar goals.

Recognizing the significance of the ripple effect means paying close attention to your own impact on groups. Your level of communication proficiency

Students and faculty wear gauze masks during an assembly at the University of the Pacific to protect themselves from the 1918 flu pandemic. Fear of the ripple effect was widespread.

or deficiency can mean success or failure of the entire group. "The power of one" should not be underestimated.

② Synergy

The whole is not necessarily equal to the sum of its parts. It may be greater than the sum of its individual parts. This effect is called synergy. **Synergy** *(syn*=together + *ergon*=work) occurs when group performance from joint action of members exceeds expectations based on perceived abilities and skills of individual members (Salazar, 1995).

working together / as a whole the group can do better than the individual

interconnected

The synergistic quality of group decision making is analogous to mixing drugs or chemicals. Some combinations of drugs, such as certain types of chemotherapy, can produce more effective results than two or more drugs taken separately. The potency of some pesticides, when mixed together, increase dramatically. One study at Tulane University found that mixing two common pesticide chemicals, endosulfan and dieldrin, didn't double their potency but instead increased their potency by as much as 1,600 times. As endocrinologist John A. McLachlan, who led the Tulane University team that did the study, explains, "Instead of one plus one equaling two, we found that one plus one equals a thousandfold" (as cited in "Playing havoc," 1996, p. 14A).

A creative synergy is often produced when talented people work together effectively. If the task calls for creativity, groups often outperform even a creative individual. That is why comedy writers for television shows frequently work as teams.

In the 1980 Winter Olympics, the U.S. hockey team was given virtually no chance of defeating the powerful Soviet Union. Two weeks before the Olympics the Soviets had demolished the same team from the United States by the humiliating score of 10–3. This was the same Soviet team that had defeated a National Hockey League All-Star team a year earlier and would do it again a few weeks after the Olympics. Nevertheless, in one of the most stunning upsets in sports history, the United States won the hockey game 4–3 and went on to win the gold medal. On the basis of individual talent the Soviets should have won easily. The inspired U.S. team, however, playing before a home crowd in Lake Placid, New York, produced synergy from collective effort melded into virtually flawless teamwork. Synergy is one reason why sports championships are decided by actually playing the game and not by relying on forecasts by experts that are based on the individual talents of players. Sometimes the underdog pulls off a synergistic miracle.

Synergy is produced only when group members work in an interconnected way. If group members work independently by completing individual assignments on their own and the group merely compiles the results without the benefit of group discussion and interaction, no synergy will occur (Fandt, 1991). For instance, if your group took an essay test and each member was assigned one question to answer, no synergistic benefit would occur if group members did not discuss rough draft answers with the whole group and make improvements prior to a final draft.

The 1980 U.S. Olympic hockey team completed a synergistic miracle by defeating the more talented Russian team 4–3.

Systems don't always produce synergy. Sometimes they produce negative synergy. **Negative synergy** occurs when group members working together produce a worse result than expected based on perceived individual skills and abilities of members (Salazar, 1995). The whole is worse than the sum of its parts. Negative synergy is like mixing alcohol and tranquilizers, causing suicidal effects. When group members know little about a subject, resist change, or share a collective bias or mindset, the result of mixing their individual contributions can produce decisions beyond bad.

One such instance occurred in the early 1980s. As part of an effort to sell Congress and the American public on the survivability of nuclear war and the necessity of spending four billion dollars to implement a civil defense plan, the Federal Emergency Management Agency (FEMA) downplayed the horror of nuclear holocaust. A December 1980 FEMA publication stated, "With reasonable protective measures, the United States could survive nuclear attack and go on to recovery within a relatively few years" (as cited in Scheer, 1983, p. 111). FEMA compounded this widely recognized absurdity with plans to evacuate whole cities (as if an aggressor would provide a week's warning in advance of an attack). Incredibly, FEMA also instructed survivors to fill out change-of-address cards with their post offices following the nuclear attack (apparently so the IRS could still collect taxes from traumatized survivors). FEMA presumed that life would return to something approaching normality soon after nuclear bombs had decimated a substantial portion of the human species (not to mention most post offices).

FEMA's *Alice-in-Wonderland* civil defense plan makes as much sense as satirical advice given in the "Meet Mr. Bomb" spoof of the plan edited by Tony Hendra (1982), in which citizens are instructed to prepare for the 4,000 degree centigrade temperature at ground zero by spending ten to fifteen minutes a day in a clothes dryer. FEMA's ludicrous civil defense directives were a jaw-dropping example of negative synergy.

On a less global scale, negative synergy can be seen in a group dialogue recorded by Hirokawa (1987). The group is deliberating a winter survival task whereby items must be ranked according to their utility in improving the group's survival in a wilderness area. Here the actual process of negative synergy becomes apparent.

B: This may sound crazy, but I say we go for the radio.
A: Why the radio? It's broken.
B: I know, I know . . . but that doesn't mean we can't use it.
C: I don't understand.
A: I think I do . . . but go ahead.
B: OK, like here's what I'm thinking. I remember, like I'm a fan of *Star Trek*, right . . . anyway, like on one show, Spock and Kirk are being held prisoners and they make this makeshift radio to call for help. So, like here's what I was thinking we could do . . . we could use the parts to build our own transmitter.
A: Right . . . like we could take the antenna and place it on a high tree . . . run wires down, and start building a transmitter, maybe then send Morse codes. We wouldn't have to talk.
B: What about power, though?
A: We could use the battery from the plane.
B: But that's not on the list here and we were told not to assume other things aside from the list.
C: We could use solar power.
B: Yeah, the sun . . . or electrical power . . . build our own generator . . . like on *Gilligan's Island*, remember where he was on a stationary bicycle?
A: Do we know codes?
C: I know SOS . . . three dots, three dashes, three dots . . .
B: Anyway, no matter. Just keep sending signals—any signals. . . .
C: So we go with the radio?
B: Yeah, I bet no one else thought of it. (p. 22)

In this illustration there is no indication that any of the group members knows anything about building a transmitter or generator. The success of such a venture would be doubtful at best even if MacGyver (to continue the group's reference to television shows) were available. Bad ideas in this group are simply compounded one upon the other—negative synergy at work.

ADAPTABILITY TO CHANGE

In a human system, **adaptability** is the modification of the structure and/or function of the system in response to changing conditions. Every system reacts to change in its own way. Two groups, for instance, that begin at the same point and experience similar environmental conditions may turn out very differently. Conversely, two groups that begin at very different points and experience dissimilar environmental conditions may turn out very similarly. In other words, groups with a similar or identical final goal (e.g., financial security) may reach that end in highly diverse ways (called *equifinality* in the somewhat ponderous systems lingo).

willingness to change.

Focus Questions

1. Why do groups establish boundaries? How do they establish boundaries?
2. Can groups ever become too open? Too closed?
3. Is it better to be more open than closed?

Openness and Change

Groups are never in a static state. Groups are in a constant state of becoming until they terminate. In human systems, change cannot cease. You do not have a choice between change and no change. The relevant choice is, "Can the group adapt to the inevitable changes that are certain to occur?"

Openness in a system refers to continuous interaction with the outside environment. Systems require input in order to function. **Input** is access to information, energy, people, ideas, and experiences from the outside environment. All living systems are open to some degree. No group, for instance, can be completely isolated from its outside environment and survive. Even cloistered monasteries require some input from outside. Outsiders must be transformed into new members or the group will eventually cease to exist. Some information is bound to leak into even the most sheltered groups.

Openness and change go hand in hand in a system. As systems open to the outside, new input inevitably disturbs the system by producing change. Admit women into a previously all-male club, boardroom, or law firm and change is inevitable. Women running for Congress in the 1992 election repeatedly argued that, if elected, they would shake up the male-dominated House and Senate, producing unprecedented change, and in many ways they did. A three-year study by the Center for the American Woman and Politics at Rutgers University was summarized this way by Debra Dodson, senior research assistant with the Center: "Women members of the 103rd Congress had an impact in every area of legislation studied, whether or not the legislation dealt with 'women's issues.' But much of their impact is missed if we look simply at floor votes. Without the efforts of women members, some legislation might never have made it to a final vote, or it might have looked very different when it got to the floor" (Goldston, 1995, p. 2A).

Openness and Boundaries

<u>Degree, rate, and desirability are three general factors that influence a group's ability or willingness to adapt successfully to change</u>. The unhappy experience of a friend of mine illustrates all three. As the owner of a small business, he decided to go high tech and computerize his office with the very latest, most sophisticated equipment. At the same time, he embarked on an office renovation project. To add to the disruption, he moved in a new partner. His office staff went berserk. They hadn't been trained to run the sophisticated computer programs and equipment. They resented the renovation, which displaced them from their normal work areas and created a huge mess that they had to work around. The new partner turned out to be a very demanding individual who thought little about expecting instant results from the beleaguered staff. The final change, however, that toppled this house of horrors was my friend's insistence that his staff work half-days on weekends until the office was returned to a more normal state. Three of the four members of his staff quit, and they were spitting fire as they stomped out of the office, never to return.

Too much change (degree) was required in too concentrated a period of time (rate) without a concerted effort to persuade the staff of the value (desirability) of the changes demanded. Groups can often adapt even to large changes if given sufficient time to absorb them and if members are convinced the changes have merit.

<u>Boundaries regulate the degree of openness and consequent exposure to change in a system</u>. When groups establish boundaries they regulate the degree, rate, even the desirability of change. This **boundary control** determines the amount of access a group has to input and influence from outsiders. Every group maintains boundary control to some extent. It is a critical group function.

The cast of the highly rated television sitcom *Friends* showed keen awareness of the necessity of maintaining boundaries. "Sharing is one thing, snitching another. Fiercely protective of each other's privacy . . . they know how to close ranks when besieged by the press" (Chin et al., 2000). In 1997, Matthew Perry, the self-deprecating Chandler Bing character in the series, became addicted to pain-killers following a jet-ski accident and lost a shocking amount of weight. Fellow cast members became intensely protective and supportive of Perry during his recovery, offering little information to the press and public about his ordeal. They erected strict boundary control to maintain group solidarity and personal friendships among cast members.

<u>Boundaries, however, are permeable</u>. They leak. No group can close off so completely to its environment that no change is possible. There is always some interchange with the environment that leaks through the boundaries.

Methods of Boundary Control   Groups establish boundaries by erecting physical, psychological, and linguistic barriers, and by establishing rules, roles, and networks. **Physical barriers** include locked doors, walls, an inconvenient location in a building to discourage people from just dropping by, partitions and cubicles in offices (sometimes derisively referred to as rabbit warrens). **Psychological barriers** make an individual feel that they do not belong in the group. Members' contributions are ignored or they are treated as outcasts. They may even be told that they are not wanted in the group. *ignore*

Linguistic barriers are the use of a private vocabulary, or *argot*, peculiar to a specific group. Those that understand the argot are presumed to be group members. Those that don't are clearly outsiders. Imagine if you heard this statement in an elevator from one business executive to another: "You could bring in a good athlete, but there's always the chance he or she could hit the windshield. Because you're worried that your VC partners have short arms, you're wondering whether to wake the giant. In any case, you're out of bandwidth: You're thinking about putting a ribbon on it and moving into sell mode. It's the living dead and about to become plankton." Translation? "You could bring in a talented executive from another field, but there's always a chance that he or she could fail. Because you're worried that your Venture Capitalist partners won't participate in a second round of funding, you're wondering whether to talk to Microsoft. In any case, you're out of time and exhausted. You're thinking about firing the engineers and selling the company. It's stagnant and about to be a small company swallowed by a larger one" (as cited in Herbold, 1998, p. 26A). This is an example of the argot of venture capitalists, or high-risk deal makers in the business world.

Rules establish who can become a group member. They also define appropriate behaviors in specified social situations. Rules may specify who can talk to whom, thus controlling input from outside. Within organizations there is usually a chain of command rule. You do not normally leapfrog your immediate supervisor and communicate directly with the president of the company. In order to prevent information overload and inefficiency, the Big Cheese will want you to talk to the Cheez Whiz.

Roles (cultural) are another way groups set boundaries. A role is a pattern of behavior exhibited by a member of a group. All roles have expectations attached to them. These expectations specify appropriate behavior, thereby fostering predictability and controlling variability. Once the pattern of behavior is associated with a group member, a boundary is set.

In the United States, managers are expected to respect the boundary between an employee's work life and private life. Commenting on a female employee's lack of a husband and informing her that she will be attending a luncheon to meet an eligible male would be viewed as clearly overstepping the boundaries separating supervisor and employee. The same reaction may not occur, however, in India where a leadership style called *paternal authoritativeness* is often preferred. Indians expect that someone in a supervisory leadership role, typically a male, will act like a father who cares about a family member. Going to the trouble of arranging a luncheon for a female employee to meet an eligible male would likely be perceived as showing personal interest and concern for the employee's welfare (Brislin, 1993). The employee would likely appreciate the gesture (and attend the luncheon), whereas in the United States charges of sexual harassment might be filed. Role boundaries and culture are inseparably interconnected.

Finally, groups set boundaries by establishing networks. Networks control the access and flow of information within the group and they may also isolate the group from outside influences. A **network** is a structured pattern of information flow and personal contact. The more open the network, the more accessible information is to a broad range of individuals. <u>Open networks encourage change while closed networks emphasize stability and permanence</u>.

In some cases, becoming a link in the network is the hard part. One study of African Americans in the banking industry (Irons and Moore, 1985) found that not being included in the network was rated as the most serious problem to advancement in their jobs by 75 percent of the respondents. Other studies of Asian Americans found similar barriers to upward mobility (see Morrison and Von Glinow, 1990).

CLOSER LOOK

Bound and Gagged: Cult Boundary Control

From the Manson Family and the Heaven's Gate Cybergroup to the Moonies and the Branch Davidians, cults small and large have emerged in the United States. Some have disintegrated in violent clashes with law enforcement or in mass suicides, while others continue to troll the waters of the disenchanted and dispossessed for new converts. Depending on the definition, there are between 3,000 and 5,000 cults in the United States with between two and five million members (Singer, 1995). These are rough estimates at best since there is no precise way to make a membership head count. These numbers do not include the millions of relatives and friends profoundly affected by individuals' membership in cults. Thus, <u>although cults are typically viewed as "fringe groups," their impact stretches far beyond the actual number of cults or size of cult membership</u>.

Singer (1995) defines a **cult** as "a group that forms around a person who claims he or she has a special mission or knowledge, which will be shared with those who turn over most of their decision making to that self-appointed leader" (p. xx). There

are four important characteristics of cults that separate them from other religious, political, or social groups (Appel, 1983; Galanter, 1989; Singer, 1995). These four characteristics are:

1. Cults have strong, charismatic leaders who exercise control in an authoritarian power structure.
2. Cults have a shared belief system whose adherents accept that they alone are gifted with the revealed truth.
3. Cults insist on regimented behavior of followers, strict obedience to authority figures, and unquestioning acceptance of the group's norms and beliefs.
4. Cults create rigid boundary control.

It is this last cult characteristic that I wish to explore here.

Cults exercise boundary control in the same ways that other groups do, just with greater enthusiasm and extremity. First, <u>they create physical isolation</u>. The most obvious examples are the Jonestown complex in Guyana and the Branch Davidian fortress in Waco, Texas. Reverend Jim

Isolated locations and fences clearly provide physical boundaries for Branch Davidian and Montana Freemen compounds. The boundaries, however, are permeable. Note the satellite dish, power and phone wires connecting the compounds to the outside world.

vidian leader built a 77-acre fortress of isolation in the middle of Texas. The Koresh cult also ended tragically in a 1993 fiery battle with federal authorities.

Physical isolation is also achieved through secrecy, in some instances. The manual of the Free Militia, a Midwest paramilitary cult, reads in part:

"The identities of cell members are known only within the cell and by their immediate superior.... All codes, passwords, and telephone networks are determined by and held in confidence within the cell. All fortified positions are determined, prepared and concealed by the cell.... The cell leader easily conveys clear orders to a small group of men. [Cell members] can communicate freely and openly while shrouding the particulars of their tactics, positions, and signals to everyone outside the group" (as cited in Conway and Siegelman, 1995, p. 344).

These cells, or subterranean secret units, are reserved for hard-core insurgent operations (Conway and Siegelman, 1995, p. 354).

A second way cults maintain rigid boundaries is through information control. As Galanter (1989) explains, if a cult "is to maintain a system of shared beliefs markedly at variance with that of the surrounding culture, members must sometimes be rigidly isolated from consensual information from the general society that would unsettle this belief system" (p. 112). Working hand in hand with physical isolation, information control is exercised partly by creating closed networks

Jones, dubbed the "Messiah from Ukiah" by the media, awash in his paranoid delusions and threatened by a series of exposés in newspapers and magazines, moved the bulk of the membership in his People's Temple from San Francisco to the jungles of Guyana, South America. There, in splendid isolation, Jones ruled his cult followers with an iron fist until it came to an end with the mass murder/suicide of 912 people, 276 of whom were children. David Koresh followed a similar pattern to Jones. Followers of this Branch Da-

that prevent outsiders such as parents, friends, and the media (unbelievers) from entering the cult's premises. A member's support network (family) is severed. Access to outside information is cut off. Cult members are encouraged to read cult literature. Of course, the best means of information control is self-censorship (Pratkanis and Aronson, 1992). Information that is not "of the cult" is labeled "of the devil," "lies of the government," and so forth. Members are made to feel guilt and shame for showing interest in such information.

Cult followers are also fed a diet of misinformation (Singer, 1995). Sheltered from outside information, the only reality for members of Jonestown, for instance, was what Jim Jones and his band of cohorts created for the group. Jonestown members were told that Los Angeles had been abandoned due to severe drought, that the Ku Klux Klan was boldly marching through the streets of San Francisco, and that the U.S. government was preparing to destroy Jonestown and kill its inhabitants. So restricted was the information entering Jonestown that even misinformation served to control the membership and create a paranoid atmosphere.

A third method of cult boundary control is the use of a group argot incomprehensible to outsiders. How, for example, are outsiders to know that *the devil disguise, just flesh relationships,* and *pollution* are derogatory terms for parents (Singer, 1995)? *Being too horizontal* is being too sympathetic to peers. Moonies refer to all relationships between people as either a *Cain–Abel* (superior–subordinate) or a *chapter 2* (sexuality) problem (Hassan, 1988). The Divine Light Mission refers to their services as *satsang* and *darshan.* Deceptive fund-raising practices are referred to by some cults as *transcendental trickery.* This **groupspeak** or cult jargon shuts down members' critical thinking. "Eventually, speaking in cult jargon is second nature, and talking with outsiders becomes energy-consuming and awkward. Soon enough, members find it most comfortable to talk only among themselves in the new vocabulary. To reinforce this, all kinds of derogatory

names are given to outsiders: wogs, systemites, reactionaries, unclean, of Satan" (Singer, 1995, p. 70).

A fourth method of cult boundary control involves erecting psychological barriers. This practice is most clearly evident in the "them versus us" in-group/out-group mentality that fosters either-or thinking within cults. You're *either* "with us" and right, redeemed, saved, *or* you're "against us" and therefore wrong, evil, unenlightened, doomed (Singer, 1995). To be an in-group member is to be a "chosen one." Those in the out-group are hated or feared as enemies (Pratkanis and Aronson, 1992). The beast in David Koresh's worldview was the U.S. government—also the object of virulent hatred from various militia cults in the United States (Conway and Siegelman, 1995). The Heaven's Gate group believed that Earth was controlled by demonic extraterrestrial "Luciferians" (Goodstein, 1997). "Fearfulness of outsiders, or xenophobia, a common characteristic of cults, is an important manifestation of boundary control. It holds groups together but it can reach the dimension of outright paranoia" (Galanter, 1989, p. 114).

Cults also erect psychological barriers against "bad thoughts." Questions that might arise in a member's mind that indicate less than total acceptance of the belief system of the cult are forcefully discouraged. These are "disagreeable thoughts," "evil," or "the work of Satan" (Pratkanis and Aronson, 1992). Members become their own mind police trying to clear their heads of Orwellian thought crimes.

Finally, cult boundary control is created by rigid rules. There are dress codes, dietary restrictions, and rules governing with whom a member may associate, marry, or talk. Some cults have rules stipulating whether members may raise their own children and where they may live (Singer, 1995). Gag rules that prohibit gossiping or "nattering" where members might express doubts or misgivings about the cult and the cult leaders are commonplace. Members are instructed to report any violations of the gag rule.

Although cults have extremely tight boundary control, no group can exist as a totally closed system. Boundaries are permeable even for cults. Seeking new converts requires some interaction with the outside world. The Branch Davidians, isolated in their fortress though they were, equipped their compound with a satellite dish, and some members, including Koresh, regularly jogged through Waco neighborhoods and shopped in local stores ("Cult compound," 1993). Members of the Heaven's Gate cult designed Internet Web sites for San Diego businesses and used their own Web sites to recruit members and proselytize their beliefs.

All groups exercise boundary control, but cults make boundary control a top priority, sometimes an obsession. This rigid boundary control is self-protective and has the effect of maintaining stability within the group and stifling change.

Questions for Thought

1. Can you have a cult without rigid boundary control?
2. Although cults are often religious or quasi-religious in nature, can cults be secular?
3. Can you have a cult without a charismatic cult leader?
4. How are cults different from the U.S. Marine Corps? The Catholic church? The Mormon church? The CIA?

Boundaries and Group Effectiveness Although all groups set boundaries, there is a strong bias in American culture that encourages openness, or loose boundaries, and discourages closedness, or rigid boundaries. We preach the value of fostering an open society and maintaining an open mind. Having a closed mind is linked to an authoritarian personality and dogmatism. A closed society is likened to China or North Korea. As I've already noted, highly closed, isolated groups are often referred to as cults. The fact that cults are excessively closed, however, shouldn't prompt the opposite problem—excessive openness. According to Klapp (1978), the belief that openness is always good and closedness is always bad is a faulty one.

The degree of openness in a system is a critical factor in a group's ability to adapt to change successfully. The pervasive bias for overly abundant openness found in U.S. society, however, is simply misguided. No group can long endure unless it closes off to *some* outside influences and restricts access to *some* information (Galanter, 1989). This is why boundary control is an essential group function.

A group must close off when both the quantity and type of input place undue stress on the group and/or prevent it from accomplishing its task. There are times, for instance, when a family seeks advice and counsel from friends and relatives (input), but there are also times when a family should close off to the intrusion from outsiders. In-laws who are overly free with advice and criticism impose stress on the family. Permitting even well-intentioned relatives and friends to hammer immediate family members with unsolicited counsel can easily lead to bickering, increased tension, conflict, even family disintegration.

The Voyeur Dorm Web site became a controversial issue in Tampa, Florida in August 1999 (Blumner, 1999). For $34 a month, customers, mostly

[handwritten margin note: At boundaries v- access / bound. control is / Not all negative / (ic FBI, CIA)]

Executive producer Paul Romer of the Dutch television show "Big Brother," stands in front of monitors used in this wildly popular "reality" TV program. Nine strangers are confined for 100 days in a house loaded with video cameras allowing viewers to watch the groups daily activities, all for a chance to win $120,000 for the "most liked" group member.

men, could observe seven female college students in their home. The women occupied a residential house wired with 34 video cameras that covered almost every part of the house. The Tampa Variance Review Board discovered this real, live "Truman Show" and ruled that the Voyeur Dorm was not a legitimate home occupation but an adult-use business. Despite what you might think of this bizarre business venture, imagine what it would be like living under the constant view of strangers in your own home. Taking a shower would be a public event. Although there was a no-sex policy in the Voyeur Dorm, practically every other personal activity was paraded before the peeping eyes of Web site subscribers. Clearly, this would be far too much openness for the vast majority of people, as was made evident in the movie *EdTV*. We need our boundaries to live our lives without the probing eyes of strangers increasing our stress.

When groups experience debilitating stress and tension, divisive conflicts, boredom and malaise, and poor productivity, members should take these as possible signs of excessive openness or closedness. Loosening or tightening boundary controls may be in order because groups must be able to adapt successfully to change. <u>Knowing whether to relax or tighten boundaries depends on whether the group is already very closed or very open.</u>

second look

Openness and Group Boundary Control

Types of Group Boundaries Regulating Change

Physical Barriers	Psychological Barriers
Linguistic Barriers	Rules
Roles	Networks

Boundary Control and Group Effectiveness

Groups should adjust their boundaries, becoming more open or closed based on how rigid or loose boundaries already are, when both quantity and type of information place undue stress on the groups and/or prevent them from accomplishing their task.

Debilitating stress/tension, divisive conflicts, boredom, malaise, and poor productivity are signs of excessive openness or closedness.

INFLUENCE OF SIZE

Size is a central element in any human system. Fluctuations in size have enormous influence on the structure and function of a group.

Focus Questions
1. What is the most appropriate size for a decision-making group?
2. What distinguishes a small group from a large one?
3. How are groups and organizations different?

Group Size and Complexity

 As groups increase in numerical size, complexity increases. There are numerous complications that increased complexity produces. In this section, I will discuss in what ways size matters in groups.

Quantitative Complexity   Bostrom (1970) observes that as the size of the group increases arithmetically (linearly), the possible number of interactions between group members increases geometrically (exponentially). These are his calculations:

Number in Group	Interactions Possible
2	2
3	9
4	28
5	75
6	186
7	441
8	1056

Bostrom shows that in a dyad, only two relationships are possible, namely, person A to person B and vice versa. A and B may not have the same perception of their relationship. Person A may perceive the relationship with B as a close friendship whereas B sees the relationship with A as merely acquaintanceship. In a triad, or three-member group, there are nine possibilities:

1. A to B	4. C to A	7. A to B and C
2. B to A	5. B to C	8. B to A and C
3. A to C	6. C to B	9. C to A and B

In a special issue of *Newsweek* on the subject of the family, a practical example of the Bostrom calculations in real life is described:

> The original plot goes like this: First comes love. Then comes marriage. Then comes Mary with a baby carriage. But now there's a sequel: John and Mary break up. John moves in with Sally and her two boys. Mary takes the baby Paul. A year later Mary meets Jack, who is divorced with three children. They get married. Paul, barely two years old, now has a mother, a father, a stepmother, a stepfather, and five stepbrothers and stepsisters—as well as four sets of grandparents (biological and step) and countless aunts and uncles. And guess what? Mary's pregnant again. (Kantrowitz and Wingert, 1990, p. 24)

Complexity increases rapidly as the size of the group grows. Adding even a single member to a group enormously complicates the group dynamics. As newscaster Jane Pauley once remarked, "Somehow three children are many more than two."

Complexity and Group Transactions

Complexity increases as groups increase in size, but does this affect group transactions in significant ways? The answer is yes. Try scheduling a meeting for a group of 15 or 20 members. Consider how difficult it would be finding a time that doesn't conflict with at least one or more members' personal schedules and preferences. Consider further what would likely occur if your group suddenly gained a new member who couldn't meet at the scheduled time. A meeting already scheduled would have to be either rescheduled (unlikely) or the new member would have to miss the meeting and be filled in later. Then there is the potential hassle that can occur when the new member misses the meeting, but strongly disagrees with the group decisions made in his or her absence. Issues decided may be raised anew, members may grow annoyed, and conflict may ensue. Adding members to a group complicates the decision-making process.

Variations in size affect group transactions in several specific ways. First, larger groups typically have more nonparticipants than smaller groups (Kessler, 1973). This occurs partly because in larger groups there is more intense competition to seize the floor (Carletta et al., 1998). More reticent members are apt to sit quietly rather than fight to be heard. This also means that the more talkative members are likely to emerge as leaders of larger groups because influence on the group comes partly from speaking (Kolb, 1997).

Second, smaller groups inhibit overt disagreement and signs of dissatisfaction more than larger groups do. Smaller groups can apply more intense pressure to conform to majority opinion than can be applied in larger groups

(Bettinghaus and Cody, 1987). Splinter groups and factions are more likely to emerge in larger groups. In a six-person group there may be only a single deviant who must stand alone against the group. In a twelve-person group, however, two or more deviants may more easily emerge, forming a supportive faction. Having an ally makes nonconformity easier to sustain.

In the movie *Twelve Angry Men*, only one juror votes "not guilty" on the first vote. Hailed by many as a dramatization of the importance of one person standing against the many in a fight for truth and justice, one scene is often overlooked. The lone holdout debates with fellow jurors for a while but eventually indicates that he is unwilling to continue if no other juror will support his position. He makes a deal with the jury. If no other juror votes not guilty on the next ballot, then he will join the majority and also vote for conviction, thereby sending the defendant to death row. When he gains an ally, the fight is continued to its dramatic conclusion. Nonconformity is easier when you don't have to stand alone against the group.

Third, group size affects levels of cooperation (Stahelski & Tsukuda, 1990). When groups of 12 to 30 members were compared, the smallest groups were found to be the most cooperative, meaning they worked together on tasks more interdependently, engaged in collaborative effort, and exhibited consensus leadership. As groups increased in size, cooperation decreased. This resulted in diminished task effectiveness, unmet goals, and increased conflicts. Other studies have found that larger groups encourage formation of **cliques** or small, narrowly focused subgroups that create a competitive atmosphere. These cliques diminish overall group performance (Carron & Spink, 1995).

Fourth, group members tend to be less satisfied with groups of ten or more (Carter & West, 1998). The overall group climate often deteriorates when groups become large. Tasks become more complex to perform, tension mounts, and dominant group members can trigger interpersonal disharmony by becoming too aggressive and forceful with other members while trying to impose order (Pavitt & Curtis, 1994).

So what is the ideal size for a group? There is no specific number. The best size for a group is the smallest size capable of performing the task effectively (Hackman, 1987; Sundstrom et al., 1990). This admittedly is somewhat imprecise advice, but there is a tradeoff between quality and speed when trying to determine ideal group size (Pavitt and Curtis, 1994). If the primary group goal is the quality of the decision, then a moderately sized group of seven to ten is advisable. (Groups larger than this, especially substantially larger, can easily become unwieldy and inefficient.) Moderate-sized groups are especially effective if there is little overlap of knowledge and skills among group members and the group task requires substantial diversity in knowledge and skills (Valacich et al., 1994). If the primary goal of the group is speed, however, then groups of four or fewer members are advisable. Larger groups typically slow down decision making and problem solving, sometimes maddeningly so.

Since juries are faced with momentous choices that significantly affect people's lives, the twelve member jury has been the norm. If your well-being depended on a jury verdict, you would certainly want the primary group goal to be the quality and not the speed of the decision. Nevertheless, as groups become larger, decision making becomes more complicated. Consensus (unanimous agreement) becomes difficult and majority vote is often used to make final decisions when groups are large. Some research (see Pavitt and Curtis, 1994) suggests five-member groups are a nice compromise when both quality and speed are important group goals. Ultimately, there is no magic number that constitutes the ideal-sized group. Even five-member groups can circumvent quality deliberations by a quick majority vote. Contextual factors (politics, legal requirements, institutional norms, availability of members, task complexity, etc.) may necessitate groups larger in size than five or even ten. Competent communicators can work effectively in larger groups, although increased size magnifies the difficulties.

Groups Versus Organizations

When groups grow, they reach a point where they may become organizations with bureaucracies. For instance, suppose you and two friends decide to open a small business together. Let's say you call it New Age Repair & Care (NARC for short). Your business specializes in "holistic healing of automobiles" in addition to conventional automotive services.

In its initial stages, the structure of your group is informal and the division of labor is most likely equal. Since the three of you work at the establishment, communication is not hampered by cumbersome chains of command, middle managers, and the paper chase of a large formal organization. Standards of operation and procedures for decision making are informally negotiated among the three of you as situations occur.

If your little enterprise booms, employees will have to be hired, thus expanding the business and increasing the complexity of the entire operation. Work schedules will have to be coordinated. Standardized codes of dress and conduct on the job may be required. Some training in New Age automotive techniques may be necessary. Formal grievance procedures may also be required to settle disputes. You may decide to open additional NARC outlets, even become a chain, selling franchises around the country. Now you must hire managers, accountants, and lawyers, establish a board of directors, sell stock in the company, and become business executives. What began as a small enterprise can grow into a large organization.

When small groups grow into larger groups, finally graduating into complex organizations, the structure and function of these human systems change. With increasing group size comes greater formality. Small groups are more personal than large organizations. Small groups usually can function well as a committee of the whole with relatively equal distribution of power. Large organizations become hierarchical, with clearly demarcated power structures and lines of authority, although recently there has been a trend toward *flattening the hierarchy* by moving away from tightly defined roles of superiors and subordinates and placing greater emphasis on teamwork. The company becomes more important than any single individual. Employees in the organization can be replaced with relative ease whereas in a small intimate group, loss of a single member may bring about the demise of the group.

The flow of information is one of the most important differences between small groups and complex organizations. Normally, <u>little negative information from below reaches the top of the corporate hierarchy, or if it does it is delayed</u> (Conrad, 1990). In the spring of 1995, software producer Intuit, Inc., confessed that there were bugs in its tax-preparation software. Those using the software would likely file erroneous income tax returns with the IRS. Intuit's tax-preparation programs were the market leaders and the timing of the announcement that the programs were defective came just six weeks prior to the April 15 income tax deadline, too late for eager beavers who filed an early return. Intuit President Scott Cook admitted at a news conference that the firm's technical support team knew about the software bugs in December 1994 but didn't pass the information up the corporate ladder for many weeks. Cook sheepishly explained, "This one is particularly embarrassing because we didn't know we knew about it. I am very disappointed that we did not act more quickly on this. We really let our customers down" (as cited in Gomes, 1995, p. 4C).

Although negative information and blunders can be hidden in small groups, it is far more difficult than in organizations. Bad decision making cannot be hidden easily when the group is small. Almost any blunder will become incandescent when the black hole of bureaucracy is not present to shroud it. If you have three people running a small business and one of the three does something boneheaded that affects the enterprise, your choices immediately narrow to two possibilities (unless, of course, you are guilty but playing dumb). One of your two partners has to be the culprit.

<u>Information distortion usually is a bigger problem in organizations than in smaller groups.</u> Managers act as gatekeepers, screening messages, selecting which ones will be brought to the attention of higher-ups. By the time a message from below reaches top executives in an organization, it can easily become unrecognizable nonsense. Similarly, information from the top can be distorted by the time it filters down to the bottom of the organization (Conboy, 1976).

telephone

---

second look

Effects of Increasing Group Size

Increases	Decreases
• Complexity	• Participation in group discussion
• Factionalism/cliques	• Cooperation (in very large groups)
• Formality—more hierarchical	• Pressure to conform—coalitions likely to form in opposition to group norms
• Information distortion	
• Quality decision making (unless group becomes too large and unwieldy)	• Member satisfaction with group experience (10 or more)
	• Access to information
• Difficulty achieving consensus—majority vote often substituted	• Flow of negative information to top of hierarchy
• Likelihood talkative members become leaders	• Speed of decision making

[handwritten margin notes: le boundries / 1. physical boundries / 2. psychological / 3. / 4. / 5. / le .]

In smaller groups, however, the communication is usually more direct with fewer opportunities for distortion, as messages are transmitted serially through several people. If the message is communicated to the entire group at the same time—a comparatively easy task if the gathering is small—then the problems of message distortion are reduced.

The Beatles as a System

In February 1966, John Lennon made the provocative and not very bright remark that the Beatles rock group was more popular than Jesus Christ. Although this offhand bit of hyperbole by the most volatile member of Britain's famous rock quartet was not well received by many Beatle fans and foes alike, there was no doubt that this rock band was an international phenomenon of no small proportion. They sold over *one billion* recordings—which is the current world record.

The Beatles' popularity continues unabated. There are dozens of Beatles' Web sites. When the Beatles *Anthology*, Vol. I, a CD of previously unreleased tracks, was made available on November 21, 1995, to coincide with a six hour ABC-TV documentary on the rock group, it sold 450,000 copies the first day. This was the highest single-day sales ever for an album ("They're still on top," 1995, p. 4A). Thirteen million of their first two anthology albums were sold in 1996 and six million of their old albums were purchased, making 1996 the best year commercially that the Beatles ever had. Their third anthology album hit the top of the Billboard chart in November, 1996. Forty-one percent of the album buyers were not even born when the Beatles split up in 1970 ("Who's the hot group," 1996, p. 2A).

1999 was another big year for the Beatles. Three Beatles' recordings were named to the National Academy of Recording Arts and Sciences Hall of Fame. The song "Yesterday" was named top song of the twentieth century in a poll released on the BBC. Paul McCartney was voted greatest composer of the millenium in a BBC on-line poll, and John Lennon was voted the greatest singer of all time in a poll by the British magazine *Mojo*. The re-release of the Beatles' movie *Yellow Submarine* was an international event.

Albert Goldman (1988) described the phenomenon of the Beatles as "the most triumphant career in the history of show business" (p. 326). Music critic Robert Christgau, writing in 1973, gave tribute to the Beatles by defining "rock" as "all music deriving primarily from the energy and influence of the Beatles—and maybe Bob Dylan . . ." (as cited in Stokes, 1980, p. 151).

The Beatles are credited with revolutionizing the economics of the music industry by inventing the rock tour on a grand scale emulated to this day by subsequent rock bands (Stokes, 1980). The Beatles seized artistic control of their recordings from record companies, leading the way for future groups and musicians. They popularized the concept album *(Sgt. Pepper's Lonely Hearts Club Band)*, convincing other rock musicians that an album didn't have to consist merely of a conglomeration of hit singles and filler recordings. "The Beatles broke down the barriers between low art and high art, the visceral and the intellectual—rock became something to think about as well as feel about. And telling us how to think and feel about the music were rock critics, something else we have the Beatles to thank/curse for" (Brumley et al., 1995, p. 8).

The Beatles serve as an interesting historical case study illustrating the groups-as-systems perspective. It is difficult to find well-researched accounts of the complete life cycle of any long-standing group. Since much has been written chronicling the decade long lifespan of this phenomenally popular group, however, all three primary elements of a system—interconnectedness of parts, adaptability to change, and influence of size—can be usefully illustrated by analyzing the Beatles.

Originally called the Quarrymen and composed of John Lennon, Paul McCartney, George Harrison, Stuart Sutcliffe (who dropped out early on), and any drummer they could find, by 1960 they had become the Beatles with Pete Best at the drums. The cohesiveness of the group did not gel, however, until Best was replaced by Ringo Starr (Richard Starkey).

McCartney described the early Beatles, who played predominantly in pubs and strip joints in Hamburg, Germany, this way: "We're all really the same person. We're just four parts of the one" (as cited in Stokes, 1980, p. 53). As the band developed and rocketed to superstardom following appearances on the *Ed Sullivan Show* in February 1964, the interconnectedness of the four became increasingly obvious. "John needed Paul's melodic sense; Paul needed John's skepticism; George needed their sense of pop; and because he kept his feet unhesitatingly on the ground, they all needed Ringo, who cherished them like a fan" (Ward et al., 1986, p. 348). Famed conductor Leonard Bernstein waxed rhapsodic when describing the synergistic effect of John and Paul's songwriting collaboration plus the meshing of all four band members: "These two [John and Paul] made a pair embodying a creativity mostly unmatched during that fateful decade [the Sixties]. . . . And yet, the two were merely something, the four were it. The interdependence was astonishing" (as cited in Stokes, 1980, p. 3).

Faced with adulation from fans on an unprecedented scale, the Beatles were forced to erect boundaries for their own protection and sanity. These boundaries included hiding away in hotel rooms during tours, ducking out back entrances to avoid shrieking throngs of Beatles worshippers, and avoiding most public establishments. In order to record their albums and most of all protect the band's initial image of whole-

someness, the prying eyes of outsiders were steadfastly blocked from view. Boundary control was so stringent that a rumor began circulating that Paul had died in a bloody traffic accident in 1966. This rumor "explained" why the Beatles had stopped touring and had sequestered themselves in recording studios where Paul's demise could be camouflaged by electronic gimmickry.

Adaptability to change became essential to the Beatles' long survival as a rock band. Some of the changes they faced included wealth and notoriety, marriages and children, serious drug use (especially by John), drug arrests (John and Paul), the death by drug overdose of their long-time manager Brian Epstein who skillfully created the image of the Beatles, and a foray into Eastern mysticism (primarily by George). Yet by closing off to the public and placing the primacy of the Beatles above petty conflicts and artistic differences, the Beatles managed to stay together despite some rocky moments. The final straw of change that broke the band's back was the arrival of Yoko Ono (Lancashire, 1970). This was one change too many (degree) and an unwanted one, besides (desirability).

John became fascinated with Yoko in 1966 but did not begin an intimate relationship with her until two years later. Their celebration of newfound love together culminated in the *Two Virgins*

Yoko Ono was the "fifth Beatle" and a disruptive, and apparently depressing, influence on the group.

album they recorded in a six hour period one night. Consisting mostly of "random bird calls, screeches, and nose-blowings" (Stokes, 1980, p. 222), the most noteworthy feature of the album was its cover displaying John and Yoko nude. The controversy surrounding this album strained the already turbulent relationships among the foursome, but when John tried to impose Yoko's musical suggestions onto the Beatles' compositions, she became an intolerable threat. When John married Yoko, the end was near. Paul, George, and Ringo had not contemplated a "fifth Beatle," yet Yoko's intrusive presence had the effect of increasing the group's size and thus magnifying complexity and conflict.

On April 10, 1970, Paul announced to the world that the Beatles were no more. Yet even in divorce, he recognized the continued intercon-

nectedness of band members. "No matter how much we split, we're still very linked. We're the only four people who've seen the whole Beatlemania bit from the inside out, so we're tied forever, whatever happens" (as cited in Lancashire, 1970, p. 1).

Questions for Thought

1. Could rock bands like the Beatles ever survive long without stringent boundary control? Why?
2. The intrusion of Yoko Ono demonstrates the significant impact a single individual can have on a group, especially when that individual is not regarded as a true group member. Can you think of similar instances where a single individual has had such a dramatic effect on a rock band?

DEFINITION OF A SMALL GROUP

Now that I have sketched the face of what a system looks like, let me provide a suitable definition of a group. A group is a system. As a system, a group is characterized by interconnectedness of its constituent parts, adaptability to change, and the influence of size. Consequently, I offer the following definition: a **group** is a human communication system composed of three or more individuals, interacting for the achievement of some common purpose(s), who influence and are influenced by one another.

A group, then, is different from a mere collection of individuals called an *aggregation* (Goldhaber, 1990). Twenty-five people standing in line to buy tickets for a movie are not a group but simply an aggregation. Since they do not interact with and influence one another to achieve a common purpose (strangers standing in line are not there expressly to help each other secure tickets), they do not qualify as a group. The same holds for a crowd shopping in a mall or waiting for a plane departure delayed by fog. In both cases the presence of other people is irrelevant to the achievement of the specific purpose (buying clothes or traveling from point A to point B). A collection of individuals must succeed or fail as a unit in a quest to achieve a common purpose in order to be called a group. Crowds, of course, can become groups if they satisfy the definition provided above.

This text will focus on small groups with special emphasis in chapters 6 and 7 given to decision making and problem solving groups. Trying to draw a meaningful line between small and large groups, however, can prove to be fruitless. When does the addition of one more member transform a small group into a large one? Over the years, some communication theorists have set the upper limit of small groups at between twelve and twenty members, with fifteen often cited. Other theorists define a small group, as distinct from a large group, as composed of few enough members to have specific impressions of each other and the ability to treat one another in a personal manner (Pavitt & Curtis, 1994). I think this approach is preferable to setting an arbitrary upper limit on group size.

Although I will not concentrate on organizations in this book, I will include examples from organizational settings because many of you can relate meaningfully to such an environment. Virtually all of what I will discuss is immediately relevant to enhancing communication competence in organizations. After all, "an organization itself may be viewed as a group of groups" (Haslett et al., 1992, p. 103).

In summary, groups are systems. The three main elements of a system are interconnectedness of parts, adaptability to change, and the influence of size. A small group is defined in terms of function and the ideal size for most decision making and problem solving groups is the smallest group capable of performing the task effectively. Having now laid the theoretical foundation for analyzing small groups, I will discuss the process of group development in the next chapter.

Questions for Critical Thinkers

1. How does the effect of a disruptive group member demonstrate the interconnectedness element of a system?
2. In groups that you belong to, what boundaries are erected?
3. Do organizations always require a hierarchical structure? Explain.
4. How far can you flatten an organizational hierarchy and still maintain effectiveness?

CHAPTER

3

Group Development

On April 24, 1997, Delta Air Lines' board of directors announced the unanimous decision not to renew the contract of Delta's Chair, Ronald Allen. Despite helping to pull Delta out of a tailspin in the early 1990s in which heavy financial losses were recorded, Allen was forced out because, as one board member put it, there was "an accumulation of abrasions over time" (Brannigan, 1997, p. A8). So what were these "abrasions" that led the board to replace Allen despite Delta's turnaround from near financial collapse? In a memo released to Delta employees, the board, without making direct reference to Allen, stated that it placed "a high value on Delta's culture of respect, unity and deep regard for our heritage." The board went on to say that it intended "to select a person as our next leader who will work well within this culture we all value so highly" (as cited in Brannigan, p. A8). Ronald Allen clearly did not engender respect, unity, and a deep regard for the worker-friendly, family atmosphere valued by the board.

Allen had a caustic management style that concentrated on the financial "bottom line" at the expense of relationships with workers. He developed a reputation for berating employees in front of other workers. He was known as autocratic, intolerant, and harsh (Brannigan, 1997). When Hollis Harris revealed to Allen that he was resigning as Delta's president to head Continental Airlines, Allen demanded that Hollis relinquish the keys to his company car on the spot, leaving him stranded without transportation home. Allen cut thousands of jobs in 1994. Employees were extremely upset with this cost-cutting measure and the heavy-handed way in which it was done. Allen acknowledged that workers were upset with his slash-and-burn tactics, but his glib response was "so be it." Soon buttons reading "So Be It" began appearing on the chests of pilots, flight attendants, and mechanics. Worker morale plunged. An exodus of senior managers began. Many experienced workers were laid off or quit. Delta service, once the envy of the airline industry, rapidly deteriorated. Dirty planes and frustrated flight attendants became the norm. On-time performance of flights sank from the top to the bottom of the industry. Passengers began joking that Delta stood for "**D**oesn't **E**ver **L**eave **T**he **A**irport." Tough measures were necessary to save Delta when Allen took over, but, as Wayne Horvitz, a Washington, D.C., labor relations consultant notes, "You don't have to be an SOB to be tough" (Brannigan, 1997, p. A1). Allen had "broken the spirit" of this once proud company. His narrow focus on the task of returning Delta to profitability ignored the vital role interpersonal relations play in group success.

This example highlights the strong connection between the task and social dimensions of groups. Put simply, how group members are treated and the quality of their relationships within a group can markedly affect task accomplishment. As groups move through phases of development, this relationship between these two key dimensions of every group can become a critical factor in achieving success or experiencing failure. The primary purpose of this chapter is to explore this interconnectedness of task and social dimensions through phases of group development. I have three related chapter objectives:

1. to explain the connection between task and social dimensions of a group,
2. to discuss task and social dimensions within the periodic phases of group development, and

3. to discuss how newcomers affect task and social dimensions of groups, with strategies offered for newcomer acceptance into groups.

TASK AND SOCIAL DIMENSIONS

Focus Questions
1. How do the task and social dimensions of groups interconnect?
2. How are the task and social dimensions integral to both the formation and development of decision-making groups?

performance

relationships impact on whole

All decision-making groups have both task and social dimensions. The **task dimension** is the work performed by the group and its impact on the group. The **social dimension** is the relationships that form between members in the group and their impact on the group as a whole. As I have already explained, groups are systems and, as such, all aspects of a group are interconnected. Thus, degree of concern for a task affects the social or relationship aspects. Conversely, degree of concern for relationships in the group affects the accomplishment of the task.

In a system, the results of a group's interactions are called **outputs.** The output from a group's task dimension is productivity and the output from the social dimension is cohesiveness. **Productivity** is the result of the efficient and effective accomplishment of a group task. **Cohesiveness**—the degree to which members feel a part of the group, wish to stay in the group (Lanfred, 1998), and are committed to each other and to the group's work (Wech et al., 1998)—is produced primarily by attention to social relationships. Cohesive groups have a We-orientation.

P107 example

Neither the task nor the social dimension can be ignored for a decision-making group to be successful. Too much attention to productivity can diminish cohesiveness by producing stress and conflict. Ronald Allen's single-minded focus on the task of returning Delta Air Lines to profitability disrupted the interpersonal harmony within the company. This disruption ultimately led to poor service, diminished worker morale, loss of valuable employees, and a negative image within the industry and among passengers. Conversely, too much emphasis on cohesiveness can produce a group of socializers who like each other a great deal but accomplish nothing in particular. This is a problem unless, of course, the purpose of the group is merely to have a good time and no task needs to be accomplished.

In general, cohesiveness enhances group productivity unless overemphasized (Evans and Dion, 1991). This relationship, however, is stronger in small groups than in larger ones, for ongoing natural groups than for artificially created groups, and for cooperative groups than for competitive groups (Klein, 1996). The nature of the task also affects the relationship between cohesiveness and productivity. The more interdependent group members must be in order to accomplish a task (e.g., flying a passenger jet, performing surgery, playing team basketball) the stronger is the cohesiveness-productivity relationship (Gully et al., 1995).

The Case of "Hormones with Feet"

Anxious to make friends and not infrequently hopeful that romance is in the offing, students preparing group symposium presentations in my classes often become sidetracked. They devote disproportionate energy toward cultivating interpersonal relationships at the expense of the group's overall performance. Sometimes this involves only certain members, and other times the total membership becomes involved in pursuing a good time at the expense of task accomplishment.

I would never wish to thwart burgeoning romance nor interfere with blossoming friendship, but there is a time and place for everything. I still remember with some amusement the couple in one group a few years back who aptly illustrated Mark Twain's definition of an adolescent as "hormones with feet." This couple's group was desperately attempting to put together a symposium presentation on some issue of national import. Meanwhile, these overheated lovers were fixated with each other. Their conversation gushed with honey-coated affection. Meaningful squeezes, tender hugs, starry-eyed gazes, the entire repertoire of longing for each other was amply demonstrated for all to observe.

I'm confident that you can predict the reaction of other group members to this overt display of adolescent behavior. At first, group members were uncomfortable, then mildly amused, irritated,

exasperated, and finally just plain hostile. Two group members self-absorbed in promoting a social relationship while ignoring the task at hand seriously undermine the entire group's ability to function productively. In other circumstances, I am certain the entire group membership would have applauded this couple's newly discovered love for each other. In this particular context, however, members viewed the couple's behavior as disruptive. This couple did not exhibit communication competence. Both individuals showed insensitivity to the needs of the group, a pronounced Me-orientation, and no commitment to group goals. They put their agenda ahead of the group's.

When whole groups decide that it is better to socialize than to work, task accomplishment obviously suffers. It is not unusual for a group to waste valuable time socializing with one another only to realize too late that deadlines are fast approaching and sufficient work has not been completed.

Questions for Thought

1. How do you know when the group as a whole has become excessively social?
2. Have you experienced a similar case of over-socializing to the detriment of task accomplishment?

So how do groups build cohesiveness? There are several ways. <u>The main strategies for instilling cohesiveness in groups are</u>:

1. *Encourage compatible membership.* When group members enjoy each other's company and share an attraction for one another, cohesiveness can be easily built. When difficult, disruptive individuals join the group, cohesiveness can suffer. Of course, a group doesn't always have the luxury of choosing who can join. Sometimes membership is mandated from outside (e.g., by an institution or corporation).

2. *Develop shared goals.* One aspect of cohesiveness is sharing a common vision.

When all group members are pulling together to achieve a goal valued by all, cohesiveness increases.

3. *Accomplish tasks.* Productive groups usually become more cohesive as a result of task accomplishment. If group members feel good about work accomplished, this often pulls the group together and promotes team spirit. As a rule, successful teams exhibit harmony. Unsuccessful teams, however, frequently manifest frustration and disappointment by sniping, sniveling, and finger-pointing. Poor productivity can lead to group disintegration.

4. *Develop a positive history of cooperation.* If group members work together cooperatively rather than competitively, cohesiveness can flourish (Klein, 1996). I will elaborate on constructing cooperation and building teamwork in small groups in chapter 4.

5. *Promote acceptance of group members.* If members make each other feel valued and err on the side of praise, not blame, then they will be encouraging each other to excel.

The task and social dimensions are integral to both the formation and development of decision-making groups. Just where these two dimensions fit into the life of a group can be ascertained by exploring the periodic phases of group development.

PERIODIC PHASES OF GROUP DEVELOPMENT

Many communication scholars have classified group development into specific stages. Tuckman (1965) describes the four phases of group development as forming, storming, norming, and performing. These phases, however, should not be viewed as sequential. Groups do not necessarily pass through these phases of development in linear fashion like a person does when growing older (i.e., youth, middle age, old age). Groups tend to be far messier than this, sometimes cycling back around to a previous phase seemingly completed (Hare, 1994). (Unhappily, such cycling back is not possible with aging.)

Admittedly, group development can be classified in terms of an initial phase where individuals join together for some reason (forming), a tension phase (storming), a standards and rules of conduct for members phase (norming), and a phase where effort is targeted toward goal achievement (performing). These phases, however, can be very periodic, meaning that they are apt to appear, disappear, and reappear, even overlap.

Let me add one other note of clarification. Forming, storming, norming, and performing are global phases of group development relevant to groups in general, large or small. I will discuss specific phases relevant to the process of decision emergence in small groups in chapter 7.

Focus Questions
1. Does why we join a group make any difference to the group?
2. Is tension in a group undesirable?
3. Where do group norms come from? Why do we conform to group norms?
4. Do groups outperform individuals?

Forming: Why We Join Groups

The reasons we join groups act as catalysts for group formation. We join groups to satisfy some need (Shaw, 1981). This need satisfaction divides into five principal categories discussed in this section.

Interpersonal Attraction   We join groups because we are drawn to its members. Human beings have a strong need to affiliate with others, particularly others who are similar to ourselves (Shaw, 1981). We seem drawn to others when we perceive them to be similar to us in personality, attitudes and beliefs, ethnic origin, sexual orientation, and economic status. Many campus clubs and support groups are attractive because of member similarity.

We also seem attracted to those who experience similar feelings to our own in distressing situations (Schachter, 1959). Victims of natural disasters are attracted to each other because of shared misery. They are bonded by trauma. Misery may love company, but the company is usually of a particular type. "Misery loves *miserable* company" (Firestone et al., 1973).

If you just flunked a big exam, chances are you'll seek out others who likewise bellyflopped and avoid those who aced the test. We seem drawn to those who are experiencing similar emotions to our own. Who wants to be around someone who glories in his or her good fortune while we sink into a blue funk over our misfortune?

Contestants on the MTV show "Singled Out" are matched on the basis of their similarities. Similarities with others is a prime reason we join groups.

Other factors influence interpersonal attraction besides similarity between individuals. Physical attractiveness is probably the most obvious source of attraction. Women seem drawn to good-looking men. There is evidence to support the common observation, however, that physical attractiveness is more important to men than it is to women as a factor influencing attraction (Ritter, 1996), a fact surprising only to someone new to the planet. Although other factors of attractiveness may be more important determinants of group membership, physical attractiveness certainly matters to some people.

Attraction to Group Activities

Sometimes we join groups to participate in the group's activities. Hackers' groups have emerged all over the United States. One such group of twelve members ranging in age from teens to a man in his fifties was interviewed by Dawn Yoshitake (1996) in the Union Station train terminal in Los Angeles. Meetings are open to anyone, including security specialists, law enforcement agents, or the curious. These hackers meet to share information about equipment and new techniques for manipulating technologies. They may also bond in the process. One hacker, a sixteen year old, put it this way, "I can't talk to a lot of my friends about computers and phone (hacking). But here, people understand. It's an acceptance thing" (p. A7).

Joining a group because you are attracted to the group's principal activity (e.g., chess clubs and debate teams) doesn't preclude the additional draw from social connection among members. When I coached intercollegiate debate, students would join primarily for the competition. Several students, however, seemed motivated to remain on the team primarily to travel around the country, cultivate friendships, fall in love, and engage in the inevitable social activities that are attached to debating. Doing well in team competition was secondary for these group members.

Softball leagues are frequently rated A, B, and C. The hard-core athletes can be separated from the Budweiser crowd. Some players are drawn to the physical activity and others are drawn to the social activity.

Attraction to Group Goals

A third reason why we join groups and wish to remain as members is an attraction to the group's goals (Reckman and Goethals, 1973). When you are drawn to a group because of its goals, commitment to it is likely to be strong. Those of you who may have worked for a political candidate know full well that commitment to the cause, namely electing the candidate, acts as an adhesive that binds members of political groups together. When the goal is achieved, such groups normally disband until the bid for re-election surfaces and groups form once again.

When you join a fund-raising group for a worthy cause, you don't have the luxury of interacting only with members that you'd enjoy inviting to dinner. You're stuck adapting to the various personalities and quirks of fellow fund-raisers. Your commitment to the goal of the group, however, may be enough to keep you coming back.

Establishment of Meaning and Identity

We sometimes join groups to make sense of our world. Consider cults, for instance. Making sense of the world is the fundamental basis of cult conversions. Individuals who join cults are in the throes of an identity crisis. They are searching for meaning in their lives, and cults offer such meaning and identity. Social psychologist George Cvetkovich notes that studies of ex-cult members reveal that 75% are recruited during an identity crisis and 25% had always been in an identity crisis (as cited in Valdez, 1983, p. 7).

Former Massachusetts Commissioner of Public Health Deborah Prothrow-Stith's (1991) study of youth violence in the United States draws this comparison between antisocial groups such as gangs and pro-social groups such as fraternities:

> Pro-social and antisocial, they satisfy the adolescent need to belong to a group, separate from one's family. Pro-social and antisocial, they provide young people with goals and objectives, a world view, and a place where they are valued. Group membership gives some purpose to life. The more adrift a young person feels, the more powerful the attraction of the peer group, but even well-adjusted young people need what groups offer. (p. 97)

When situations are ambiguous, and we're looking for answers, we often join groups as a means of better understanding ourselves, our world, and others who cross our paths (Goethals and Darley, 1987). Joining a group can give meaning and purpose to our lives.

Fulfillment of Unrelated Needs Finally, we join groups to satisfy needs that are unrelated to the group's task, goals, members, or even our desire to belong. Sometimes we join because it looks good to do so or because it may further our career. We may become group members to enhance our resume or establish business contacts. In some cases we are told by persons in authority to join a group and we think it wise to comply lest we suffer unhappy consequences. The instructor of your class may put you into a group of people who interest you very little. If you are pragmatic, you will make the best of a less than satisfactory situation since your grade may depend on it.

The reasons individuals join groups have noticeable effects on the productivity and cohesiveness of those groups. If you join because you are attracted to the other members, the likelihood of cohesiveness in the group is cer-

second look

Why We Join Groups

- Interpersonal attraction (we are drawn to members of the group)
- Attraction to the activities of the group
- Attraction to group goals
- Establishment of meaning and identity
- Attraction to the fulfillment of needs outside of the group

tainly more probable than if you join to meet self-oriented needs. If you join because you are attracted to the group's goals, productivity is likely to be enhanced. If you join groups for personal gain only, you'll likely end up as dead
weight and drag the entire group down. The reasons you join groups influence
the outcomes of the group. Exhibiting a sensitivity to the needs of the group during the forming phase is therefore vital.

The competent communicator can show sensitivity to the needs of
the group during the forming phase in the following ways (Andersen, 1988):

1. *Express positive attitudes and feelings*. Avoid disagreement and disagreeableness.
This phase is the getting-acquainted stage of group development. This is not an
appropriate time to be deviant (e.g., embarrassing lapses in social etiquette,
abrasive remarks, provocative statements, outrageous dress). Don't put your foot
in your mouth. Put your best foot forward.
2. *Appear friendly, open, and interested*. Be approachable by establishing eye contact
with group members, initiating conversation, and responding warmly to interactions from others.

Storming: Tension in Groups

The inevitability of change within a system ensures stresses and strains in any
group. These stresses and strains usually surface in the form of conflict. All
groups experience some social tension because change can be an ordeal. Tension among group members should be viewed as a positive force. We are usually

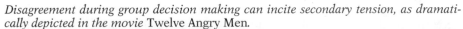

*Disagreement during group decision making can incite secondary tension, as dramati-
cally depicted in the movie* Twelve Angry Men.

change causes tension

at our best when we experience some tension. Athletes perform best when they find the proper balance between complete relaxation and crippling anxiety. Excessive tension, however, can produce damaging conflict that may split the group apart. The relative absence of tension in a group can result in lethargy, haphazard attention to the task, and nonproductivity. Finding the level of tension that solidifies the group and effectively managing group tension are important factors in successful group development.

There are two types of social tension—primary and secondary (Bormann, 1990). All groups experience both types.

initial

Primary Tension   When you first congregate in a group you normally feel some jitters and unease. This is **primary tension.** Instructors meeting classes for the first time usually experience some primary tension. When you initially meet roommates, classmates, or teammates, primary tension occurs. Even groups that have a lengthy history can experience primary tension at the outset of every meeting. This is especially true if groups such as the PTA or homeowners associations meet infrequently.

There are many signs of primary tension. Group members may become cautious and hesitant in their communication. Long periods of uncomfortable silence and tentative statements are all indicators of primary tension. Group members are often overly polite and careful to avoid controversy. Interruptions normally invoke immediate apologies.

Primary tension is a natural dynamic of group life, so understand it and deal with it; don't run from it. In most instances primary tension tends to be short-lived and cause for little concern. With time, you become comfortable with the group and your primary tension diminishes. Joking, laughing, and chatting about your interests, experiences, and beliefs on noncontroversial subjects all serve to reduce primary tension. Superficial conversation on frivolous topics (e.g., the weather, sports, fashion) is appropriate. You're not trying to "Free Tibet," "Save the Whales," or "Convert the Unbelievers." Your purpose is to become acquainted with other group members and to work out how you will relate to each other. As you get to know one another better, there is less perceived threat and consequently less primary tension.

If a group is too anxious to get down to business and foregoes the small talk, however, primary tension is likely to create an atmosphere of formality, stiffness, and insecurity. Communication will be stilted and hesitant. The ability of the group to work on a task will be hindered by excessive and persistent primary tension.

Engaging in small talk to relieve primary tension has cultural variations. In the United States, we tend to view small talk as wasting time, especially if our primary focus is on a task (e.g., finalizing a business agreement). Many Asian (e.g., Japan, China, and Korea), Middle Eastern (e.g., Saudi Arabia), and Latin American (e.g., Mexico, Brazil, and Chile) cultures, however, view small talk as a necessary ritual engaged in over many cups of coffee or tea for several hours or even several meetings during which the group's task may not even be mentioned (Samovar and Porter, 1995). Ethiopians attach prestige to tasks that require a great deal of time to complete. Lengthy small talk, viewed by most Americans anxious to do business as "doing nothing," is considered highly significant and purposeful.

Secondary Tension   The stress and strain that occurs within the group later in its development is called **secondary tension.** Having to make decisions produces secondary tension. Disagreements and conflicts—storming—inevitably emerge when group members struggle to define their status and roles in the group. Shortage of time to accomplish a task or make a decision can induce tension. A deviant member can rattle the tranquillity of a group. Whatever the causes, secondary tension should be expected. Low levels of secondary tension may mean that the group is highly harmonious. It may also mean that group members are unmotivated, apathetic, and bored.

Signs of secondary tension are many and varied. Frequently, secondary tension is marked by an abrupt departure from the group's routine. A sharp outburst, a sarcastic barb, or hostile and antagonistic exchanges between members signal secondary tension. Rules of polite communication may be replaced by shouting matches. Extreme secondary tension is unpleasant for the group. If left uncontrolled, the group's existence may be threatened.

Secondary tension was palpable during the second Rodney King trial, a 1993 civil suit against Los Angeles police officers who beat King following a traffic stop. According to interviews with three of the jurors, tempers flared on the fifth day of deliberations. Jurors argued over taking time off. The foreman quarreled with another juror and refused to apologize, claiming that if he tried he'd probably end up punching her in the face. Another juror questioned the masculinity of a thirty-year-old engineer on the jury who had insisted that deliberations terminate early because his brain couldn't absorb any more information. The young man responded to this insult by threatening to beat up his detractor. Half the jurors broke into tears as the emotional bloodletting continued. One juror demanded to see his doctor (Rohrlich, 1993). Similar tension was evident during jury deliberations in the trials of the Menendez brothers, O. J. Simpson, and Oklahoma-bombing accomplice Terry Nichols.

Let me emphasize that the goal is not to eliminate secondary tension. All decision-making groups will unavoidably experience secondary tension. Within tolerable limits, such tension can be a positive force. Tension can energize a group, challenge the members to think creatively, and bring the group together.

As we will see when I discuss the problems associated with groupthink, trying to avoid or camouflage secondary tension merely tricks us into believing the group is functioning well. Beneath the surface, the group may be disintegrating or the decisions coming from the group may be ill-conceived, even disastrous.

The real challenge facing competent communicators is to manage secondary tension within tolerable limits. But how do we know when tension exceeds the limits? There is no mathematical formula for such a determination. Every group operates as a unique system of interconnected parts. Some groups can tolerate a great deal of disagreement and conflict. Other groups are more vulnerable to disintegration because members are more thin-skinned or insecure and view disagreements as personal repudiations and attacks. Some families operate well in an atmosphere of considerable screeching and yelling. Other families function successfully only in an atmosphere of civility; raising a voice would be most unsettling for the group. Communication appropriateness, thus, is contextual.

A group's inability to accomplish tasks and to maintain a satisfying social climate is a general rule of thumb for determining excessive tension in a group (Wilson and Hanna, 1990). In the trial of defendants accused of seriously beating trucker Reginald Denny during the Los Angeles upheaval precipitated by the verdict in the first Rodney King trial, jurors clearly experienced excessive tension. One juror was dismissed by the judge at the request of the other eleven exasperated jurors for "failure to deliberate." One female member of the sequestered jury became so upset about not being able to see her boyfriend that she ran down a hallway of the courthouse yelling, "I can't take it anymore" (Kramer, 1993, p. 1A). The judge gave jurors the weekend off from their deliberations to recharge their batteries and to reduce the tension so they could finish their task.

A competent communicator can exhibit sensitivity to the needs of the group during the storming periodic phase of group development by handling secondary tension as follows (Andersen, 1988):

1. *Tolerate, even encourage, disagreement and deviance.* Suppressing differences of opinion will likely increase tension and exacerbate conflict. The trick is to keep the disagreement and deviance within tolerable limits. One way to do this is to focus the disagreements and deviance on the task (unless, of course, the conflict is social in nature). Resist the temptation to drift into irrelevant side issues, especially contentious ones.

2. *Keep a civil tongue.* When disagreements become more social than task related (e.g., personal attacks and disparaging remarks), they easily degenerate into interpersonal combat. Disagree without being disagreeable. You want to foster a cooperative, not a competitive, atmosphere for discussion. You can express opinions with conviction and exuberance without going psycho on those who do not agree with you.

3. *Be an active listener.* Encourage all group members to express their opinions and feelings. Clarify significant points that are confusing. Resist the temptation to interrupt, especially if this produces defensive behavior from group members. Make an honest effort to understand the point of view that is in opposition to your own.

There are numerous sources of conflict within a group that raise the level of tension. Reasons for stormy transactions in groups and strategies for effectively managing them will be discussed in greater detail in later chapters. For now, recognize that conflict and tension are a normal part of the group experience. Dealing with tension may be smooth sailing for some groups and whitewater rafting for others.

Norming: Regulating the Group

A group will establish rules or standards. Rules define appropriate behaviors in specified social situations. "They stipulate what a person must do (obligation), ought to do (preference), or must not do (prohibition) in order to achieve certain goals" (Smith, 1982, p. 63). In other words, rules regulate behavior. In groups, these rules are called **norms.**

Types of Norms   There are two types of norms, explicit and implicit. Explicit norms are rules that expressly identify acceptable behavior. Such rules are codified in constitutions and bylaws of fraternal organizations, religious orders, and the like. All laws in our society act as explicit norms.

Most norms in small groups, however, are implicit. You ascertain implicit norms by observing uniformities in the behavior and expressed attitudes of members and by noticing what fosters negative consequences and thus constitutes deviance for a particular group.

A college seminar illustrates the difference between explicit and implicit norms. If participating in a seminar qualifies as a new experience for you, group norms could be determined in several ways. Usually, the professor teaching the seminar will provide a syllabus explicitly specifying what students are expected to do during the term. Such norms as "Refrain from tardiness and absenteeism," "All assignments must be turned in on time," "All papers must be typed—no exceptions," and "Active participation in class discussions is imperative" are some of the possible explicit rules.

One colleague of mine refused to tolerate even minor instances of tardiness. She used to tell her students that she would lock the classroom door exactly at the start of the hour when class was supposed to begin. Any student who was late for any reason would be barred from entry. This worked well until the professor was sued by one of her students. The claim was made that the professor's strict, no-exceptions policy caused her student, who was running late, to drive unsafely one day in order to avoid being locked out when an important exam was scheduled. The student lost control of her car and suffered serious injuries when she crashed her automobile.

The implicit rules for the seminar class might be such things as "Don't interrupt the professor when he or she is speaking," "Sit in chairs stationed around the rectangular table," "Be polite when disagreeing with classmates," and "Don't hide the professor's notes, even in jest" (you had to be there). These norms are ascertained by observing the behavior of your classmates and the professor.

Purpose and Development of Norms   The main purpose of norms is to achieve group goals. Consider the group Overeaters Anonymous (Shimanoff, 1992). Change (i.e., losing weight) is regulated by rules, one of which is that members are permitted to talk about food only in generic terms (carbohydrates, protein, etc.) but not in terms of specific foods (Twinkies, burgers, cookies). The rule is based on the assumption that references to particular foods will stimulate a craving for those foods and make goal achievement more difficult, while references to foods in generic terms will produce no such cravings. Apparently you won't hear the refrigerator calling your name when merely talking about carbohydrates, but mention Häagen-Dazs and there better be a clear path to the Frigidaire or someone is going to get trampled.

The norming process takes place almost immediately in groups. When a group is formed, members cast about trying to determine what behavior will be acceptable and what will be unacceptable. Part of the primary tension in a group may stem from this concern for proper group etiquette.

There are three principal sources of norms in small groups. First, some norms are from systems outside the small group. Standards of excellence and specific norms of performance for work teams within organizations can be and often are externally influenced by management outside of the team (Sundstrom et al., 1990). Charters and bylaws of local chapters of fraternal organizations, therapeutic groups, and others are usually set by parent organizations or agencies. In a clear case of interconnectedness of parts in a system, the small groups work within the normative framework set by the organization. These small groups have varying degrees of freedom to develop unique norms not stipulated externally.

A second source of small group norms is the influence of a single member. Research shows that a single person can influence the group to accept higher standards of behavior and performance than would exist without the influence of this member. Even when that influential member leaves the group, the norm typically remains (MacNeil and Sherif, 1976). Sometimes these influential individuals are designated group leaders and sometimes they are newcomers joining an established group.

A third source of small group norms is the group itself. Small group norms most often develop from transactions within the group. Sometimes this is explicitly negotiated (e.g., juries deciding what procedures will be used to arrive at a verdict), but most often it emerges implicitly from trial and error ("Oops, the group disapproves—guess I'll try something else.").

Conforming to Norms   The propensity toward **conformity,** the adherence to group norms, can be seen from a study of bulimia, a disorder characterized by binge eating followed by self-induced vomiting (Crandall, 1988). Bulimia is typically found in certain social groups such as cheerleader squads, sports teams (e.g., gymnastics), dance troupes, and sororities. Norms are established within these groups, which promote the binge and purge behavior. Instead of viewing this bizarre behavior as abnormal or unhealthy, sororities studied by Crandall promoted bulimia as a reasonable method of controlling the weight of members. Group norms even established a preferred rate of binging and purging. Popularity in the group depended on sticking to this standard. Even those group members who initially felt no desire to binge or urge to purge began to follow the crowd.

Conformity isn't always a negative experience. Peer pressure can be applied for pro-social reasons. At Shaker Heights High School in Ohio, a group of black upperclassmen dressed in shirts and ties march conspicuously down the hallway to the auditorium where underachieving black freshmen wait to explain their poor grades. "You think D's and F's are funny?" a senior says to a grinning 15-year-old student. "This is mediocre," claims another, flashing a report card in front of a clearly uncomfortable underclassman. The Minority Achievement Committee, a group of high-achieving African American male students are working to establish the norm that being smart and doing well in school is cool, not "acting white." Junior Justin Taylor reflects the committee's point of view, "What, only white people study? That's just plain stupid and insulting" (as cited in Clemetson, 1999, p. 37). Students must earn at least a 2.8 GPA to gain membership into the Minority Achievement Committee. Weekly MAC meetings begin with a firm handshake and the MAC credo, "I pledge to uphold the name of the African American man. I will do so by striving for academic excellence." Raji Bey, a senior, comments on the MAC effort, "These guys have the grades, the respect *and* the girls. Who wouldn't want to be like them?" (as cited in Clemetson, 1999, p. 37). Cullen Buie, a MAC scholar, puts it this way, "We create positive peer pressure. We make success seem like something real" (p. 37).

So why do we conform to norms in groups? In a society as individualistic as the United States, why do we adhere to the rules of acceptable behavior in groups? We conform for three reasons that flow from the purposes for norms.

First, conforming to group norms reduces ambiguity and makes functioning in a group a smoother operation. Maintaining order—controlling change—is the first purpose of norms. Conforming to norms in a group manifests a desire for order and a reduction of ambiguity. Most people are not comfortable with rapid, unregulated change. We conform because we like things orderly and predictable.

A second reason we conform to norms is that conformity results in social acceptance, support, companionship, and recognition. We must "go along to get along." Loyalty to the group is manifested in conformity to group norms and is rewarded with approval from the members. Norms create solidarity with group members. Our natural desire to belong makes such solidarity attractive. Individual goals such as making friends or increasing social activities can be satisfied by conforming to group norms. Why shouldn't we want to conform?

Third, groups have informational power. Group norms "serve as frames of reference for assessing the reasonableness of one's own opinions and behaviors" (Smith, 1982, p. 171). We match our view of the world with that of the group. We thus learn whether we are in step or out of step with prevailing points of view. In addition, groups can act as a source of information for evaluating or perfecting our abilities and for accomplishing certain ends. A chess team, writers' group, bridge club, or work group may have its social function, but such groups also provide information on our level of skill and accomplishment and they assist us in improving our abilities. Failure to conform to the norms of the group will often mean the withholding of valuable information that can assist us in our quest for personal improvement.

CLOSER LOOK

High School Cliques: A Lesson in Conformity

When the school lunch bell rings at high schools across the country, kids pour out of their classrooms and almost instantly sort themselves into small groups or cliques. In a field investigation of cliques at three Santa Cruz county California high schools, students split into a myriad of small groups—jocks, preps, dirts, surfers, skaters, Goths, nerds, and a variety of ethnic groupings (Townsend, 1999). We all remember cliques in high school. For some of you it may still be a fresh memory.

Students join cliques because the pressure to belong, to be accepted by peers, is intense. In some cases the outcasts rejected by more established cliques form their own group. As one girl at Soquel High School revealed, "We're outcasts, but at least we're outcasts together" (as cited in Townsend, 1999, p. A8). As Margarita Azmitia, professor of developmental psychology at University of California Santa Cruz notes, "Some kids don't want to be in deviant cliques, but that's their only option" (as cited in Townsend, p. A8). The clique gives them an identity, and some protection from harassment by more favored cliques on campus.

High school cliques typically divide into a competitive hierarchy with jocks on top and nerds on the bottom. This competitive hierarchy often leads to in-group versus out-group hostility. Name-calling, threats, water balloons, and food rain down on those who belong to the less popular cliques. "They throw stuff at us all the time" says one 18-year-old male student, indicating a collection of surfers, jocks, and popular kids. "I've had yogurt thrown at me, apples, oranges," says another student dressed entirely in black. "They call me dirt, faggot, queer" (as cited in Townsend, 1999, p. A1). A student athlete, one of the popular kids at Aptos High School looks across the open quad where cliques have fanned out like ripples on a pond and says, "I hate 'em, I don't care." Another jock adds, "They smell and they

listen to Marilyn Manson. I hate Marilyn Manson. And they don't wear shoes." A 15-year-old female student expresses her anguish regarding the abuse heaped on her by competing cliques, "A lot of people yell at us. They say, 'You freak of nature. You Satanist.' We've had people harass us to tears. I've come back crying. They yell, 'Go back to hell, no one wants you.' It hurts." "It's almost as bad as racism," says an 18-year-old male student who is one of the objects of jock derision. "We are who we are, and we can't be someone else" (as cited in Townsend, 1999, p. A8). Misery loves miserable company so the outcasts and the derided join cliques for identity and for self-protection.

Conformity to the norms of the clique is strong. At least there is some protection from harassment when you aren't facing it alone. Some students are so desperate to fit in, to belong in a group, that they will do almost anything to gain membership and to stay in a clique. Professor Azmitia explains that cliques are typically ten to twelve members in size. This sets up an intense competition to get into the cliques, especially the most favored ones, and to remain members once admitted. Even minor deviance from clique norms, such as wearing the wrong clothes, hanging with someone from an outcast clique, or missing a clique party can get a member ousted. As a ninth grader at Aptos High confessed, "I wasn't comfortable with myself so I tried to conform. I felt pressure to look a certain way. To party, to use drugs and alcohol." She would get "weird looks" when she wore a colorful scarf wrapped around her short blond hair. "They were too uptight about everything" (as cited in Townsend, 1999, p. A8). Eventually she left her popular clique, but she quickly joined an outcast group.

Cliques can provide social acceptance, support, companionship, and recognition for members. Friendships can blossom from participation in cliques. Nevertheless, cliques can also encourage blind, desperate conformity, especially when intergroup competition erupts into hostility and abuse.

Questions for Thought

1. Do you remember your experiences with cliques? Were your experiences mostly positive or negative?

2. Did you experience an intense pressure to conform as a clique member? Did intergroup rivalry exist that produced harassment of members from other cliques?

Conditions for Conformity to Norms   There is greater conformity to group norms when certain conditions exist. First and foremost, <u>the stronger the cohesiveness in the group, the greater is the conformity to group norms</u> (Shaw, 1981). The relationship between cohesiveness and conformity is hardly surprising. Cohesiveness, by definition, is the degree of attraction we have to a group and our desire to be a member. If there is minimal attraction to the group and nebulous desire to be a member, then there is scant reason to adhere to the rules of behavior. A group has little leverage against apathetic or scornful members. How can the group command conformity when you don't care if you're unceremoniously booted out of the group? Conversely, individuals who are strongly attracted to the group and wish to remain members in good standing are much more likely to conform and to bow to pressure for uniformity of opinion and behavior.

Second, <u>conformity is greater when individuals expect to be group members for a long time</u> (Smith, 1982). After all, you must live with this group. Why make your life unpleasant by not conforming, particularly in job situations where economic considerations may make job switching impractical?

Melanie Singer, a Los Angeles Highway Patrol officer called to testify on behalf of the accused officers in the second Rodney King trial in 1993, admitted on the witness stand that she didn't give medical assistance to the hogtied, bleeding King following his horrific beating because she didn't want her fellow officers to start heckling her ("Fearing heckling," 1993). When your life's profession forces you to live with a certain group you tend to conform to implicit norms of behavior even when your conscience may dictate otherwise.

CLOSER LOOK

Hazing Rituals

Recognizing the strong link between cohesiveness and conformity to norms, groups will sometimes go to great lengths to foster cohesiveness. Hazing rituals of college fraternities purposely subject prospective members to a series of activities, often ludicrous and sometimes dangerous, designed to test the limits of physical exertion, psychological strain, and social embarrassment. Cialdini (1993) lists numerous examples of silly, stupid, dangerous, and lethal activities actually

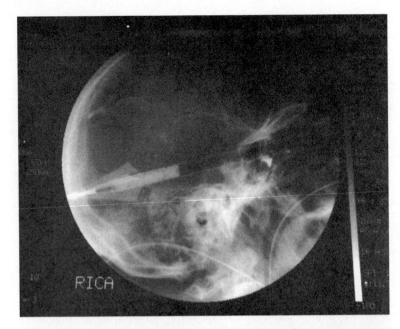

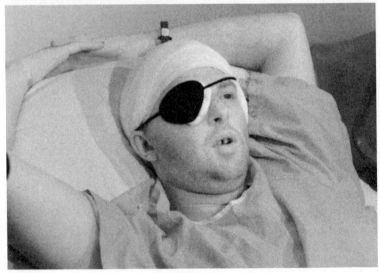

Anthony Roberts took an arrow through his eye and into his brain (see his X-ray above) in a hazing ritual that went very badly.

out suitable clothing, repeatedly punching the stomach and kidneys of pledges who forget parts of ritual incantations, and incarcerating pledges in a locked storage closet for two days with only salty foods, no liquids, and only a small plastic cup to catch urine.

Dennis Jay, a fraternity pledge, was forced to drink huge quantities of alcohol from a beer bong—a funnel contraption. He was rushed to a hospital in a coma. His blood alcohol level was .48, six times the legal definition of drunk in most states and .02 below the normal fatal dose (Grogan, B. et al., 1993). When he recovered he remained loyal to his fraternity and refused to admit that hazing was the cause of his near-death experience. It was only after he discovered that fraternity members lied and said he had stumbled into the fraternity house drunk and that frat brothers had taken him to the emergency room as an act of concern for his well-being that he reported the truth to officials.

Dozens of college students have died from hazing incidents ("The hazards," 1986). By 1986, seventeen states had outlawed hazing. Other states and numerous colleges and universities have followed suit. Stopping hazing, however, is not easy. When Richard Swanson, a University of Southern California student, gagged on an oil-soaked hunk of liver, then choked to death before anyone could help him, the university applied stringent rules to initiation practices. Students

required by some fraternities as part of Hell Week initiations. Examples include forcing pledges to swallow quarter-pound hunks of raw liver slathered with oil, abandoning pledges on mountain tops or in remote areas in bitter cold conditions with-

rioted in protest. Outlawing hazing is more likely to drive it underground than to eliminate the practice.

Hazing or initiation rituals in groups is widespread. Clubs, gangs,and even some businesses subject new members to hazing. Anthony Roberts lost his right eye and almost his life when, as part of an initiation ritual into a rafting and outdoor group called Mountain Men Anonymous, he stood with a fuel can on his head so a group member could shoot it with a bow and arrow. The arrow missed the can and passed through his eye into his brain. Miraculously he survived with no serious brain damage. He said he felt "really stupid" ("Man survives," 1993, p. 9A).

Five teenage girls had unprotected sex with an HIV-infected male gang member as part of an initiation rite to gain entrance into a gang. Jo Ann King-Sinnett, spokeswoman for Planned Parenthood of San Antonio, Texas, explains the teens' behavior this way: "If the test (for HIV) came up negative, then it was like they were brave enough to have unprotected sex and they were tough enough, and their body was tough enough to fight the disease" ("Unsafe sex," 1993, p. 4A).

Rohlen (1973) cites an elaborate initiation ritual required by a Japanese bank. Over a three month period, new employees are forced to meditate and fast together at a Zen monastery, participate in rigorous basic training at an army base, perform community service, vacation at an isolated youth hostel, and complete a strenuous twenty-five-mile hike. All this so employees can cash checks for customers and turn down their loan applications.

West Point cadet John Edwards experienced an ironic twist to the hazing controversy. In 1988, he was expelled from the U.S. Military Academy because as an upperclassman he refused to subject first year cadets to the ritual hazing. He felt it was absurd and dehumanizing behavior, not to mention dangerous.

Why do groups insist on such bizarre and risky membership rituals? Moreland and Levine (1987) cite several reasons. First, groups harshly initiate their newcomers because the harder it is to get into a group the greater will be the loyalty and commitment to the group once membership has been attained. We tend to value more that which is difficult to achieve than that which requires minimal effort. The more severe the hazing ritual, the more desirable a group appears to be. In one experiment, the more electric shock a woman received as part of the hazing ritual, the more she convinced herself that the group and its activities were valuable, interesting, and desirable despite the clear effort of the experimenters to make the group appear uninteresting and worthless (Gerard and Mathewson, 1966). A study by Young (1965) of fifty-four tribal groups found that those with the most severe and difficult initiation rituals had the greatest group solidarity.

If you had to swallow a slimy, oil-soaked slab of raw liver, freeze off the southside of your anatomy, or risk your life in order to gain membership, chances are quite good that you would slavishly conform to the norms of the group once you were admitted as a member. Deviance is not likely to emerge from a tight-knit group bonded by ordeals.

Second, a harsh initiation provides the group with valuable information about the newcomers. If newcomers refuse to be initiated, fail the initiation tasks, or participate in the rites of passage grudgingly, then this informs the group that such newcomers are not likely to fit in with the group. They probably will not conform to group norms.

Third, a harsh initiation discourages newcomers who have a weak commitment to the group or have a half-hearted desire to join the group. The sooner such individuals leave before becoming members, the less trouble they are likely to pose for group members. Troublemakers can destroy the cohesiveness of the group.

Fourth, a harsh initiation may convince newcomers how dependent they are on longtime members (old-timers). The old-timers make the decisions regarding who is granted membership and who is not. The old-timers must be convinced that the newcomers are worthy of that membership.

Questions for Thought

1. Have you ever participated in hazing either as the perpetrator or the recipient? Was it for the reasons stated above?

2. Should hazing rituals, especially the high-risk ones, be outlawed? Would outlawing such practices stop them?

3. Is it possible to have hazing rituals that are not dangerous and still serve the purpose of creating cohesiveness and subsequent conformity in the group?

---

second look

The Norming Process

Types of Norms
Explicit—preferences and prohibitions specifically stated in some form
Implicit—preferences and prohibitions determined from observation

Sources of Norms
Other larger systems outside the small group
Influence of a single member
Transactions within the group

Why Group Members Conform to Norms
Reduction of ambiguity
Social acceptance, support, companionship, and recognition
Information—assesses reasonableness of one's opinions/behaviors

Conditions for Conformity to Norms
Stronger the cohesiveness, greater the conformity
Greater conformity when individuals expect to be group members for a long time
Greater conformity when individuals perceive they have lower status in group

---

Third, conformity is greater when individuals perceive that they have somewhat lower status in the group than other members or are not completely accepted by the group (Smith, 1982). Higher status members have earned the right to dissent but lower status members must still earn that right to occasional nonconformity. Lower status members also feel a greater need to prove themselves to the group, to show fealty.

Nonconformity   Since behavior in groups is governed by rules, a violation of a norm can be quite disturbing for group members. A colleague of mine once told me of a surprising incident that occurred in her elements of public speaking class. She asked all students to give a four-minute introductory speech to loosen everyone up. She instructed students to describe a significant event that they had experienced that had a profound impact on their lives. She expected to hear straightforward presentations on trips taken to foreign countries, geographic relocations, the college experience, and so forth. She did hear this—and more. After most of the students had given their presentations, a woman in her thirties gave her speech. She began by telling the class that she had never achieved sexual fulfillment in her life until the previous weekend when she and her lover experienced carnal bliss. She then proceeded to tell the astonished class in graphic detail what it was like experiencing her very first orgasm.

It is difficult to imagine what could possibly have possessed this woman to believe that such a revelation was appropriate for this environment. Communication competence is a real issue here. As Littlejohn and Jabusch (1982) observe, "One of the signs of communication competence is the ability to move in and out of a variety of communication situations with ease, adapting to the rule systems of others" (p. 38). This woman clearly exhibited scant awareness of which rule system was appropriate for this situation. Her revelation and description of sexual fulfillment might have fit the rules system in a professional counselor–client relationship, even perhaps in a conversation with a close friend, but in front of a group of relative strangers in a formal classroom situation? Her unpredictable behavior produced plenty of red faces and eyes cast downward from embarrassed classmates.

Groups usually do not appreciate nonconformity except within fairly limited boundaries. How groups deal with nonconformity, especially in its intentionally bold form—defiance, will be discussed at length in chapter 9.

The norming periodic phase of group development provides a structure for appropriate communication. Norms are rules that regulate change, promote group solidarity, and serve as a reference for assessing the reasonableness of our opinions and behavior. The norms of different groups vary greatly. Group norms are maintained until they no longer serve functional purposes. If a norm tends to divide a group rather than solidify it, for instance, or thwarts achievement of group goals (i.e., establishes an overly open or excessively closed system), then it becomes dysfunctional and needs to be changed.

A competent communicator exhibits a sensitivity to the needs of the group during the norming periodic phase of development as follows:

1. *Adapt communication to the norms of the group.* As previously noted, communication becomes inappropriate when, without sacrificing goals, violation of norms could be averted by more prudent action.
2. *Encourage change when norms are excessively rigid.* Norms are not sacrosanct. Some norms can be suffocatingly rigid—too closed to permit adaptation to change in the system. Norm rigidity fosters nonconformity and disruption. Violating the norm is one avenue of change if rational argument proves unsuccessful, but expect backlash from the group. Leaving the group is certainly an option. Failure to loosen norms from within may require intervention from without, such as court suits and protests.
3. *Encourage change when norms are too elastic.* Excessive openness in a system can be counterproductive. The same guidelines for changing overly rigid norms apply here as well.

Performing: Group Output

If I had a dollar for every time I have been told that a camel is a horse designed by a committee, I would be sipping Mai Tais on a white sand beach in the tropics enjoying a blissful state of very early retirement. Then there is the equally moth-eaten description of a committee as "a group of people who can do nothing individually but, as a group, can gather and decide that nothing can be done." Along the same line is this anonymous offering: "Trying to solve a problem through group discussion is like trying to clear up a traffic jam by honking your horn." Winston Churchill, always armed with his sardonic wit, fired this salvo: "A committee is the organized result of a group of the incompetent who have been appointed by the uninformed to accomplish the unnecessary." On my own campus, committees metastasize like malignant cancer, eating up professors' and administrators' time and sucking the lifeblood from the institution. There was even a recent proposal to establish a committee on committees, ostensibly to bring this blood-sucking monster under control, but nothing ever came of the proposal.

In terms of performance, groups as decision-making units are in need of better public relations. Too many people are inclined to believe that groups are assembled to stymie progress and to serve as roadblocks to decision making, not to produce better alternatives. Grouphate is real.

So, are groups as inept as the moldy jokes and acerbic assessments indicate? Berg's (1967) study of 124 discussion groups is not very encouraging. He found that groups pursued their discussion topics for an average of only 58 seconds at a time before diverting to an irrelevant topic. The range varied from a low of 28 seconds to a high of 118 seconds. One group leader in this study described his job as "chairman of the bored." Other studies support Berg's results. "Whether groups were composed of women in a Lebanese college, Japanese graduate students, university undergraduates, first-line managers at IBM, or educators in public-health nursing, the average attention span for all the groups was about one minute" (Bormann and Bormann, 1988, p. 120).

Although the tired jokes about groups and the research on the group attention span suggest that groups hinder rather than help solve problems and make decisions, the evidence is far more mixed. One of the most researched areas of group communication is the comparison of individual to group performance. The key issue from this research is not whether individuals or groups are superior performers. The central point is under what conditions do groups outperform individuals and vice versa? Since grouphate is often a result of poor group productivity, group versus individual performance seems to be a significant issue to explore.

Individual versus Group Performance   Groups will probably outperform individuals when certain conditions exist (Forsyth, 1990; Pavitt and Curtis, 1994). First, when the task requires a wide range and variety of information and skills, groups tend to be superior to any individual. One study found that the group scored significantly higher than its highest scoring member (Stasson and Bradshaw, 1995). It did this by *pooling knowledge.* When the highest scoring member didn't know the answer to a question, another member typically knew the answer to that specific question. Thus, the group as a whole benefited because members had nonoverlapping knowledge. As humorist Will Rogers once said, "Everybody is ignorant, just on different subjects." A key to successful group performance is putting together a team composed of members who do not share ignorance, but instead pool nonoverlapping areas of knowledge (Stasson and Bradshaw, 1995).

Dr. Don Wukasch spent nineteen years as part of a high-performance cardiac surgery team. He cites an instance of effective team performance that resulted from pooling nonoverlapping knowledge (Larson and LaFasto, 1989). When he performed surgery at the Texas Heart Institute a hurricane hit during one procedure and the power was knocked out. The heart–lung machine quit, leaving about a minute or two before the patient would start to die. Wukasch didn't know how to restore the heart–lung machine, but functioning as a cohesive, well-trained unit, team members began hand-cranking the machine and surgery continued within fifteen seconds.

Besides pooling knowledge, another reason groups outperform individuals when the task is comprehensive is the *group remembering* phenomenon or collective recall of information. Quantitatively, the research on group remembering has consistently shown that groups are superior to individuals (even compared to the best individual) in recall of information (Clark and Stephenson, 1989).

Why is group remembering significant? Juries more often than not arrive at verdicts on the basis of recall of the evidence and pertinent information reflecting guilt or innocence. In one study, individual jurors averaged only a 60 percent accuracy rate on recall of specific evidence and less than 30 percent on questions pertaining to the judge's instructions to the jury. As a group, however, the jury scored 90 percent accuracy on evidentiary material and 80 percent accuracy on the judge's instructions (Hastie et al., 1983). "The group memory advantage over the typical or even the exceptional individual is one of the major determinants of the superiority of the jury as a legal decision mechanism" (Hastie et al., 1983). Not surprisingly, larger sized (twelve member) juries have superior recall of evidence compared to smaller sized (six member) juries (Hastie et al., 1983).

Group remembering can be a significant benefit for a group such as personnel-interviewing panels that often must sift through huge amounts of information and listen to hours of oral responses to questions from numerous candidates for a job. Group remembering is also a significant advantage for student study groups preparing for an exam.

Second, groups generally outperform individuals when both the group and any individual compared are without expertise on the task. Here *synergy* is at work. As Johnson and Johnson (1987) remark in somewhat overstated fashion, "None of us is as smart as all of us" (p. 131). In a recent study, even though no individual group member knew the correct answer on a test question, the group as a whole selected the correct answer in 28 percent of the cases. Individual members working alone, however, selected the correct answer only 4 percent of the time (Stasson and Bradshaw, 1995).

Third, groups will usually outperform an individual when both the group and the individual have expertise and the task is an especially complicated and complex one. The ability of a group to divide labor, to *share the load*, will normally result in a better decision than any overburdened individual could manage. Legal cases such as the Microsoft antitrust suit in 1999 and the O. J. Simpson trial in 1995 require armies of attorneys. In cases such as these, a single attorney would be easily overwhelmed by workload and by information overload without extensive assistance from other attorneys.

A group of experts is especially effective when members are highly motivated and they are trained to work as a team. One study found that expert groups outperform their best member 97 percent of the time (Michaelson et al., 1989). *Teamwork* allows a group to coordinate efforts and to work at optimum effectiveness.

Fourth, even when comparing a group of reasonably bright and informed nonexperts to an individual with special expertise, group decisions are sometimes superior. One of the reasons for this superiority is that when groups are functioning effectively, members perform an *error correction* function for the group (Hastie et al., 1983). Assumptions are challenged and alternatives are offered that an individual might overlook. In addition, the collective energy and chemistry of the group may produce a synergistic result.

Although groups frequently outperform individuals, this is not always the case. Under certain conditions, individuals outperform groups. There are five such conditions supported by research.

First, groups composed of uninformed laypersons will not usually outperform someone with special expertise, such as a doctor or lawyer on issues of medicine and law. There is certainly no advantage to be gained from *pooling ignorance*. As already noted, however, even in uninformed groups, synergy sometimes compensates for lack of knowledge. *Negative synergy*, nevertheless, is more likely when group members are uninformed.

Second, individuals outperform groups when groups establish norms of mediocrity. Some groups are composed of members who are satisfied with relatively low productivity. If norms of mediocrity prevail in a group, performance will be lackluster or worse (Stogdill, 1972). Even individual members who may wish to perform at a higher level will become discouraged because of *insufficient motivation to excel*. Since the group rewards middling performance, why bother trying harder than the rest?

Third, when groups become too large, individuals outperform groups. Again, the rule of thumb is to select the smallest sized group capable of performing the task effectively. Quality performance is usually enhanced in moderately sized groups (i.e., seven to ten members). Much larger than this, however, and *problems of coordination and efficiency increase*. Just assembling a dozen members can be daunting when schedules have to be coordinated. More important, however, is the problem of **social loafing**—the tendency of individual group members to reduce their work effort as groups increase in size (Gerow, 1995). Social loafing is displayed by members goofing off when performance is needed in a group, by missing meetings, showing up late, or failing to start or complete individual tasks. Please note here that reticence to participate in group discussion because of shyness does not constitute social loafing. Loafers put out little effort because of poor motivation, disinterest, or a bad attitude.

CLOSER LOOK

Social Loafing: Sapping a Group's Vitality

Social loafing can suck the energy from a group. A group cannot ignore a social loafer because a group is a system of interconnected parts. Social loafing is not an insignificant problem for groups. When groups become populated predominantly with social loafers, nothing much gets accomplished and negative synergy can result.

Social loafing has been observed in groups working on a variety of tasks, among both males and females, people of all ages, and in many different cultures (Forsyth, 1990). Social loafing occurs more often in larger groups because sluggards can idle away their time less noticeably than in smaller gatherings (Zimbardo, 1992). Since other members presumably can pick up the slack resulting from loafers' listless participation, larger groups act as breeding grounds for loafers.

Social loafing is more common in an individualist culture such as the United States than it is in collectivist cultures such as Taiwan, Singapore, China, and other Asian countries (Early, 1989; Gabreyna et al., 1985). In a collectivist culture, social striving or the desire to produce for the group because group membership is highly valued is strong. Personal efforts and achievements are less visible in a group and more likely to go unrecognized, however, so social loafing is more likely in an individualist culture.

So what can you do about social loafers? Here are several steps that can be taken to address the problem (see also Lumsden and Lumsden, 1993):

1. *Establish a group responsibility norm.* Emphasize as a group individual responsibility to the team and the importance of every member contributing a fair share to the successful completion of a task.

2. *Note the critical importance of each member's effort.* Impress upon all members that their individual effort is special and essential to the group's success.

3. *Hold members accountable.* Provide each member with specific and easily identifiable tasks and set aside time for the group to assess each member's contribution to the overall project. Gerow (1995) claims that social loafing can be "virtually eliminated" by combining Step 2, making each member's effort seem valuable and essential, and letting members know that their individual tasks will be clearly identified and that they will be held accountable for their performance. Despite Gerow's optimism, however, I know from experience that more is sometimes required.

4. *Talk to the individual privately.* The first three steps attempt to prevent loafing. This step calls for either the leader of the group or a designated member to approach the loafer and ask why the lethargic attitude exists. Encourage stronger participation, reaffirm the importance of the loafer's contribution to the team effort, and solicit suggestions regarding how the group might help the person become a contributor.

5. *Confront the loafer as a group.* Identify and describe the problem behavior in specific detail. Ask the loafer directly how the problem can be solved. Do not name-call or personally attack the recalcitrant member.

6. *Consult a higher power* (not to be confused with divine intervention, although that would be impressive). When all of the above steps fail, consult a supervisor, teacher, or someone with greater authority than the group members and ask for advice. The authority figure may need to discuss the problem with the loafer.

7. *Boot out the slacker.* This is a last resort. Do not begin with this step as many groups would prefer to do. You may not have this option available, however.

8. *Sidestep the loafer.* Reconfigure individual responsibilities and tasks so even if the loafer contributes nothing to the group effort, the

group can still maneuver around the loafer and produce a high-quality result.

Questions for Thought

1. Does the group task have any bearing on the frequency of social loafing? Explain your an-swer. Give examples from your own experience.

2. Do you agree that an individualist culture such as the United States has a bigger problem with social loafing than a collectivist culture? Explain.

Fourth, <u>when the task is a simple one</u> groups are not superior to individuals. When faced with a remedial task there is no special advantage in having a group work on it. Minimal resources are required. If any individual can likely do the task, why involve a group?

Finally, <u>when time is a critical factor</u>, groups usually perform less effectively than individuals. In emergency situations or in circumstances where speed and efficiency are paramount, individuals can often perform better than groups, especially large groups. The reason is simple. Groups tend to be abominably slow. There are exceptions, however, such as a disaster team trained to perform under pressure and time constraints. Most groups, though, are not trained to operate swiftly and efficiently under pressure. As previously noted, small groups are usually faster than larger groups, but even small groups can lag behind a single individual in the performance of a task.

Groups outperform individuals in a variety of conditions. There is no magic, however, in assembling groups to perform tasks. There are conditions in which groups perform abysmally.

second look

Individual versus Group Performance

Group Superior to Individual

Conditions	Reason(s)
• Broad-range task	• Pool knowledge, group remembering
• Neither have expertise	• Synergy
• Experts, complex task	• Share the load, teamwork
• Individual expert, informed group	• Error correction, synergy

Individual Superior to Group

Conditions	Reason(s)
• Individual expert, uninformed group	• Pooling ignorance, negative synergy
• Groups establish mediocrity norms	• Insufficient motivation to excel
• Group becomes too large	• Difficulty coordinating, social loafing
• Simple task	• Minimal resources required
• Time critical factor	• Groups too slow

Risk-Taking and Polarization   Jason Allen, a 20-year-old student at Carteret Community College in Morehead City, North Carolina, died after swallowing dozens of caffeine pills on a dare from a fellow student. His caffeine intake was equivalent to drinking about 250 cups of coffee. We can be goaded by another person into taking unreasonable risks. Imagine how much more powerful is the influence to take risks when the majority of a group does the goading.

Researchers of small group decision making used to believe that group members inevitably influence each other to take greater collective risks than members' initial preferences. This was called the *risky shift phenomenon*. Teenagers who goad each other to engage in goofy and dangerous group actions is a common example. Excessive alcohol consumption, or binge drinking, by college students with its potential for hazardous consequences has been tied to the social influence of groups (e.g., fraternities and sororities). The frequency within these groups of talking about drinking is a particularly important influencing factor (Dorsey et al., 1999). Terrorists concoct riskier, bolder, fanatical acts of violence when they discuss their schemes in a group (McCauley and Segal, 1987). After hundreds of studies, however, there is ample evidence that groups sometimes have a conservative shift rather than a risky shift (Levine and Moreland, 1990). Thus, group decisions tend to polarize.

Group polarization is the group tendency to make a decision after discussion, that is more extreme, either riskier or more cautious, than the initial preferences of group members. (Group polarization does not mean that disagreement among group members becomes more pronounced, or polarized.)

What influences the direction of the polarization? Groups tend to polarize decision making if there is a clear majority leaning one way (risk) or the other (caution). If most members of a group lean slightly toward risk taking initially, the group will become more prone to take even greater risks than any in-

make more extreme either way than you would do on your own depends on group

Groups often promote risk-taking, such as binge drinking by college students.

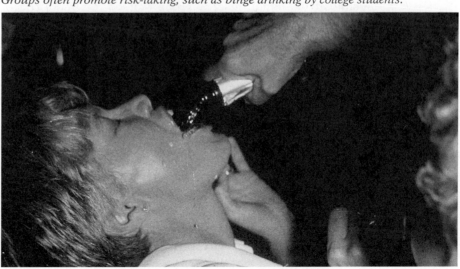

dividual member might have initially preferred, and if most members of a group lean slightly toward playing it safe, the group will likely become even more cautious than it was initially. It is unlikely that a group will polarize when group members are about evenly split between risk taking and playing it safe. This is where compromise, or depolarization, may result.

Research also indicates that group decisions will likely shift toward risk taking when groups are large, when members do not know each other well, and when members are knowledgeable and well-informed about the problem. Groups will likely shift toward more cautious decision making when the decision is steeped in uncertainty, when the results could be severe, and when the probability of successful risk taking is questionable (BarNir, 1998). The direction of the group polarization also appears strongly influenced by culture. For instance, U.S. groups are more likely to polarize in the direction of risk while Chinese groups are more likely to polarize in the direction of caution (Hong, 1978). Risk could produce disharmony, especially if it turns out badly.

There are two primary explanations for why group polarization occurs (BarNir, 1998). The first is social comparison (normative influence). The assumption here is that an individual uses the group norm regarding riskiness or caution as a point of reference. The individual is inclined to shift after group discussion in order to conform more closely to the perceived expectations of the group in this regard. The individual member compares his or her position on risk or caution to that of the group as a whole. If most group members initially tend toward riskiness, cautious members are inclined to move in the direction of the majority. If most members initially favor caution, all members feel pushed to be cautious.

A second explanation for the group polarization effect is persuasive argumentation (informational influence). Individuals in a group will move toward either greater risk or caution when exposed to arguments and information that were not available to members when they made their initial decision. In general, the greater the number of arguments advanced during discussion that support the initial majority group opinion, the more cogent, reasonable, and persuasive they seem to be, and the more original or nonredundant the arguments are, the greater will be the group polarization (Smith, 1982). Naturally, if the majority is predisposed toward risk taking (or caution), the number of arguments advanced will usually favor that predisposition.

The performance phase of group development is a complex process. I have merely laid the groundwork for more detailed discussion of group performance in later chapters. Nevertheless, I can give some general advice at this juncture regarding communication competence. A competent communicator exhibits a sensitivity to the needs of the group during the performance periodic phase of group development as follows:

1. *Focus on the task.* Since task and social dimensions of groups are interconnected, focusing on the task to the detriment of social relationships among members obviously makes little sense. Nevertheless, when there is work to be done, the primary focus is on the accomplishment of the task. Cohesiveness can be built when the pressure to perform has lessened. Task accomplishment also increases cohesiveness.

2. *Encourage participation from group members*. The group needs to utilize its resources fully, which means that even social loafers may have much to contribute. A <u>note of caution</u> here: Encouraging member participation should not be a blanket rule. Some group members should not be encouraged to participate because they disrupt the group's decision-making process (more on this in chapter 7).

Communication competence requires flexibility. What is appropriate communication in one phase of group development will prove to be inappropriate in other phases. As Andersen (1988) summarizes, "Competent communicators are skilled in all phases of group development, and they are adaptable enough to implement effective communication behavior at the appropriate phase of group development. You can improve your overall group competence by becoming sensitive to group phases and the appropriateness of your communication skills" (p. 456).

---

second look

Competent Communication and Group Development

Forming Periodic Phase
- Express positive attitudes and feelings
- Appear friendly, open, and interested

Storming Periodic Phase
- Tolerate, even encourage, disagreement and deviance
- Keep a civil tongue
- Be an active listener

Norming Periodic Phase
- Adapt communication to the norms of the group
- Encourage change when norms are excessively rigid
- Encourage change when norms are too elastic

Performing Periodic Phase
- Focus on the task
- Encourage participation from group members (in most instances)

NEWCOMERS AND GROUP DEVELOPMENT

The interconnectedness of all components of a system makes the entry of even a single new member into a group a highly significant event. Moreland and Levine (1987) note that as groups develop, relationships among members stabilize and the roles and norms in the group become more complex. "The entry of a newcomer into the group can threaten this development by forcing members to alter their relationships with one another" (p. 156).

Nature of Group

Several characteristics of a group directly affect the acceptance of a newcomer (Moreland and Levine, 1987). First, <u>the level of group development has a direct bearing</u>. Katz (1982) studied several research and development groups in a large corporation for four months. Members of those groups which had been in existence for a relatively short time communicated more with newcomers and were more open to their ideas than were members of older groups. A newcomer in a younger group is less disruptive since he or she enters early on in the group development process. Entering a long-standing group, however, where development has progressed far beyond the initial stages can be a far greater shock to the system and requires greater adaptation by the members. The newcomer seems more like an outsider in older groups than in younger ones.

Second, <u>the level of group performance affects the acceptance of newcomers</u>. When the system is functioning well, group members may not want to take a chance on altering a successful formula. Accepting a newcomer may pose a big risk. When a group is performing poorly, however, there is a strong impetus for change. The arrival of a newcomer may be perceived as a welcome addition. The newcomer might turn the group around.

Third, <u>the number of members affects acceptance of a newcomer into a group</u>. Those groups that have too few members to perform necessary tasks well usually are eager to accept newcomers. Newcomers mean less work for each member and potentially greater success for the group. Groups that have too many members to function efficiently, however, will probably view a newcomer as an additional burden.

Finally, <u>the degree of turnover in a group also affects acceptance of newcomers</u>. Groups accustomed to frequent entry and exit of members will accept newcomers more readily than groups unaccustomed to turnover.

In Alan Alda's movie *The Four Seasons*, a longtime (older) group of close, successful, middle-aged friends whose group membership had not changed in years (no turnover) is thoroughly disrupted when one member marries a young woman after divorcing his wife. Initially, the young woman is given an icy reception. The friends quarrel as a result of the perceived intrusion of this outsider. Having experienced a long period of stability with no exits of old members and no entrances of new members before this, they are unskilled in adapting to such change. The period of adjustment to this newcomer is lengthy.

Newcomer Strategies

There are several strategies newcomers can employ to improve their chances of gaining acceptance from a group (Moreland and Levine, 1987). First, <u>conduct a thorough reconnaissance of the group</u>. Most newcomers do a poor job of scouting out a group to determine whether they and the group are a good match (Wanous, 1980). Newcomers should exploit all available sources of information about the group in order to form a reasonably accurate assessment of the group they contemplate joining.

Second, <u>play the role of newcomer</u>. Seek the advice of longtime members, avoid disagreements with old-timers, and talk less than they do. This shows respect. This obviously is not a permanent role. As you become more accepted by the group your communication can move away from the newcomer role pattern.

Third, <u>seek patrons within the group</u>. Patrons are old-timers who help newcomers become accepted by the group. The best patrons are called mentors. Mentors are old-timers who develop a close personal relationship with the newcomer and assist the newcomer's entry into the group.

Fourth, <u>collaborate with other newcomers</u>. When more than one newcomer enters a group, they stand to gain from banding together with a common purpose. Newcomers can lend emotional support and encouragement to one another. They can provide useful information about the group. They can act as a friendly face, making the group climate more inviting.

---

second look

Newcomer's Entry into a Group

Characteristics Affecting Newcomer's Acceptance

- Level of group development
- Level of group performance
- Number of members (too many or too few members)
- Degree of member turnover

Newcomer's Strategies for Acceptance

- Conduct thorough reconnaissance of group
- Play the role of newcomer
- Seek patrons within the group
- Collaborate with other newcomers

FOCUS *on gender/culture*

Gender/Ethnicity and Group Development

Women and ethnic minorities have typically experienced unequal treatment in small groups (Forsyth, 1990). There are significant differences between groups composed of diverse members (mixed company) and groups whose membership is homogeneous (nondiverse). Unfortunately, the focus of research in this area has mostly ignored ethnic minorities and concentrated on gender differences. Unquestionably, however, female ethnic minorities experience the greatest disadvantage because they face a double bias (Morrison and Von Glinow, 1990).

In mixed-sex groups, men are normatively assumed to be the task experts whereas women are assumed to be the relationship experts (Acker, 1990). This assumption puts women at a disadvantage in task groups. The norm emphasizes a lower status role for women (i.e., keeping the peace) while dictating a higher status role for men (i.e., making important decisions and solving problems).

Do women perform as well as men in small task groups? The answer depends on the gender balance. If a woman is alone in an otherwise all-male group, her performance will be adversely affected. As Taps and Martin (1990) explain, "The opportunities for a solo woman to speak, or to show she is competent and has a contribution to make, are low in otherwise male groups; and the larger the size of the group, the lower these odds are" (p. 475). Balanced gender in groups can overcome the normative bias of mostly male task groups.

There is definitely a benefit to women and, by extrapolation of the research, ethnic minorities when group composition is more diverse. One study showed that gender diversity in small groups enhanced the team performance even on male-oriented tasks (Rogelberg and Rumery, 1996). In situations where group composition can be considered during the forming phase (e.g., task force or ad hoc groups), a maximum effort should

be made to have a diverse membership with women and ethnic minorities fairly represented. The **Twenty Percent Rule** is an important minimum standard to achieve in this regard. Researchers have observed that discrimination against minorities, and presumably women, drops substantially when no less than 20 percent of a group, and not fewer than two members, are from a minority (Pettigrew and Martin, 1987).

Questions for Thought

1. Why does the Twenty Percent Rule work to diminish discrimination against minorities and women?
2. How important do you think it is to have a diverse group membership? Is there any connection to group synergy? Explain.

In summary, all groups have a task and social dimension. The output of the task dimension is productivity. The output of the social dimension is cohesiveness. Productivity can affect cohesiveness and vice versa.

Group development encompasses four periodic phases: forming, storming, norming, and performing. These periodic phases do not occur in rigid sequence. They frequently overlap and groups may jump around between phases depending upon the circumstances and situations groups face. Some groups never progress beyond the forming and initial storming phases. These are groups that dissolve for many reasons because they do not work.

Finally, the entry of newcomers into a group can be a disturbing event. Competent communicators learn about the nature of the group to which they seek membership, and they learn the strategies that will assist their acceptance into the group. Women and ethnic minorities, who are often in the newcomer role, have had a difficult time gaining acceptance into groups.

Questions for Critical Thinkers

1. When is it appropriate to be a nonconformist in a small group?
2. Are there ever times when the task is so important that concern for the social dimension of the group must be ignored?
3. Should group members make an effort to integrate newcomers into the group or is it primarily the task of the newcomer to adapt to the group?

CHAPTER

4

Developing the Group Climate

IDEO, a design firm in California's Silicon Valley, produces 90 products on average each year. IDEO has designed, among other things, the Macintosh Duo docking system for laptops, Apple's original point-and-click mouse, AT&T's new line of answering machines and telephones, the insta-cholesterol test, virtual reality headgear, and Levolor blinds (O'Brien, 1995).

What IDEO has accomplished, however, is not nearly as impressive as how the firm accomplished it. David Kelley, the founder and driving force behind IDEO, is the most uncorporate corporate executive you're likely to find. Kelley has established a corporate climate that is the antithesis of what you're likely to see in most of the Fortune 500 companies and in most small businesses as well. Kelley wanted three things when he established IDEO: to work with friends, to have no bosses in charge of employees' lives, and to eliminate jerks from the workplace (O'Brien, 1995).

IDEO has a flattened hierarchy characterized by few titles, no bosses, and no time clocks or specified vacation schedules. Kelley organizes weekly company bike rides, hosts birthday celebrations for workers according to their zodiac signs, and often conducts Monday morning meetings seated on the floor of a purple-and-aqua room devoid of furniture.

At IDEO, employees are treated as equals who set their own schedules (typically fifty- to sixty-hour workweeks) while meeting demanding standards and strict deadlines. The open, freewheeling climate at IDEO is a large part of its appeal (O'Brien, 1995). Bob Sutton, a Stanford professor of organizational behavior, spent fifteen months studying IDEO to understand the secret of its success. His conclusion: "The secret is simple but complex. It's about people who aren't focusing on office politics" (p. 25). At IDEO, developing and maintaining a positive group climate free of negative in-fighting is essential.

A communication climate permeates all groups and affects every aspect of a group's social and task dimensions. A positive climate exists when individuals perceive that they are valued and treated well by the group. A negative climate exists when group members do not value and respect one another, when trust is minimal, and when members perceive that they are not treated well.

The purpose of this chapter is to identify and explain those communication patterns and processes that build a positive group climate and those that create a negative climate with its typically ineffective and unproductive outcomes.

I have three objectives related to this purpose:

1. to discuss the effects of competitive and cooperative group climates on group effectiveness,
2. to explore ways to construct cooperative teamwork in small groups, and,
3. to provide a specific plan for dealing with difficult members who disrupt the group climate.

The underlying premise fundamental to this discussion is that prevention is preferable to cure. Establishing a positive group climate of trust, openness, directness, and accomplishment will prevent many problems from occurring, thus making cures for hostile conflict and disruptive dissension among members largely irrelevant. A positive climate is far more likely to develop in a

<u>cooperative instead of a competitive atmosphere</u>, a theme that will be explored extensively in this and later chapters.

COMPETITIVE VERSUS COOPERATIVE CLIMATES

Our culture pays lip service to the desirability of human cooperation, while our behavior shows a clear preference for competition. The belief is widespread that we live in a dog-eat-dog world. Mutts get devoured by Dobermans. It's better to be a Doberman.

I will train an analytical eye on the competitive mindset that permeates American culture. I will make a special effort to compare the effects of competition versus cooperation on small group climate and goal attainment.

Focus Questions

1. What is the relationship between communication competence and competition/cooperation?
2. Does competition increase motivation to succeed? Group cohesiveness?
3. Does competition improve achievement and performance?
4. Does competition build self-esteem and character?

Definitions

Alfie Kohn (1992) in *No Contest: The Case against Competition* defines **competition** as a process of "<u>mutually exclusive goal attainment</u> (MEGA)" (p. 3). When transactions in groups are competitive, your success is achieved at the expense of other group members. *Competition, by definition, necessitates the failure of the many for the success of the few.* There is only one World Series champion in baseball, one world chess champion, one female and one male world figure skating champion, and one woman crowned Miss America. Competition for a job produces a single happy candidate and, in some cases, hundreds, even thousands of disappointed applicants. In the fall of 1996, the city of San Francisco solicited applications for 50 new firefighters. More than 10,000 individuals applied. That's 50 winners and more than 9,900 losers. Pick any contest and the disproportionate number of losers compared to winners is usually enormous.

Linda Putnam (1986) describes competitive climates in the group setting this way: "In competitive climates, decision outcomes emerge from the suspicion and distrust of group members. . . . The tensions inherent in decision dilemmas are managed through power plays by dominant members who control decision rules, procedural directives, and topics of discussion. Ineffective decisions often emerge from the constrained patterns of communication that typify these competitive climates" (p. 179).

Cooperation can be defined as a process of <u>mutually inclusive goal attainment</u> (MIGA). Your success is tied directly to the success of other group members. The spirit of cooperation was captured and its logic was communicated succinctly by Benjamin Franklin when he reputedly remarked upon signing the Declaration of Independence, "We must all hang together—or, most assuredly, we shall all hang separately."

Putnam (1986) describes a cooperative climate in the group setting this way: "In cooperative climates, decision outcomes emerge from coping effectively with differences of opinion, personality clashes, and rival alternatives for courses of action. Group supportiveness, commitment, and interdependence constitute the content themes of cooperative climates" (p. 179).

Independently attempting to attain a goal previously unrealized, such as performing more push-ups than ever before or earning a higher grade on a calculus exam than at any other time in your academic life, is neither competition nor cooperation. It is, however, often mistakenly referred to as "competing with oneself." When Mariah Nelson (1998) asked 1,030 girls and women from ages 11 to 49 to indicate with whom they compete generally, 75% responded "with myself; my own standards and goals." The effort to improve on a previous performance is not competition unless the aim is to defeat another party to achieve such a goal (which means that if you "compete with yourself" you have to try to beat yourself and be victorious at the same time). If being number one requires a number two, three, four, and so forth, then we are competing. If being better than before is attained at no one else's expense, then this is **individual achievement** not competition.

For conceptual clarity it is important that we understand the difference between competition and individual achievement. As Kohn (1992) notes, competition requires interaction. It is not a solitary undertaking. Claiming that we compete with ourselves is like saying we arm wrestled with ourselves. Arm wrestling is an interactive phenomenon necessitating at least one other party. Competition is likewise interactive.

Prevalence of Competition

Fisher and Ury (1981) tell a story that reflects the preoccupation of individualist cultures with competition. "In 1964 an American father and his twelve-year-old son were enjoying a beautiful Saturday in Hyde Park, London, playing catch with a Frisbee. Few in England had seen a Frisbee at that time and a small group of strollers gathered to watch this strange sport. Finally, one Homburg-clad Britisher came over to the father: 'Sorry to bother you. Been watching you a quarter of an hour. Who's winning?'" (p. 154)

Our inclination to view most human interactions in a competitive light is real and pervasive. Kohn (1992) argues that life in America "has become an endless succession of contests. . . . It is the common denominator of American life" (p. 1). Nathan Miller bitingly asserts that "conversation in the United States is a competitive exercise in which the first person to draw a breath is declared the listener" (as cited in Bolton, 1979, p. 4). Paul Wachtel (1983), author of *The Poverty of Affluence,* declares, "Competition is almost our state religion" (p. 284). Psychologist Elliot Aronson (1999) claims that "we manifest a staggering cultural obsession with victory" (p. 263).

Competition in the United States is everywhere. Our economic, judicial, and political systems are based on competition. U.S. universities are "intensely individualistic and highly competitive. Student is pitted against student through the grading system, and faculty member against faculty member for

The toddler race and children's chess match show that emphasis on competition begins at an early age.

promotion and other academic favors" (Smith, 1990, p. 13). According to one report, academic competition "will intensify over the next ten years" (Bronner, 1999, p. 13A). In 1999, a new Web site (www.ecollegebid.org) appeared that was modeled after priceline.com. Instead of bidding for airline tickets and hotel reservations, however, this new Web site created by Tedd Kelly, a Virginia-based marketing consultant, auctions off admissions to U.S. colleges. Students name what they are willing to pay annually for a college education, provide their grades, test scores, and financial aid eligibility information. Colleges that have subscribed to the Web site try to outbid each other by presenting the most competitive financial package to attract the student. Although highly controversial, Catholic University's John Dolan, dean of enrollment management, offers this spin, "People are screaming about this (site), but Tedd recognizes that they're really screaming about the competitiveness of the college recruiting and financial aid marketplace" (as cited in Feder, 1999, p. 16A).

The competitive obsession in the United States is graphically illustrated by an incident that occurred in Lakewood, California. On March 19, 1993, police arrested eight members of a high school boys' clique called the "Spur Posse" (named after the San Antonio Spurs professional basketball team). The boys, ages 15 to 19, were charged with 20 counts of various sex crimes involving girls from ages 10 to 16. The boys readily admitted that one of the main activities of this group was to "hook up" (have sex) with as many girls as possible (Seligman, 1993).

The boys, many of them top athletes at their high school, coolly admitted to investigators that they kept count of the young girls with whom they had sex. Billy Shehan boasted 66 conquests, the most of any Posse member

Members of the Spur Posse argue with a female antagonist on a talk show.

("Who's keeping score," 1999). Apparently, this was more of a contest about "scoring" than simply having sex. As sociologist Donna Eder of Indiana University explains, "They take the competitive sense and move it into the realm of sexuality" (as cited in Gelman & Rogers, 1993). Contests in the United States can be about almost anything.

FOCUS *on gender*

Gender and Hypercompetitiveness

Competition is everywhere in the United States, but is it predominantly a male fascination? After all, Tannen (1990) argues that men view conversations from a status (competitive) perspective but women view them from a connection (cooperative) perspective. Mona Harrington (1995) studied female attorneys. She claims that female lawyers reject the combative approach to settling disputes typical of male lawyers. Female lawyers prefer finding common ground, not trying to conquer adversaries. Nelson (1998) isn't "terribly concerned that women will follow in men's footsteps" (p. 24) and adopt what she calls the "Conqueror's way," the win-at-all-costs approach typical of male culture in America. Nevertheless, she admits "the Conqueror's way demands our attention, complicating and influencing any female or feminist form of competition that we might imagine" (p. 25).

According to Kohn (1992), women—although not as competitive as men overall—are becoming more competitive as they enter the workforce in larger numbers. A study of conflict management practices in the workplace found that women are no less competitive than men when conflicts arise (Gayle, 1991). In some instances, women who have advanced in their professions exhibit the "Queen Bee Syndrome" (Mathison, 1987). They climb up the competitive ladder of success and then, instead of assisting other women in doing likewise, they protect their position as top woman in the company. They do this by making it tough for other talented women, who are seen as possible rivals, to advance. Consequently, women, especially those who support

Women have become increasingly competitive in the United States.

traditional gender roles "continue to be an important obstacle in keeping other women from being successful in leadership positions" (Cooper, 1997, p. 483).

In business, sports, entertainment, medicine, law—virtually all facets of our society—women increasingly are pressured to emulate the previously male preoccupation with competition (Kohn, 1992). Pat Heim (1992), in her book *Hardball for Women,* advises women in the workplace, "Drop comments about his (a male coworker) incompetence, point out his past cost overruns to your superiors, or even conveniently 'lose' his files and sabotage his progress—in short, pull out all the stops to undermine his winning the project" (p. 29). Resisting such questionably ethi-

cal advice may prove difficult for women in a hypercompetitive climate where generous salaries, promotions, and perks are given typically to the Conquerors.

Questions for Thought

1. Do you believe that women have become increasingly competitive to succeed in a hypercompetitive society? Explain.
2. How should you deal with the Conqueror mentality in a workplace, for example, when you would rather be more cooperative?
3. Is there any advantage to adopting the Conqueror mentality at work? Is it ethical?

Let me clearly state my point of view here so there is no misunderstanding. It is the *pervasiveness and intensity of competition,* not competition itself, that is the principal problem. We don't have to replace one extreme (hypercompetitiveness) with another (ultracooperativeness). There will be numerous times in groups where despite Herculean efforts to cooperate, competition prevails. In some cases a cooperative alternative may not exist. How does a hiring committee, for example, transform the competition among hundreds of candidates into a cooperative endeavor when there is only a single position? In such cases, the competent communicator has to have the flexibility of skills to adapt to an adversarial, competitive situation. As we will see when conflict management is discussed in the final chapter, sometimes a competitive communication style is required in order to manage a conflict effectively. Competition, however, should be significantly de-emphasized in small groups, and cooperative systems should be established in groups whenever possible.

But if cooperation is We-oriented (working together) and competition is Me-oriented (working against others), how can competitive patterns of interaction be anything but incompetent communication? First, communication competence is a matter of degree. Drinking a small amount of alcohol does not make you an alcoholic and it may be beneficial in some instances, if kept to a minimum. Likewise, a small amount of competitiveness in groups does no harm and may be beneficial to the group. Second, although competent communication requires a We-not-Me orientation, this does not exclude any consideration of individual needs. Orientation implies primary, not exclusive focus. The emphasis matters, not the mere presence of occasional competitive, individualistic communication patterns.

CLOSER LOOK

Competing for No Good Reason

The mental set that predisposes us to compete easily pervades situations that do not demand a win–lose mentality. An interesting instance of this occurred in my group communication class. Students were assigned a symposium project. The assignment required a discussion of the full range of viewpoints on a topic of national or international import.

Three of the term groups working on this assignment were extremely reluctant to indicate their topic choice when asked for this information by a representative of the fourth group. Despite the fact that I had not ruled out the possibility of two groups presenting a symposium on an identical topic, such a restriction was assumed by all. When we discovered that two of the four term groups had chosen rain forests as their topic, the winds of competitiveness blew chill indeed. One of the groups that chose rain forests immediately negotiated with me to present its symposium first, thereby hoping to steal the thunder of the other group. When members of the competitor group overheard the negotiations, they screamed foul. Bitter recriminations flew between the antagonists. I stepped in to calm tempers. I instituted a random drawing to designate the order of presentation. Despite my assurance that both groups could work on the same topic and that grades would not be determined on any comparison between groups, the competitors seemed unmollified.

Outside of class the antagonism continued. Members of the two competing groups verbally accosted each other during lunch in the cafeteria. When class resumed, both groups could be heard muttering unflattering comments about their adversaries. On her own initiative, one member asked to speak to the rival group, but her rivals curtly ordered her to leave.

A contest of sorts ensued. Members of one group swarmed the library, hoping to preempt efforts by members of the competing group to secure necessary informational resources. Library books were jealously guarded. Magazines were checked out and hoarded. Independent sources of information, such as interviews with professors, material garnered from environmental groups, and the like, were kept secret.

What is most interesting about this feud is that neither group needed to compete, yet cooperation never seemed to enter the consciousness of participants in this skirmish. Since their grades would be determined by a set of criteria applicable to all groups, and no comparison between groups would transpire, neither of the rivals had any good reason to compete. They both had excellent reasons, however, to collaborate and share information. If they were worried about the redundancy of two identical presentations, the antagonists could have worked together and organized their symposiums in such a way that redundancy could have been kept to a minimum. By pooling resources, they could have improved both of their final presentations. Instead, the two groups became instantly rigid and systemically hostile, each demanding that the other group choose a different topic. The result? Both groups gave mediocre symposium presentations.

The We-not-Me orientation of the competent communicator necessitates less emphasis on competitive win–lose and more emphasis on cooperative win–win approaches to these kinds of conflicts of interest. In my students' defense, they learned from their experience of competing when competition wasn't necessary. Their second symposium was a more cooperative effort and a better overall performance.

Questions for Thought

1. Why do you think the two groups were unable to break their competitive mindset? Why didn't

they see the wisdom of cooperation and act accordingly?

2. Can you think of experiences you've had in groups that closely parallel these two groups?

Effects of Competition versus Cooperation

The pervasiveness of competition in American society and the vehemence with which it is defended makes competition difficult to challenge. Bruce Ogilvie, a professor emeritus at San Jose State University and a pioneer in sports psychology, states, "We have to be careful in our country about ever attacking winning. It's a deeply embedded ethic in our culture" (as cited in Kutner, 1994, p. D2). Nevertheless, a sober, analytical review of the research comparing the effects of competition and cooperation is warranted, if for no other reason than to base our conclusions on evidence.

Achievement and Performance   In September 1989, President George Bush expressed his belief in the merits of competition. He called for "a new spirit of competition between students, between teachers and between schools" (as cited in Jacobs, 1989, p. 5B) in order to improve student achievement and performance in the classroom. Republican presidential candidate Bob Dole echoed the Bush sentiment in his acceptance speech at the Republican national convention in the summer of 1996 when he called for "school choice and competition to improve education in the United States" (as cited in Baxter, 1996). This belief in the merits of competition is cultural dogma accepted by most Americans without question.

Do we function more effectively in groups when the climate is competitive? Almost without exception, the resounding answer is NO! Johnson and Johnson (1981, 1987, 1998) reviewed hundreds of studies on the effects of competitive, cooperative, and individualistic learning. They concluded that cooperation, not competition, clearly leads to higher academic achievement. As David Johnson concludes, "There's almost nothing that American education has seen with this level of empirical support" (Kohn, 1987, p. 54).

Members of the victorious Brazilian World Cup soccer team express their jubilation. Members of the second-place Russian Olympic gymnastics team appear to be attending a funeral, not receiving silver medals at the Olympic games.

The clear advantage of cooperation compared to competition is reflected in other arenas besides education. Robert L. Helmreich, a professor of psychology at the University of Texas, conducted seven studies with a wide variety of subjects (e.g., scientists, businesspeople, airline pilots, and airline reservation agents). All seven studies (Kohn, 1992) showed clear advantages of cooperation over competition on achievement and performance.

A large group of studies by Dean Tjosvold (1986) of Simon Fraser University in British Columbia echoed Helmreich's results. "Cooperation makes a work force motivated," but "serious competition undermines coordination" (p. 29). More recently, another study (Van Oostrum & Rabbie, 1995) was added to the growing mountain of research showing the superiority of cooperation over competition on achievement and performance. When competitive groups were compared to cooperative groups within an organization, overall the cooperative groups vastly outperformed the competitive groups. Even the *worst* cooperative groups that were relatively weak on task accomplishment, on average, outperformed the *best* competitive groups.

Kohn (1992) offers three primary reasons why cooperation promotes and competition dampens achievement and performance for most groups and individuals. First, attempting to achieve excellence and trying to beat others are different goals. A series of studies conducted at a business school at Cambridge University makes the point. Teams composed of members with high-IQ scores performed worse than teams whose members had more ordinary IQs. Why? High-IQ members spent a great deal of time in competitive debate, attempting to outshine all other members of the team so they would be recognized as the intellectual star (Belbin, R., 1996). Trying to beat other group members diverts attention from achieving group excellence.

Second, resources are used more efficiently in a cooperative atmosphere. A cooperative climate promotes the full utilization of information by a group, whereas a competitive climate typically promotes information hoarding (Johnson et al., 1986). When group members work interdependently toward a common goal, not competitively to advance individual goals, there is likely to be less duplication of effort, better utilization of members' skills, and greater pooling of information and knowledge. The synergistic effect already explained is more likely to occur in a cooperative climate.

Third, competition diminishes performance because of the antagonism associated with beating others. The goal of competition is victory over opponents. Since your opponents stand in the way of your victory, they are the enemy. Any system that is structured in a zero-sum fashion—I win only if you lose—is bound to create hostility, even hatred and aggression toward those who block your path to victory (Kohn, 1992). A Little League organization in Albuquerque, New Mexico cancelled the baseball season for 500 kids because of hostility and fights among parents, coaches, and league officials. One coach in Whitehall, North Carolina, slashed the throat of a rival coach, spattering blood on one of the Little Leaguers. A teen umpire was shot at by an assistant coach in East St. Louis, Illinois, over a perceived bad call (Corcoran, 1993). So widespread is the aggressive behavior of parents at youth sporting events that Fred Engh, president of the National Alliance of Youth Sports has begun the Parents

Association of Youth Sports to teach parents sportsmanship (Dreyfuss, 1999). As Engh notes, "Because sports are so popular in our society, it's anathema for us to think our child will sit in the dugout. We desperately have to have our child be the star" (Dreyfuss, 1999, p. A9).

Pressure to win and achieve stardom encourages kids to quit competitive sports. A study of kids involved in Little League revealed that the more winning is emphasized, the higher is the dropout rate. Highly competitive coaches had a team dropout rate *five times greater* than teams coached by a more cooperative manager who emphasized skill development, not winning ("Put enjoyment ahead," 1994). Anywhere <u>from 50 to 80% of adolescents who participate in sports quit because they aren't having any fun and the pressure to win is too great</u> (Brue, 1989; Orlick, 1978). As sports psychologist Terry Orlick (1978) observes, "For many children competitive sports operate as a failure factory which not only effectively eliminates the 'bad ones' but also turns off many of the 'good ones'" (p. 129). Achievement and performance cannot be enhanced if a hyper-competitive, aggressive climate provokes kids to quit.

Group Cohesiveness   Closely associated with group achievement and performance is group cohesiveness. Does competition enhance intragroup cohesiveness? *Intra*group competition (within the group) usually increases hostility and aggressiveness among group members. But what about *inter*group competition (between groups)? Doesn't wanting to defeat another group increase cohesiveness within your group? This is true to an extent. Van Oostrum and Rabbie (1995) found "weak indications" that intergroup competition generates internal group cohesion. This is primarily true, however, when your group has to pull together to face a common foe. In the long run, however, cohesiveness is enhanced primarily for winning teams. Losing teams typically fall apart and members look for someone to blame (Van Oostrum & Rabbie, 1995).

<u>Even if intergroup competition stimulates internal group cohesion, however, this method is a questionable way to achieve such a result</u>. The group will have to manufacture enemies to defeat in order to maintain cohesion within the group. Cohesion, then, is artificially induced. It doesn't flow naturally from group interaction. Once the foe has been bested, the reason for cohesion is removed (Filley, 1975). A cooperative group climate, on the other hand, enhances the social relationships within the group thereby increasing cohesiveness and group productivity as a by-product (Rabbie, 1993).

Self-Esteem   Jules Henry (1963) noted that "a competitive culture endures by tearing people down." While many adolescents quit sports because they fear failure and they can't handle the pressure of intense competition, many others never try out because they wish to avoid the embarrassment of not making the team. Remember those agonizing moments in childhood when you engaged in the ritual of choosing up sides for basketball, soccer, or some other competitive game? If you were considered a star by your schoolmates your inclusion on the team was assured. Your main concern was the prestige and enhanced self-esteem that accompanies being chosen first, second, or third. If you were viewed as inept at sports by schoolmates, however, then your main concern was whether you would suffer the humiliation of being taken last in the playground draft.

In a competitive environment, the most skillful are valued. The less skillful just make defeat more probable and thereby become a burden on the team. Olympic swimming sensation Amy Van Dyken, winner of four gold medals in the 1996 Games, took 7 years to win her first race. While she was in high school, she overheard her relay teammates complaining that "with Van Dyken anchoring [the race], we're not even going to get second." Van Dyken recalls that "I found out later that some of them had gone to our coach several times and said they would refuse to be in the relay with me because I was so terrible" (as cited in Meacham, 1996, p. 8DD). To her credit, Van Dyken plugged away for years, quitting at one point in college but coming back "because of how greasy my hair got when I wasn't in the pool two times a day" (p. 8DD). Hers is a story of incredible persistence against the forces that tried to beat her into submission. Most people quit rather than absorb the torment of being called a loser. As Aronson (1999) notes, "We reward winners and are disdainful of losers" (p. 263).

Psychologist Roger Johnson makes the point this way: "You know where self-esteem comes from? It comes from peers, from being liked, accepted, connected. Competition offers a very different message. The minute you lose, your value ends. That's a terrible thing to tell a kid," says Johnson, "or an adult" (Kohn, 1987, p. 54). Daniel Gould, professor of exercise and sports science at the University of North Carolina in Greensboro, makes this assessment: "We find that children believe that if you win, you're worthy, but if you lose, you're not worthy. They pick up the subtle message that outcome is the only thing that counts" (Kutner, 1994).

The true story of "Kathy O." makes this point dramatically. Kathy was a top student and a champion distance runner in high school. She broke three state track records. She was valedictorian for her graduating class, and her high school celebrated a day in her honor. She had it all. In college, she continued her winning ways. In 1985, she set an American collegiate track record for the 10,000 meters. In 1986, Kathy fell a few strides behind the lead pack of runners in the NCAA 10,000 meter final. This was an unaccustomed position for her. Nevertheless, the crowd assumed, as the favorite to win the race, that Kathy would eventually make her move. She did, but in a wholly unexpected way. She left the track in the middle of the race, climbed a 7-foot fence, raced down a side street, and leaped off a 50-foot bridge. She smacked the concrete below. At age 22, Kathy survived her attempted suicide, but she was paralyzed from the waist down. Why did such a gifted athlete with so many victories try to end her life? Her father thought the pressure to win had something to do with it. Kathy later revealed to an interviewer that she felt a terrifying fear of failure as she found herself losing the race. She knew she couldn't catch the lead pack of runners and this made her angry and embarrassed (Zimbardo, 1992).

Unquestionably, competition has an effect on an individual's self-esteem and this effect is mostly negative, except for the disproportionate few

who have the skills to be winners and remain victorious. <u>Cooperation en-</u>
<u>hances self-esteem</u> (Aronson, 1999; Deutsch, 1985; Ebbeck & Gibbons, 1998).
Of 82 studies conducted on the effects of competition and cooperation on
self-esteem, 81 show an advantage for cooperation and *only one* gives the advantage to competition (Johnson & Johnson, 1989). Cooperation bolsters individual self-esteem, but for most individuals, competition does not enhance
self-esteem.

Character Building and Ethics   You've heard the claim. Competition
builds character. It teaches you, in the words of an editorial in the *San Jose Mer-*
cury News lamenting the demise of spelling bees in the Gilroy, California, school
district, "how to work hard, to sacrifice, to concentrate and to lose" ("It spells
success," 1991, p. 5B). The editorial concludes, "We don't need less healthy competition in our schools, we need more. Kids need to learn how to lose if they are
going to learn how to win" (p. 5B).

Such sweeping claims of character building are typically offered as
self-evident truisms with not the slightest effort to support such generalizations
with evidence. Wilmot and Hocker (1998) claim that losing "does not build character; it builds frustration, aggression, or apathy" (p. 85). Sports psychologist
Susan Butt (1976) states that "the traditional assumption that competitive sport
builds character is still with us today in spite of overwhelming contrary evidence" (p. 54). There is "no empirical support for the tradition that sport builds
character" (Ogilvie & Tutko, 1971, p. 61).

The evidence actually shows that competition typically produces
cheating and dishonesty. In business, insider trading scandals made headlines
more than once. In education, cheating among students is epidemic (Derber,
1996). A February 18, 1999, NBC News report stated that 70% of college students admit cheating on tests, and 84% admit cheating on term papers, usually
by buying them off the Internet. Intense competition for grades is given as a primary reason for cheating.

On the other side of the podium, professors fake research results published in scholarly and scientific journals far more frequently than we care to
admit, and the dishonest practice of piggy-backing, attaching one's name to a
publication for which little or no work was performed, is widespread (Sykes,
1988). <u>When much is at stake and few can be winners, cheating and dishonesty</u>
<u>flourish in a hypercompetitive climate</u>. As Sissela Bok (1978), in her widely ac-
claimed book *Lying*, explains, "The very stress on individualism, on competition,
on achieving material success which so marks our society also generates intense
pressures to cut corners . . . such motives impel many to participate in forms of
duplicity they might otherwise resist" (p. 258).

By contrast, in a cooperative system, where the focus is placed on
working together to achieve a common purpose, not on beating an adversary to
gain personal advantage, there is no incentive nor benefit derived from dishonesty and cheating. In a cooperative system, group pressure is aimed at discouraging individualism and a Me-orientation. Rewards come from working and
achieving as a team.

FOCUS on Culture

Competition and Culture

The pervasiveness of competition in the United States can easily delude us into believing that humans are competitive by nature. But where is the evidence that humans must compete because nature makes it inescapable? Even the depiction of life in the animal world as "survival of the fittest" and "red in tooth and claw," to use Tennyson's metaphorical description, vastly overstates the competitive aspects of life on Earth. Anne Fausto-Sterling (1993) observes that "research in the past two decades shows that cooperation among species plays at least as big a role as violent struggle" (p. 24). Zoologist Frans de Waal notes, "Aiding others at a cost or risk to oneself is widespread in the animal world" (Boyd, 1996). Cooperation, according to this new school of thought, has survival value. Animals that help each other find food and ward off predators do better than those that go it alone (Boyd, 1996).

Comparing cultures reveals that "it is the norms of the culture that determine its competiveness" (Kohn, 1992, p. 39), not human nature. Anthropologist Margaret Mead (1961) claimed that "it is the way the structure of the society is built up that determines whether individual members shall cooperate or shall compete with one another" (p. 481).

Consider the typical case of an elementary student who experiences difficulty discerning the correct answer to a math problem. The teacher urges the student to "think harder," applying further pressure to the intimidated youngster desperately hoping for a flash of brilliance. Meanwhile, fellow classmates are frantically waving their hands, certain in their own minds that they have deduced the right answer. Finally, giving up on the perplexed child, the teacher recognizes another student who excitedly shouts the correct answer. One child's misery is another child's triumph. Henry (1963) summarizes this commonplace competitive situation in U.S. classrooms this way: "So often somebody's success has

been bought at the cost of our failure. To a Zuni, Hopi, or Dakota Indian, [besting another student] would seem cruel beyond belief, for competition, the wringing of success from somebody else's failure, is a form of torture" (p. 35).

Chuck Otterman's experience coaching football to students at Arizona's Hopi High School illustrates the normative nature of competitiveness. Football, with its emphasis on hitting opponents, psyching up for the game, and total commitment to victory, contradicts almost nine centuries of Hopi culture and religion.

Located on a reservation, Hopi High hardly embraced football. As Otterman (Garrity, 1989) explains, "They aren't used to our win-at-all-costs, beat-the-other-man mentality. Their understanding of life, of what it means to be a good Hopi, goes against what it takes to be a good football player" (p. 11). Hopi football players did not initially understand the game. Hopi fans didn't know what to do at games, so Otterman had to be both coach and cheerleader, frequently urging the slim crowds to stand up and shout their support for the team.

In the second year of the program, the team went a respectable 6–4 thanks to an excellent quarterback and sure-handed wide receivers. Nevertheless, their quarterback, Jarrett Huma, was uncomfortable with his impressive record-setting personal statistics. Huma and his teammates felt more comfortable when his proficiency at quarterback fell off the next season. Otterman observed that individual success made them uneasy.

After three seasons of bringing football to a community that was skeptical from the outset, Otterman resigned, citing lack of community support for the program. Otterman explained, "These people (were) just waiting to say, 'Football is bad, we don't want it.' And maybe they're right. I really don't know. I don't think the Hopis knew what they were getting into" (p. 16).

There is abundant evidence demonstrating

that American hypercompetitiveness flows primarily from an individualist cultural value system, not a biological imperative (Chatman & Barsade, 1995). Collectivist cultures tend to be far less competitive than the United States (Cox et al., 1991). Two separate studies comparing American groups (highly individualist) with Vietnamese groups (highly collectivist) found that Americans were competitive but the Vietnamese exhibited an "extraordinarily high rate" of cooperation, even when faced with competitive strategies from others. The authors of these studies concluded: "The difference between the extremely individualist and extremely collectivist cultures was very large and consistent with cultural norms" (Parks & Vu, 1994, p. 712). Cultural norms heavily influence the degree of competitiveness in a society.

Questions for Thought

1. In your judgment, was it appropriate to introduce football to the Hopis? Explain.
2. Is it possible for a subcultural group to remain mostly cooperative when the predominate culture is largely competitive?
3. Have you had experience with other cultures where cooperation is emphasized?

Whether the arena is business, education, politics, medicine, or even religion, competition prevails in America. So how do we reverse this emphasis? How does the competent communicator establish greater cooperation in small groups? Not simply, but persistently.

second look

Cooperation Compared to Hypercompetition

Cooperation	Hypercompetition
Improvement of achievement/ performance	Diminishment of achievement/ performance
• efficient utilization of resources	• hoarding of resources
• goal of achieving excellence	• goal of beating others
• promotion of harmonious relationships	• fostering of antagonism/divisiveness
Increased cohesiveness	Diminished cohesiveness for "losers"
Enhancement of self-esteem	Creation of "failure factory"
Encouragement of openness/honesty	Encouragement of cheating/dishonesty

TEAMWORK: CONSTRUCTING COOPERATION IN GROUPS

Urgent pleas and pious pronouncements will rarely produce cooperative teamwork in groups, even if our intentions are noble. Teamwork must become systemic. For teamwork to become systemic in a small group, *cooperation has to be structured into the framework of the group for the benefit of all members*. There are six elements necessary to establish a cooperative team structure: interdependence, equality, participation, individual accountability, cooperative communication patterns, and noncompetitive listening approaches. Leave out any one of these elements and you diminish the teamwork potential of the group.

Interdependence   When we all work together in order to achieve a desirable goal, we exhibit **interdependence.** The goal is unattainable without the cooperation of group members, so we depend on each other for success. Success is not defined individually but in terms of the group. Cooperative goals can be reinforced by an <u>interdependent division of labor and resources within the group</u>. The story of Fred Beasley, a fullback drafted by the San Francisco 49ers in 1998, illustrates interdependence in action.

Fred's father died when he was 12 years old, leaving a wife and nine children to survive on a paltry Social Security income. The interdependent family goal following the loss of Fred's dad was to keep the family intact. This was accomplished by sharing labor and resources interdependently. Alma Beasley, Fred's mom, got jobs cleaning houses. All nine kids found odd jobs. Whatever income was earned from these jobs was pooled to cover family, not individual, needs. Four boys slept in the same room. Dresser drawers were divided among the kids. Household chores were everybody's responsibility. Alma Beasley explains how the family remained together through difficult times: "It was tough on all of us. . . . I just did the best I could. I think we all pulled together" (Judge, 1998, p. D8).

Sometimes groups choose a cooperative goal of simply doing the best they can for all members of the team. The first women's team to be invited to climb Mount Kongur in China didn't set as its target getting one team member on top of the mountain. Instead, the team chose a cooperative goal to get as many team members as high up the mountain as possible (Larson & LaFasto, 1989). Here success is determined by everyone pulling together to produce the best results for every member—no winners or losers.

Equality   There are essentially three ways rewards can be distributed in a group: winner-take-all, equitable distribution (proportional), and equal distribution. Deutsch (1985) discovered that when success depends on group members working together, an equal distribution of rewards gives the best results and the competitive winner-take-all system gives the poorest results (p. 163).

A merit system of rewards (winner–take–all) is intrinsically competitive. Only the winners receive the rewards. This sets up a win–lose dichotomy and sets in motion all the negative consequences associated with competition already discussed. Merit systems may motivate the few who believe they have a reasonable chance of being "number one." Everyone else, however, is demoralized or indifferent because the rewards are forever out of reach. The final report of the Merit Pay Task Force of the California State University Academic Senate (Charnofsky et al., 1998) noted that almost 3,000 studies show either no positive results or serious disadvantages, such as divisiveness and demoralization, from merit pay schemes. The report also noted that other countries such as Japan believe merit pay is ridiculous because it embarrasses employees. The individualist value system of American culture, however, maintains the belief in the wisdom of competitive merit pay despite the evidence. In a survey of 2,022 adults by the Public Policy Institute of California, more than 80% supported merit pay for teachers (Aratani, 1999).

Profit-sharing programs based on equitable reward distribution (i.e., the more a member contributes to the team success the higher the bonus) is preferable to winner-take-all schemes. The biggest drawback, however, to equitable reward distribution is identified by Brislin (1993), "The goal is to reward the efforts of *individuals* in the group rather than to ensure that the group will survive into the future. The quest for individual rewards often leads to a great deal of tension when benefits are to be distributed. People disagree if they do not receive as much as expected" (p. 53).

Schuster (1984) studied 28 firms engaged in some form of financial sharing plan. The majority showed productivity gains from the plans, but the productivity improvements occurred more frequently in firms with system-wide distribution of bonuses that were equally distributed.

The incentive of system-wide equal distribution plans is to share the rewards of a team effort to excel. Equal distribution of rewards provides potential motivation for all group members and, as Deutsch (1979) notes, enhances mutual self-esteem and respect, group loyalty, and congenial personal relationships within the group. The superiority of equal rewards distribution is supported by the results of hundreds of studies (Deutsch, 1985).

Both interdependence and equality as means of structuring cooperation in a group were experimentally tested in a school setting by psychologist Elliot Aronson (1999), using what he terms the "jigsaw classroom." Students were formed into small learning groups to prepare for an upcoming examination. Each student was given only a portion of the material, a piece of the overall puzzle, necessary to pass the test. Everyone needed each other, and test scores were determined on the basis of how well the group did, not on individual performance. Thus, group members had to teach each other and work together in order to do well. So the group goal and division of labor were interdependent, and the rewards (grades) were distributed equally (all group members received the same grade).

When the jigsaw method was used by Aronson in classrooms that had been recently desegregated, impressive results were obtained. Jigsaw learning produced significantly more friendships and less prejudice between ethnic groups than occurred at the same school using competitive learning techniques. Self-esteem, test scores, and liking for the school experience all improved for minority students. White students also experienced similar positive results.

 Participation Group members must have a stake in the outcomes for cooperation to occur. Participative decision making is essential to the institution of cooperation in groups. Collaborative effort will disintegrate if group members feel that their cooperation merely rubber-stamps decisions already made by others with more power.

Participative decision making occurs at two levels. First, group members' participation in decision making is valued, encouraged, and respected. Members feel they are a part of a team making important decisions. Second, the decisions of the team (subsystem) are valued, encouraged, and respected by the system as a whole. Teams are given a great deal of autonomy to determine their own success. Team decisions are not vetoed by upper management. Cooperation occurs in a climate of trust. If the team is not trusted to make careful, deliberative decisions, and if the team's choices are not respected, then participative decision making will quickly be perceived as a deceptive game that only creates the illusion of choice.

A review of 47 studies revealed that meaningful participation in decision making increased worker productivity and job satisfaction (Miller & Monge, 1986). When participative decision-making programs fail, they typically fail because participation was minimal, only some individuals were allowed to participate, the program was too short-term, the decisions teams were allowed to make were relatively inconsequential, or the team's choices were essentially ignored by upper management (Kohn, 1993). I will discuss participative decision making in greater detail in chapter 7. Meaningful participation is essential to the establishment of teamwork in groups.

Individual Accountability   Interdependence, equality, and participation all sound great, I picture you saying, but what about social loafers who could benefit from the toil of others? Group effort is not truly cooperative if some members are slackers who let others do all the work. You must have a mechanism for individual accountability in order to discourage freeloading (Johnson & Johnson, 1987).

I discussed in chapter 3 a plan to deal with social loafing. Institute it. If loafing continues despite the group's best efforts, however, then deny the loafer some rewards as a last resort. Distribution of rewards among all group members should be based on a genuine effort to produce for the group (We-orientation), not merely on equal rewards for all members who still register a pulse. Individual accountability establishes a *minimum standard of performance* in order to share the fruits of team labor. The standards should not be set so high that they assure failure. Opportunities for loafers to redeem themselves should be available. The focus should be on raising all team members above the minimum standards, way above if possible, not on looking for ways to designate failures. Minimum standards agreed to in advance by the group might include the following: no more than two missed meetings, no more than two tardies or early exits from meetings, work turned in to the group on time, and work of satisfactory quality as determined by the group.

Individual accountability is not the same as rank ordering of group members' performances or distributing rewards based on merit. Individual accountability merely establishes a floor below which no one should drop, not a ceiling that only a very few can reach.

Cooperative Communication Patterns

All of the other criteria are largely irrelevant if the communication patterns in the group are competitive, not cooperative. Learning cooperative communication patterns is vital if you hope to build teamwork. Consequently, I will devote the next section to a detailed discussion of defensive (competitive) versus supportive (cooperative) communication.

noncompet. listening? listen completely

CLOSER LOOK

Habitat for Humanity

In 1993, it became the 17th largest homebuilder in the United States. More than 400,000 people in more than 1,200 U.S. cities and towns and in 48 other countries have donated their time and energy to the cause of building new homes for the world's poor (Gaillard, 1996). By 1997, Habitat for Humanity was building homes at a rate of 20,000 per year. On September 13, 1999, Habitat dedicated its 85,000th home built worldwide ("Building on faith," 1999).

The success of Habitat for Humanity is a case study in cooperative team building. Habitat was begun in 1968 by Millard Fuller, a lawyer and businessman who became a self-made millionaire but gave away his riches and dedicated his life to helping poor people own decent homes. Habitat embodies the first four criteria for establishing teamwork and constructing cooperation in groups.

First, Habitat structures interdependence into every housing project. Building houses for Habitat is a community project, not the work of unrelated individuals. As Fuller (1995) explains, "We are all connected. Who doesn't want their community to flourish? And as long as there are shacks in any community, the community is less than well. A Habitat home can be the first step to bringing those who've been left behind into the fullness of community life. The community is always the better for it" (p. 10).

The building of Habitat homes is based on interdependent teamwork. Work crews composed of volunteers divide the labor, with each small subgroup erecting portions of the total structure a section at a time. Work crews are synergy in action. Most volunteers who

build Habitat homes have no expertise in such tasks. In fact, one Habitat construction team in Bend, Oregon, calls itself Chris's Bad Girls and advertises on the Internet, encouraging women ages 16 to 100, "experienced or inexperienced, walking or in a wheelchair, sighted or unsighted" to volunteer their labor to build Habitat homes. On their first project, women from ages 16 to 84 volunteered to build a Habitat home constructed entirely by women (at the time only the third such all-female construction project of its kind in the United States). With the exception of Chris, who was the leader of the group and a general contractor, none of the women were builders. The second-in-command was picked because she had once built a doghouse. Nevertheless, they successfully constructed a Habitat home by working together as a team of committed volunteers with a common goal.

Second, Habitat promotes the equality criterion. Qualifications to own a Habitat home are applied equally to all applicants. All Habitat homeowners are given no-interest home loans. Habitat does not make any profit on the homes

An all-woman construction team works cooperatively to build a Habitat home.

so there is no winner-take-all or equity reward system. Mortgage payments are sunk back into new Habitat construction projects. All houses are basic structures with no frills; just solid, standardized houses varying in size only on the basis of number of family members who will occupy the homes.

Third, Habitat also encourages participation in several ways. The entire community is involved in fund raising, land acquisition, donation of construction materials, and plans for building Habitat homes. Volunteers contribute their time and effort and for this they are valued, encouraged, and respected members of a team. Future homeowners participate along with volunteers, helping to build their own homes.

Fourth, individual accountability is an essential part of Habitat's success. Future homeowners are not accepting charity. As Fuller (1995) puts it, "Habitat is a hand up, not a handout. It's empowerment on the most basic level. Each homeowner family is expected to help build their own house and others" (p. 8). Fuller calls the minimum contri-

bution the future owners must make to the home-building effort "sweat equity." Homeowners are expected and required to contribute 500 hours of labor on their own home and other Habitat projects. They also pay an average of $240 per month in mortgage payments. They are accountable for their loans like any other homeowner. An impressive 89% of Habitat homeowners make their mortgage payments on time and fewer than 1% of all Habitat loans end in foreclosure (Fuller, 1995, p. 125). Habitat, a Christian-based organization that practices what it preaches, helps people help themselves in an exemplary exhibition of cooperation in groups.

Questions for Thought

1. What problems do you think Habitat runs into when developing plans to build low-income homes? How might it overcome these problems?
2. Do you see any limitations on Habitat's ability to achieve its stated goal, to wipe out all substandard housing in the world?

Jack Gibb (1961), in an eight-year study of groups, identified specific communication patterns that both increase and lessen **defensiveness**—a reaction to a perceived attack on our self-concept and self-esteem. These patterns are:

Defensive	**Supportive**
1. Evaluation	1. Descriptive
2. Control	2. Problem orientation
3. Strategy	3. Spontaneity
4. Neutrality	4. Empathy
5. Superiority	5. Equality
6. Certainty	6. Provisionalism

As I discuss each of these communication patterns, see if you recognize any of them in your own experience with groups.

Evaluation Versus Description

A friend of mine was in his townhouse when the 6.9 magnitude Loma Prieta earthquake hit Santa Cruz, California in October 1989. Objects flew across the rooms, kitchen cabinets emptied onto the counters and floor, and glass shattered throughout his home. When the 15 seconds of rocking and rolling to Mother Nature's syncopation subsided, a momentary quiet ensued. Then from the back room came the timid, frightened little voice of his five-year-old daughter: "Daddy, it wasn't my fault." We are quick to evaluate each other in American society, especially negatively, and we are ready to defend ourselves even when no evaluation is offered.

Negative evaluations include criticism, contempt, and blame. Positive evaluations include praise, recognition, and flattery. Negative evaluations produce defensiveness. A study of 108 managers and white-collar workers found that criticism produced more conflict in the workplace than mistrust, personality clashes, pay, or power stuggles (Baron, 1990). In another study, harsh criticism demoralized participants, reduced their work effort, and led to refusals to work with criticizers on future tasks (Baron, 1988).

Who criticizes us does make a difference. A study in West Germany (as cited in "Ditch hubby," 1989) revealed that 86.5% of the women surveyed "willingly accept" criticisms from their best female friends. Another survey by Simmons Market Research Bureau/Bright Enterprises ("Criticism that hurts," 1989) revealed that criticism from a spouse's parents produces the greatest defensiveness, followed closely by criticism from a mate, then criticism from a subordinate at work. Men resent criticism from their children more than women do. What is criticized also influences our level of defensiveness. The Simmons survey revealed that respondents were most hurt by criticism questioning their integrity.

Praise, on the other hand, is usually welcomed unless we suspect an ulterior motive prompts the positive evaluation. A survey of 150 executives from Fortune 1,000 firms by Robert Half International found that scant praise and limited recognition were the main reasons employees left their companies. Robert Half, who conducted the research, notes, "Praising accomplishments provides psychological rewards that are critical to satisfaction" ("Praise the employees," 1994).

Besides giving praise and recognition, description can substitute for negative evaluations and neutralize defensiveness. **Description** is a first person report of how an individual feels, what the individual perceives to be true, and what behaviors have been observed in a specific context. There are three primary steps necessary to become more descriptive.

1. *Use first person singular language* (Narcisco & Burkett, 1975). First person singular uses **I**-statements, not you- or we-statements at the beginning of a sentence. Typically, first-person singular statements begin with an identification of the speaker's feeling, followed by a description of behavior linked to the feeling. "**I** feel excluded and isolated when my contributions receive no response from the group" is an example of a first-person singular descriptive statement. Such an **I**-statement focuses the attention on the person speaking.

    A you-statement, however, places the focus on someone who is an object of attack. "You have excluded me from the group and you make me feel isolated" is a statement dipped in the acidic juices of accusation and blame. Finger-pointing invites defensiveness.

2. *Make your descriptions specific, not vague.* "I feel weird when you act inappropriately around my boss," is an inexact description. "Weird" and "inappropriately" require specific elaboration. Get to the point. "I feel awkward and embarrassed when you tell my boss jokes that ridicule gays and women," is much more specific.

3. *Eliminate editorial comments from descriptive statements.* This is perhaps the most challenging step. Some I-statements are undisguised personal assaults. "I feel ashamed when you act like a social retard in front of my colleagues" uses the I-statement form without the supportive intent or phrasing. Even an I-statement that may appear to be a specific description devoid of judgment sometimes inadvertently travels into evaluative territory. "I get irritated when you waste the time of this committee by commenting on trivial side issues" loads the statement with provocative phrasing. "Waste time" and "trivial" retain the evaluative and attack elements likely to induce defensive responses. Simply jettison the loaded language.

Textbook-perfect, first-person singular, specific, editorial-free statements, of course, induce no supportive climate if the tone of voice used is sarcastic or condescending, eye contact is threatening, facial expressions and body language are intimidating, and gestures are abusive. We must be willing and able to place the focus on our own feelings and spotlight the specific behaviors we find objectionable without sending mixed messages composed of verbal descriptions and nonverbal negative evaluations.

Control versus Problem Orientation

English poet Samuel Butler once said, "He who agrees against his will, is of the same opinion still." Jack Brehm (1972) developed a theory of **psychological reactance** to explain our resistance to efforts aimed at controlling our behavior. Simply put, psychological reactance means the more someone tries to control us by telling us what to do, the more we are inclined to resist such efforts, even to do the opposite. The following bit of wisdom from advice columnist Ann Landers captures this well: "There are three ways to make sure something gets done—do it yourself; hire someone to do it; forbid your kids to do it" (Landers, 1995).

Tell someone they can't do something and, typically, it is what they want to do most. Levine (1984), in his 15-year study of "radical groups" involving more than a thousand subjects, concluded that the coercive practice of "deprogramming" individuals to give up their cult membership "can drive young people back into their group, or into a pattern of cult-hopping, for years" (p. 27).

We help prevent a defensive climate from emerging when we collaborate on a problem and seek solutions cooperatively. The orientation is on the problem and how best to solve it, not on how best to control those who have less power. The problem needs to have a kind of separateness from the individuals involved. Personality conflicts and power struggles have to fade into the background while the spotlight illuminates the problem, and the solution is explored by all parties together.

A study of decision making at 356 U.S. companies discovered that 58% of strategic plans were rejected when executives overseeing the plans attempted to impose their ideas on colleagues. When executives asked instead for problem-solving ideas from colleagues, however, 96% of the plans were approved (McNutt, 1997).

Wanting to be less controlling and more oriented towards problem solving is not the complete answer. The competent communicator must know how to problem solve, have the requisite skills, and be committed to finding solutions. More will be said on problem solving and on how to develop a problem orientation in later chapters.

Strategy versus Spontaneity   The experience of buying a new car is a trial for me. I loathe the initial fake friendliness from the salesperson. I recoil when the salesperson starts in with the transparent compliments (e.g., "You look like a smart guy" or "You strike me as the kind of guy who can spot a steal when you see one"). I retreat (usually out of the showroom entirely) when the auto hucksters try to double-team me, one on each side, with their transparent stereophonic sales pitch.

Most people resent and resist being manipulated. If you are like most people, simply knowing that someone is attempting to influence you for his or her own benefit is repellent. If you suspect that dishonesty is part of the stratagem, you are probably doubly put off.

Hidden agendas, personal goals of group members that are not revealed openly and that can interfere with group accomplishment, can create a defensive atmosphere. I have seen several efforts by part-time instructors to denigrate other part-timers with greater seniority in a ploy to bolster their own image and position in the department. All of these attempts backfired. Their strategy was seen as disruptive to the department, creating conflict and intrigue where none needed to exist. In one instance, the offending instructor was terminated.

Gibb (1961) calls for spontaneity as the answer to strategic communication. I consider the term ill chosen for two reasons. First, how do you manufacture spontaneity, and if you do, is that not strategic? Second, spontaneity can also mean off-the-top-of-your-head, ill-conceived, inappropriate remarks—the kind that a competent communicator would edit. Impulsive behavior doesn't seem like a useful model for competent communication.

What Gibb seems to be calling for is not so much spontaneity, but straightforwardness—directness and honesty. If we are straightforward with others they will often be straightforward with us. Straightforwardness sends a clear message: DON'T PLAY GAMES WITH ME. I DON'T LIKE IT. In the long run, defensiveness is reduced by a consistent, straightforward pattern of communication. How to be straightforward without being hostile or sounding threatening will be discussed when I outline the essential elements of assertiveness in chapter 9.

Neutrality versus Empathy   We like being acknowledged when we are present in a group. We dislike being treated like a piece of the furniture, sitting alone in a corner. Indifference to group members, or what Gibb calls neutrality, makes us defensive. Making little or no effort to listen to what a member of your group has to say exhibits indifference and treats the communicator as a non-person.

Failure to acknowledge another person's communication effort either verbally or nonverbally is called an **impervious response** (Sieberg & Larson, 1971). Such indifference is disconfirming.

You counter indifference with empathy. Howell (1982) defines **empathy** as "thinking and feeling what you perceive another to be thinking and feeling" (p. 108). Empathy is built on sensitivity to others, a quality of the competent communicator. Empathy requires that we try to see from the perspective of the other person, perceiving the needs, desires, and feelings of a group member because that is what we would want others to do for us. "How would you like it if I treated you the way you treat me?" is a plea for empathy from others.

Rosenfeld (1983) determined that creating a supportive climate in the college classroom was a key determinant of whether classes would be liked by students. In liked classes instructors show interest in the problems students face, exhibiting a perception of subject matter as students see it, and make students feel that the instructor understands them. Showing that we understand and relate does make a difference.

Superiority versus Equality

A superior attitude is a turn-off for most people. The Rosenfeld (1983) study on defensiveness in the college classroom found that the behavior of instructors in disliked classes is characterized as predominantly superior. "My teacher makes me feel we are not intelligent" was one of the key factors attributed to classes disliked by students. One of the key factors characterizing liked classes was "My teacher treats us as equals with him/her."

Whatever the differences in our abilities, talents, intellect, and the like, treating people with respect and politeness, as equals on a personal level encourages harmony and productivity. Treating people like they are IRS agents at the awards ceremony for the state lottery winner will invite enmity and retaliation.

Equality does not mean we all have the same abilities. Equality from the standpoint of group climate means that we give everyone an equal opportunity to succeed. We accord all group members respect unless they earn our disrespect. We do not make people feel stupid. Despite variability in talent, ability, achievements, money, and so forth, we do not make issues of these differences in the group. We do not sabotage the efforts of one person in the group by demeaning that member as inferior. Task accomplishment is thwarted by diminishing the self-esteem of any member. The diminishment of even one member may send a system-wide message to all members—you could be the next target. *Be on guard*.

Certainty versus Provisionalism

There are very few things in this world that are certain—death, taxes, and your clothes dryer will eat your socks are a few that come to mind. Communicating certainty to group members, however, is asking for trouble. I listened to students in my class argue with one of their group members who insisted that crystals really do have healing powers and that only pigheadedness kept the group from accepting the truth of what he was adamantly asserting. This individual would entertain no contrary point of view, so certain was he of the unalterable correctness of his belief, nor would he accede to requests from members for hard evidence of crystals' healing power. He was certain he was right and anyone who couldn't accept this truth must be stupid. This was dogmatism in action.

Dogmatism is the belief in the self-evident truth of one's opinion. The dogma, or declaration of truth, warrants no debate in the mind of the dogmatist. A dogmatic individual exhibits closed-mindedness and rigid thinking. Alternative ideas are not seriously considered. Interestingly, the word dogma spelled backwards is *am-god*. Dogmatists act god-like in the certitude of their own point of view. These self-appointed deities can easily inflame the tempers of group members. Some people derive pleasure from trying to prove the dogmatist wrong. Competitive contests fought over assertions of truth by dogmatists and their antagonists can degenerate into adolescent bickering.

Leathers (1970) conducted a study where typical dogmatic statements were introduced into group discussions. The five statements used were:

1. That's a ridiculous statement. I disagree.
2. Are you serious in taking such an absurd position?
3. You are wrong. Dead wrong!
4. I don't understand why I ever agreed with you.
5. That's downright foolish.

Subjects responded to these statements of certitude (and evaluation) with increased tension (e.g., rubbing hands together nervously and squirming in their seats). These statements also elicited opinionated statements from group members. A climate of inflexibility was produced and trust among group members deteriorated.

Provisionalism, the view that shuns absolutes and encourages openness to new possibilities, counters certainty. You approach problems in groups as issues to be investigated. Provisionalism does not require you to be open to nonsense, however. Some issues have been settled for all practical purposes and necessitate no further discussion unless startlingly new evidence surfaces that challenges accepted beliefs. Generally, however, you want to encourage full discussion of issues and avoid absolute statements.

Reciprocal Patterns   The moment we begin to interact with another person we establish a communication climate. Once this climate develops, it can set in motion a reciprocal pattern—like begets like (Adler, Rosenfeld, & Towne 1989). One such famous tit for tat exchange occurred between Lady Astor, the first female member of the British Parliament, and Winston Churchill. Exasperated by Churchill's opposition to several of the causes she espoused, Lady Astor acerbically remarked, "Winston, if I were married to you, I'd put poison in your coffee." Churchill replied, "And if you were my wife, I'd drink it" (Fadiman, 1985, p. 122). Verbal attack begets verbal attack.

One study (Burggraf & Sillars, 1987) found that supportive/confirming communication patterns by one party during a conflict elicited similar responses from the other party. The same held true for defensive/disconfirming communication patterns. Sundell (1972) verified this in a study of junior high school teachers and students. Confirming teachers were confirmed by their students while disconfirming teachers were disconfirmed by their students.

The challenge in any group experience is to maintain the positive reciprocal pattern of support and to break the cycle of the negative reciprocal pattern of defensiveness. A positive reciprocal pattern of support and cooperation must emerge from the communication transactions among group members. Group leaders may play an important role in this process by setting a cooperative tone for the group. The responsibility, however, for establishing a positive group climate rests on all group members. Norms of cooperation emerge from patterns of group interaction. You must encourage cooperation, suggest ways to cooperate rather than compete, discourage competitive communication patterns, and model the appropriate communication behavior for a positive climate to develop.

CLOSER LOOK

The Robbers Cave Experiment

Social psychologist Muzafer Sherif and his colleagues conducted studies in 1949, 1953, and 1954 on intergroup conflict and cooperation (Sherif, 1966). These studies are noteworthy because they took place in a natural environment (campsites in remote areas), not in a laboratory setting, and because the magnitude of the endeavor has never since been duplicated (Sherif et al., 1988). Many experiments have since confirmed the findings of these three studies (Brewer, 1979; Brewer & Miller, 1984), but not one of these efforts alone was nearly as ambitious in scope.

The 1954 study, commonly referred to as the Robbers Cave experiment in reference to the Oklahoma state park where it was conducted, is the most important of the three experiments. The subjects were 22 11-year-old boys from established middle-class Protestant families. Two groups of 11 boys apiece were formed by the experimenters and matched on the basis of observed skills and athletic ability. The reduction of intergroup tension and conflict was the primary focus of this study.

The experiment had three stages. Stage One brought the two groups of boys to the campsite on separate days. Neither group even saw each other until the end of the first week. Activities and problem situations with common appeal to the boys that necessitated interdependent action were created to induce cooperation within each group. Toward the end of the first week, each group adopted a team name. One called itself the Rattlers and the other designated itself the Eagles.

Stage Two was the friction phase. The two groups were brought together to participate in a tournament. Competitive events in the tournament included several tug-of-war contests, baseball games, a touch football game, tent pitching, cabin inspections judged by staff members, a skits and songs contest, and a treasure hunt. Prizes were awarded to the winning team based on accumulated points.

Stage Three was the friction-reducing phase. This stage had two parts. First, the Rattlers and the Eagles came in contact with each other in situations varying in duration from 15 minutes to an hour. These situations were meant to test the effects of pleasant contacts on intergroup conflict. The second part introduced goals that were compelling for both groups, the attainment of which was beyond the efforts and resources of either group alone. Sherif referred to these as **superordinate goals**. The staff sabotaged the water supply to encourage the two groups to pitch in together and discover the source of the problem. A copy of *Treasure Island* was rented after both groups pooled their money to secure the film. The Eagles and Rattlers worked together to help start a stalled truck used to bring in food supplies. All of the boys had to pull on a rope attached to the truck. This tug-of-war with the truck was required on more than one occasion.

The results of this study were many and varied. First, when the Eagles and the Rattlers, physically separated from each other, worked interdependently on goals with common appeal value within their groups (e.g., learning to pitch a tent, make meals, and an unplanned group effort to kill a copperhead snake eight feet from the campfire), cooperation was promoted. This cooperation, however, did not transfer to intergroup relations. The realization that a second group was present at another part of the campsite immediately induced a "them versus us" mentality.

When the competitive interactions between the two groups commenced, conflict escalated. Boys on both teams took the tournament extremely seriously. Both sides prayed for victory.

The tournament produced reciprocal patterns of attack–counterattack. Competition produced aggression and hostility, even hatred. Name-calling and invective became standard practice. The Eagles and Rattlers hurled insults back and forth. They called each other "cowards," "yellow bellies," "braggarts," "sissies," "little babies," even "communists" and "nigger campers." Evaluation was met with counter-evaluation, insult with insult. Assertions of superiority ("Our pitcher's better than yours") were immediately countered ("Our catcher's better than yours").

The competitive phase of this experiment provoked territoriality. Both groups made frequent reference to "our diamond," "our swimming hole," "our Upper Camp," and the like. The Rattlers tried to lay claim to the ball field by placing "their flag" on the backstop. It was burned later by the Eagles. Fistfights broke out and challenges to fight were frequent. Both groups raided each others' cabin, turning over beds, ripping screens off windows, and stealing personal possessions. One member of the Eagles, just prior to the tournament, expressed the opinion that "maybe we could make friends with those guys and then somebody would not get mad and have any grudges" (Sherif et al., 1988, p. 98). During the tournament this same individual became one of the most enthusiastic name-callers. A competitive system produces competitive individuals.

During the final stage of the experiment, mere contact in pleasurable activities did not reduce the friction and antagonism between the two warring groups. In fact, these contact situations merely provided additional opportunities for both groups to wage war on each other. Putting the Eagles and Rattlers together in the mess hall produced several food fights. Whenever the Rattlers entered a building ahead of the Eagles, they were taunted with the remark, "Ladies first."

The establishment of superordinate goals succeeded where mere contact failed. At first, the boys returned to bickering and name-calling following their joint effort. Gradually, however, their hostility diminished as they worked together for the common good. Members of both groups began to intermingle.

A comparison of friendship choices by members of both groups graphically shows how successful superordinate goals were in reducing friction and promoting cooperation. At the end of Stage Two (friction phase), only 6.4% of the Rattlers identified members of the Eagles as their friends. At the end of Stage Three (friction-reducing), this figure had increased to 36.4%. Among the Eagles, the figures were 7.5% after Stage Two and 23.3% at the end of Stage Three. Perhaps even more impressive were the unfavorability ratings of the former "enemies." At the end of Stage Two, 53% of the Rattlers' ratings of the Eagles were unfavorable but only 4.5% were unfavorable after Stage Three. Similarly, 76.9% of the Eagles' ratings of the Rattlers were unfavorable after Stage Two. After Stage Three, however, only 22.6% were unfavorable (Sherif et al., 1988).

Clearly, when groups perceive advantages to cooperating, they will cooperate. Sherif (Trotter, 1985) sums up the essence of this remarkable study: "In short, hostility gives way when groups pull together to achieve overriding, superordinate goals which are real and compelling to all concerned" (p. 59).

Questions for Thought

1. Do you think the results of the Robbers Cave experiment would have been similar if the subjects had been eleven- and twelve-year-old girls? Adults? Why?
2. Can superordinate goals be established to prevent or resolve any conflict?
3. Can you think of examples where intergroup rivalry such as occurred in this experiment produced similar results? Different results?
4. Do you think the results of this study would be the same if we replicated this experiment today?

Noncompetitive Listening

A report from the U.S. Department of Labor (1991) reveals that the average worker spends about 55% of time on the job listening to others. Another study found that college students devote more than half of their communicating time to listening (Barker et al., 1981). Despite the obvious importance of listening well in groups, evidence shows that for the most part we don't listen very well. One report (Adler & Towne, 1999) discovered that only 12% of college students were actively listening to a class lecture and another 20% were mildly attentive. The remaining students were pursuing erotic thoughts (20%), reminiscing (20%), or worrying, daydreaming, or thinking about lunch or religion (8%). Active listening is focused listening. We make a conscious effort to focus our attention on the speaker and his or her message. Too often when sitting in groups we do not make the effort to actively listen. We allow our minds to wander.

Competent listening, however, goes far beyond actively listening to other group members. How we listen is also extremely important. In this section I will briefly discuss competitive and noncompetitive listening.

Shift Response versus Support Response

Listening can become a competitive event. When we vie for attention during a group discussion, our listening becomes competitive. Conversation becomes a contest. An attention-*getting* initiative by a listener, called the **shift response,** is a key competitive listening strategy. Here the listener attempts to shift the focus of attention from others to oneself by changing the topic of discussion. The shift response is Me-oriented. The **support response,** in contrast, is an attention-*giving,* cooperative effort by the listener to focus attention on the other person, not on oneself (Derber 1979; Vangelisti et al., 1990). Consider this example:

MARIA: I'm feeling very frustrated by our group's lack of progress on our
         project.
MICHAEL: I was more frustrated by Jerry's snotty attitude during yesterday's
         meeting. (Shift response)

Notice how Michael does not respond to Maria's frustration. Instead he shifts
the focus to his own frustration about another issue in the group.
         Now compare this shift response with a support response:

MARIA: I'm feeling very frustrated by our group's lack of progress on our
         project.
MICHAEL: I hear you. What do you think we should do about it? (Support
         response)

Here the response from the listener keeps the focus on the speaker and encourages Maria to explore the topic she initiated.
         A shift response can easily provoke shift responses from other group
members in a competitive battle for attention. For example:

BETH: I don't think our project fulfills the requirements of the class assign-
         ment. I'm worried that we will get a bad grade.
GREG: The project was too difficult. I never did understand what we were sup-
         posed to do. (Shift response)
CARLA: The project wasn't too difficult. It was really interesting and fun. I'm
         looking forward to the next project, aren't you? (Shift response)
BETH: But what about our report on this current project? I still don't think
         we've fulfilled the assignment. (Shift response to refocus attention on ini-
         tial topic)
GREG: You worry too much. I need help on my speech. What's the main point I
         need to make first? (Shift response)

Although the shift response may be appropriate in some instances where individuals drift from the main topic of conversation and need to be refocused, competent communicators emphasize support responses and use shift responses
infrequently. Background acknowledgment ("really," "uh-hum," "yup"), a supportive assertion ("That's super," "Nicely done") and a supportive question
("How do you think we should proceed?") are the types of supportive responses
that encourage cooperative discussion, not competitive struggles for attention.

Competitive Interrupting   Competitive interrupting is closely related to
the shift response. It differs, however, in one key way. Listeners who use the
shift response usually observe the "one speaker at a time" rule of conversation.
Competitive interrupters do not.
         Interrupting becomes competitive when the listener attempts to seize
the floor from the speaker and dominate the conversation. Not all interrupting,
of course, is competitive. Sometimes group members interrupt to express support ("I agree with Joe") or enthusiasm ("Great idea"), seek clarification ("I'm
confused. Could you explain that again before we move on?"), warn of danger

("Look out. You're falling over backwards") or cut short a talkaholic's nonstop monologue that prevents other group members from participating (James & Clarke, 1993).

Competitive interrupting is Me-oriented. The focus is on individual needs, not group needs. Competitive interrupting creates antagonism, rivalry, hostility, and in some cases withdrawal from group discussion by frustrated members. Group members often mirror the interrupting patterns of others. If one member interrupts to seize the floor, another member will likely interrupt to seize it back. If members rarely interrupt, and when they do, primarily offer support, however, others will likely follow suit and keep the conversation supportive and cooperative.

Ambushing   When we are ready to pounce on a point made by a speaker, we are listening with a bias. The bias is to attack the speaker verbally, not try to understand the speaker's point of view. This is called **ambushing.** Ambushing is clearly competitive listening. Ambushers aim to defeat a speaker in a verbal jousting match. Preparing a rebuttal while a speaker is still explaining his or her point shows little interest in comprehending a message. In competitive debates, message distortion is a common problem. The focus is on winning the argument, not discerning a message accurately.

Should we ever debate ideas? Debating ideas is a useful and important process in a democratic society. Ambushing, however, puts the caboose in front of the train engine. Defeating an opponent becomes the driving force for ambushers, not clarity of messages. During group discussion, we need to understand messages clearly and accurately *before* evaluating them. Otherwise, we may be evaluating and refuting ideas that were never advanced by any group member.

Probing and paraphrasing can short-circuit ambushing. **Probing** means seeking additional information from a speaker by asking questions. Probing includes clarifying questions ("Can you give me an example of an important goal for the group?"), exploratory questions ("Can you think of any other approach to this problem?"), and encouraging questions ("Who can blame us for making a good effort to try a new approach?").

Paraphrasing "is a concise response to the speaker which states the essence of the other's content in the listener's words" (Bolton, 1979, p. 51). Paraphrasing should be concise and precise. For example:

GABRIELA: I'm so sick and tired of working and working on this report and we have so little to show for it. If we'd started earlier, we would be done by now.

FRANK: You seem frustrated and unhappy with the group's effort.

GABRIELA: I am frustrated, but I'm not unhappy with our group. We've all worked hard. None of us could arrange our schedules to begin any sooner on this.

Paraphrasing can reveal misunderstanding. Ambushing merely assumes a message is understood without checking. Noncompetitive listening is a useful communication skill.

second look

Structuring Teamwork

Interdependence
- Establish cooperative goal structure (interdependent individual/group goals)
- Develop interdependent division of labor and resources

Equality
- Avoid winner-take-all reward distribution
- Avoid equity reward distribution
- Share rewards equally among group members

Participation
- Establish participative decision making on important issues
- Give teams decision-making autonomy
- Value, encourage, and respect group members' participation

Individual Accountability
- Keep groups small—discourages loafing
- Employ plan to stop social loafing (see chapter 3)
- Establish minimum standards of performance—denial of rewards

Cooperative Communication Patterns
- Avoid defensive communication patterns
- Encourage supportive communication patterns

Noncompetitive Listening
- Use support responses, not shift responses
- Avoid competitive interrupting
- Don't ambush; paraphrase and probe

DEALING WITH DIFFICULT GROUP MEMBERS

Unfortunately, it is not uncommon to have a member of a group who hasn't learned supportive communication patterns or who chooses competitive defensive patterns regardless. Jerry Talley of Edgewise Consulting in Mountain View, California, estimates that dealing with difficult individuals consumes a minimum of 10% of a company's time, and can easily grow to 30–40% if the company is truly dysfunctional (Townsend, 1999). Difficult individuals can prevent a group from operating as a cohesive, fully functioning team. Gouran (1988) notes, "Disruptive behavior perhaps is the one occurrence with which the average participant in a decision-making or problem-solving group feels least equipped to cope" (p. 202). There are several fundamental steps that should be taken by the group when dealing with a difficult member.

First, make certain the group climate is cooperative. You can hardly expect others to be supportive and cooperative when the group hasn't made the effort. "There are evil people on the planet and some of them get jobs," notes

Talley (Townsend,1999, p. C2), but most difficult people are created by a competitive system (Aguayo, 1990). Create a ruthlessly competitive, politicized climate in a group where decision making is influenced by rumor mongering, back stabbing, deal making, and sabotaging of coworkers' projects, and difficult group members will appear like flies at a summer picnic. As Talley states in somewhat overstated fashion, "In a lot of ways, organizations are training grounds for insanity" (Townsend, 1999, p. C2).

Second, <u>change your communication in relation to a difficult person's behavior</u>. Communication in groups is a transaction operating within a system. What one party does affects the other parties. So how do you act in relation to the difficult member? You discourage disruptive behavior by doing the following:

a. *Don't placate the troublemaker.* Laughing nervously when the disrupter cracks sexist or racist jokes or makes offensive remarks about group members merely encourages further moronic behavior. Permitting frequent interruptions from the offending party, enduring this ploy for conversational control, is a strategy of appeasement with little potential for success. Allowing the disrupter to manipulate the group so an illusion of harmony can be maintained rewards the troublemaker for objectionable behavior.

b. *Refuse to be goaded into a reciprocal pattern.* Don't counter abusive remarks with abusive remarks of your own. <u>Be unconditionally constructive</u> (Ury, 1993). Disrupters thrive on provoking retaliation. Your insistence that the dogmatist is "completely wrong" will only brand you as dogmatic and unyielding. Becoming aggressive with aggressors escalates into intractable power struggles. So don't take the bait. Keep telling yourself that if you do, you're engaging them on their terms and on their familiar ground, to your disadvantage. As Nancy Heischman, director of the Conflict Resolution Center in Aptos, California, notes, "You're not going to win if you enter into a competition with these people" (Townsend, 1999, p. C2). Resisting the temptation to "fight fire with fire" requires self-control (and in some cases deserves a medal of commendation). In some extreme cases it won't be possible.

c. *Have an out-of-body experience* (Lulofs, 1994). Remove yourself mentally from the conflict. Listen to the disrupter as if you were an uninvolved third party with no energy in the outcome. Picture yourself as a mediator whose job it is to resolve the problem.

d. *Don't provide a soapbox for the troublemaker.* On two occasions in my teaching career, I have had a disruptive student interrupt me in the middle of a lecture/discussion to complain about the class. On the first occasion, I handled the situation poorly. My difficult student blurted out in a loud voice, "Can we do something relevant for a change? I'm tired of discussing other people's problems." I mistakenly took the bait and tried justifying what I had been doing in the class. Not surprisingly, he was unmoved by my response and undeterred in his obnoxious behavior. He was more than happy to mount the soapbox and focus attention on his personal agenda. The rest of the class became restless and annoyed with this interruption. I felt angry and ineffectual.

On the second occasion, my disrupter demanded to know why I was "wasting so much time on the relationship between gender and communication patterns." In this instance, I immediately deferred to the entire class, "Do the rest of you agree that this is a waste of time?" When they indicated that they did not, I then asked the class, "Do you want to take class time to discuss his complaint?" They again indicated that they did not. With the support of the group, I then deferred a confrontation with this student until the class was over. He was ill-prepared to challenge the entire group. Notice, however, that I said *deferred* the confrontation. You can't ignore disruptive behavior, especially when it becomes chronic.

Third, <u>attempt to convert disruption into a constructive contribution</u> (Gouran, 1988). Suppose in the middle of a group discussion your disrupter blurts out, "That's a completely stupid suggestion, but typical of a woman" (I didn't say this was going to be easy). You could reply in kind, thereby setting in motion a reciprocal pattern of derision. Instead, you could attempt to divert the disrupter away from abusive remarks and toward constructive contributions to the group by responding, "Perhaps you could provide a better suggestion." This response does not invite your obnoxious member to mount a soapbox and launch into an irrelevant monologue. You are requesting a pertinent contribution. Bell's (1974) research indicates that substantive comments in a group discussion encourage a focus on content not on relationship conflicts. Disrupters are less likely to continue their abuse when they are focused on the substance of the discussion. If the disrupter does not respond appropriately to your invitation to be constructive, then you can proceed to the next step.

Fourth, <u>confront the difficult person directly</u>. If the entire group is upset by the behavior of the difficult person, then the *group* should confront the disrupter. Even truly abrasive individuals whose behavior seems to indicate a complete lack of regard for the group will find it tough to ignore pressure from group members. Confrontations, of course, should be descriptive not evaluative.

Fifth, <u>separate yourself from the difficult person if all else fails</u>. Communication is not a panacea for every problem that comes up in groups. Some individuals leave no other option except ostracism (a competitive choice) by the group. Removing the troublesome individual is one way of ridding the group of the disruption. If the difficult person is powerful, however, ostracism may not be an option. In this case, try putting physical distance between you and the problem person. Stay out of each other's way whenever possible. Keep interactions to a minimum. In a few instances, you may have to leave the group in order to restore your sanity. Some jobs, for instance, are just not worth keeping when abuse is heaped on you daily by an individual with more power than you have.

I have presented you with a rational model for handling troublemakers. I encourage you to try these methods. I am confident that they will work well for you. Nevertheless, we are not strictly rational beings. Difficult people can provoke intense anger and deep frustration from group members. In my own experience, I have found that even if I lost my temper and let my emotions get the better of me, this response is not as problematic as simply ignoring or enduring the disruptive behavior. Even if your anger translates into personal

second look

Dealing with Difficult Group Members

Make certain the group climate is cooperative
Change your behavior in relation to the difficult person's difficult behavior
• Don't placate troublemakers
• Refuse to be goaded into a reciprocal pattern (tit-for-tat)
• Have an out-of-body experience—become a third party observer
• Don't provide a soapbox for troublemakers
Try to convert disruption into a constructive contribution
Confront the difficult group member directly
Separate yourself from the difficult group member if all else fails

attacks, at the very least you have served notice on the troublesome group member that his or her pattern of behavior is unacceptable and will not be suffered in silence.

I do not counsel emotional explosions as a means to resolving conflicts with difficult individuals, yet I know that occasionally we give in to our impulses. Sometimes it just feels s-o-o-o-o-o g-o-o-o-o-d to tell off our tormentors. If you do lose your self-control, at least follow up at a later time with direct confrontation. You may find that your initial outburst got the attention of your troublemaker. A more rational, deliberate strategy may still work even after a shouting match.

In summary, there is perhaps no greater challenge nor more important task in a group than establishing a positive, cooperative climate. A negative, competitive climate will bode ill for your group. Defensive climates promote conflict and disharmony in groups. Supportive climates do not free groups entirely from conflict, but such an atmosphere enhances the likelihood of constructive solutions to conflict in groups.

Questions for Critical Thinkers

1. Why do you think supervisors faced with poor employee performance use predominantly controlling, not problem-solving, strategies?
2. Are there instances when you should act as a model of cooperative behavior even though other group members will take advantage of you?

Roles and Leadership in Groups

In a study of a surgical team at St. Joseph's Hospital in Ann Arbor, Michigan, the distinction between the role of doctor and nurse was evident. During a coronary bypass operation, the two surgeons (both males) began swapping stories about the Detroit Tigers while loud rock music played in the background. Two nurses (both women) assisting with the operation began a quiet discussion of their own, only to be reprimanded by the head surgeon, who bellowed, "Come on people, let's keep it down in here" (Denison & Sutton, 1990, p. 301). Nurses did not have the same leeway to talk, laugh, and joke with each other as did surgeons. Surgeons, by necessity, were in charge of the operation. Surgeons were in the leader role and nurses were in the follower role, expected to do the bidding of the surgeons without question. Surgical teams have clearly defined roles. Nurses, nevertheless, complained bitterly that the doctors were unnecessarily oppressive in exercising their superior power (i.e., used defensive communication patterns of control and superiority). Nurses complained that they were "slaves" and often were expected to perform demeaning tasks when ordered by surgeons to do so.

In the drama of life we play many roles. A group **role** is the pattern of behavior expected of a group member. Individuals act out their roles in transactions with group members. What may have begun as a casual or unnoticed pattern of behavior may quickly develop into an expectation. What has occurred becomes what ought to be. You tell a few jokes during the initial meeting of your group. You may have just assumed the role of tension reliever without even noticing. Other group members, however, may come to expect you to interject humor into tense situations.

Roles are not static entities. When the composition of your group changes, when phases of development change, when the group climate shifts either toward or away from a cooperative/supportive one, or when you move from one group to another, you have to adapt to these changes in the system. The required behaviors for your role may change as a consequence or the roles members play may change.

In this chapter, I will discuss roles with special focus on the prime group role of leader. My principal <u>objectives</u> are:

1. to explain the significance of roles in groups,
2. to identify the different types of group roles,
3. to discuss the role emergence process,
4. to explore how members gain and retain group leadership, and
5. to discuss how to be an effective leader in groups.

GROUP ROLES

Norms and roles form the basic structure of a group. **Structure** is the systematic interrelation of all parts to the whole. Structure provides form and shape for a group. Norms designate appropriate behavior for all group members while roles stipulate how particular group members should behave. A norm for a group might be that every member works hard on all tasks. Roles, however, specify different task behaviors for a manager and a worker. In this section I will discuss the effects of roles on behavior, types of roles, role emergence, and role fixation.

Focus Questions

1. Are there some group roles that the competent communicator should avoid?
2. When two roles conflict, which role is likely to prevail?

Effects of Roles

The expectations attached to roles can have a marked influence on group members' perceptions. This influence was demonstrated in a study in which pairs of students performed the roles of questioner and contestant in a college bowl-type quiz game (Ross et al., 1977). Questioners were instructed to think of 10 difficult questions for which they knew the answers. They then were to ask contestants these questions. Both students and the audience knew that the roles of questioner and contestant were randomly assigned. Yet, both the audience and the contestants thought that those students playing the questioner role were smarter than those students playing the contestant role. Questioners, of course, looked more impressive asking difficult questions for which they already knew the answers, while contestants looked less impressive trying to answer the questions and sometimes making mistakes. Despite the obvious advantage given to the questioners and despite the fact that students playing both roles were equally intelligent, the predominant perception was markedly influenced by the role each student played.

I have seen the effects of acting out roles in my own classroom. I conduct a simple exercise where I randomly assign roles to individuals in groups. The roles, however, are known to the group but not known to the individuals assigned the roles. The group then works on a task together, adapting to the roles each person is expected to play. When an individual is assigned the role of leader, for example, the group looks to that person for direction. If a person is assigned the role of an isolate, the group ignores that person. Individuals quickly recognize what role they have been assigned.

I have had some very interesting results from this simple exercise. When groups laugh at the "clowns," the clowns usually become instant comics and enjoy the attention. I have seen individuals who have never made a humorous comment in class, become genuinely funny playing the clown role. When isolates are ignored they usually struggle to get recognized for a time, then give up in disgust and become an isolate sitting in silence. When "leaders" are looked to for direction, they usually end up leading the group.

The effects of roles on perceptions can be seen in a dramatic way by doing a **role reversal,** which is stepping into a role distinctly different from or opposite a role we usually play. In a study (Geis et al., 1984) of the impact of high-status versus low-status roles, the power of role reversal was evident. Viewers of television commercials depicting a man in a high-status important person role (his wishes, needs, and preferences were the central concern of the commercial) and a woman in the relatively low-status helpmate role (her wishes, needs, and preferences were never addressed or acknowledged) described the man as a "rational, independent, dominant, ambitious leader." The woman, by contrast, was described as an "emotional, dependent, submissive, contented follower." A markedly different result from these stereotypic depictions of male-female interactions occurred when the roles were exactly reversed. When the woman in the commercial performed the high-status role and the man acted out the low-status role, viewers described the woman as a "rational, independent, dominant, ambitious leader" and the man as an "emotional, dependent, submissive, contented follower."

Role status, the relative importance, prestige, or power accorded a particular role, apparently nurtures stereotypic perceptions of males and females (Hoffman & Hurst, 1990). The implication of this finding is significant. One way to shatter the stereotype that women are followers and not leaders is to reverse roles—place more women in the high-status leadership role and fewer women in the lower-status follower role. Let women be seen more often in power positions and less often in subservient positions. This conclusion would seem to apply to ethnic minorities as well.

The effects of roles can be seen in another way. When we find ourselves playing roles in different groups that contradict each other, we experience **role conflict.** Usually we are forced to make a choice between the two. For instance, when a disastrous fire in the 1950s in Texas City, Texas, endangered the entire city, police officers were faced with a serious role conflict. Should they continue to protect the citizens of the city in their role as police officers, or should they consider their role of parent and spouse as more important? They couldn't do both. In every case except one they chose their family role over their professional role. The exception was a man who knew his family was safe in another city (Killian, 1952). Which role would you choose if faced with such a dilemma?

Similarly, students who have children are often faced with conflict between their student role and their parent role. Do you take the final exam or do you stay home with your sick child? Women with careers and families are increasingly concerned with this perceived role conflict. When a woman is in an important business meeting where colleagues depend on her input and she receives a phone call from her child's school, what does she do? Let me note that the same role conflict could exist for a man as well, but women are still typically cast as the primary caretaker except in single-parent situations. The perception that family demands will intrude upon a woman's work world more than on a man's acts as an impediment to women's advancement in organizations (Haslett et al., 1992).

An extensive review of 42 studies on role conflict (Fisher & Gitelson, 1983) showed significant effects. When individuals felt role conflict within organizations, they exhibited an increased tendency to leave an organization. They also showed decreases in commitment to the organization, involvement in the job, satisfaction with the job, and participation in decision making.

Some roles have a greater impact on us than others. The role that has the greatest importance and most potent effect on us is usually the one we choose when we have to decide between conflicting roles.

The Stanford Prison Study

It happened one Sunday morning. Police officers with sirens screeching swept through the college town and arrested 10 male students. Charged with a felony, they were searched, handcuffed, and taken to police headquarters for booking. Then they were blindfolded and transported to the Stanford County Prison located in the basement of the Stanford University psychology building. Upon arrival they were stripped naked, issued a smock-type uniform with an ID number across the front and back, and made to wear a cap made out of nylon to simulate a shaved head. Each prisoner received towels, soap, a toothbrush, and bed linen. Jail cells were sparsely furnished—cots and bucket toilets. Personal belongings were prohibited.

The 10 inmates were guarded by 11 college students. These guards carried billy clubs, handcuffs, and whistles. They dressed in khaki uniforms and wore reflecting sunglasses to make eye contact impossible. They remained nameless.

Guards established a set of rules that the prisoners were to follow without hesitation or resistance. The rules were rigid: no talking during meals, rest periods, or after lights were out. Head counts were taken at 2:30 A.M. Troublemakers faced loss of "privileges." At first, these privileges included opportunities to read, write, or talk to other inmates. Later, privileges were defined as eating, sleeping, and washing.

The inmates revolted against the repressive conditions. Some barricaded the doors of their cells with cots. Some engaged in hunger strikes. Several tore off their ID numbers. The guards became increasingly abusive and authoritarian in response to the revolt. They used a fire extinguisher to quash the rebellion. Punishment for disobedience included cleaning toilets with bare hands, doing push-ups, and spending time in solitary confinement (a closet). Head counts were used as a means of harassment. Head counts took ten

minutes or less on the first day. By the fifth day, the head counts lasted several hours as the guards vilified prisoners, who were standing at attention the entire time, for minor infractions of the rules.

Within a short time some of the prisoners began to act depressed, dependent, and disturbed by their incarceration. Several prisoners experienced severe stomach cramps. One prisoner wept uncontrollably. He flew into fits of rage and experienced disorganized thinking and bouts of severe depression. Three other inmates developed similar symptoms. Another inmate developed a psychosomatic rash over his entire body when his "parole" was denied.

The chief form of communication initiated by the guards to the prisoners consisted mostly of

Roles can become too real, as depicted in this photo of the Stanford Prison study.

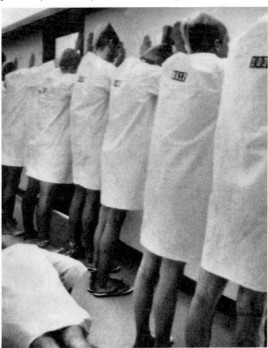

commands, insults, verbal and physical abuse, degrading references, and threats. The principal form of communication used by the prisoners when interacting with the guards consisted mostly of resistance and ridicule in the beginning, but became more compliant later (e.g., answering questions and giving information).

Stanford psychologist Phillip Zimbardo (1992), who conducted this mock prison study, terminated the experiment after only six days. The study was originally planned for a two-week period, but he decided that the roles had become real. As Zimbardo (1992) concluded: "In guard roles, college students who had been pacifists and 'nice guys' behaved aggressively—sometimes even sadistically. As prisoners, psychologically stable students soon behaved pathologically, passively resigning themselves to their unexpected fate of learned helplessness" (p. 576).

Zimbardo had taken 21 healthy, well-adjusted male students who exhibited no signs of emotional instability or aberrant behavior when given extensive personality tests and clinical interviews prior to the experiment and had transformed them into pathological guards and compliant prisoners. The guard and prisoner roles were randomly assigned by the flip of a coin, so pathological behavior cannot be explained by looking for character flaws in the men acting as guards. Clearly, the young men in this controversial field study became the product of their designated roles.

Questions for Thought

1. Considering the effects this experiment had upon its subjects, do you have any ethical concerns about conducting similar studies?
2. Can you think of roles outside of a prison environment that exert similar influence and power over individuals' lives as exhibited in this experiment?
3. Would you have preferred to be a prisoner or a guard? Why?
4. As a guard, would you have treated the prisoners abusively? Are you uncertain of how you would have behaved? Explain.
5. As a prisoner, would you have been docile or rebellious? Are you uncertain of how you would behave in the prisoner role? Explain.

The expectations associated with group roles and the perception of the value, prestige, influence, status, or stigma attached to each role by both the group and the individual can strongly affect us. The types of roles we play, of course, can have a direct bearing on the effect playing roles can have on the person and the group.

Types of Roles

It is not possible to enumerate all the roles a person can play in groups. In the broadest sense, roles are categorized as formal and informal. **Formal roles** are assigned by an organization or group partly to establish order. This type of role identifies a position. Titles such as president, chair, and secretary usually accompany formal roles. Especially within larger organizations, a set of expected behaviors to fulfill the role is explicitly spelled out. A job description used to hire an individual to fill a specific position is an example. Formal roles exist within the structure of the group or organization. They are designated. They do not emerge naturally from communication transactions. Formal roles are often independent from any person filling the role.

In smaller groups, the roles are mostly informal. The roles emerge from the group transactions. **Informal roles** emphasize functions, not positions. A group member may fulfill leadership functions, that is, perform as a leader, without any formal designation. No single informal role is found in all or even most groups with the probable exception of leader.

Actual duties and specific behaviors expected from a group member playing an informal role are implicitly defined by communication transactions among members. The group does not tell an individual explicitly how to be a good leader, but members do indicate degrees of approval or disapproval when an individual assumes the role. Informal role playing is improvisational, not scripted.

Informal roles are typically classified into three types: task, maintenance, and self-centered (Benne & Sheats, 1948; Mudrack & Farrell, 1995). **Task roles** move the group toward the attainment of its goals. The central communicative function of task roles is to extract the maximum productivity from the group. **Maintenance roles** focus on the social dimension of the group. The central communicative function of maintenance roles is to gain and maintain the cohesiveness of the group. Self-centered or **disruptive roles** serve individual needs or goals (Me-oriented) while impeding attainment of group goals. Individuals who play these roles often warrant the tag "difficult group member." The central communicative function of self-centered, disruptive roles is to focus attention on the individual. This focus on the individual can diminish group productivity and cohesiveness. Competent communicators avoid these roles. Table 5.1 provides samples of task, maintenance, and disruptive roles with corresponding communication behaviors.

Table 5.1 Sample of Informal Roles in Groups

Task Roles

1. *Initiator-Contributor:* Offers lots of ideas and suggestions; proposes solutions and new directions.
2. *Information Seeker:* Requests clarification; solicits evidence; asks for suggestions and ideas from others.
3. *Opinion Seeker:* Requests viewpoints from others; looks for agreement and disagreement.
4. *Information Giver:* Acts as a resource person for group; provides relevant and significant information based on expertise or personal experience.
5. *Clarifier-Elaborator:* Explains, expands, extends the ideas of others; provides examples and alternatives.
6. *Coordinator:* Draws together ideas of others; shows relationships between facts and ideas; promotes teamwork and cooperation.
7. *Secretary-Recorder:* Serves group memory function; takes minutes of meetings; keeps group's records and history.
8. *Director:* Keeps group on track; guides discussion; reminds group of goal; regulates group activities.

continued

9. *Devil's Advocate:* Challenges prevailing point of view for the sake of argument in order to test and critically evaluate the strength of ideas, solutions, or decisions.

Maintenance Roles

1. *Supporter-Encourager:* Bolsters the spirits and goodwill of the group; provides warmth, praise, and acceptance of others; includes reticent members in discussion.
2. *Harmonizer-Tension Reliever:* Maintains the peace; reduces tension through humor and by reconciling differences between members.
3. *Gatekeeper-Expediter:* Controls channels of communication and flow of information; encourages evenness of participation; promotes open discussion.
4. *Feeling Expresser:* Monitors feelings and moods of the group; suggests discussion breaks when mood turns ugly or when energy levels flag.

Self-Centered or Disruptive Roles

1. *Stagehog:* Seeks recognition and attention by monopolizing conversation; prevents others from expressing their opinions fully; wants the spotlight.
2. *Isolate:* Deserts the group; withdraws from participation; acts indifferent, aloof, uninvolved; resists efforts to be included in group decision making.
3. *Clown:* Engages in horseplay; thrives on practical jokes and comic routines; diverts members' attention away from serious discussion of ideas and issues; steps beyond the boundaries of mere tension reliever.
4. *Blocker:* Thwarts progress of group; does not cooperate; opposes much of what group attempts to accomplish; incessantly reintroduces dead issues; makes negative remarks to members.
5. *Fighter-Controller:* Tries to dominate group; competes with members; abuses those who disagree; picks quarrels with members; interrupts to interject own opinions into discussion.
6. *Zealot:* Tries to convert members to a pet cause or idea; delivers sermons to group on state of the world; exhibits fanaticism.
7. *Cynic:* Displays sour outlook (a person who "smells flowers [and] looks around for a coffin"—H. L. Mencken); engages in fault-finding; focuses on negatives; predicts failure of group.

Playing roles is a fluid process. During a single committee meeting an individual may play several roles. A group member may even adopt a disruptive role following an unsuccessful attempt to play a maintenance role such as tension reliever or encourager. Individuals in a system are so interconnected that what one group member does can influence significantly the roles other group members play.

Role Emergence

In large groups and organizations roles are largely determined by their formal structure. Even within this formal structure, however, role emergence occurs.

Functional roles operate in smaller group meetings within the organization or in factional subunits of large groups.

Role emergence, however, is a relevant concern primarily to small, informal leaderless groups without a history. These groups can be ad hoc project groups set up within formal organizations (e.g., self-managed work teams), classroom discussion groups formed for the purpose of completing a class project, or a jury in a criminal trial. The roles each member will play have not been designated in advance but emerge from the transactions conducted among group members. How roles emerge in zero-history groups has been studied extensively at the University of Minnesota (Bormann, 1990).

Individuals initially make a bid to play a role. They may bid for a role because they have special skills that suit the role or they succumb to gender role stereotyping. **Group endorsement** of the bid to play a specific role must occur before a person gets to play that role. This endorsement may be difficult for women to obtain if they seek high-status roles. In a competitive culture, high-status roles are generally perceived to be those that are task oriented. Accomplishing tasks brings "victories," tangible accomplishments, and recognition. The roles of director, initiator-contributor, information-giver, and devil's advocate are high-status roles because individuals are perceived as doers—they accomplish important tasks for the group's success.

Despite their critical importance to group success, maintenance roles are often viewed as lower status in a competitive culture such as the United States. Those who play maintenance roles are viewed as the "helpers" not the doers. Helpers typically receive less status than doers in our society (e.g., surgeons are viewed as the doers and nurses are seen as the surgeon's helpers). Women have been socialized to play primarily the lower-status maintenance roles. As Wood (1997) notes, "Women remain disproportionately represented in service sectors and human relations divisions of companies, while men are moved into executive positions. Women are still asked to take care of social activities on the job, but men in equivalent positions are seldom expected to do this" (p. 63). Thus, group roles such as supporter-encourager, harmonizer-tension reliever, feeling expresser, and secretary-recorder (a task role that is lower status and helping in nature) are roles traditionally played more by women than men (Wood, 1997). When women are underrepresented in groups, it is particularly difficult to break through the stereotyping and receive the endorsement of the group to play nonstereotypic, higher-status roles or to enhance the perceived status of maintenance roles.

The endorsement process proceeds by trial and error. A group member tries out a role, perhaps initiator-contributor, for example. If the group does not reinforce the effort (e.g., ignores the contributions), then the member will try another role hoping to get endorsement. An individual who persists in an effort to play a specific role in the face of group resistance may be characterized as inflexible and uncooperative.

Once a role for a member has been endorsed by the group, **role specialization** occurs. An individual member settles into his or her primary role. If the group wants you to be an information giver, then that will be your principal function. This specialization doesn't preclude you from assuming other roles, however. Role specialization does not grant a monopoly to a single member. There may be more than one harmonizer in the group, although there is likely to be only one member with the primary responsibility. Too much effort to operate in what is perceived to be another member's primary role territory can invite negative feedback from the group.

Role Fixation

In the movie *The Great Santini*, Robert Duvall plays a Marine Corps pilot. He is a rather odd character because he interacts with members of his family as if they were military recruits at boot camp. He orders his children to stand at attention early every morning while he inspects them. The children are required to address their father as "Sir" in a snappy voice. Duvall expects absolute obedience from his kids as he would from his subordinates in the military. He is aggressive and savagely competitive with his son. Duvall's character is fixated in a single role. Despite the inappropriateness of this role acted out in a family context, despite the disruption it causes his wife and children, Duvall's character seems incapable of playing any role other than that of officer in the military.

Competent communication requires the ability and the willingness to adapt communication behavior to changing situations. Some individuals, however, get locked into the mindset that they must play a certain role and there are no good substitutes. Leader, information giver, feeling expresser, and tension reliever are among the most likely candidates for **role fixation**—the acting out of a specific role and that role alone no matter what the situation might require (Postman, 1976).

Professional comedians sometimes don't know when to be serious in social gatherings. They are always "on." Lawyers who cross-examine their spouses as they do hostile witnesses on the stand at a criminal trial may find their role fixation is a ticket to a court of a decidedly civil sort.

Role fixation in decision-making groups can occur when an individual moves from one group to another, or it can happen within a single group. If you were a gatekeeper in your last group, you may insist on performing the same role in your new group. There may be another member, however, who can play the role better. If you insist on competing for the role instead of adapting to the new group by assuming another role, you will be a source of conflict and disruption. If the other member is truly better in the role than you are, then the resources of the group will not be utilized to their fullest if you continue to fight for the role.

Sometimes the group insists on role fixation to its own detriment. The reluctance of men to accept women in a leadership role, for instance, can lead to role fixation against a woman's wishes. Expecting women to play feeling expresser in all or most groups erects overly restrictive boundaries within the system and uses group resources inefficiently. Women should have the opportunity to play roles that require more than nurturing (e.g., supporter-encourager) or low involvement (e.g., secretary-recorder).

So what suggestions do I offer regarding communication competence and group roles? <u>The competent communicator exhibits a sensitivity to the needs of the group in relation to group roles as follows</u>:

1. *Demonstrate flexibility*. Playing a variety of maintenance and task roles adapts to the needs of the group. Fighting for roles perceived to be more prestigious and desirable may leave vital group needs unattended.
2. *Avoid disruptive roles*. Show commitment to group effectiveness, not self-centeredness at the expense of group success.
3. *Be experimental*. Try different roles in different groups. Don't get locked into playing the same role in all groups. You'll become role fixated.

LEADERSHIP

Gibb (1969) observes: "Almost every influential thinker from Confucius to Bertrand Russell has attempted some form of analysis of leadership" (p. 205). Scholars, philosophers, social scientists, even novelists have exhibited an intense interest in the subject. When Geier (1967) interviewed 80 students, males and females, who participated in 16 discussion groups, all but 2 reported they would like to be the group leader. Bormann (1990) accumulated case studies outside of the academic setting indicating that the desire to provide leadership for a group is widespread.

Why do most people want to be leaders? There are numerous reasons, but the most obvious ones are *status* that comes from running the show, *respect* from group members for doing a good job of guiding the group, and *power* accorded leaders that allows them to influence others and produce change.

Wanting to be a leader in decision-making groups, however, is hardly sufficient. The competent communicator must acquire the knowledge and the skills necessary to be an effective leader. In this section I will define leadership, discuss how to gain and retain leadership, and explore several perspectives on what constitutes effective group leadership.

Focus Questions

1. How is the process for retaining the leader role different from the process for emerging as group leader?
2. Are women and ethnic minorities equally as capable as white males as leaders in small groups? Does your experience parallel the research results on this question?
3. After considering all the perspectives on leadership, what is the central overriding point that can be made about leadership in small groups?

Definition of Leadership

There are numerous definitions of leadership. As far back as 1949, there were at least 130 different definitions of leader and leadership (Bass, 1960). Marak

(1964), however, writes, "The most common definition of leadership . . . and the one closest to ordinary usage describes leadership in terms of interpersonal influence-compliance relationships" (p. 174). But what kind of influence-compliance relationship?

Shaw (1981) claims: "Leadership is an influence process which is directed toward goal achievement" (p. 317). Since no particular goal achievement is specified, however, an individual goal achieved at the expense of group goals might qualify as leadership. Wilson and Hanna (1990) argue that Shaw's definition is satisfactory if it is slightly amended to read: "**Leadership** is an influence process which is directed toward *group* goal achievement."

Despite the differences among the various definitions of leadership, there does seem to be agreement that leadership is a social influence process (Husband, 1992). This consensus serves as a basis for indicating what I consider leadership to be and not to be.

First, leadership requires followership. The two roles either exist together or they exist not at all. A leader must have someone to lead and followers must have someone to follow. Behavior labeled as leadership in the absence of followership "is no more leadership than the behavior of small boys marching in front of a parade, who continue to strut along Main Street after the procession has turned down a side street toward the fairgrounds" (Burns, 1978, p. 427).

Second, leadership implies change. As Husband (1992) explains: "People expect leaders to bring change about, to get things done, to make things happen, to inspire, to motivate. To influence someone is to change them—their behavior, their attitude, their beliefs or their values" (p. 494). Standing still is losing ground in a world of constant flux. The world will pass you by.

Leadership, as noted historian James MacGregor Burns (1978) argues, can be transformational. The transaction between a leader and followers can elevate, mobilize, inspire, and uplift. Groups that are transformed—changed—seek higher goals, loftier purposes, and experience increased levels of motivation.

Third, leadership is a transactional power relationship. Viewing leadership as a transaction signifies a two-way influence process. The social influence occurs with the consent of the governed. Leaders influence followers, but followers also influence leaders by making demands on them, requiring them to meet members' expectations, and evaluating their performance in light of these expectations.

Fourth, leadership is a communication process. Leadership is exercised through communication within the group (Barge & Hirokawa, 1989). Managers, for instance, spend a majority of their work time communicating with others (Luthans et al., 1988). The communication competence of the leader is therefore central to any discussion of leadership.

Fifth, leadership should not be determined exclusively on the basis of outcomes. Leadership is a communication process, not an outcome. I am not arguing that outcomes are irrelevant to leadership. If the group never attains its goals, then members might contemplate a change in leadership. The group goal, however, may not always be attainable, or the goal may be unrealizable in the short term. Within organizations, leaders of work groups may be thwarted from achieving change by inflexible institutional policies or by veto power from upper management.

Ethics and Leadership

Approximately $150 million is spent annually by U.S. businesses on controversial group-training programs for employees (Singer, 1995). These group-training programs include an amazing conglomeration of techniques to incite worker motivation, enhance cooperation, and improve productivity. According to the Equal Employment Opportunity Commission (EEOC), a federal oversight agency, training programs include mysticism, faith healing, aura readings, meditation, guided visualization, self-hypnosis, therapeutic touch, biofeedback, yoga, and fire walking (I've heard of lighting a fire under your employees but this takes the metaphor a bit literally). In one case, a woman who perceived herself to be very overweight was told to wear a bikini, go out on the street, and act like a Pied Piper singing and trying to get a band of men to follow her. In another instance, people cross-dressed and acted out caricatured versions of the opposite sex. Then there is the "rebirthing" exercise called Cocktail Party where group trainees writhe on the ground while exorcising their personal demons and shout at one another for up to 2 hours while trainers hand out vomit bags and exhort the trainees to purge their emotions (Singer, 1995). The list of controversial training programs is extensive: Actualizations, Direct Centering, the Forum, Lifespring, MSIA/Insight Training Seminars, PSI World, Silva Mind Control, Sterling Management Systems, and Transformational Technologies are just a few cited by Singer (1995).

Ethical leadership is an important issue. The consequences of unethical leadership can be serious. Singer (1995) notes, "Besides making complaints to the EEOC, many employees have filed civil suits objecting to training program content or related pressures at the workplace. Some lost their jobs by objecting. Other employees have suffered psychological decompensation as a consequence of what occurred in the training programs" (p. 191).

In chapter 1, ethical standards for competent communication were identified: honesty, respect, fairness, and choice. These standards should be applied to group training programs:

1. *Honesty.* Ethical leaders avoid intentionally deceptive or harmful messages. Many of the training programs I referred to are deceptively packaged as seminars on job-related skills when they are actually confrontational, psychologically intense therapy groups (Goleman, 1998; Singer, 1995).

2. *Respect.* Ethical leaders treat all members with equal respect unless they earn disrespect (e.g., by exhibiting racist, homophobic, or sexist attitudes toward other group members). Treat others as you would want others to treat you. Trainers that abuse individuals in training programs show disrespect that individuals have not earned.

3. *Fair-mindedness.* Ethical leaders apply and enforce policies and decisions without favoritism or cronyism. Racism, sexism, and homophobia have no place in decisions made by leaders.

4. *Choice.* Leadership is a transactional power relationship. Do more powerful managers, supervisors, and leaders of small groups have a right to compel less powerful employees and group members to participate in a program they find offensive, immoral, or potentially

harmful? At best, such practices are questionably ethical. In addition, coercive training programs often produce lackluster participation from group members, resentment, and sometimes exit from the group (Goleman, 1998).

Leaders frequently face ethical dilemmas where no clear answers emerge. If leaders are guided by the ethical criteria of respect, honesty, fair-mindedness, and choice, however, they are making a sincere effort to do what is right, and that is the essence of ethical leadership.

Questions for Thought

1. Should a group member have an absolute right to refuse to participate in a training program if he or she finds it offensive or objectionable? Should training programs ever be a requirement of employment?
2. Can you think of exceptions to each of the ethical criteria as applied to training programs?
3. What should be done with group members who refuse to take training because they perceive it to be offensive or pointless, even though these members are deficient in important skills?

Conceptualizing what constitutes leadership is a far cry from knowing how to exercise leadership in a group. How leaders emerge and the ways to retain leadership in groups will be discussed next.

Gaining and Retaining Leadership

Some zero-history groups never do settle on who will lead and who will follow. In Geier's (1967) study of 16 such groups working for as long as 12 weeks, almost a third of the groups never had a leader emerge. These leaderless groups were uniformly unsuccessful at their tasks and were socially unsuccessful as well. Strife predominated. Time was wasted and members became frustrated. Cohesiveness suffered and members began skipping meetings rather than suffer more disharmony. In contrast, groups that had leaders emerge and that developed stable roles for their members were successful (De Souza & Kline, 1995). The emergence of leaders, therefore, is a significant event in the life of a group.

How Not to Become a Leader   It is often easier to determine what you shouldn't do if you wish to become leader than what you should. We know that corruption or sex scandals, for instance, can send the media into a feeding frenzy and can torpedo a promising political career, but the absence of such scandals won't capture any headlines. Having a spotless character may just brand you as dull in some people's minds. Lack of negatives do not necessarily equal positives.

Before I discuss how you should communicate in groups in order to improve your chances of emerging as the leader, I will indicate first what you should avoid. The competent communicator who wishes to emerge as group leader should heed the following dictums (Bormann, 1990; Fisher & Ellis, 1990; Geier, 1967):

1. *Thou shalt not show up late for or miss important meetings.* Groups choose individuals who are committed, not members who exhibit an insensitivity to the

group. As an anonymous wit once observed, "Absence makes the heart grow fonder—of someone else."

2. *Thou shalt not be uninformed about a problem commanding the group's attention.* Knowledgeable members have a greater chance of emerging as leaders. The clueless need not apply.

3. *Thou shalt not manifest apathy and lack of interest by sluggish participation in group discussions.* Group members are not impressed by "vigor mortis." Indifference provokes defensiveness. Participation is a sign of commitment to the group, and commitment to the group and its goals is part of the leadership process (De Souza & Kline, 1995).

4. *Thou shalt not attempt to dominate conversation during discussion.* Learning when to shut up is a useful skill.

5. *Thou shalt not listen poorly* (Bechler & Johnson, 1995). Leadership is not a monologue; it's a dialogue. As someone once said, a monologue is "the egotist's version of a scintillating conversation." Dialogue means leaders and followers listen carefully to each other.

6. *Thou shalt not be rigid and inflexible when expressing viewpoints.* A hardened position is plaque on the cortex. It decays the mind and contracts the brain.

7. *Thou shalt not bully group members.* Browbeating members to do your bidding will gain few admirers. There may be no way to avoid issuing orders in some situations (e.g., in the military), but watch out for psychological reactance. Bullies get banished to the playground.

8. *Thou shalt not use offensive and abusive language.* Blue language produces red faces. This will surely alienate many, if not most, group members.

Geier (1967) found that some of these counterproductive communication patterns were more likely than others to prevent someone from becoming a group leader. The three he found most relevant, in order of importance, were being uninformed, not participating, and being rigid and inflexible.

General Pattern of Leader Emergence   The extensive research conducted at the University of Minnesota under the direction of Ernest Bormann (1990) discovered a pattern of leader emergence in small zero-history groups. In general, a group selects a leader by a process of elimination where potential candidates are systematically removed from consideration until only one person remains to be leader. We may be quite clear on what we don't want in a leader but not as sure about what we do want. This narrowing of the candidate field makes good sense. As we eliminate candidates, complexity is reduced. The breadth of possibilities is narrowed while the depth of understanding of each candidate's qualifications for the role is increased.

There are two phases to the process-of-elimination explanation of leader emergence. During the first phase, roughly half of the members are eliminated from consideration. The criteria for elimination are crude and impressionistic. Negative communication patterns—the "thou shalt nots"—weigh heavily. Quiet members are among the first eliminated. Nonparticipation will leave the impression of indifference and noncommitment. There was not a single instance in the Minnesota studies of a quiet member who became a leader.

Conversely, talkativeness also influences the leadership emergence process. Those who talk the most are perceived initially as potential leader material (Pavitt & Curtis, 1994). Group members who blather, or who make pronouncements on subjects without making a great deal of sense, however, are quickly eliminated by the group from consideration as leader. Such individuals are reminiscent of William Gibbs McAddo's characterization of President Warren G. Harding as "an army of pompous phrases moving over the landscape in search of an idea." Windbags gain no favor.

The members who express strong, unqualified assertions are also eliminated. These individuals are perceived to be too extreme and too inflexible in their points of view to make effective leaders. The attitude of certitude will provoke defensiveness from group members.

The uninformed, unintelligent, or unskilled are next in line for elimination. Groups look for task-competent individuals who are committed to the group goals to emerge as leaders (De Souza & Klein, 1995). Inept members distract the group from goal attainment.

In the second phase, about half the group still actively contend for the leader role. This part of the process can become quite competitive. Frustrations and irritations can mount. Of these remaining contenders, those who are bossy or dictatorial and those whose communication style is irritating or disturbing to group members are eliminated.

So who emerges as leader if more than one member survives the elimination rounds? There are several possibilities. First, if the group feels threatened by some external or internal crisis (e.g., inability to choose a topic for a symposium presentation or members with expertise fall sick or leave the group), the group often turns to the member who provides a solution to the crisis and he or she becomes the leader. Second, those members perceived to be effective listeners can make a strong bid to be chosen leader (Johnson & Bechler, 1998). Third, members who remain active contenders for the leader role often acquire lieutenants. A lieutenant is an advocate for one of the contenders. He or she boosts the chances of the contender becoming the group leader. If only one of the members gains the support of a lieutenant, then this person will likely become the leader. If two members each gain a lieutenant, then the process of leader emergence can be drawn out, or can even end in stalemate.

The general tendency is for groups to accept as leader the person who provides the optimum blend of task efficiency and sensitivity to social considerations. This tendency, of course, does not translate into a tidy formula or precise recipe. Some groups prefer a leader who concentrates more on task accomplishment and less on the social dimension of the group. Other groups prefer the opposite.

Ultimately, if you want to become the leader of a group you should take the following steps (Bormann, 1990):

1. Manifest conformity to the group's norms, values, and goals.
2. Display proper motivation to lead.
3. Avoid the "thou shalt nots" previously identified.

Deviants, dissenters, and disrupters will be eliminated early as potential leaders. Groups prefer leaders who will assist them in the attainment of their goals, who will defend the group vigorously against threats, and who will remain loyal to the group. Since most group members think of a leader as the single individual who does most of the work, anyone hoping to be leader must also demonstrate a willingness to work hard for the group (Hollander, 1978).

FOCUS *on gender/culture*

Gender and Ethnic Leadership Bias

The problem of gender and ethnic bias complicates the pattern of leader emergence just described. The research on gender bias is far more voluminous than it is on ethnic discrimination.

Studies of gender bias in the workplace, where emerging leaders live their daily lives and engage in small group communication, provide mixed results. The issue of a **glass ceiling**, an invisible barrier of subtle discrimination that excludes women from top jobs in corporate and professional America, is apparent. According to a report on NBC Nightly News, only three women were CEOs of Fortune 500 companies and only seven women were CEOs of Fortune 1000 companies when the report was aired on August 10, 1999. According to the same report only 5% of senior management positions (vice-president and higher) in the United States are filled by women. A mere 2.7% of the top income earners are women.

That's the bad news. The encouraging news is that women are making huge strides in several areas. Economic consultant Nuala Beck argues that women are well positioned to advance in the new knowledge-based economy driven by the microchip. She claims that the Fortune 500 companies, and women's place in their hierarchy, are largely irrelevant—a relic of the manufacturing economy that is dwarfed by the knowledge-based industries. The ratio of female-to-male knowledge workers (engineers, technicians, scientists, professionals, and senior managers) is almost one to one (Collingwood, 1997). The new economy is based primarily on the knowledge and skills of the workers instead of seniority, a decided advantage for women. Consider the evidence.

Twenty-five years ago fewer than 4% of MBA degrees went to women. Now, more than one-third of all MBAs are earned by women (Jacobs, 1996). At the turn of this century, women occupied only 4% of management positions in the United States. Almost half (44%) of all managers in the United States today are women (Samuelson, 1999). Nearly half of all law students in the country are women (Epstein, 1996). In 1960, fewer than 3% of all law degrees conferred in the United States were earned by women. Now it is close to half (Jacobs, 1996). In 1971, only 3% of all lawyers in the United States were women. Now a quarter of all U.S. lawyers are women ("Equality still," 1996), and if law school enrollment of women continues at the present rate, 40% of the U.S. legal profession will be composed of women by the year 2010 ("Sexism prevails," 1996). Women earn almost half of all doctoral degrees ("Study shows," 1997). In the 1960s, only a handful of women were tenured college professors. Currently, almost a quarter of the nation's tenured faculty are women (Koury, 1996). In the medical profession, fewer than 6% of all M.D. degrees were earned by women in 1960. Now it is almost 40% (Jacobs, 1996). According to the Center for the American Woman and Politics at Rutgers University, three decades ago only 4% of state legislators were women. At the end of the

Jane Hull, Betsey Bayless, Janet Napolitano, Carol Springer, and Lisa Graham were elected to the five top statewide offices in Arizona—a political first for women.

millenium, 22% of legislators and 28% of state executive officials were women. In the state of Washington, 41% of legislators were women (as cited in Jacobs, 1999a).

Even the wage–salary disparity between men and women has narrowed substantially. On average, women earn 74 cents for every dollar men earn ("Heat's on," 1999). As an hourly wage (men work more hours on average than women), however, it jumps to 82 cents (Jacobs, 1996). Young women in their late twenties and early thirties earn 83 cents, and those under 25 earn 94 cents for every dollar men in the same age bracket earn (Jacobs, 1999b). Post and Lynch (Jacobs, 1996) conclude: "The gender pay gap virtually disappears when age, educational attainment, and continuous time spent in the workforce are factored in as wage determinants" (p. 7B).

Despite these historic gains in fields that prepare women for leadership roles, women still have difficulty becoming leaders despite convincing evidence that women and men are equally capable (Eagly et al., 1995; Haslett et al., 1992; Morrison & Von Glinow, 1990). In fact, a study conducted by the Hagberg Consulting Group and reported on NBC Nightly News on August 10, 1999 revealed that women scored better than men on 41 of 47 management skills. Richard Hagberg, head of the consulting firm, concludes that women have "a much more team oriented

style" of leadership appropriate for today's workplace. Nevertheless, in a variety of group settings, men are typically favored over women when leaders are selected and evaluated, even when no differences in actual leadership behavior occur (Forsyth et al., 1997).

This is a good news–bad news record, but, overall, the outlook for the future is optimistic. Jane Freedman, CEO of Harper/Collins Publishing Company, during an interview on NBC Nightly News on August 10, 1999, concludes, "American business is about to say the best *person* will have the job."

Although the research on gender bias is substantial, the issue of ethnic bias and leader emergence has been largely ignored (Morrison & Von Glinow, 1990). Nevertheless, there are some indicators. The U.S. Labor Department's Glass Ceiling Commission, in its final report, noted that African, Asian, and Hispanic Americans occupy only a scant 1% of the executive management jobs at Fortune 500 companies ("Glass ceiling intact," 1994). The report also noted that the glass ceiling is apparent in federal jobs as well. Minorities hold 28% of all federal jobs but fill only 8% of the top posts. Female ethnic minorities tend to have the toughest time emerging as leaders because they face a double bias (Morrison & Von Glinow, 1990). Even among professionals, where a pay gap should be far less because of equivalent education and training required for job entry, a huge discrepancy is apparent. African American and Asian American women earn 53% of the average white male salary, and Hispanic American women earn a mere 47% (Kleiman, 1998). Despite these figures, there is some room for optimism. According to the Joint Center for Political and Economic Studies, the number of African American elected officials has increased almost sixfold since 1970 to roughly 9,000 (Cose, 1999). One-fifth of black American adults are in management or professional jobs compared to 31% for whites ("Moving forward," 1999).

How do we combat this gender–ethnicity bias in emergent leadership in groups? First, the Twenty Percent Rule again comes into play. When women and minorities find themselves flying solo in groups, the chance that they'll land in a leadership position is remote. <u>As the number of women and minorities increase in a group, however, the likelihood that a woman or a minority will emerge as leader also increases</u> because bias decreases (Shimanoff & Jenkins, 1996). When women and ethnic minorities are no longer perceived as tokens, but instead form a substantial portion of group membership and increasingly occupy top leadership positions, then competence will be judged less on gender and ethnic bias and more on actual performance.

Second, <u>if group members are allowed to mingle, interact, and work on a project before determining a leader</u>, the decision is more likely to be made on the basis of individual performance rather than gender (or ethnicity if we extrapolate the research findings). Small groups that met for six to fifteen weeks on a project were as likely to name a woman as their leader as they were a man (Goktepe & Schneier, 1989). Allowing women and minorities to display their strengths increases their chances of emerging as group leaders.

Third, <u>engaging in task-relevant communication behavior is a key to emerging as leader of a small task-oriented group</u> (Hawkins, 1995). Task-relevant communication includes initiation and discussion of analysis of the group problem, establishment of decision criteria, generation of possible solutions to problems, evaluation of possible solutions, and establishment of group operating procedures. Task-oriented female group members are as likely to emerge as leaders of small task groups as are task-oriented male group members (Hawkins, 1995).

Fourth, <u>if women and minorities are among the first to speak in the group and they speak fairly frequently</u>, their chances of emerging as leaders increase (Shimanoff & Jenkins, 1996). Speaking early and often without dominating discussion is perceived as assertive. Speaking early is more important for women and minorities than it is for men.

Finally, women and minorities can advance their chances of becoming leaders in small groups by <u>honing their communication skills and abilities</u>. Developing competence in communication by using skills appropriately and effectively can go a long way toward combating gender and ethnic leadership bias (Hackman & Johnson, 1996).

Questions for Thought

1. Should group members encourage women and minorities to speak early and often by inviting their participation?
2. Do you feel that the glass ceiling will shatter soon as the number of women and minorities in the middle ranks of leadership swell? What might prevent this from happening?
3. What responsibilities do white males have regarding the issue of leadership bias?

---

second look

Pattern of Leader Emergence

GENERAL PATTERN

(Process of Elimination)

Phase One

- Quiet members eliminated
- Members who express strong, unqualified assertions eliminated
- Uninformed, unintelligent, and/or unskilled eliminated

Phase Two, part one

- Bossy, dictatorial members eliminated
- Members with irritating or disturbing communication style eliminated

continued

Phase Two, part two
- Member who provides solution in time of crisis considered
- Member who exhibits effective listening skills considered
- Member who acquires a lieutenant considered
- If more than one member acquires lieutenant—possible stalemate

HOW TO BECOME LEADER
- Manifest conformity to group norms, values, and goals
- Display proper motivation to lead
- Avoid the "thou shalt nots"

MODIFYING FACTORS OF LEADER EMERGENCE
- Gender bias
- Ethnic bias

Retaining the Leader Role   The process for retaining the leader role is not the same as the process for emerging as the group leader. An individual could conform to group norms, display a strong motivation to lead the group, and avoid the thou shalt nots and still not retain the role of leader, as many political leaders have learned. A leader is sometimes deposed if his or her performance is felt by members to be unsatisfactory. There are three primary qualifications for retaining leadership (Wood et al., 1986):

1. You must demonstrate your competence as leader.
2. You must accept accountability for your actions.
3. You must satisfy group members' expectations.

Retaining the role of leader can be a tricky business. Groups can be fickle. What seems to satisfy members one day may enrage them the next. Take, for instance, the case of Ann Reynolds. From 1982 to 1990 she was the chancellor of the California State University system. In December 1989, the *San Jose Mercury News* (Philp 1990) reported several disturbing facts regarding the chancellor's behind-the-scenes maneuvering for executive perks and salary increases. Under her leadership, $99,999 (one dollar under the legislative limit) was quietly spent on six cars for vice chancellors, $240,000 was spent on Reynolds' state-owned Bel-Air home, and members of the board of trustees for the CSU system were given a 43% raise. Members of the public and the state legislature were incensed, especially since all this had been done in secret.

Trustees for the CSU system expressed embarrassment publicly and turned on the chancellor for allegedly misleading them on the propriety of using the secret delegation method for increasing executive salaries. Her competence to retain the leadership position was in question. Members of the board of trustees felt Reynolds misled them. She failed to meet their expectations— specifically, to keep the board out of public controversy on sensitive issues. Ultimately, she was held accountable by the trustees and the public. Reynolds resigned just before a move was made to oust her as chancellor.

Retaining leadership in a group requires competent communication. The leader must adapt to ever-changing situations. Group expectations of the leader may shift as circumstances alter. Members' confidence in and loyalty to their leader may be shaky. A leader must demonstrate competence and satisfy group expectations on a continuing basis or member loyalty may disappear quickly. Last year's success may not compensate adequately for this year's failure as many athletic coaches have learned.

Perspectives on Effective Leadership

Scholarly perspectives on leadership have changed greatly over the three-quarters of a century since the first serious research was conducted on this central group role. In this section, I will examine the primary perspectives that have generated considerable interest.

Traits Perspective   This is the "leaders are born not made" perspective. The earliest studies on leadership set out to discover a universal set of traits applicable to all those who become leaders. A huge number of traits were studied. We know, for instance, that height, weight, and physical attractiveness have a bearing on social influence. Tall individuals usually have greater influence with others than do shorter individuals. In the last 25 U.S. presidential elections, 22 have been won by the taller candidate. Very heavy or skinny people have less influence than more "ideal weight" types (Hickson et al., 1989). Good-looking individuals can influence a group.

So why don't all tall, fit, physically attractive individuals become leaders instead of short, dumpy, plain-looking individuals? How did Michael Dukakis (short and registering zero on the charisma meter) become the Democratic candidate for president in 1988? Explain how Rush Limbaugh, rotund, balding radio talk show host, achieved such popularity and influence? How did diminutive Barbara Boxer and Barbara Mikulski become United States senators? And what are we to make of Microsoft's CEO, Bill Gates, who is a walking advertisement for *Revenge of the Nerds*? NBC News anchor Tom Brokaw remarked after conducting a roving interview with Gates at a Comdex computer show in Las Vegas, "It's like walking the Vatican with the Pope" (Levy, 1995, p. 54). Then, of course, there is the "billionaire Boy Scout" and former presidential candidate H. Ross Perot, frequently described by political pundits as "jug-eared" and "squeaky-voiced." Fellow Texan Molly Ivins (1992), a newspaper columnist, described Perot as "a seriously short guy who sounds like a Chihuahua" (p. 38). Contrasting sharply with Perot is Jesse Ventura, a former professional wrestler, who was elected governor of Minnesota in 1998. Garrison Keillor, host of the public radio show "A Prairie Home Companion," describes Ventura as a "great big honking bullet-headed, shovel-faced mutha who talks in a steroid growl and doesn't stop" (Ventura, 1999, p. A2). I'm sure you can cite many examples of individuals in groups you belong to where no specific set of traits explains why this person is the leader.

Leader emergence and leadership effectiveness, however, are not identical. The characteristics necessary even to be considered for the leader role

The traits perspective explains little about leadership. Which traits do Bill Gates, Colin Powell, Barbara Boxer, Bill Clinton, and Jesse Ventura share that would explain their rise to leadership positions: Good looks? Height? Physical size? Charisma? Intelligence? Personality? Ethnicity? Gender?

in a small group (e.g., talkative, confident, motivated, knowledgeable, punctual, adaptable, good listener) don't assure your emergence as leader. You may possess other traits that the group finds annoying or obnoxious. More importantly, such traits don't assure success if you become a leader.

What traits make a leader effective? Fiedler and House (1988) claim that "effective leaders tend to have a high need to influence others, to achieve, and they tend to be bright, competent, and socially adept, rather than stupid, incompetent, and social disasters" (p. 87). Perhaps intelligence, social and verbal skills, integrity, sense of humor, extroversion, confidence, or some other list of characteristics accounts for effective leadership in groups. These and other traits seem appropriate, even essential for a leader to possess. These traits, however, may be *necessary yet not sufficient* to be an effective group leader. Certain basic traits move you into the leadership arena. They are the irreducible minimum qualifications to become a leader, but to retain the role of leader and ultimately to perform effectively in this role other factors play a more important part.

The principal problem with the trait approach to effective leadership is the assumption that leadership resides in the person, not in transactions conducted within the group context (Northouse, 1997). As Hollander (1985) observes, *"Leadership is a process and not a person"* (p. 487). Why do individuals become leaders in some groups, but not in others if an individual possesses the requisite leadership traits? If traits explain leadership, how could mass murderer Charles Manson inspire such fanatical obedience from his little "family" of compliant followers yet produce such revulsion from most of society? Some people saw cult leaders Marshall Applewhite, Jim Jones, and David Koresh as messiahs; others saw only lunatics. If they had the requisite leadership traits for one group, why not all groups? Obviously, there is more to effective leadership than the trait approach can explain.

Styles Perspective   Unsatisfied with the trait approach to leadership, Kurt Lewin and his associates developed a new approach based on three leadership styles: autocratic, democratic, and laissez-faire (Lewin et al., 1939). Autocratic style exerts control over group members. The autocratic leader is highly directive. This leadership style does not encourage member participation. Douglas McGregor (1960) describes autocratic leadership as a "my way or the highway" approach: do what I say or hit the road. Autocratic leaders are not concerned about making friends or getting invited to parties. The autocratic style puts most of the emphasis on the task with little concern for the social dimension of the group (high task, low social).

The democratic style is nondirective and participative. It encourages participation and responsibility from group members. Democratic leaders work to improve the skills and abilities of group members (Gastil, 1994). Followers have a say in what the group decides. The democratic style puts a balanced emphasis on both the task and social dimensions of the group (high task, high social).

The laissez-faire style is not really leadership at all and was eventually dropped from serious consideration in most of the research. It is a do-nothing

How could these seriously weird individuals (Charles Manson, Jim Jones, David Koresh, and Marshall Applewhite) become leaders? The traits perspective doesn't explain much about the emergence or influence of these "misleaders."

approach to the group. The laissez-faire style provides no direction and no regard is accorded the social transactions in the group (low task, low social).

The extensive research comparing autocratic-directive and democratic-participative leadership styles, presents mixed results (Northouse, 1997). Both directive and participative styles can be productive, and, although the participative style fosters more member satisfaction than does the directive style (Van Oostrum & Rabbie, 1995), the difference is neither large nor uniform (Gastil, 1994). Participative leadership seems to work best when it springs naturally from the group itself. Not all small groups, however, want nor expect their leaders to adopt the participative leadership style. Some cultures prefer the "paternal authoritative" (benevolently directive) style to the participative style (Brislin, 1993). In such cultures, the participative style may not work as well as the directive style.

Gender also plays a role in the leadership style-effectiveness equation. Male and female leaders are evaluated by group members as equally competent when the democratic-participative style is used (Eagly et al., 1992). When the autocratic-directive style is used, however, group members evaluate women as substantially less competent leaders than men. Apparently, group expectations influence judgments of leader competence. Female leaders are expected to adopt the participative leadership style, which complements the desire for connection, but groups are unaccustomed to seeing women use the directive style, which places more emphasis on independence and power than on connection (Tannen, 1990). Men clearly have more flexibility in choice of leadership style. With time, this stereotype that locks women into a single style of leadership should virtually vanish as women challenge the expectation.

One weakness of the participative-directive leadership style duality is that these styles are viewed as extreme opposites. Individuals operate either as participative or directive leaders, but not both. Realistically, though, a combination of participative and directive leadership styles is required in small groups. Intuitively, we know this is the case. When you're sitting white-knuckled in the jumbo jet that is experiencing engine trouble, do you want the captain to be democratic and take a vote on what should be done? Does it not make more sense to have someone in charge who takes action and tells the crew what to do immediately without pausing for conversation and debate? This is an emergency situation.

Or, consider the situation in which a person is a "temp worker" and is new on the job. Should this person be consulted on how the job should be accomplished when he or she doesn't even have a good idea what the job entails? Should teachers consult their students before determining course content when the students know little or nothing about the subject? Should military commanders seek the advice of their troops before launching an offensive? "All those in favor of attacking the heavily armed enemy hidden among the rocks and trees signal by saying aye; those opposed, nay. Okay, the nays have it. We'll stay put and live another day." Group members can't always meaningfully participate in decision making.

No one style of leadership will be suitable for all situations. This realization has led researchers to explore yet another approach to leadership—the situational or contingency perspective.

Situational (Contingency) Perspective This is the "it depends" approach to leadership. Since no one style of leadership is appropriate for all situations, effective leadership is contingent upon matching styles with situations.

There are two principal situational models of leadership effectiveness. The first is Fred Fiedler's (1967) contingency model. Fiedler's model, however, does not offer guidance on how to become a more effective leader once you're in a group. In this sense it has rather limited application for our purposes, so I will spare you an explanation of his complicated model.

A more flexible and useful situational model of leadership effectiveness has been offered by Hersey and Blanchard (1988). Although their model is targeted at organizations, it applies well to groups large and small, especially ones with long life cycles. Their model is also well-suited to a systems perspective. Acknowledgment of the interconnectedness of leader and followers plus the recognition of the importance of leader adaptability to change are emphasized.

Hersey and Blanchard have combined <u>three variables in their situational model</u>:

1. The amount of guidance and direction *(task emphasis)* a leader provides.
2. The amount of relationship support *(socio-emotional emphasis)* a leader provides.
3. The *readiness level* in performing a specific task, function, or objective that followers demonstrate.

The interplay among these three variables will indicate the level of leadership effectiveness.<u>Effective leadership is dependent upon the transactions that take place between the leader and followers</u>. For Hersey and Blanchard this is the vital, paramount contingency upon which leadership effectiveness rests.

There are four leadership styles in the Hersey and Blanchard model. The **Telling style** (high task, low relationship emphasis) is directive. A leader using this style provides specific instructions regarding a task and closely supervises the performance of followers but places minimal focus on developing social relationships with followers. The **Selling style** (high task, high relationship) is also directive. A leader using this style explains and clarifies decisions but also tries to convince followers to accept directives. The **Participating style** (low task, high relationship) is nondirective. A leader using this style encourages shared decision making with special emphasis on developing relationships in the group. The **Delegating style** (low task, low relationship) is nondirective. A leader using this style allows the group to be self-directed. Responsibility for decision making and implementation of decisions rests with the group. <u>The key to leadership effectiveness is matching the appropriate style to the group environment</u>.

Fisher (1986) criticizes the situational approach to leadership by arguing that it is "intuitively reasonable" but "the number of variables which are potentially contingent on leadership and the possible combinations of those variables of situation, leader, and followers are virtually impossible to comprehend" (p. 203). Hersey and Blanchard agree with the thrust of Fisher's criticism. No leader could ever consider all possible situational variables before making a decision. Hersey and Blanchard contend, however, that there is no need to consider all or even most variables. The relationship between the leader and followers is the prime consideration because if group members decide not to follow the leader, then all other situational variables (nature of the task, time involved, expectations, etc.) are irrelevant.

The primary situational variable that the leader must consider when adapting leadership styles to the specific group is the readiness level of followers. Originally called "maturity," Hersey and Blanchard (1988) define **readiness** as "how ready a person is to perform a particular task" (p. 175). They identify two principal components of readiness: ability and willingness. "Ability is the knowledge, experience, and skill that an individual or group brings to a particular task or activity" (p. 175). They define willingness as "the extent to which an individual or group has the confidence, commitment, and motivation to accomplish a specific task" (p. 175). This all sounds remarkably like communication competence.

Decisions are leader directed at lower levels of readiness while decisions are follower directed at higher levels of readiness. As readiness levels increase, effective leadership requires reduced guidance and direction from the leader and less socio-emotional support for followers. These relationships are depicted in Figure 5.1.

Followers, for whatever reasons (e.g., divorce, midlife crisis, lack of challenges), may regress in their readiness levels, losing motivation or slipping

Figure 5-1

The Telling (S1), Selling (S2), Participating (S3), and Delegating (S4) leadership styles related to follower readiness. Situational Leadership® is a registered trademark of the Center for Leadership Studies, Inc. Reprinted with permission. All rights reserved.

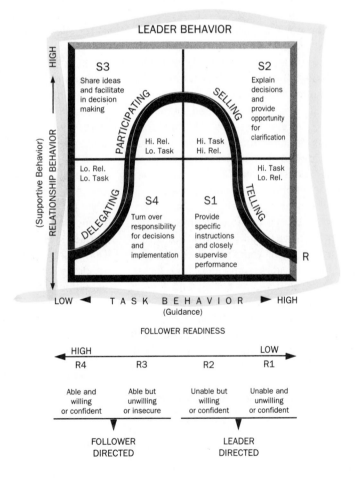

in their skill performance. In such cases, the leader moves backward through the styles curve (i.e., from delegating to participating or even telling), adapting to the change in circumstances.

CLOSER LOOK

Effective versus Ineffective Leadership

A friend of mine once worked in county government. She was hired to fill an administrative position in the personnel office. Her immediate supervisor employed the laissez-faire leadership style, which is to say no leadership at all was ever exercised. Upon my friend's arrival at her new job, she was delegated authority and responsibility for which she had little preparation. Office procedures were not explained. She was expected to perform by trial and error without direction or training. When she made mistakes, she was held accountable, while her supervisor literally sorted through his list of music tapes and CDs on a computer file in his office, disappeared on extended lunches, and attended numerous "meetings" (i.e., coffee breaks). My friend received no useful training from her supervisor during the first six months of her employment.

Here was a case of ineffective leadership. The supervisor employed an inappropriate style right from the beginning. When you start a job, you don't even know where the coffeemaker is located, much less the details of how you're expected to perform in your new position. An effective leader provides some direction for an employee at the start (some telling and lots of selling). The employee's input regarding decisions is solicited (participating) as he or she masters the relevant tasks, and eventually you delegate authority and responsibility to the employee because he or she can be trusted to perform well.

A second example illustrates effective leadership. A friend of mine, a gifted individual working for a "temp agency," was assigned to work in the international finance division of a large computer software company. She had no background in international finance but is a quick learner. Her supervisor, a bright young woman, was a skillful leader. During the first week, the supervisor trained my friend, indicating what she needed to know in order to perform her job. Soon her supervisor solicited her opinions. Gradually, her supervisor delegated new responsibilities and tasks to her as her readiness level increased. What began as a temporary, short-term, expedient employment opportunity grew into an offer of permanent employment in a responsible position. Effective leadership is good for the leader and good for the followers.

Effective leadership requires adaptation of styles to individuals within the group. Some members will require a telling or selling style for a longer period of time than will others. Some members may require a great deal of encouragement and support while others will require little. In the above cases, the ineffective leader had a "one style fits all" approach—the laissez-faire or sit-on-your-derriere style. He "managed" all of the employees in his department exactly the same way. Conversely, the effective leader adapted to the readiness levels of each individual employee within her department. She exhibited the flexibility of the competent communicator because she tailored her leadership style to the needs of each follower.

Questions for Thought

1. Have you had a similar problem with a supervisor who exhibited poor leadership?
2. What should you do if faced with an ineffective leader in a group?

Is situational leadership effective? A study at Xerox Corporation (Gumpert & Hambleton, 1979) revealed that highly effective managers knew more about and used situational leadership more frequently than less-effective managers. When situational leadership was applied according to the Hersey and Blanchard model, subordinate job performance was higher than when it was not. Hersey and Blanchard (1988) cite additional studies in educational settings (e.g., classrooms, college boards of trustees) where situational leadership has proven to be highly effective.

Functional Perspective   Unlike the previous approaches to leadership that assume a leader has already been designated or emerged in the group, the functional perspective views leadership in terms of certain functions that must be performed for the group to be successful. Typically, these functions fall into two categories: task requirements and social or maintenance needs.

The functional perspective can be divided into two schools of thought. The first has been dubbed by William Schutz as the **leader as completer** viewpoint. Leaders are thought to perform those essential functions within a group that other members have failed to perform. Typically, the list of possible functions falls into the standard task requirements and social or maintenance needs categories. The list of task and maintenance roles previously identified indicates functions essential to a group (e.g., giving information, coordinating, directing, gatekeeping, and relieving tension). Leadership, then, is seen as an adaptive role. Leaders step in and assume whatever role in the group is required at a particular time that has not been filled by any other member (e.g., researching background on group task, making list of group members' phone numbers).

A second school of thought, the **vital functions** viewpoint, sees leaders performing a list of vital group functions different in kind and/or degree from other members. Fisher and Ellis (1990) offer a list of such functions:

Group Procedures

1. *Plan an agenda*. Group meetings proceed more smoothly when the leader has constructed a list of topics for discussion and decision making. (See Appendix C.)
2. *Handle routine "housekeeping" details*. These include taking roll, calling the meeting to order, making important announcements, modifying the agenda before discussion proceeds, and so forth.
3. *Prepare for the next meeting*. Announce the time, place, and date of the next meeting. Plan ahead by making certain that the meeting room is appropriate in size and physical conditions.

Task Requirements

1. *Initiate a structure*. The leader identifies issues to be discussed, proposes procedures for such discussion, guides the discussion, focuses members on the agenda, and may suggest possible solutions to problems.
2. *Seek information*. More so than other members, the leader requests facts, asks for clarification of points that are unclear, and asks questions.

3. *Give information.* Leaders are the most prepared group members. They research the important issues in advance. They can inform other group members when there are gaps in their knowledge.

4. *Offer informed opinions.* Leaders give opinions based on evidence and sound reasoning. So as not to stifle discussion, these opinions will usually be offered after other group members have had their say.

5. *Clarify, summarize, and elaborate.* The leader provides closure for the group. Points agreed to and points still disputed are identified.

Social Needs

1. *Facilitate involvement and communication.* Leaders encourage participation from all members. Keeping meetings lively and fast-paced can prevent the non-participation that results from boredom.

2. *Harmonize.* The leader is responsible for establishing a supportive climate. This may mean confronting members who are disrupting meetings or creating competitiveness. Humor helps relieve tension and improve the group climate.

3. *Express feelings.* A leader expresses feelings when appropriate and promotes a supportive environment in which others can express their feelings.

Of the two functional viewpoints, <u>the leader as completer seems to have the greater merit</u>. A large-scale investigation of the question, "Which communicative functions do leaders perform more frequently or more characteristically than nonleaders?" revealed no unique functions associated with the leader role (Drecksel, 1984). <u>The set of leader behaviors listed are essential for the effective functioning of the group</u>, but Fisher (1986) also observes that "there is no particular reason to believe that leaders should or do contribute more of those functions than other members" (p. 212).

Reasonably, a leader has no preset list of functions to perform for the group, with the possible exception of certain procedural acts (e.g., constructing an agenda, arranging for an appropriate meeting room). A leader acting as a competent communicator, however, is responsive to the specific needs of the group. If tension needs to be relieved, the leader provides that function. If the group requires certain information, the leader can provide it. The leader as completer viewpoint does have merit.

CLOSER LOOK

Leadership and Teambuilding

In the previous chapter, ways to transform a small group into a team by establishing cooperation were discussed. Leadership is a key element in this process. The functional approach to leadership is a useful perspective in this regard. Building a team requires every member to work on three initial functions: establishing goals, developing a team identity, and designating clear roles.

A group needs a purpose to become a team. Not every group, of course, can become a team.

Boards of directors, student and faculty senates, and standing committees are not usually teams because members may have individual goals, representative of diverse factions that clash. Thus, they do not necessarily share a common purpose. Teams require a common purpose, and goals provide the team focus. Teams work best when goals are decided, not just by the team leader, but by all members together.

Team goals should be clear and challenging. Vague goals such as "make a good effort" or "improve our performance" give no clear direction. "Complete a study of all security needs on campus by the end of the term" or "raise $50,000 in contributions for a student scholarship fund within one year" are clear, specific team goals. Goals should also be challenging. Trivial goals motivate no one. Randy Wigginton, a member of the team that created the original Macintosh computer, notes, "We believed we were on a mission from God" (Bennis & Biederman, 1997, p. 83). Steve Jobs, the team leader of the Macintosh group, convinced team members that together they were going to construct a computer that would "put a dent in the universe" (p. 80).

A team also needs to develop an identity. There is no single way to build a team identity. A uniform or common mode of dress, a team name, an identifiable style, certain rituals or ceremonies unique to the group, even possessing a shared secret unknown to those outside the team are some ways to establish a team identity. James Carville, chief strategist for Bill Clinton's 1992 presidential campaign, helped establish an identity for Clinton's campaign team. The main headquarters for the team was located in Little Rock, Arkansas. It became known as the War Room and members were part of the War Room team. Carville also emphasized speed as a defining element of the campaign. There was a constant air of immediacy. War Roomers didn't walk to copy machines, they ran. Every attack from the Bush campaign, every mistake or stumble by Clinton was responded to with lightning speed by the team. T-shirt and jeans, Carville's preferred style of dress, became the uniform of the War Roomers, not because Carville insisted, but because team members embraced it.

Finally, roles need to be designated in teams. Unlike informal small groups where roles simply emerge, teams require more structure than this. A football team can't function effectively if team members decide for themselves which roles they plan to play. You might end up with 15 quarterbacks and no cornerbacks. A team must have every group function covered by a qualified member playing a specific role so there is little or no duplication of effort. A surgical team has clearly designated roles for each member. Nurses aren't supposed to step in and begin performing heart surgery. Every function is critical to the success of the team. If only some roles are played but others are ignored, several important team functions will be sacrificed with sometimes disastrous results. The team leader may designate the roles, as a coach does on a soccer or baseball team. Sometimes, however, team members volunteer for specific roles. The key point is that certain functions necessary to establishing a team during its infant stage—clear and challenging goals, a team identity, and designated roles—must be performed. The team leader alone cannot perform these functions. The team as a whole, under the guidance of a strong leader, must accomplish these goals together.

Questions for Thought:

1. Can you think of any teams that don't require clear, challenging goals, a team identity, and designated roles?
2. Can a team identity be established that doesn't conform to the team leader's preference?
3. How much say do you think a team member should have when roles are designated? Should this be the exclusive choice of the team leader?

From the functional perspective, leadership is a shared responsibility. If the group strays off task, any member can and should refocus the group. If a minority point of view has been ignored, any member can and should encourage the group to listen and give a fair hearing to a differing viewpoint. If conflict is smoldering beneath the surface of group discussion, any member can and should confront this. The group leader monitors the overall group process and progress, but the leader is not solely responsible for how the group performs.

Communication Competence Perspective   What do we really know about leadership in groups? With so many perspectives and viewpoints, what makes sense? Ultimately, effective leadership depends on competent communication. As Hackman and Johnson (1996) put it, "Extraordinary leadership is the product of extraordinary communication" (p. 81). No specific set of traits, particular style, situational readiness, or set of functions will produce effective leadership without the knowledge, skills, sensitivity, commitment, and ethics to provide group leadership.

The central, overriding point to make is that leadership in groups is an adaptive process. Leaders have to function within a system, and change is unavoidable in any system. As the most central role in a small group, the leader must be the most adaptive. Leaders have to be sensitive to the needs of group members and to changing situations. The "one leadership style fits all" approach is doomed to fail much of the time.

The leader sets the emotional tone for the group. Chief executives who fail typically do so because they exhibit insensitivity to group members, are brutally critical, and too demanding (Goleman, 1998). Ineffective leaders put their ego ahead of the needs of the group. When a group leader criticizes, shows contempt for members, berates those who make mistakes, humiliates members in front of others, and exhibits arrogance and mean-spiritedness, the entire group is tarnished by the incompetent communication (Goleman, 1998). Emotional outbursts, or what Birgitta Wistrand, CEO of a Swedish company, calls *"emotional incontinence,"* create a ripple effect that spreads fear, mistrust, and anger in all directions. This is not a climate conducive to effective leadership and group performance. As the old maxim goes, "A fish rots from the head down."

Steve Jobs, when he was the young leader of Apple Computer in the 1980s, was noted for what his employees dubbed "management by walking around." Jobs would appear at a work site without warning, stroll past work stations where employees were toiling away, then savage workers with brutal criticism. His favorite comment was "This sucks!" (Bennis & Biederman, 1997). Jobs's youth, arrogance, and mercilessly directive leadership style provoked derisive jokes from employees. "What's the difference between Apple and the Boy Scouts?" went one such joke. Answer: "The Boy Scouts have adult supervision" (Bennis & Biederman, 1997, p. 81). In 1985, Jobs was forced out of the company he helped to found. In 1997, he returned, a more mature and wiser leader, to resurrect Apple Computer from near collapse. On October 5, 1999, Jobs unveiled three new versions of the popular iMac computer to a packed house of appreciative Apple employees and members of the news media. Jobs acknowledged the effort of Apple employees who "burned the midnight oil" to resurrect the company. "I get the applause when you guys do all the work," he told his employees (Claymon,1999, p. 1C). David Lynch, a senior engineer, expressed the enthusiasm Apple employees have regarding Jobs as their leader. "He's a winner. He's the kind of guy you can follow" (p. 12C). Effective leaders create a supportive, cooperative group environment (Goleman, 1998).

CLOSER LOOK

"Chainsaw Al" and Aaron Feuerstein: A Lesson in Contrasts

He's been called "the most cold-blooded businessman around . . . brutal, heartless, and arrogant" (Plotz, 1997, pp. 1, 3). He's been nicknamed "Rambo in Pinstripes" and "Chainsaw Al" for his savage "downsizing" tactics when he is called in to "save" a company. He wrote a self-promoting book entitled *Mean Business*.

Albert Dunlap is a notorious corporate turn-around specialist, a hired gun who is given the position of CEO in a company. He uses this position to "turn around" the company by eliminating thousands of employees' jobs, increasing stock values, and selling off the remaining shell of a business. Dunlap slashed 18,000 jobs when he was CEO of Scott Paper Company. He cut more than 6,000 jobs when he took over the helm at Sunbeam. In the bargain, he received a 3-year, 70 million dollar contract with Sunbeam. He bragged, "You can't overpay a great executive . . . Don't you think I'm a bargain?" (Byrne, 1999, p. 185)

"Nothing that is valued by less steely businessmen—loyalty to workers, responsibility to the community, relationships with suppliers, generosity in corporate philanthropy—matters to Dunlap" (Plotz, 1997, p. 2). In his book, Dunlap offers this glib advice to those who lose their jobs and livelihood to his slash-and-burn tactics, "Those whose jobs will be eliminated in a restructuring should still consider the outcome philosophically, and have enough confidence in themselves to know

they will have opportunities somewhere else. A company is not your high school or college alma mater. Don't get emotional about it" (Dunlap 1997, p. 272). "Don't get emotional" he tells workers who must find a way to pay their mortgages and support their families after abruptly losing their jobs—this advice coming from a multimillionaire. As former Labor Secretary Robert Reich remarked when he heard that Dunlap planned to cut thousands of employees at Sunbeam, "There is no excuse for treating employees as if they are disposable pieces of equipment" (Byrne, 1999, p. 68).

Dunlap's leadership style consisted of intimidation and fear (Byrne, 1999). As Richard Boynton, president of the household products division of Sunbeam Corporation, put it, "It was like a dog barking at you for hours. He just yelled, ranted, and raved. He was condescending, belligerent, and disrespectful" (Byrne, 1999, p. 5).

Ironically, Dunlap himself was fired as CEO of Sunbeam in June 1998. His trademark downsizing strategy faltered. The company's board of directors lost faith in Dunlap's leadership. Those employees who remained at Sunbeam after the downsizing reportedly cheered when they heard he had been fired.

Aaron Feuerstein is a leader of a markedly different sort. In 1995, Feuerstein saw his family business, a textile company named Malden Mills, in Lawrence, Massachusetts, burn to the ground.

He was advised by everyone—family members, the board of directors, and other executives—to collect the insurance money and retire to his hammock leaving 2,400 employees to fend for themselves. Instead, Feuerstein did something remarkable and wholly different from the Dunlap approach. He maintained his entire workforce on his payroll while a new mill was built. It cost him 15 million dollars (Teal, 1996). Exhibiting an admirable We-orientation, Feuerstein believed that if he closed the mill the city of Lawrence would disintegrate. "I wasn't going to be the guy to finish it off. We have a responsibility to our community. Keeping the mill open helps to keep the town alive" (Amparano, 1997, p. E3).

Feuerstein was given the Lincoln Award for Ethics in Business in 1997 for his seemingly selfless act, but was it entirely selfless? Feuerstein did claim that "it was the right thing to do, and there's a moral imperative to do it irrespective of the consequences" (Lorant, 1996, p. 2). Thomas Teal, a former senior editor at *Harvard Business Review,* however, sees it as a good practical business move, not the act of a saint. "Why in the world should it be a sign of divinely inspired nuttiness to treat a work force as if it was an asset, to cultivate the loyalty of employees who hold the key to recovery and success, to take risks for the sake of a large future income stream, even to seek positive publicity? These are the things Aaron Feuerstein has done, and most people

stand in amazement as if they were witnessing a miracle or a traffic accident" (Teal, 1996, p. 1). Teal is correct. Before the fire, employees produced, on average, 130,000 yards of fabric per week. When the mill reopened, workers produced 200,000 yards of fabric each week (Amparano, 1997). Workers repaid Feuerstein's commitment to them with hard work and increased productivity. Competent leadership is good business.

The differences between the leadership of Al Dunlap and Aaron Feuerstein are stark and meaningful. Dunlap exhibited insensitivity and disrespect toward workers. He created a defensive work climate. Feuerstein showed amazing sensitivity to and respect for workers. He created a supportive, cooperative work climate. Leaders establish the emotional tone of a group. Dunlap created fear, anger, and mistrust. Feuerstein, by contrast, promoted loyalty, devotion, trust, and commitment from workers. For whom would you prefer to work, Dunlap or Feuerstein?

Questions for Thought

1. Should we always view Dunlap's approach to business as deplorable?
2. Can Feuerstein's compassionate leadership model be applied in all groups?
3. Why is getting rid of fear a desirable goal for groups?

In summary, there are many roles to play in small groups. Competent communicators learn to play a variety of roles. Leaders emerge in a process of elimination. There are different requirements, however, for gaining the leader role and retaining it once the role has been secured. The key to effective leadership is communication competence, whose keystone is adaptability to changing situations and needs in the group.

I've discussed how groups develop and how to create a cooperative/supportive climate during that development, and I've explained the roles we play during the life of a group and how to function effectively in those roles. Now I will examine the principal work that most groups perform. In the next two chapters I will analyze first defective, then effective decision making and problem solving in small groups.

Questions for Critical Thinkers

1. Have you experienced role fixation? Have you observed it in others?
2. Do Adolf Hitler, Joseph Stalin, Jim Jones, David Koresh, Charles Manson, and Marshall Applewhite qualify as leaders? Explain your answer in terms of leadership perspectives.

Group Discussion: Defective Decision Making and Problem Solving

Irving Janis (1982) relates the story of a tragedy that occurred in the mining town of Pitcher, Oklahoma, some years ago. The local mining engineer warned the inhabitants that due to an error, the town was in danger of imminent cave-in from undermining. Residents were advised to evacuate immediately. The warnings went unheeded. At a meeting of the local Lion's Club, leading citizens of the town joked about the doom-and-gloom forecast. One club member evoked raucous laughter from the membership when he entered the meeting wearing a parachute on his back in mock preparation for the predicted disaster. Within a few days, several of the club members and their families died when parts of the town caved in, swallowing some of those who spoofed the warnings.

Why would people ignore the threat? We read and hear stories every year of similar collective misjudgments and disasters. How do scandals such as Watergate, the Iran-Contra affair, and Whitewater ever occur in the first place? On a more local level, how do clear glass windows in a men's restroom at my college get installed to replace opaque windows when the new windows leave men standing at the urinals plainly visible to passersby? What gives rise to poor decision making in groups? How can group fiascos be averted? These are some of the questions that will be addressed in this chapter.

The terms decision making and problem solving are sometimes used synonymously. I see the terms as interconnected but not identical. <u>A decision requires a choice between two or more alternatives</u>. Groups make decisions in the process of finding solutions to problems (e.g., where to meet, what process to use in making choices, what is the best solution to the problem, how to implement the solution). Problem solving necessitates decision making, but not all decision making involves a problem to be solved. Although I will often use both terms together, when I use either term alone I am indicating a primary emphasis on one or the other.

In this chapter, I have four <u>objectives</u>:

1. to analyze the adverse effects of excessive or insufficient information quantity on group decision making/problem solving,
2. to explain the role of mindsets in defective decision making/problem solving,
3. to explore the contribution of collective inferential error to defective decision making/problem solving, and
4. to describe and analyze groupthink as an ineffective group decision-making process.

In other words, <u>this chapter explores ways in which small groups manifest defective critical thinking, a major cause of bad decisions and poor solutions to problems</u>. **Critical thinking** requires group members to analyze and evaluate ideas and information in order to reach sound judgments and conclusions. Critical thinking, therefore, is central to any discussion of small group decision making and problem solving.

One note of caution, however. Russian author Fyodor Dostoyevsky once remarked that "everything seems stupid when it fails." Determining degrees of decision-making and problem-solving effectiveness simply on the basis of outcomes would be misleading and inaccurate. Although suggestive, bad outcomes do not automatically signal defective decision making and problem solving because bad luck, sabotage, poor implementation by those outside the group, or misinformation may have caused the undesirable result.

INFORMATION: THE RAW MATERIAL OF CRITICAL THINKING

Information is critical to decision making and problem solving in groups. Faulty information processing by a group will likely lead to low-quality decisions, but sound information processing will likely lead to high-quality decisions (Hirokawa, 1987). Faulty information processing is partly the result of too much or too little information on which to base decisions.

Focus Questions

1. Which is the bigger contributor to defective decision making/problem solving in groups—information overload or underload?
2. Which method of coping with information overload is potentially the most effective?

Information Overload

Richard Wurman (1989) claims, "Information has become the driving force in our lives" (p. 32). With the advent of rapidly proliferating databases and the World Wide Web, information overload has become *the* problem of the new

Information overload can be a formidable problem that impedes critical thinking and decision making.

millenium. <u>When the rate of information flow into a system and/or the complexity of that information exceeds the system's processing capacity, **information overload** (excessive input) has been reached</u> (Farace et al., 1977). This section will examine the scope and consequences of information overload and ways decision-making and problem-solving groups can cope with it.

Scope of the Problem Jeff Davidson (1996) puts the problem succinctly, "This generation is more besieged by information than any that preceded it, and perhaps more so than all previous generations combined" (p. 495). More information has been produced in the last 30 years than was produced in the previous 5,000 years. A single edition of *The New York Times* contains more information than the average person was likely to be exposed to in an entire lifetime in seventeenth-century England (Wurman, 1989). With the rise of the Internet, we are rapidly approaching a point in which more information will be generated in *one hour* than could be processed and absorbed in your lifetime (Davidson, 1996).

Every day, Americans send 2.2 *billion* e-mail messages (Baran, 1999). Some virtual groups operate across time zones and conduct business almost exclusively by e-mail (Lipnack & Stamps, 1997). According to a study by Yankelovich Partners, a telecommunications marketing firm, employees receive an average of 11 voice mail messages each day at work, and 6.5 answering machine messages at home per day (Wen, 1999). In a survey of 1,300 business managers from Great Britain, the United States, Australia, Singapore, and Japan by Reuters Business Information, 43% of senior managers claimed that information overload made them ill ("Businesspeople suffering," 1996). Nearly two-thirds of these same individuals said that their personal relationships had also suffered and that they had experienced diminished job satisfaction because of information overload. In another Reuters' study of 1,000 managers in the United Kingdom, the United States, Germany, Singapore, Hong Kong, and Ireland, 46% claimed that they work longer hours just to keep up with the flood of information and 61% believe that they receive too much information (Veitch, 1997).

Consequences There are four main consequences of information overload relevant to group decision making and problem solving. First, information overload *impedes critical thinking* (Shenk, 1997). A glut of information makes it very difficult to distinguish useless from useful information. Critical thinking and effective decision making are hampered because group members have trouble digging through the garbage heap of useless information to discover the treasured nugget. Halpern (1984) cites a riddle illustrating this point. It reads as follows:

> Suppose you are a bus driver. On the first stop you pick up six men and two women. At the second stop two men leave and one woman boards the bus. At the third stop one man leaves and two women enter the bus. At the fourth stop three men get on and three women get off. At the fifth stop two men get off, three men get on, one woman gets off and two women get on. What is the bus driver's name? (p. 201)

Don't reread the riddle! Have you figured it out? The answer, of course, is your name since the riddle begins, "Suppose *you* are a bus driver." All the information about the passengers is irrelevant and merely diverts your attention from the obvious and correct answer.

Students working on group projects recognize the problem of information overload and its disruptive quality. When surrounded by a Mount Everest-size pile of books and articles or a stack of printouts from the Internet related to a group project, you lose sight of the larger picture. How does all this information fit together into a coherent package? Simply sorting through the gigaheaps of information on a subject leaves little time for group members to examine the information critically.

CLOSER LOOK

The McMartin Preschool Case

All decision-making groups are adversely affected by information overload. Information is the lifeblood of decision making in groups, but if there is a hemorrhaging of information, then the capacity to make decisions is impaired. This can be seen by examining the McMartin Preschool child molestation court case (Goldston & Torriero, 1990; Schindehette et al., 1990), the most expensive criminal trial in American history, lasting 28 months and costing $15 million.

The case began when Judy Johnson, who claimed she had divine powers and whom the courts described as a psychotic alcoholic (Baker, 1996), charged that her two-and-a-half-year-old son had been sexually abused at a daycare center in Manhattan Beach, California. Ultimately, 65 sex abuse and conspiracy charges were filed against two defendants: Raymond Buckey, 31, and his 63 year old mother, Peggy McMartin Buckey. Testimony in the trial was taken from 124 witnesses. One ten-year-old boy was on the witness stand for 16 days.

Weeks of testimony were devoted to the meaning of turtle shells that children in the case claimed were part of threatening satanic rituals used to silence them. The jury was faced with the nearly impossible task of sifting through 63,000 pages of sometimes complicated testimony and 917 exhibits in order to determine the guilt or innocence of the defendants. Jury deliberations commenced a full year and a half after the last of nine children testified at the trial. The jury deliberated for *nine weeks* before acquitting the defendants on 52 counts but deadlocking on 13 others. The jurors admitted afterward that they believed someone had committed child molestation at the daycare center but weren't sure who.

Critics argued afterward that the prosecution filed too many charges. They claimed that a case should have been built around a few strong charges and fewer children should have been involved (originally 400 children were interviewed and more than 200 charges filed, contributing to overload right from the start). How can one feel confident that justice has been served when the sheer quantity of information overwhelms the jurors' ability to absorb it and think critically? As Michael Marien observes, "Paradoxically, as more information is made available to us, we become less well-informed and decisions become harder to make" (Didsbury, 1982, p. 63).

Raymond Buckey was retried on the 13 charges that deadlocked the original jury. After yet another lengthy and expensive courtroom drama, the second trial ended in a hung jury. Charges against him were ultimately dismissed after he had served 5 years in a county jail awaiting trial and his entire family fortune of $3 million had been exhausted on lawyers' fees.

Questions for Thought

1. If you were on a jury such as the one in the McMartin case, how would you proceed to deal with the massive quantity of information?
2. Are there effective ways to present information so jury members aren't overwhelmed by the sheer volume of testimony and details?

A second consequence of information overload is that it *promotes indecisiveness* (Shenk, 1997). Paradoxically, the technologies that have ushered in the Information Age speed up almost everything enormously (see Closer Look: "Technology and the Bias of Speed"), but a group's ability to make decisions is slowed. "The psychological reaction to such an overabundance of information . . . is to simply avoid coming to conclusions (Shenk, 1997, p. 93). We become overly concerned that some new instantly available fact or statistic that would invalidate a group decision will be overlooked, making the group look foolish.

A third consequence of information overload is what Wurman (1989) dubs information bulimia. **Information bulimia** is a binge-and-purge cycle of information processing. For example, students cram facts into their heads, regurgitate them for a test or group presentation, then quickly purge them from their minds forever (sound vaguely familiar?). We become so focused on the quantity of information that we hardly notice if the quality is substandard. No meaningful decisions have been made in the process; no vital answers to problems have been discovered.

 *CLOSER LOOK*

Technology and the Bias of Speed

"Much time is lost by slow moving passengers who make no effort to hurry," claimed the president of Otis in a 1953 sales pitch for automated elevators. "They know the attendant will wait for them. . . . But the impersonal operatorless elevator starts closing the door after permitting you a reasonable time to enter or leave." He noted, "People soon learn to move promptly" (Gleick, 1999, p. 29).

Our technology makes "faster" possible, even necessary. As soon as faster becomes possible, it becomes our expectation. We perceive a "need for speed" whether or not it is required. Thus, computer printers of a dozen years ago seem painfully slow by today's standard even though they were viewed as almost miraculously swift in their day. Waiting even a few seconds to log onto our computers produces agitation for many users. When the push-button phone was invented, the rotary dial seemed interminably slow by comparison, but now we have a speed-dial button. Some telephone-answering machines have quick-playback buttons. The speed of the message when played back can be increased by 25 percent. Federal Express ushered in overnight mail service. Suddenly, regular mail service seemed annoyingly slow. The advent of e-mail initiated speed-of-light transmission of messages. Now regular mail service is "snail mail." Everything compared to e-mail seems like the pace of a caterpillar on tranquilizers. "Faster is better" has become the modern maxim.

Faster, however, may seem better because we supposedly "save time," yet all these technologies that accelerate the pace of our lives don't actually provide most of us with free time to make careful, deliberate decisions. We now have to "multitask" to keep pace (Gleick, 1999). Harvard economist Juliet Schor explains, "Technology reduces the amount of time it takes to do any one task, but also leads to the expansion of tasks people are expected to do ... It's what happens to people when they get computers and faxes and cellular telephones and all of the new technologies that are coming out today" (Shenk, 1997, p. 56). Where once a group might be given a month to finish a report, it now might be expected to finish a professional-looking report in only a few days. Little time is available to reflect, think, analyze, evaluate, or decide. We can become paralyzed into indecisiveness or forced to make rash decisions by the unrelenting pressure to act swiftly.

Group discussion can seem interminably long in a fast-track society. Allowing every group member to express his or her point of view seems like "wasted time." The pressure is to act, not deliberate. We become impatient with searching for creative solutions to complex problems. We feel a need to move quickly to the next problem, not linger on an "old" one. Crises and emergencies proliferate because everything becomes "last minute." "This is the Information Age, which does not always mean information in our brains. We sometimes feel that it means information whistling by our ears at light speed, too fast to be absorbed" (Gleick, 1999, p. 87). Technology is rapidly eliminating the pauses in our lives, and group decision making is probably not the better for it.

Questions for Thought

1. Have you experienced the difficulties associated with group decision making when faster is perceived to be better? How do you cope with it?
2. Should we try to slow the pace? How could this be done?
3. Is ever-increasing pace an inevitable product of technology?

A fourth consequence of information overload is a kind of *group Attention Deficit Disorder* (ADD). People with ADD, a brain syndrome, find that it is extraordinarily difficult to concentrate on any one thing for more than a fleeting moment. Similarly (though not literally), the megamountains of information competing for group members' attention makes focusing on any one idea, concept, or problem extremely difficult. Add to this what Shenk (1997) calls our "electronic leashes"—cell phones, pagers, faxes—that either distract our attention or make us wary that an interruption is imminent, and you can appreciate the problem. When cell phones and pagers go off during group meetings, classes, and the like everyone is distracted and attention is diverted from decision making and problem solving.

Coping with Information Overload   You can cope with information overload in several ways. *Screening information,* much like you do phone calls, by simply choosing to ignore much of the information, is one possibility. If you find 100 e-mail messages waiting for your attention when you return from a vacation, how do you cope? One way is to use a software program that automatically screens e-mail messages from designated senders. E-mails from virtual group members may be given highest priority. E-mails advertising rental housing may be deleted. A more low-tech screening method is to merely delete unread messages based on the title and author of the message.

A closely related method to screening is *shutting off the technology*. Information overload is largely a problem of too much openness in a system. Access to information needs to be closed off some. A standard rule for most group meetings should be that all cell phones and pagers will be shut off to prevent interruptions. Computers can be turned off, although this may require some individual discipline.

Specialization is a third method for coping with information overload. When you specialize you can manage to know a lot about a little. When a group's knowledge is limited in scope it becomes more dependent on experts, more vulnerable to their characterizations and perceptions of reality, and more prone to let them do the thinking for the group. If group members know little or nothing about the law, for instance, they may be forced to trust the advice of a lawyer counseling the group on some legal issue. Although some specialization is undoubtedly necessary to cope with information overload, increasing specialization will probably not improve decision making in groups, and may worsen it. Specializing can mean we know more and more about less and less. Ideas may go unchallenged because we form chat groups with like-minded individuals with similar biases and assumptions.

Selectivity is a fourth method of coping with information overload (Klapp, 1978). Since group members can't attend to all information bombarding them, they should choose selectively on the basis of group priorities and goals. Setting group priorities helps select which information requires members' urgent attention and which can be delayed or ignored entirely. Setting priorities distinguishes what we *need* to know from what there *is* to know. Selecting what information specifically is required avoids burial by the information dumptruck.

Limiting the search is a fifth way of coping with information overload. The search must stop at some point to allow time to reflect and evaluate information. There is a time for searching and a time for thinking and deciding. Setting deadlines for group decisions is critical. Deadlines force a group to bring a search for information to a halt. This means, however, that the search for information should begin early, not be postponed until the last minute. Otherwise, the search for relevant information due to time constraints may be far too limited to be effective.

Pattern recognition is a sixth means of coping with information overload and potentially the most effective. Discerning patterns is a group's best defense against information overload. As Klapp (1978) notes, "Once a pattern is perceived, 90% of information becomes irrelevant" (p. 13). Pattern recognition allows us to digest and process greater quantities of information if for no other reason than it assists our memory and helps us chunk information. **Chunking** is a process of recoding information into larger more meaningful patterns.

Consider the following example: 1776181218611917194119501964. Without chunking, these 28 numbers would overwhelm the average person's memory and render the numbers useless. A closer examination, however, reveals that the above digits easily break into the generally accepted official starting dates for the United States' entry into major wars. These 28 digits recode into seven more manageable chunks: 1776 1812 1861 1917 1941 1950 and 1964.

In order for chunking to help group members cope with information overload, the units must be meaningful. You can't chunk units into just any pattern. For instance, look at the following set of letters: FEA TSO FST REN GTH AMA ZEF RIE NDS. This form of chunking offers no meaningful pattern. In the absence of a meaningful pattern, the sets of letters become clutter. Yet a recoding of the same letters results in the more meaningful and memorable message: FEATS OF STRENGTH AMAZE FRIENDS.

Chunking can be used effectively by groups to cope with information overload. Football teams preparing for a game against an opponent could not possibly perform effectively without a specific game plan. A team's game plan acts as a chunking device. Only a small number of plays are chosen. The players are instructed by the coaches to concentrate on a few key strategies: establish the running game, contain the opponent's quarterback, double-team the wide receivers. No player can concentrate on more than a few crucial strategies. The plan simplifies the team's approach to the game. It establishes recognizable patterns for players.

second look

Coping with Information Overload

Screening—limit exposure to information

Shutting off the technology—turn off cell phones, pagers, etc.

Specialization—know a lot about a little

Selectivity—attend to information that relates directly to group goals and priorities

Limiting the Search—set time for searching and time for deciding

Pattern Recognition—chunk information into meaningful units

Information Underload

Although information overload is a far more prevalent and significant problem, information underload can also present problems for groups. **Information underload** refers to an insufficient amount of information (inadequate input) available to a group for decision-making purposes.

Kruglanski (1986) argues that the 1986 *Challenger* space shuttle disaster was partly a result of information underload. He claims that the compartmentalized deliberation and small-group discussion process at NASA prevented vital information concerning potential sources of an accident from being communicated to the responsible decision makers. This conclusion was supported by the Report of the President's Commission on the Space Shuttle *Challenger* Disaster (1986).

As tragic as the loss of the Challenger crew was, however, this flaw in group decision making could have been infinitely more serious if the faulty

The Challenger space shuttle explodes, partly the result of information underload.

O-rings had failed on the very next shuttle flight scheduled, instead of during the *Challenger* flight. According to Berkeley professor Dr. John Gofman, codiscoverer of Uranium 233, if the O-rings had failed one flight later you could have "kissed Florida good-bye" (as cited in Clanton, 1988). The next shuttle flight after the Challenger was scheduled to carry 47 pounds of Plutonium 238. According to Dr. Helen Caldicott in her book, *Nuclear Madness,* one ounce of Plutonium 238 could induce lung cancer in every person on earth. Effective group decision making is serious business.

Information underload can pose a problem in a variety of arenas. Conrad (1990) notes that a consistent finding in studies of organizational communication is "subordinates want their supervisors to 'keep them informed' and feel that they receive too little relevant and useful information from their supervisors, especially about events, policies, and changes directly involving them or their jobs" (p. 132). Supervisors do not usually provide enough job-related information to subordinates (Goldhaber, 1986).

The problem of unshared information in small groups is serious. Groups that pool information have an advantage over individual decision makers. This potential advantage of pooling information in groups, however, often goes unrealized because group members who have unique information fail to share that information with other members (Schittekatte & Van Hiel, 1996).

Not only is a potential advantage lost from unshared information, but disaster may occur because vital information was not shared with the group. A study (Foushee & Manos, 1981) of cockpit crews flying large commercial planes revealed that crews who shared little information did not perform as well as crews who shared a greater quantity of information. Seventy percent of all civil aviation accidents and near-misses during a 5-year period reported by the NASA Safety Reporting System were caused by either improper transmission of information from one crew member to another or by failure to transmit vital information at all (Burrows, 1982). Fewer errors related to mishandling of the engines, hydraulic systems, fuel systems, misreading and missetting instruments, and failing to use ice protection were found when sufficient information was communicated to all crew members.

Information underload is usually a problem of too much closedness in a system. The general solution to this problem is greater openness in the lines of communication. All members of the group must have access to the relevant information in order to make quality decisions. Finding the balance between too little and too much information, however, requires critical thinking skills. The competent communicator must acquire sufficient knowledge to recognize within a specific context what information is directly relevant to the task and what is irrelevant or marginal. Increasing the quantity of irrelevant or minimally useful information will confuse the group, not assist it in making effective decisions and solving problems.

MINDSETS: CRITICAL THINKING FROZEN SOLID

Perceptual **mindsets,** psychological and cognitive predispositions to see the world in a particular way—such as biases, preconceptions, and assumptions—interfere with effective group decision making and problem solving. Cognitively we are prepared to receive only certain messages and ignore others. We are conditioned to view the world narrowly.

Try this demonstration of a mindset on your unsuspecting friends. Have them spell the word *shop* out loud. Now ask them to respond immediately to the question, "What do you do when you come to a green light?" The vast majority will unthinkingly reply, "stop." Why? Because spelling the word *shop* narrows our focus to rhyming words even though the correct answer does not rhyme. Our minds are set to view the world in a particular way even if this is inappropriate. You may be surprised by the power of mindsets. Follow the "shop–stop" demonstration with this version of the same illustration: Spell *joke* out loud. "What do you call the white of an egg?" Most people will be victimized a second time by answering "yolk."

Focus Questions
1. Why does confirmation bias lead to defective decision making/problem solving?
2. Why is dichotomous (either–or) thinking called false?

Confirmation Bias

Confirmation bias is a prime example of a mindset that can produce defective decision making and problem solving. **Confirmation bias** is a tendency among all of us to seek information that confirms our beliefs and attitudes and to ignore or distort information that contradicts our currently held beliefs and attitudes (Hunt, 1982).

Consider this real example of confirmation bias. A man sued the phone company for several million dollars when he was seriously injured by an automobile that crashed into the phone booth he was occupying. The insurance industry has cited this as an obvious example of a frivolous lawsuit. Obviously, the injured man sued the "deep pocket," the party with the megabucks, not the party truly responsible for the injury, namely, the driver of the car. If you already hold a strong opinion that Americans suffer from lawsuit mania, then you probably would seek no additional or contradictory information regarding this case. Why look any further when your predisposition is confirmed? You give up the investigation before you have a chance to discover contradictory information that would challenge your confirmation bias.

The facts, however, paint a more complex picture. The phone company had been notified on many occasions that the particular phone booth in question had a defective door. The door stuck regularly and trapped occupants in the booth. Even in normal circumstances this could pose a danger and obviously a considerable inconvenience to occupants. In the case in question, an automobile spun out of control and headed for the phone booth. The man tried desperately to escape from the phone booth but was unable to do so because the door jammed. The automobile crashed into the booth and permanently crippled the man. The victim won the suit because of negligence on the part of the phone company.

The predisposition many people have that Americans are lawsuit-happy acts as a filter for the facts in the case just described. Since our bias is to search for information that supports our points of view, once we think we've had a confirmation, there is little motivation to search any further. Our minds slam shut on the subject.

Confirmation bias is alive and well in small groups (Schittekatte & Van Hiel, 1996; Stasser & Titus, 1987). Janis (1982) notes the strong tendency among group members to "show interest in facts and opinions that support their initially preferred policy and take up time in their meetings to discuss them, but they tend to ignore facts and opinions that do not support their initially preferred policy" (p. 10).

The consequences of confirmation bias to decision making and problem solving in groups are serious. Hirokawa (1985) found that assessing "the negative qualities or consequences associated with alternative choices" (p. 218) was an important determinant of high-quality group decision making. In other words, looking for the potential weaknesses and disconfirming evidence regarding decisions and solutions is a significant element of effective group decision making and problem solving. Assessing positive qualities or consequences is not nearly as important. Thus, groups that resist confirmation bias and actively search for possible flaws in decisions and solutions usually make better choices than groups that don't.

There is more to confirmation bias, however, than simply seeking confirmation of viewpoints and ignoring disconfirmation. Confirmation bias can also distort evidence that disconfirms our viewpoints and perceptions. The Heaven's Gate group exhibited such distortion. Members purchased a high-powered telescope so a clearer view of the Hale-Bopp comet and the spaceship they steadfastly believed was traveling in its wake—a spacecraft that was to transport Heaven's Gaters to a new cosmic life—could be discerned. The telescope was returned, however, and the store owner was politely asked for a refund. When the owner asked what was wrong with the telescope, he was informed, "We found the comet, but we can't find anything following it" (Aronson, 1999, p. 3). The Heaven's Gaters thought the telescope must be defective, not the original belief of a spaceship trailing the comet. This is distorting the evidence to maintain a strongly held belief.

The perpetuation of unwarranted beliefs is the natural result of confirmation bias. False beliefs that pollute the decision-making/problem-solving group process won't be corrected when we aren't open to refutation of such beliefs. We can't see the world accurately so our group decisions have greater validity and our solutions to problems have more efficacy when we insulate ourselves from disconfirming information.

So how does the competent communicator combat confirmation bias? The competent communicator combats the problem of confirmation bias as follows:

1. *Seek disconfirming information and evidence.* Since most group members will be predisposed to seek confirming evidence, someone will have to perform an error-correction function for the group. Consider it your personal responsibility to find the disconfirming information. If, after a concerted effort, you find little negative evidence of note, then your decision or solution has an excellent chance of turning out well.

2. *Vigorously present disconfirming evidence to the group.* Be persistent. Members will usually ignore negative news unless you assert yourself. Messengers with bad news aren't always killed. Sometimes they're received as heroes when they prevent the group from making an embarrassing error.

3. *Play devil's advocate.* The term *devil's advocate* originated many centuries ago with the Roman Catholic Church (Forsyth, 1990). Investigations of claims of sainthood were viewed by the church as so important that a formal position called devil's advocate was instituted for the express purpose of challenging the qualifications of candidates. Develop the habit of asking yourself and others the question, "So what's another side of the issue?" Challenge the assumptions and claims of those defending a decision or solution in your group—play devil's advocate. Do it in the spirit of problem orientation (supportive), not as an effort to force your will on the group (defensive). Clearly indicate your intentions so there will be no misunderstanding of your motives or intent. Anyone may play devil's advocate in a group. If groups establish a norm of devil's advocacy, the responsibility won't fall on only one member's shoulders.

4. *Gather allies to help challenge confirmation bias*. Women and ethnic minorities especially profit from developing support with those members of a group who are respected and open-minded.

False Dichotomies

Dichotomous, either–or thinking is the tendency to view the world in terms of opposites and to describe this dichotomy in the language of extremes. Dichotomies are usually false because in most instances there are more than two opposing possibilities, thus, the term **false dichotomy.** Describing objects, events, and people in such extreme polarities as moral–immoral, good–bad, rich–poor, corrupt–honest, intelligent–stupid locks us into a mindset of narrow vision. Most objects, events, and people are more accurately described in shades of gray, not black or white (pregnancy being a rare exception since it is difficult to be "sort of pregnant").

For instance, when does success turn into failure? When does a small group become a large group and vice versa? Dichotomous descriptions of events and objects are usually false because most of reality consists of more-to-less, not either–or.

False dichotomies contribute to defective group decision making and problem solving. When group members are predisposed to see problems and solutions only in extremes, the vast middle ground goes largely unexplored. City councils, faced with reduced revenues during a recession, see only layoffs and reductions in public services when they think dichotomously (i.e., tax revenues up—fund services and jobs; tax revenues down—cut services and jobs). They may fail to explore other avenues for raising revenues besides taxes.

Dichotomous thinking can lead to a friends–enemies duality when controversy brews. Group members may then shrink from making hard decisions or be provoked into making decisions from less than pure motives. Even the decision to make a decision can be a product of dichotomous thinking. Groups locked into the mindset that a decision has to be made may never consider a third alternative besides voting for or against some proposal. Postponing the decision until adequate study of the problem can take place and potential solutions can emerge may be a more viable option.

The competent communicator combats the problem of false dichotomies in small groups as follows:

1. *Be suspicious of absolutes*. When group members argue only two extreme possibilities (e.g., a solution is either all good or all bad), look for a third or even fourth possibility.
2. *Employ the language of qualification*. When engaged in group discussion, speak in terms of degrees (i.e., to what extent an argument is true). You'll be using terms such as *sometimes, rarely, occasionally, mostly, usually,* and *moderately*. This is not the language of the wishy-washy fence-straddler. This is the language of precision in matters of human discourse.

CLOSER LOOK

Blue Eyes versus Brown Eyes

In-group bias, a product of our tendency to dichotomize the world, is a source of racism, sexism, and discrimination. The in-group bias occurs when one group of individuals is differentiated from another group of individuals. The differentiations may be quite arbitrary and meaningless in any important sense (e.g., individuals wearing basic blue jeans versus individuals wearing designer clothes). Nevertheless, both groups will quickly develop a "them" versus "us" mentality. This we–they thinking between groups fosters a superior attitude toward your own group (the in-group) and a perception of inferiority toward the other group (the out-group). Once the superiority-inferiority dichotomy is established, hostility targeted at the out-group easily emerges. Perceived differences between the groups, even trivial ones, are magnified.

A remarkable demonstration of the arbitrariness of the in-group versus out-group phenomenon was devised by Jane Elliott (1977), a third-grade teacher in Riceville, Iowa. Elliott wanted her students from an all-white, rural community of about 900 people to experience prejudice and discrimination firsthand in order to appreciate its viciousness.

She divided her class into two groups according to eye color. Quite arbitrarily she designated the brown-eyed children as "superior" to the "inferior" blue-eyed children. "Brown-eyed people are better, cleaner, smarter, more civilized than blue-eyed people," she informed her wide-eyed pupils. Brown-eyed students were given special privileges, while blue-eyed children were told to obey certain demeaning rules that applied to them exclusively.

With their teacher constantly reminding the blue-eyed children of their inferiority and the brown-eyed children of their superiority, the we–they false dichotomy quickly affected the children's performance and self-esteem. The blue-eyed children im-mediately began to perform poorly in their schoolwork and became downcast, sullen, and angry. Brown-eyed children transformed from "marvelously cooperative, thoughtful children" into "nasty, vicious, discriminating little third-graders."

The following day, Elliott informed her class that she had been wrong the day before. The blue-eyed children were really the superior people and the brown-eyed children were inferior. Almost immediately the two groups switched behavior and self-perceptions. Now the brown-eyed children described themselves in derogatory terms such as stupid, dull, and bad while the blue-eyed children chose complimentary terms such as nice, good, and sweet. This was a complete turnaround for both groups from self-reports the day before. Academic performance suffered for the new "inferior" group and was enhanced for the new "superior" group.

The simplism and false perceptions fostered by dichotomous labeling of groups during this demonstration were apparent. The distinctions drawn by Elliott between the blue-eyed children and brown-eyed children were unequivocally either–or: superior or inferior designations with no in-between. The distinctions were obviously false since the two groups flip-flopped on the second day and suddenly became the opposite of what they were designated the previous day.

In addition to demonstrating the falseness of dichotomous, either–or thinking, Elliott's classroom experiment also clearly illustrates confirmation bias. Inappropriate or disruptive behavior by members of whichever group happened to be designated inferior was seized upon by Elliott as "proof" of their inferiority, and admirable behavior by members of the superior group was noted as proof of the group's superiority. In one instance, when brown-eyed children were labeled inferior, Elliott exclaimed, "Everyone's ready except Lori—she's a brown eyes."

When the blue-eyed children were designated as the inferior group, Elliott shook her head when a blue-eyed child had trouble reading, then allowed a brown-eyed child to read the passage correctly. Turning to one blue-eyed child she asked, "Russell, where are your glasses?" He had forgotten them. "Susan has her glasses—she's a brown eyes," noted Elliott to the class. No matter what the children did, Elliott selectively spotlighted behavior that seemed to confirm the arbitrary designation of either superiority or inferiority. Throwing away a plastic cup was "wasteful" if done by a child in the inferior group, while keeping it might be labeled "unsanitary". Elliott, however, was not immune from confirmation bias. When she accidentally flipped up a screen while trying to pull it down, one of her pupils shouted, "What do you expect, she's blue-eyed."

Weiner and Wright (1973) found results similar to Elliott's when they conducted a controlled experiment with a third-grade class. In addition, however, they also found that a classroom experiment like the one Elliott created can significantly diminish racial prejudice among children.

Children are suggestible. Adults, however, are more sophisticated. Nevertheless, Elliott duplicated her results when she tried her experiment with adult groups, most notably with officials and employees at an Iowa state penitentiary. At first I didn't believe these results could be duplicated with adults. When I saw a movie on Jane Elliott and her experiments, however, I became a believer.

No matter how arbitrary and trivial the distinctions are between groups, human beings easily slip into a we-they frame of mind. Once the designation has been made regarding who the "we" are and who the "they" are, almost any behavior can be twisted to confirm a predisposition. In this way, prejudice is excused and nurtured.

Questions for Thought

1. Do you think Elliott's experiment should be conducted in public schools across the United States to combat racism fostered by confirmation bias and dichotomous thinking?
2. In your opinion is this experiment with third-graders ethical? Could children suffer serious psychological trauma from such an experiment?

COLLECTIVE INFERENTIAL ERRORS: UNCRITICAL THINKING

Two American women—a matronly grandmother and her attractive granddaughter—are seated in a railroad compartment with a Romanian officer and a Nazi officer during World War II. As the train passes through a dark tunnel, the sound of a loud kiss and an audible slap shatters the silence. As the train emerges from the tunnel no words are spoken but a noticeable welt forming on the face of the Nazi officer is observed by all. The grandmother muses to herself, "What a fine granddaughter I have raised. I have no need to worry. She can take care of herself." The granddaughter thinks to herself, "Grandmother packs a powerful wallop for a woman of her years. She sure has spunk." The Nazi officer, none too pleased by the course of events, ruminates to himself, "This Romanian is clever. He steals a kiss and gets me slapped in the process." The Romanian officer chuckles to himself, "Not a bad ploy. I kissed my hand and slapped a Nazi."

This story illustrates the problem of inferential error. **Inferences** are conclusions about the unknown based on the known. They are guesses varying by degrees from educated to uneducated (depending on the quantity and quality of information on which the inferences are based). We draw inferences from previous experiences, factual data, and predispositions. The facts of the story are that the sounds of a kiss followed by a slap are heard by all members of the group. Based on what is known, the three individuals who do not know for sure what happened all draw distinctly different and erroneous inferences.

Making inferences is not a problem in itself. The human thinking process is inferential. Our minds "go beyond the information given" (Nisbett & Ross, 1980). We could not function on a daily basis without making inferences. You can't know for certain that the grocery store is open. It may have burned down or closed due to a power outage. You draw the conclusion that it is open on the basis of what is known. If the store has always been open 24 hours, 7 days a week, then you infer it will be open now, which is a relatively safe inference. <u>The principal problem with inferences is that we too often assume our inferences are mere descriptions of fact even when they rest on insufficient or faulty information</u>, and, as the Felix Unger character in an episode of the old TV program *The Odd Couple* once explained, "To *assume* is to make an *ass* out of *u* and *me*." This can pose serious problems for group decision making. If we don't exercise our critical thinking abilities by closely examining important inferences central to decision making in groups, bad decisions are highly likely to result.

Focus Questions
1. What are the primary general sources of collective inferential errors?
2. Should we avoid making inferences?
3. Why are most correlations noncausal?

Prevalence of the Problem

The centrality of inferences to decision making and problem solving in groups is made apparent by Gouran (1982) when he explains:

> In virtually every phase of discussion, inferences come into play. Whether you are assessing facts, testing opinions, examining the merits of competing arguments, or exploring which of several alternatives best satisfies a set of decisional criteria, you will have occasion to draw inferences suggested by the information you are examining. How well you reason, therefore, can have as much to do with the effectiveness of a decision-making discussion as any other factor that enters the process. (pp. 96–97)

Individuals are inclined to make inferential errors (see Closer Look: "The Uncritical Inference Test" p. 170). The problem can be magnified in groups. Gouran calls this collective inferential error.

The research regarding group polarization suggests that when a group exhibits a predominant initial tendency, group discussion seems to amplify the initial position of group members. If the inference is a bad one, the group may engage in collective misjudgment. Studies by Gouran (1981, 1982, 1983) have established the prevalence of inferential errors in groups. As many as

Look at the college basketball coach pictured above. How did you decide which individual was the coach? Did you assume that the male is the coach? If so, you made an inaccurate inference. Laura Mitchell, at the time of this photo, was the coach of the University of California at Santa Cruz women's basketball team.

half of a group's discussion statements may be inferences. Groups often accept these inferences uncritically.

Gouran (1983) examined student group discussions in which 80 inferences were made regarding questions of policy. Only one inference was challenged. The rest were reinforced, extended, or new inferences were added. Why is this significant? Because Hirokawa and Pace (1983) and Martz (1984) found that <u>ineffective decision-making groups that arrived at faulty decisions displayed more inferential deficiencies in their discussions than did effective groups</u>.

The Uncritical Inference Test

Individuals are prone to make inferential errors (Nisbett & Ross, 1980). See if you have such a tendency. Read the following story. For each statement about the story, circle "T" if it can be determined without a doubt from the information provided in the story that the statement is completely true, "F" if the statement directly contradicts information in the story, and "?" if you cannot determine from the information provided in the story whether the statement is either true or false.

Dr. Chris Cross, who works at St. Luke's Hospital, hurried into room #314 where Yoshi Yamamoto was lying in bed. Pat Sinclair, a registered nurse, was busy fluffing bed pillows when Dr. Cross entered. Dr. Cross said to the nurse in charge, "This bed should have been straightened out long ago." A look of anger came across Nurse Sinclair's face. Dr. Cross promptly turned around and hurried out the door.

1. Chris Cross is a medical doctor who works at St. Luke's Hospital. **T F ?**
2. Dr. Cross is a man in a hurry. **T F ?**
3. Yoshi Yamamoto, who is Japanese, was lying in bed. **T F ?**
4. Pat Sinclair was in room #314 when Dr. Cross entered and found her fluffing bed pillows. **T F ?**
5. Dr. Cross was irritated with Nurse Sinclair because the bed was not straightened out. **T F ?**
6. Yoshi Yamamoto is a patient at St. Luke's Hospital. **T F ?**
7. Nurse Sinclair's face reddened because Dr. Cross was stern with her. **T F ?**
8. When Dr. Cross entered he became the third person in room #314. **T F ?**
9. This story takes place at St. Luke's Hospital. **T F ?**
10. This story concerns a series of events in which only three persons are referred to: Dr. Cross, Nurse Sinclair, and Yoshi Yamamoto. **T F ?**

I created this version of what Haney (1967) originally devised and called "The Uncritical Inference Test." I have given it to students for more than 15 years. The huge majority incorrectly identify all or most of the statements as "T." If you circled "?" for *all* of the statements above, then you are not likely to make inferential errors unless you get sloppy. "?" is the correct answer for all of the statements. Without exception, these statements are based on assumptions—guesses regarding what is likely but not verifiably true from the information provided. All of the statements involve uncertainty—some more than others. The reasons these statements are uncertain are as follows:

1. Chris Cross is a doctor of some sort but not necessarily a medical doctor (Dr. Cross may be a Ph.D., chiropractor, dentist, etc.)
2. Dr. Cross is not necessarily a man.
3. Yoshi Yamamoto has a Japanese name, but isn't necessarily Japanese (married name, assumed name).
4. Pat Sinclair may be a *male* not a "her."
5. This requires an inference that Dr. Cross is irritated and that Nurse Sinclair and "the nurse in charge" are one and the same person, which cannot be ascertained from the information provided.
6. Yoshi Yamamoto may be an orderly taking a break or a visitor resting, not a patient.
7. This requires an inference that a "look of anger" automatically produces a "reddened face." Again, Nurse Sinclair may be male.
8. There may have been four people in room #314 if Nurse Sinclair and the nurse in charge are not the same person.
9. Dr. Cross works at St. Luke's. Nowhere does it say this story occurred there.
10. Again, four people may be in the story: Dr. Cross, Nurse Sinclair, the nurse in charge, and Yoshi Yamamoto.

If we don't even recognize that we've made an inference, then we're not likely to notice when the inference is a bad one. If individually you do poorly on recognizing and critically evaluating inferences, imagine the quality of decision making in a group when most or all of the members are inclined to make inferential errors.

Questions for Thought

1. Is The Uncritical Inference Test merely splitting hairs over relatively minor assumptions or does the test sensitize us to an important and common deficiency in our critical thinking process?
2. Assuming some inferential errors are more serious than others, how do you determine the more serious from the less serious?

General Sources of Inferential Errors

Inferences that rely on a quality information base in plentiful supply are educated guesses—not always correct, but nevertheless probable. Inferences that are drawn from a limited, faulty information base, however, are "uneducated" guesses—likely to produce inferential errors (Gouran, 1989). <u>The two general sources of inferential errors, then, are a faulty information base or misinformation, and a seriously limited information base.</u>

Inferential errors from a faulty information base are common. Hirokawa (1987), in a study of ineffective decision making in small groups, provides an example of collective inferential error resulting from a faulty information base. The group task was to choose 10 items from a list of 30 salvageable articles most crucial to surviving 5 days in a remote wilderness area of Canada in the middle of winter following a plane crash. In one group, the following discussion took place:

B: I think we should go with the wine next. . . . That would be helpful for survival, I would think.
C: How so?
B: Well, uh, first, it can help to keep us warm—we established that as one of our needs . . . plus, you know, like wine can be used for medicinal purposes.
A: I don't understand.
B: What? About wine keeping us warm? Medicinal value?
A: Yeah.
B: Well, OK, wine . . . have you ever drunk wine, you have, haven't you? It warms you up, right? That's because of the alcohol in it, but also, that alcohol, that's how it can be used for medicinal purposes. Say if someone got cut, we could wash it with it, cleanse it, keep it from getting infected.
C: Plus, also, if we need to, I guess we could also use it to help us get a fire going. Like if the twigs and sticks were wet, and wouldn't burn, we could pour some wine over them and light it.
A: Like lighter, or what, yeah, charcoal-lighting fluid?
B: Yeah, right, same idea. So, see, the wine has several uses. . . .
C: Yeah, let's go with the wine. (pp. 17–18)

There are several bad inferences in this example of negative synergy because the information used to draw the inferences is faulty. The feeling of warmth from drinking alcohol does not mean the body is heated by drinking wine. Alcohol dilates the blood vessels in the skin, which in turn chills the blood when a person is exposed to very cold weather. An intoxicated person is more likely to get hypothermia. The low level of alcohol in wine also makes it ineffective as a disinfectant; and have you ever tried to ignite wine? There isn't a high enough level of alcohol in wine to act as a fire starter.

Inferential error resulting from severely limited information is equally problematic for a group. Foushee (1981) notes that there have been several documented near-collisions in the sky because pilots made faulty inferences. He cites an example where a critical alarm went off in the cockpit of a plane. Shortly thereafter, the alarm went silent, leading the captain to infer that it was probably a false warning. After landing, however, the pilot learned that the flight engineer had pulled the circuit breaker for the alarm system, that it was not a false warning, and that the alarm could have been potentially serious.

Upon questioning, the flight engineer revealed that he had asked the captain if he wanted the alarm turned off. When the captain made no reply, the flight engineer wrongly inferred that he was complying with the captain's wishes by switching off the alarm. The engineer based his inference on the extremely limited information that the captain did not specifically tell him to keep the alarm operational and check for the source of the problem. The captain inferred that the alarm was a false one simply because it stopped. That's very limited information on which to draw such a significant inference.

The problem here is not that groups make inferences. Decision making requires inferences. Thinking is inferential. <u>The problem is that we are prone to make inferences based on extremely limited or faulty information without even realizing that we've made a guess, and not identified a fact</u>. If no group member challenges the validity of inferences made during discussion, if members just assume as fact that alcohol makes you warm because you get a warm feeling from it, or that silence means consent, then groups may stack one faulty inference upon another. This makes a poor basis for quality group decision making.

CLOSER LOOK

The Blandina Chiapponi Case

A dramatic example of inferential error made international headlines in 1989 (Brecher, 1989). A woman named Blandina Isabella Chiapponi said she had been raped by a man named Steven Lamar Lord, an unsavory character, in a Denny's parking lot in Fort Lauderdale, Florida, at 3:00 A.M. The case went to trial and the jury acquitted the defendant after 2 hours of deliberations. One of the jurors, Ray Diamond, gave the verdict worldwide attention when he explained after the trial that the jury all felt she was asking for it, the way she dressed (Brecher, 1989, p. B1). Blandina Chiapponi was wearing a lace miniskirt, tank top, white high heels, and no underwear on the night in question.

Within days, the 22-year-old woman was an international celebrity. On both Oprah Winfrey's and Larry King's talk shows, she claimed, "I was kidnapped, I was beaten, I was almost murdered before being raped three times. My life has been ruined, not only by the brute who raped me, but by a jury who decided I was to blame because of what I was wearing" (p. B1). The media had a field day. The *London Daily Mail* described her as "an innocent, convent-educated girl from a close-knit Catholic family who are standing by her" (p. B1). Blandina Chiapponi, so went the story, had been victimized twice—once by her brutal rapist and again by the jury. A "Take Back The Night" march on the county courthouse made her case a central issue. On the basis of her version of the incident and the one inflammatory comment of a juror (who later "explained" that he simply meant that Chiapponi was a prostitute whose form of dress purposely advertised her desire to sell sex), most people seemed to think that the jury had performed a terrible injustice.

On closer inspection, the following inconsistencies and errors in Blandina Chiapponi's story created a reasonable doubt in the minds of jurors:

1. She said she was with friends the night of the incident, but she couldn't remember their names.
2. She asserted that she was going into Denny's for something to eat, yet she had no money nor any place to keep money on her person.
3. She changed her story on the witness stand regarding where the rape allegedly took place.
4. She told the investigating officer that she was wearing underpants, then admitted during the trial that she wasn't.
5. She claimed she worked at a modeling and talent agency, which was false; she actually worked at a massage parlor thought by police to be a front for prostitution.
6. After charging rape, she later refused to cooperate with the prosecution and was arrested for ignoring subpoenas—she resisted arrest.
7. She claimed she had inherited a substantial amount of money, which was never proven.
8. She asserted, "I was hit over the head and cut up and left for dead," but although there was evidence of sexual intercourse, there was no evidence of physical violence except for a small finger wound that looked like a paper cut.
9. She claimed she had a close-knit family who staunchly stood behind her—this also proved to be untrue.

In fact, the jury did not decide its verdict on the basis of what this woman wore (Brecher, 1989). In their discussions, despite the later misleading remark by Ray Diamond, the jurors agreed that what she wore and how she lived her life were irrelevant to the verdict. The case ultimately was decided on whose story the jury believed—Chiapponi's or Lord's (he claimed she was a prostitute looking for money and cocaine). The fact that she was shown to be a liar of no small proportions left the jury with a reasonable doubt. Elinor Brecher (1990) summarizes:

What mattered to the jury was this: Blandina Chiapponi had clearly misrepresented herself under oath, not once but several times. Although it pained them, in a case where the physical evidence was inconclusive, the jury had no choice but to look to the victim's credibility in order to remove that last shred of reasonable doubt, as the law demands. They looked but they still doubted. (p. B1)

Blandina Chiapponi may have been raped. It's not likely the truth will ever be ascertained. The inference that the jury had failed in its duty and had perpetrated an abomination, however, cannot be drawn validly from the facts. The jury in the Blandina Chiapponi case was an effective decision-making group since individuals in the group performed an error-correction function and overcame the serious temptation to make inferential errors. The fact that Steven Lamar Lord was an unsavory character, who even may have looked like a man capable of rape, and the attire of Blandina Chiapponi did not sway the jury to make faulty inferences. They drew conclusions from the facts available, not from assumptions concerning what could have happened or how they might have wanted the verdict to come out.

The public, in general, and the media, in particular, were guilty of collective inferential error, of jumping to a conclusion unsupported by the facts available. Based on the slimmest information—one inflammatory statement by Ray Diamond—the inference was drawn that this jury had perpetrated an outrageous injustice. Later, this faulty inference was bolstered by Blandina Chiapponi's one-sided and erroneous presentation of the "facts." It is understandable that Ray Diamond's comment would incite an angry response from the public. His was an example of communication incompetence. He made an insensitive, completely inappropriate remark. Yet, why assume he spoke for the entire jury of 12 members? <u>Since faulty inferential leaps are more likely when the issues are emotionally charged, as was the case in the Chiapponi trial, scrutinizing inferences is all the more important when the issues are combustible.</u>

Questions for Thought

1. Do you agree that the jury in this case was an effective decision-making group? Explain.

2. Can you think of instances when you have jumped to conclusions very much like the public reaction to Ray Diamond's incendiary statement?

Specific Sources of Inferential Errors

There are several specific sources of inferential errors that can adversely affect group decision making. I will discuss three of the most prevalent.

Vividness   The graphic, outrageous, shocking, controversial, dramatic event draws our attention and sticks in our minds. This is called the **vividness effect.** Producer Gary David Goldberg captured the essence of the vividness effect when he pointedly observed, "Left to their own devices, the networks would televise live executions. Except Fox—they'd televise live naked executions" ("TV or not TV," 1993, 5E).

  We tend to overvalue a shocking example and undervalue statistical information that shows patterns and trends. Barry Glasner (1999) in his book *The Culture of Fear,* identifies numerous examples of the vividness effect in action. He notes, "Producers of TV newsmagazines routinely let emotional accounts trump objective information. In 1994 medical authorities attempted to cut short the brouhaha over flesh-eating bacteria by publicizing the fact that an American is 55 times more likely to be struck by lightning than die of the suddenly celebrated microbe. Yet TV journalists brushed this aside with . . . stomach-turning videos of disfigured patients" (p. xxii).

  The infamous shootings at Columbine High School in Littleton, Colorado by Eric Harris and Dylan Klebold on April 20, 1999, left 14 students and one teacher dead. The vivid carnage was international news. A *Newsweek* poll of 757 randomly selected adults conducted 2 days after the school massacre revealed that 63% of the adults thought a shooting incident similar to Columbine was very or somewhat likely at their children's school ("Anatomy of a Massacre," 1999). School boards around the country deliberated proposals to protect students from such violence. Swat teams performed drills in several high schools. Yet among the 20,000 secondary schools in the United States, only six similar incidents occurred in the 5 years prior to Columbine—six too many, but hardly an epidemic of random violence worthy of national hand-wringing and breast-beating about our violent youth (Glassman, 1998). Among the 52 *million* public school students in the United States, fewer than 4,000 are expelled annually for bringing weapons of any kind to school (Ramirez, 1999). Only 10% of public schools each year report even *one* serious violent crime (Adler & Springen, 1999). Vigilance is appropriate, but gross exaggeration of the problem by vivid media coverage merely distorts our perceptions and can precipitate overreactions, even panic, and faulty group decision making.

  The power of the vivid example to shape and distort group decision making is real. The potency of the vividness effect is so real that Stanovich

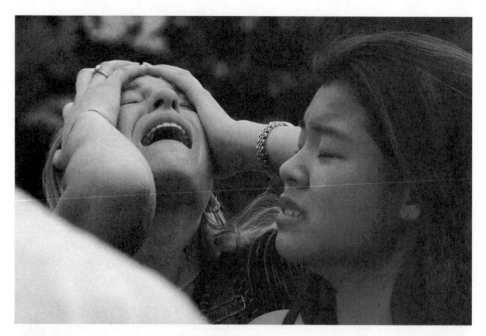

The vividness of the Columbine High School massacre provoked SWAT team drills in schools around the United States.

(1992) concludes that it "threatens to undermine the usefulness of any knowledge generated by any of the behavioral sciences" (p. 141). Be immediately wary of any claim that rests on the veneer of the vivid example.

Unrepresentativeness   When we make a judgment, we assess the resemblance or accuracy of an object or event presumed to belong to a general category. Is a specific example representative of a general category? If the answer is yes, then the inference drawn from the representative example is on solid footing. If the example is unrepresentative, however, inferences drawn from it are likely to be erroneous. If the example is both unrepresentative and vivid, then the potential for inferential error is magnified.

Ray Diamond did not speak for the Chiapponi jury, yet the public and the mass media assumed that he represented all 12 members. If you said to yourself as I related the details of the Chiapponi case that you wished I hadn't chosen this example to illustrate collective inferential error because the issues are sensitive and some might erroneously assume that her conduct was typical of rape victims, then you have manifested an appreciation for the potential dangers of unrepresentativeness. Those who would assert from the Chiapponi case that rape victims frequently lie in such trials and therefore testimony from such victims is highly unreliable make a huge inference based on a single unusual instance. This inference has as much validity as asserting that because your second cousin is a pathological liar most of your family must be too. Blandina Chiapponi hardly qualifies as a representative complainant in a rape trial.

A study by Quattrone and Jones (1980) illustrates inferential error resulting from unrepresentativeness in a group context. College students indicated their belief that if one member of a group made a particular decision, then all members of the group would make the same decision. This was especially true if the students were observing the decisions of students from other colleges. In other words, we stereotype an entire group on the basis of a single individual who may or may not be representative of the group as a whole.

Correlation   A third specific source of inferential error is correlation. A consistent relationship between two or more variables is called a **correlation**. There are two kinds of correlations: positive and negative. A positive correlation occurs when X increases and Y also increases (e.g., as you grow older your ears grow larger—nature's practical joke on the elderly; as you increase in height your weight also increases). A negative correlation occurs when X increases and Y decreases (e.g., as adults increase in age their capacity to run long distances decreases; as cars increase in age they decrease in value).

Most correlations are not perfect; a perfect correlation has no exceptions. Not everyone who grows taller increases in weight, especially if a teenager aggressively diets to slim down as he or she grows. Not every automobile loses value as it ages, especially if it is an antique classic car. The main problem with correlations is the strong inclination people have for inferring causation (x causes y) from a correlation (sometimes called a *post hoc ergo propter hoc* fallacy). A large research team collected data in Taiwan to determine which variables best predicted use of contraceptive methods for birth control (Li, 1975). Of all the variables, use of birth control was most strongly correlated with the number of electric appliances (i.e., toasters, ovens, blenders, etc.) found in the home. Birth control usage increased as the number of electric appliances increased (GE doesn't bring good things to life?). So does it make sense to you that a free microwave oven or electric blender for every teenager in high school would decrease teen pregnancy rates? I'm confident that you can see the absurdity of such a suggestion.

The birth control–electric appliances correlation is an obvious case where a correlation, even though a very strong one, is not a causation. The number of electric appliances more than likely is a reflection of socioeconomic status and education levels, which undoubtedly have more to do with the rates of birth control usage than do the number of electric irons and toasters found in the home.

Stephen Jay Gould (1981) explains that "the vast majority of correlations in our world are, without doubt, noncausal" (p. 242). The fact that most correlations are noncausal, however, does not prevent most people from making the inferential error of correlation mistaken for causation. As Gould states, "The invalid assumption that correlation implies cause is probably among the two or three most serious and common errors of human reasoning" (p. 242).

I have witnessed the correlation as causation inferential error in my own classes. Consider the following discussion that took place in a small group in one of my classes:

J: I think we should choose capital punishment for our topic. I just did a paper on it. We can show that capital punishment works. In a lot of states that have it, murder rates have decreased.

A: Yeah, did you ever see that video where they show executions? Really gross. You know most criminals would think twice about killing someone if they realize they'll fry in the electric chair.

B: Well, I heard that when they execute a guy, the murder rate goes up right after. I don't think capital punishment is a very effective solution to murder.

In this brief conversation, group members managed to allege the truth of an asserted causation based only on a correlation, affirm the validity of the inferential error with a little commonsense reasoning, then refute the effectiveness of capital punishment by introducing yet another correlation assumed to be a causation. Correlations are not causations.

second look

Source of Inferential Errors

General Sources of Inferential Errors
- Seriously limited information base (insufficient quantity of information)
- Faulty information base (poor-quality information)

Specific Sources of Inferential Errors
- Vividness
- Unrepresentativeness
- Correlation (*post hoc ergo propter hoc* fallacy)

Error Correction: Practicing Critical Thinking

In order for the error-correction function of group discussion to kick in, competent communicators must recognize the sources of inferential errors just discussed. Assertively focusing the group's attention on sources of inferential error can help prevent faulty decision making from occurring. In other words, group members must put their critical thinking abilities into practice if effective decision making is to take place. As Hirokawa and Pace (1983) found, group discussion promotes higher-quality decision making when:

1. The validity of inferences are carefully examined.
2. Inferences are grounded in valid information.
3. At least one member of the group exerts influence to guide the group toward higher-quality decisions.

Notice the last point. A single individual can prevent or minimize inferential error in group decision making because one person can affect the entire system. Communication competence can be contagious. Collective inferential error, the manifestation of defective critical thinking by a group, is the product of the communicative efforts of individual members. Hirokawa and Scheerhorn (1986) note that "an individual can prevent the occurrence of errors by influencing the group to accept correct information and conclusions" (p. 78). Learning how to evaluate information to prevent inferential error will be discussed in the next chapter. If one person can create problems for a group, one person can also help a group perform effectively.

GROUPTHINK: CRITICAL THINKING IN SUSPENDED ANIMATION

What are we to make of the monumental blunder at Pearl Harbor? How could this country have been caught so flat-footed that infamous morning of December 7, 1941? There were ample warnings that Japan was preparing for a massive military operation. On November 27, 1941, Admiral Stark in Washington, D.C., sent Pearl Harbor a "war warning" predicting an attack from the Japanese somewhere "within the next few days" (as cited in Janis, 1982, p. 75). Since Pearl Harbor was not specifically cited as a likely target for the Japanese attack, however, the warning was discounted. No special reconnaissance was ordered to provide a sufficient alert that Japanese aircraft carriers were steaming toward Pearl Harbor. Two army privates spotted large unidentified aircraft on a radar screen heading toward Pearl Harbor an hour before the actual attack. They reported this to the Army's radar center. Again, the information was discounted. Patrols encountered hostile submarines in advance of the bombings. No action was taken.

As Vice Admiral William S. Pye testified after the disaster, with even 10 minutes warning, the Japanese airplanes could have been shot down before inflicting much damage on our vulnerable fleet. Incredibly, no alert was even sounded until the bombs were actually exploding. Eight battleships, three cruisers, and four other ships were sunk or damaged. More than 2,000 men were

The sinking of the USS Arizona with its huge loss of life during the Japanese attack on Pearl Harbor was the tragic result of groupthink.

killed and at least as many were wounded or missing. Pearl Harbor was our worst military disaster. How could it have happened?

Focus Questions

1. What causes groupthink?
2. Do groups have to display all the symptoms of groupthink to exhibit poor quality decisions that accompany full-blown groupthink?

Definition

Sociologist Irving Janis (1982), who has extensively analyzed decision-making debacles, argues that Pearl Harbor, the Bay of Pigs fiasco, Watergate, the escalation of the Vietnam War, and other blunders of recent U.S. history sprang from a defective decision-making process he calls groupthink. Janis defines **groupthink** as "a mode of thinking that people engage in when they are deeply involved in a cohesive in-group, when the members' strivings for unanimity override their motivation to realistically appraise alternative courses of action" (p. 9).

Cohesiveness and its companion, concurrence-seeking, are the two central features of groupthink. Janis does not argue that all groups that are cohesive and seek agreement among its members exhibit groupthink. These are necessary but not sufficient conditions for groupthink to occur (Mullen et al., 1994). Obviously, a noncohesive group can spend most of its time and energy on social upheaval, diverted from task accomplishment, and cohesiveness in a group can be a very positive factor (Miranda, 1994).

Groupthink is rooted in *excessive* cohesiveness and a resulting pressure to present a united front to those outside of the group. The more cohesive a group is, the greater is the danger of groupthink. This is especially true as the size of the group increases (Mullen et al., 1994). Critical thinking and effective decision making are sacrificed when members are *overly concerned* with reaching agreement, avoiding conflict, and preserving friendly relations in the group. A study (Cole, 1989) of 275 members of high-level management teams at 26 major U.S. companies by Robert Lefton and V. R. Buzzotta of Psychological Associates, Inc., found that 19% of the team members carried on business by "not making waves" and another 9% revealed that their teams preferred getting along instead of getting things done.

Wood and her associates (1986) point out that groupthink is "a result of system forces that arise out of the interaction among members" (p. 103). No group member has to squash dissent openly. The concurrence-seeking norm is so firmly established in the group system that critical faculties are often paralyzed seemingly without notice. Frequently, members fail to see issues that should be challenged, positions that should be questioned, and alternatives that should be explored. Even if they do recognize such problems, they choose to go along in order to get along.

Groupthink is not the cause of every decision-making fiasco. Information overload or underload, mindsets, collective inferential error, and sometimes the plain stupidity of decision makers may be primarily responsible for blunders. As Janis (1982) argues, however, groupthink often is a contributing cause and sometimes is a primary cause. In this next section, I will summarize some of the evidence that supports the Janis groupthink explanation for abominably bad group decision making.

Identification of Groupthink

How do you recognize groupthink? Janis lists eight specific symptoms of groupthink, which he then divides into three types. I will discuss the eight symptoms within the context of these three types.

Overestimation of the Group's Power and Morality   Repeatedly, the main decision makers associated with the Pearl Harbor debacle communicated a sense of invulnerability. Pearl Harbor was thought to be impregnable, much as the French Maginot Line was thought to be an impenetrable defense until the Germans in World War II proved that to be a laughable notion. The U.S. command in Pearl Harbor ridiculed the idea of a Japanese attack. Torpedo planes were discounted because U.S. torpedoes required a water depth of at least 60 feet to function and Pearl Harbor had a 30-foot depth. Little consideration was given to the possibility that the Japanese had developed a torpedo capable of striking a target in shallow water. The <u>illusion of invulnerability</u> exhibited by the fleet command at Pearl Harbor exploded with nightmarish rapidity.

The U.S. sense of higher moral purpose contributed to the Bay of Pigs invasion. The purpose, after all, was to upend a communist dictator and free the Cubans. The Iran-Contra affair was partially the result of an excess of moral righteousness. The Reagan administration was trying to secure the release of the hostages. Sometimes you have to engage in unsavory dealings (so went the logic), such as trading arms for the hostages, when your purpose is righteous. This <u>unquestioned belief in the inherent morality of the group</u> is symptomatic of groupthink.

Closed-Mindedness   Closed-mindedness is manifested by <u>rationalizations</u> that discount warnings or negative information that might cause the group to rethink its basic assumptions. David Stockman (1986), Ronald Reagan's budget director from 1981 to 1985, cites just such an instance of rationalization. In November 1981, as the country was sliding into a recession destined to be the most severe since the Great Depression, the president met with his advisors on the budget. Having been convinced that the "Reagan Revolution" was headed toward a balanced budget, you can imagine the consternation when the economy didn't cooperate as predicted. The Office of Management and Budget predicted huge budget deficits, reaching a high of $146 billion in 1984 alone. Even the "optimistic" budget forecasts of the Department of the Treasury showed a 1984 deficit of $111 billion.

When this gloomy news was communicated to President Reagan, according to Stockman, "the words he found most soothing were those of his Treasury Secretary" (p. 373). Reportedly, Donald Regan's soothing words were a rationalization encouraging the president to accept what was later dubbed the rosy scenario—a set of economic forecasts built on wishful thinking, not on sound economic calculations and assumptions. Regan said, "Mr. President, your program has only been in effect 33 days. Let's not write it off yet. There's no reason for all the gloom and doom. We at the Treasury think these figures are too pessimistic. They assume your tax cut isn't going to work" (p. 373). Little corrective action was taken. The federal government accumulated deficits even *larger* than what was predicted by the pessimists.

Another aspect of closed-mindedness leading to groupthink is <u>negative stereotyped views of the enemy</u> as weak, stupid, puny, or evil. This characterization helps justify the recklessness of the group. The Japanese were characterized as a "midget nation" by the command at Pearl Harbor. Lyndon Johnson reputedly characterized the North Vietnamese during the war in this racist fashion: "Without air power, we'd be at the mercy of every yellow dwarf with a pocket knife" (Lewallen, 1972, p. 37). President Kennedy's advisors considered Castro and his military force to be a joke. The real joke was the invasion plan that sent 1,400 Cuban exiles up against Castro's military force of 200,000. Simple arithmetic should have shot down that idea.

Pressures toward Uniformity   The last type of symptom of groupthink is the pressure to maintain uniformity of opinion and behavior among group members. Sometimes this pressure is indirect and in other cases it is very direct. An indirect form is manifested when group members engage in <u>self-censorship</u>, assuming an apparent consensus exists in the group. The importance of doubts and counterarguments are minimized as a result of the perceived uniformity of opinion. Silence is considered assent, which can lead to what some have called "pluralistic ignorance." Other group members have their doubts, but everyone assumes agreement exists, no one wants to rock the boat, so no one questions or raises an objection. Thus, an <u>illusion of unanimity</u> is fostered.

The film adaptation of Tom Wolfe's bestseller *The Bonfire of the Vanities* was a $50 million box-office bomb. Many people involved in making the movie, starring Tom Hanks and Melanie Griffith, had doubts about the casting choices and changes in the storyline, but they never voiced these doubts to the director, Brian De Palma (Stern, 1992). Apparently, De Palma also had some reservations, but because no dissent was voiced, he convinced himself that he had made the correct decisions. The illusion of unanimity led to a disastrous motion picture.

In order to maintain the uniformity of the group, <u>direct pressure</u> is applied to deviants. David Stockman became the center of a cyclone when he was quoted in an *Atlantic Monthly* article by Bill Greider characterizing the tax-cut portion of Reaganomics—the Reagan administration's policy of minimalist government—as a Trojan horse: a most unflattering metaphor. Here was President Reagan's budget director seeming to expose the fantasy of achieving a balanced budget, vigorous economic growth, and minimal inflation in part by lowering taxes. The winds of controversy swirled around the White House following the Stockman admission.

Reagan's group of advisors was furious with Stockman for his apparent treason. The president's chief of staff, Jim Baker, called Stockman into his office and coldly issued the following directive:

> My friend, he started, I want you to listen up good. Your ass is in a sling. All of the rest of them want you . . . canned right now. Immediately. This afternoon. If it weren't for me, he continued, you'd be a goner already. But I got you one last chance to save yourself. So you're going to do it precisely and exactly like I tell you. Otherwise you're finished around here. . . . You're going to have lunch with the president. The menu is humble pie. . . . When you go through the Oval Office door, I want to see that sorry ass of yours dragging on the carpet. (Stockman, 1986, p. 5)

Stockman was thrashed back into line with the group. Intellectually, he was convinced that a tax cut was economic folly. In order to remain a member of Reagan's inner circle, however, Stockman was coerced into an act of public humiliation—a confession of his supposed rhetorical excesses.

Finally, uniformity is maintained by information control. <u>Self-appointed mindguards</u> protect the group from adverse information that might contradict shared illusions. The system closes off to negative influences, protecting uniformity. Once John Kennedy had decided to proceed with the ill-fated

Bay of Pigs invasion, his brother Robert dissuaded anyone from disturbing the president with any misgivings about the mission.

Dissent of group members is often suppressed or ignored. One study (Laughlin & Adamopoulos, 1980) found that in almost 75% of the cases, the one person in a six-member group who knew the correct answer to a problem was unable to convince the group because the group suppressed the divergent point of view.

A group does not have to display all the symptoms to experience the poor quality decisions that accompany full-blown groupthink. As Janis (1982) explains, "Even when some symptoms are absent, the others may be so pronounced that we can expect all the unfortunate consequences of groupthink" (p. 175). He argues that "the more frequently a group displays the symptoms, the worse will be the quality of its decisions, on the average" (p. 175).

Preventing Groupthink: Promoting Vigilance

In order to prevent groupthink, groups must become vigilant decision makers. Vigilant decision making requires several steps be taken (Janis, 1982; Wood, Phillips, & Pedersen, 1986). First, and most obvious, members must recognize the problem of groupthink as it begins to manifest itself. Knowledge is required of the competent communicator. If even a single member recognizes groupthink developing and points this out energetically to the group, the problem can be avoided.

Second, the group must minimize status differences. High-status members exert a disproportionate influence on lower-status group members. High-status leaders who use strongly directive leadership styles are particularly problematic (Street, 1997). The resulting communication pattern is one of deference to the more powerful person (Milgram, 1974). Such deference can produce ludicrous, even disastrous consequences.

Michael Cohen and Neil Davis (1981), Temple University pharmacy professors and authors of *Medication Errors: Causes and Prevention*, argue that the accuracy of a doctor's prescription is rarely questioned even when a prescribed treatment makes no sense. Nurses, for example, are used to being told what to do by doctors (directive leadership). They cite one comical instance of blind deference to high-status authority. A physician ordered application of eardrops to a patient's right ear to treat an infection. The physician abbreviated the prescribed treatment to read, "Place in R ear." The duty nurse read the prescription and promptly administered the eardrops where they presumably would do the most good to "cure" the patient's "rectal earache." Neither the nurse nor the patient questioned the doctor's rather unconventional treatment.

On a more serious level, airline industry officials have become alarmed at what has been dubbed "Captainitis" (Foushee, 1984). The status and decision-making authority of the flight captain make it difficult for crew members to correct obvious errors that could lead to a plane crash. One study by a major airline showed that passengers have something extra to worry about besides wind shear, metal fatigue, and baggage being sent mistakenly to the Falkland Islands. In the experiment, crews were subjected to flight simulations under conditions of severe weather and poor visibility. Unknown to the crew members, the captains feigned incapacitation, making serious errors that would lead to certain disaster. Airline officials were stunned to learn that 25% of the flights would have crashed because no crew member took corrective action to override the captain's faulty judgment. Weick (1990) claims that this contributed to the Tenerife air disaster in 1977.

Thus, status differences in groups can encourage groupthink, especially when these status differences are magnified by a directive style of leadership (Mullen et al., 1994). Of particular concern is the form of directive leadership manifested when the leader promotes one idea initially instead of seeking many ideas from members (Flippen, 1999). John Kennedy, anxious not to commit another blunder like the Bay of Pigs, instituted several new procedures for top-level decision making. One of these procedures was leaderless group discussions. On occasion, primarily during the initial stages of discussion where alternatives were being generated, Kennedy would absent himself from the proceedings. Robert Kennedy, the president's brother and close advisor, commented, "I felt there was less true give and take with the president in the room. There was the danger that by indicating his own view and leanings, he would cause others just to fall in line" (Janis, 1982, p. 142).

The group leader, as high-status member, has the primary responsibility to minimize the influence of status differences. The leader could withhold his or her point of view from the group until everyone has had an opportunity to express an opinion. As management training consultant Michael Woodruff explains, "If I present an idea as something that I am excited about, then my staff has to go against me. But if I present it neutrally, they will be more likely to speak out if they think it is wrong. Staffers will seldom criticize what the boss has endorsed" (Stern, 1992, p. 104). The high-status group member could also indicate ambivalence on an issue, thereby encouraging the open expression of a variety of viewpoints.

Seeking information that challenges an emerging concurrence is a third way to prevent groupthink. Assessing the negative consequences of choices is a mark of an effective decision-making group (Hirokawa,1985). Closely related to this, developing a norm in the group that legitimizes disagreement during discussion sessions is a final way to prevent groupthink. This norm may have to be structured into the group process. Groupthink is more likely to occur when there is no structured method in place for evaluating alternative ideas during group discussion (Street, 1997).

There are several ways to accomplish these last two ways of preventing groupthink. First, assign one or two group members or a subgroup to play **devil's advocate.** The primary group presents its proposals and arguments and the devil's advocates critique it. This process can proceed through several rounds of proposals and critiques until the group, including devil's advocates, is satisfied that the best decision has been made. This is a very effective method of overcoming the excessive concurrence-seeking characteristic of groupthink (Stasser & Titus, 1987).

Second, institute a **dialectical inquiry** (Sims, 1992). This procedure is very similar to devil's advocacy, except in dialectical inquiry a subgroup develops a counterproposal and defends it side by side with the group's initial proposal. Thus, a debate takes place on two differing proposals. One or the other may be chosen by the group, both may be rejected in favor of further exploration and inquiry before a final decision is made, or a compromise between the two proposals may be hammered out. Both devil's advocacy and dialectical inquiry are effective antidotes to groupthink, but dialectical inquiry may be slightly more effective (Pavitt & Curtis, 1994).

Third, assign a group member to play the **reminder role** (Schultz et al., 1995). This is a formally designated role. The reminder raises questions in a nonaggressive manner regarding collective inferential error, confirmation bias, false dichotomies, and any of the myriad symptoms of groupthink that may arise. The reminder role is an effective method of combating groupthink tendencies (Schultz et al., 1995).

Groupthink can be a primary source of poor decision making in groups (Hensley & Griffin, 1986; Herek et al., 1987; Leana, 1985; Moorhead & Montanari, 1986). Recognizing the symptoms of groupthink and taking steps to prevent it from occurring play an important role in any effort to improve the quality of group decisions.

---

second look

Groupthink

PRIMARY SYMPTOMS

Overestimation of Group's Power and Morality
- Illusion of invulnerability
- Unquestioned belief in the inherent morality of group

Closed-Mindedness
- Rationalizations
- Negative stereotyped views of the enemy

Pressures toward Uniformity
- Self-censorship of contradictory opinion
- Illusion of unanimity
- Direct pressure applied to deviants
- Self-appointed mindguards

PREVENTING GROUPTHINK
- Recognize groupthink when it first begins
- Minimize status differences
- Seek information that challenges emerging concurrence
- Develop norm that legitimizes disagreement

In summary, group members must exercise their critical thinking abilities. The quality of decision making and problem solving in groups is significantly affected by problems of information quantity, mindsets, inferential errors, and groupthink. If groups learn to cope with information overload and underload, recognize and counteract mindsets, avoid or correct collective inferential errors, and avoid groupthink, then decision making and problem solving will be of higher quality.

Questions for Critical Thinkers

1. Why is information overload such a problem when we have labor saving technologies such as desktop computers to process huge quantities of data?
2. Why are collective inferential errors more likely when issues are emotionally charged?
3. If cohesiveness is a positive small group attribute, why can it lead to groupthink?

Group Discussion: Effective Decision Making and Problem Solving

While Jimmy Carter was president, an incident occurred that illustrates the difficulty even the most powerful leader in the world can experience when trying to make decisions and resolve problems. A mouse that had climbed inside a wall in the Oval Office of the White House died, leaving an intolerable odor. President Carter was scheduled to meet a foreign dignitary in the Oval Office, but the smell from the dead mouse presented a real problem. The General Service Administration, which manages federal property, was called. The GSA, however, refused to handle the problem, insisting it had exterminated all mice in the White House so the dead mouse must have entered from outside. Consequently, the Department of Interior should be summoned. The Interior Department insisted that, despite its name, a mouse inside the White House was not its responsibility. Exasperated, Carter summoned the heads of both governmental departments to his office. "I can't even get a damn mouse out of my office" he complained to them. A special task force was created to solve the mouse in the White House problem (Hughes et al., 1996). Effective decision making and problem solving can be challenging.

In the previous chapter, I discussed *defective* decision making/problem solving. In this chapter, I will address the process of *effective* group decision making/problem solving. Toward this end I have four <u>objectives</u>:

1. to explain procedures for conducting productive group discussions that will result in effective decisions and solutions to problems,
2. to discuss ways to gather and evaluate information necessary for effective decision making and problem solving,
3. to explore the pros and cons of participation in the decision-making/problem-solving process and ways to encourage productive participation, and
4. to explain several techniques of creative group problem solving.

Both creativity and reasoned discourse have an important place in group discussion. <u>Competent communicators manifest flexibility by exercising both their creativity and their reasoning skills when making decisions and discovering solutions to problems.</u>

DISCUSSION PROCEDURES

In this section, guidelines and procedures for conducting effective group discussion will be presented. Special emphasis will be given to the Standard Agenda.

General Considerations

Effective decision making in groups through group discussion doesn't just happen miraculously. As you will see, there is much to consider.

Focus Questions

1. How should group members proceed systematically to engage in productive discussion?

2. How does Standard Agenda relate to the functional perspective on effective group discussion procedures?
3. What constitutes a true consensus?

Periodic Phases of Decision Emergence   The term *phase* suggests an orderly, step-by-step, one-directional development as in "phases of the moon" (i.e., the moon never travels from its half-moon back to its quarter-moon phase without first becoming full) or "phases in child development" (i.e., children never return to the terrible twos phase—for this we can be thankful). In chapter 2, I argued that group development generally does not progress in an orderly, sequential fashion from one phase to another. Phases are periodic, with stops and starts along the way. The same is true of group decision making.

The most widely accepted phasic model of group decision making is Poole's (1983) *multiple sequence model* of decision emergence. The multiple sequence model pictures groups moving along three activity tracks—task, relational, and topic. Groups do not necessarily proceed along these three tracks at the same rate or according to the same pattern. Some groups may devote a significant amount of time to the relational (social) activities of groups before proceeding to a task discussion, while other groups may start right in on the task.

Groups take three principal paths in reaching decisions (Poole & Roth, 1989a, 1989b). The first path is called the *unitary sequence*. Groups on the unitary sequence path proceed in the same step-by-step fashion toward a decision. The second path is called *complex cyclic*. These groups engage in repeated cycles of focusing on the problem, then the solution, and back again to the problem, and so forth (periodic phases). Finally, the third principal path to decision making is *solution oriented*. Here the group launches into discussion of solutions with little focus on an analysis of the problem. The complex cyclic path is chosen most frequently by groups, followed by the solution-oriented path, with the unitary sequence path used infrequently.

Poole's multiple sequence model of decision development highlights that group discussion does not necessarily proceed along a single predictable path. There are several ways that decisions occur in groups.

Functional Perspective   Discussions that follow some systematic procedure tend to be more productive and result in better decisions than relatively unstructured discussions (Hirokawa, 1985; Schultz et al., 1995). In this regard, two generalizations are supported by research. First, effective group decision making requires an analysis and understanding of a problem *before* members search for solutions (Hirokawa, 1985). The solution-oriented path to decision making does just the opposite.

Second, effective decision-making groups normally engage in creative exploration of unusual, even deviant, ideas during initial discussions (Bormann & Bormann, 1988). At some point, the group ceases generating ideas and begins focusing on which ideas are best and should be implemented. This does not mean, however, that the group never considers a new idea once the winnowing process begins. Nevertheless, there is a time for freewheeling, open-ended, creative discussion and there is a time for more organized, systematic deliberation.

Let me add that following a set of steps stipulated in a systematic discussion procedure (e.g., The Standard Agenda) in sequential rigid fashion is probably too inflexible for natural discussion to take place. The unitary sequence path is probably too rigid for most groups. Steps in any systematic discussion procedure should be looked at as guidelines, not commandments. Some allowance should be made for cycling back to steps previously addressed as group members discuss problems and solutions. The complex cyclic path to decision making does this.

There is no single systematic discussion procedure that guarantees effective decision making and problem solving. Gouran (1982) explains that you should not "assume that by simply going through a set of steps a group will automatically make a good decision. What happens at each stage and how well necessary functions are executed are the real determinants of success" (p. 30). Systematic discussion procedures work best when the group decision matters to group members and when members have received training and practice using such procedures (Pavitt & Curtis, 1994).

Hirokawa (1986) discovered that variations in the quality of decisions by groups can be accounted for by the relative ability of members to perform four critical decision-making functions. These four functions are the effective assessment of each of the following: the problem, the requirements for an acceptable choice, the positive qualities of alternative choices, and the negative qualities of alternative choices. This *functional perspective* is reflected in The Standard Agenda discussion procedures.

The Standard Agenda

John Dewey (1910) described a process of rational problem solving and decision making that he called *reflective thinking*. The Standard Agenda is a direct outgrowth of Dewey's reflective-thinking process. It is a highly effective, structured method for decision making and problem solving in groups.

Systematic Procedures   The Standard Agenda places the emphasis on the problem initially in order to counteract premature consideration of solutions. Let me briefly walk you through the six steps.

1. *Problem Identification:* Let's suppose the problem area is smoking in the college cafeteria—a problem faced on my campus. The problem should be formulated into a question identifying what type of problem the group must consider. Questions may be phrased as fact, value, or policy. The choice will identify the nature of the problem. A **question of fact** asks whether something is true and to what

extent. "Is secondhand smoke hazardous to nonsmokers?" is a question of fact. A **question of value** asks for a judgment—to what extent is something good or bad, right or wrong, moral or immoral, and so forth. "Is jeopardizing the health of nonsmokers with secondhand smoke morally justifiable?" is a question of value. A **question of policy** asks whether a specific course of action should be undertaken in order to solve a problem. "What changes should be made regarding smoking in the college cafeteria?" is a policy question. This is the question I will discuss here.

2. *Problem Analysis:* The group gathers facts, tries to determine how serious the problem is, what the harm associated with the problem is, if the harm is serious and widespread, and what causes the problem. For example, the college cafeteria is a place for students across the campus to congregate. The facility is small, not well ventilated, and has primary access through the main door that opens onto the smoking section, forcing nonsmokers to travel through a carcinogenic cloud before reaching fresh air. Smoking and nonsmoking sections exist, but smoke drifts into the nonsmoking section. Nonsmoking students complained repeatedly to their student senators about this situation. In an open hearing instituted by the Student Senate on the question, tempers flared. One student, defending the "rights of smokers," told nonsmokers to "quit school if you don't like our smoking." A student defending nonsmokers' rights vehemently retorted, "Polluters have no rights." Another nonsmoker facetiously suggested "public floggings as a penalty for smoking in the cafeteria." One note of caution here: Although analyzing the problem is important and should be undertaken before exploring potential solutions, bogging down by analyzing the problem too much can also thwart effective decision making. **Analysis paralysis** prevents a group from ever getting on with business and making a decision.

3. *Solution Criteria:* Criteria are standards by which decisions and solutions to problems can be evaluated. In the summer of 1998, the American Film Institute released its list of 100 Best American Movies. *Citizen Kane* topped the list. For most college students of today, this must seem a perplexing choice. Even those few students who have viewed the film may be scratching their heads in puzzlement. *Citizen Kane* has no real body count, the action is plodding by today's frenetic standards, and the special effects probably seem goofy compared to the blockbuster movies of today. Without knowing the criteria used by the Film Institute to judge the quality of movies, it is very difficult to understand many of the choices that made the Best 100 list and the rankings. Even if you knew the criteria used, you may still disagree with the decisions made, but at least you would have a basis for discussion. Criteria help us determine whether our decisions make sense and are likely to be effective.

The group should establish criteria for evaluating solutions *before* solutions are suggested. Not all criteria, however, are created equal. The group must consider the relevance and appropriateness of each criterion. For example, Jose da Silva, a civilian who watchdogged the police in Sao Paulo, Brazil, ran into an unexpected roadblock when he attempted to stop police killings of civilians, which had reached a hundred per month. Many civilians considered the body count to be a criterion of police competence in solving crime and they approved of eliminating rather than arresting suspects ("Sao Paulo," 1996). (A training program was introduced to dissuade police from killing suspects.) Some relevant and appropriate criteria on the smoking question might be: protect the health of nonsmokers, maintain a comfortable and attractive environment in the cafeteria for all students, cost less than $5,000, and avoid alienating either group (smokers or nonsmokers). The criteria should be ranked in order of priority. The health of students is unquestionably the most important criterion.

4. *Solution Suggestions:* The group brainstorms possible solutions without evaluating any suggestions until the best alternatives are likely to have been discovered. Some possibilities on the smoking issue include ban smoking from the cafeteria, switch smoking and nonsmoking sections, build a partition between the two sections, improve the ventilation of the smoking section, and move smokers to an adjacent lounge area away from the main entrance and closed off from nonsmokers.

5. *Solution Evaluation and Selection:* The story of a military briefing officer asked to devise a method for raising enemy submarines off the ocean floor illustrates the importance of this step. The briefing officer's solution? Heat the ocean to the boiling point. When bewildered Pentagon officials asked him how this could be done he replied, "I don't know. I decided on the solution; you work out the details." The devil is in the details. Explore *both* the merits and demerits (avoid confirmation bias) of suggested solutions. Devil's advocacy and dialectical inquiry (see chapter 6) are useful techniques for accomplishing this aspect of the Standard Agenda. Consider each solution in terms of the criteria established earlier. For instance, banning smoking satisfies the criterion "protect the health of nonsmokers" but clearly "alienates smokers." Switching smoking and nonsmoking sections may help reduce nonsmokers' contact with polluted air but wouldn't eliminate drifting smoke, and the smoking section is a much smaller area than the nonsmoking section. Thus, the criterion on comfortable environment will likely remain unmet. Building a partition between sections would protect students' health, maintain a comfortable environment, and probably wouldn't alienate either group. The cost, however, might be prohibitive and it probably would not look attractive. Moving smokers to an adjacent lounge seems, on the surface, to satisfy all the criteria, but segregating smokers from nonsmokers doesn't entirely protect the nonsmoker from secondhand smoke since nonsmokers may need to interact with smokers in the lounge for a variety of reasons. Improving the ventilation in the smoking section seems like a Band-Aid solution. None of the criteria are fully satisfied. This is a partial solution at best. Since no solution satisfied all criteria completely, how the criteria were prioritized then becomes significant. Since health of students is the top priority, my campus decided to ban smoking from the cafeteria (and eventually banned smoking from all campus locations except parking lots).

6. *Solution Implementation:* A common failing of decision-making groups is that once they arrive at a decision there is, like the backhand of an inept tennis player, no follow-through. Making the decision is one thing; implementing it is another.

Murphy's Law

In October 1999, the $125 million Mars Climate Orbiter flew too deep into the Martian atmosphere and disintegrated. A simple math error was responsible for navigating the spacecraft into a disastrously low orbit. Navigators failed to convert calculations from feet and inches (used by the contractor Lockheed Martin) into meters and millimeters (used by NASA). "That is so dumb," stated John Logsdon, director of George Washington University's space-policy institute. "There seems to have emerged over the past couple of years a systematic problem in the space community of insufficient attention to detail" (Hotz, 1999, p. 1A).

The Japanese government and nuclear experts were slow to respond to the nuclear accident in Tokaimura, Japan that occurred just hours prior to the Mars Orbiter mishap. Taisuke Sasanuma, a graduate of the John F. Kennedy School of Government, relates a conversation he had with a Kennedy School classmate who works for Japan's Science and Technology Agency that oversees nuclear power plants in Japan, "When I asked about safety training, he told me it was totally meaningless and a waste of time to discuss it. 'It is obvious that Japanese power plant systems are safe,' he told me. 'We never had a problem, so why think about it?'" (Zielenziger & Lubman, 1999, p.20A). An unidentified chief executive of Tokyo Electric Power added this, "If you assume that one [an accident] might happen, that will only make people scared. So we try not to generate people's fear. Accidents can't happen" (p. 20A).

Murphy's Law states that anything that can go wrong likely will go wrong—somewhere, sometime. A common mistake made by groups is failure to plan for Murphy's Law to minimize the chance of error or mishap. Human error or simply bad luck must be considered. The more complex the system, the more likely serious errors can and will occur. Failure to plan for errors or unusual occurrences can be catastrophic. Imagine if Boeing built airplanes that could fly only if all engines worked perfectly. Would you want to travel on such a plane?

The enormously successful rover called Sojourner, which explored the surface of Mars in 1997, was extensively tested prior to its launch. David Gruel, an engineer assigned the task of creating any conceivable problems Sojourner might encounter, tested the rover in a "sandbox" that simulated the surface of Mars. The Sojourner team needed to know in advance whether the rover could meet any difficulty it might face. Gruel and his team took into account Murphy's Law. Sojourner passed every test in the sandbox. Expected to operate for about a week, Sojourner explored the Mars surface and gathered data for almost 3 *months* and covered more than 10 times the territory anyone thought possible (Shirley, 1997).

During the solution evaluation and selection phase of discussion, groups should address possible mishaps and mistakes. Backup plans and emergency procedures should be developed. By doing so, likelihood of success, while not guaranteed, is certainly markedly improved. At worst, the consequences of actual mishaps are minimized.

Questions for Thought

1. Can you provide examples of group decision-making errors that could have been avoided or minimized had the group accounted for Murphy's Law?
2. Is planning for what might go wrong with a decision or plan the group wants to implement always a good idea?

Problems of Implementation The problems associated with implementation of small-group decisions spring from the natural resistance of human beings to change. Social philosopher Eric Hoffer titled one of his books *The Ordeal of Change*. Change does not come easily to most of us. Surgeons at one time would perform operations on one patient after the next without washing their hands or sterilizing instruments. Even when it was shown that surgeons who washed thoroughly, changed their surgical aprons, and cleansed all instruments before operating had more patients that survived surgery, the sterile operating room was slow to catch hold, especially with older surgeons.

The keyboard on most computers is called a QWERTY after the first six letters on the upper left side. The QWERTY arrangement of keys was originally designed to *slow* the typist because mechanical keys on typewriters would jam if typing was too rapid. There are several keyboard configurations superior to the QWERTY, and modern computer keyboards can handle typing speed many times faster than the ordinary typist can tap the keys, but QWERTY remains the standard keyboard nonetheless (Aguayo, 1990).

Change poses risks. Playing it safe may seem like the wisest choice for a group, yet no system can stand still. Change is ubiquitous and inevitable. Every system must learn to adapt to change, which requires overcoming resistance to change.

Five primary factors influence our resistance to change in a group (Tubbs, 1984). First, as noted in the last chapter, people are more likely to accept change when they have had a part in the planning and decision making. Imposing change produces psychological reactance and therefore increases resistance to change.

Second, changes are more likely to be accepted if they do not threaten the security of group members. When management at colleges and universities start talking about "program review," faculty often become alarmed. In the past, this process has frequently served as a mechanism for eliminating faculty positions. In the context of a threat, changes suggested by a program review committee will likely be stubbornly resisted.

Third, changes are more likely to be accepted when the need for change affects individuals directly. Discovering for yourself that change is required is more convincing than having someone else tell you it is so. Candy Lightner started MADD (Mothers Against Drunk Driving) after her daughter was killed by a drunk driver. MADD chapters have sprung up all over the country, usually composed of individuals who have suffered the loss of a loved one from an accident caused by a drunk driver.

Fourth, there will be less resistance to change when the change is open to revision and modification. Since there is no room for revision or modification in the complete abstinence school of alcoholic treatment, alcoholics usually have to hit bottom before they will join Alcoholics Anonymous because treatment calls for total lifelong sobriety.

Finally, the three factors (degree, rate, and desirability) affecting a group's ability to adapt to change in a system also affect resistance to change. For instance, individuals often resist changing their eating habits because dieting seems like such a huge alteration in lifestyle and most diets relegate their victims to a lifetime of grazing on rabbit food. Facing a diet of foods that taste like cardboard is discouraging. The first three letters of the word diet are, after all, D-I-E. Some people would rather die than diet because the change is too great (degree), it requires a sudden alteration in lifestyle (rate), and it is perceived as wholly unpleasant (desirability). This is why Weight Watchers groups emphasize that members can eat well and enjoy great food while losing weight gradually.

When the five conditions above are not met, resistance to change and difficulty implementing a group's decisions increase. Overcoming resistance to change may be the most serious problem groups face once decisions have been made.

second look

The Standard Agenda

Six Steps
- Problem identification
- Problem analysis
- Solution criteria
- Solution suggestions
- Solution evaluation and selection
- Solution implementation

Overcoming Resistance to Change (Solution Implementation)
- Participation in group planning and decision making reduces resistance
- Change is more easily accepted if it does not threaten security of group members
- Change is more easily accepted when need for change affects group members directly
- There is less resistance to change when change is open to revision and modification
- Small changes (degree), implemented over time (rate), that are viewed positively (desirability) reduce resistance

PERT   **PERT** (Program Evaluation Review Technique) is a decision-making method that stipulates systematically how to implement small group decisions. The steps in the PERT method are:

1. Determine what the final step should look like (e.g., a no smoking policy for the cafeteria will be instituted).
2. Specify any events that must occur before the final goal is realized (e.g., the Board of Trustees must endorse the Student Senate decision on banning smoking in the cafeteria).
3. Put the events in chronological order (e.g., secure the support of the college president before going to the board for endorsement).

4. If necessary, construct a diagram of the process in order to trace the progress of implementation (useful only if there are numerous steps).
5. Generate a list of activities, resources, and materials that are required between events (e.g., hold a strategy session before student senators meet with the president to gain endorsement).
6. Develop a time line for implementation. Estimate how long each step will take.
7. Match the total time estimate for implementation of the solution with any deadlines (e.g., end of school year approaching). Modify your plan of action as needed (e.g., take any appointment time available with president that will move along the process).
8. Specify which group members will have which responsibilities.

Group Decision-Making Rules

Decision making is guided by rules. As I stated earlier, rules help groups achieve their goals. They foster stability and reduce variability in a system. The three principal decision-making rules are majority, minority, and unanimity rules. Any of these decision-making rules can be applied to the Standard Agenda format.

Majority Rule   No one should be surprised that majority rule is a popular method of decision making in the United States because the U.S. democratic po-

Some group decisions should not be made by majority rule. Surgical decisions are usually made by minority rule; that is, by the chief surgeon who is the designated authority.

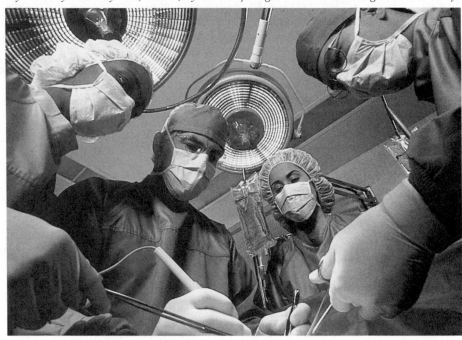

litical system relies on it. Majority rule in groups, however, is not exactly the same as majority rule in our political system. Minorities are protected by the Bill of Rights. Congress is guided by the realization that legislation must not violate constitutional guarantees of individual liberties. Most small groups provide no similar protection for minorities.

Studies comparing juries using the unanimous decision rule and majority rule (Oregon requires a 10–2 majority and Louisiana a 9–3 split for felony convictions) found several deficiencies in majority rule applicable to most small groups (Abramson, 1994; Hastie et al., 1983). First, deliberations are significantly shorter and less conscientious. Deliberations typically end once a requisite majority is reached. Consequently, less error correction takes place, sometimes resulting in faulty decisions. Second, minority factions participate less frequently and are less influential, thereby underutilizing the group's resources. Third, jurors' overall satisfaction with the group is lower. Minorities

Majority rule can produce bigoted group decision making.

feel that their point of view is ignored and the style of deliberation is typically more combative, forceful, and bullying.

The quality of the group's decision is a particularly troublesome problem with majority rule. Majorities can sometimes take ludicrous, even dangerous positions. In 1970, the National Guard was ordered onto the campus of Ohio's Kent State University in the midst of student protests against the Cambodian invasion during the Vietnam War. At one point, the Ohio National Guard inexplicably opened fire on students. Nine students were wounded and four were killed (none of whom were involved in the protest). A public opinion poll was conducted in Kent, Ohio, following the shootings. The majority of subjects polled felt that the National Guard should have shot *more* students (Michener, 1971). Mob rule is a manifestation of the tyranny of the majority. Racism, sexism, and other bigotry in the United States have been the product of majority rule.

Despite the disadvantages of majority rule, there are some advantages. When issues are not very important, decisions must be made relatively quickly, and when commitment of all members to the final decision is unimportant, majority rule can be useful. Majority rule is efficient and provides quick closure on relatively unimportant issues. As groups become larger, majority rule may be necessary for democratic decision making to take place as consensus becomes increasingly difficult the larger the group becomes.

Minority Rule   Majorities don't always make the decisions. Minority rule as a group decision-making method occurs in several forms. First, the *group designates an expert to make the decision*. This method relieves group members from devoting time and energy solving problems. Decision by designated expert, however, is mostly ineffective. Trying to determine who is the clear expert in the group is often difficult, even impossible. Lack of group input also fails to capitalize on synergy.

Second, a *designated authority* (usually from outside the immediate group) makes the decision for the group, either after hearing discussion from group members or without their consultation. Decision by designated authority is popular in business organizations because it reinforces hierarchical power structures and it is efficient. Sometimes the group acts in an advisory capacity and sometimes not. Since the group has no ultimate authority, however, this method of decision making has drawbacks.

The quality of the designated authority's decision will depend a great deal on how good a listener he or she is. If the group discussion is merely a formality, then none of the benefits of group discussion will accrue. Since power is unevenly distributed, group members are likely to vie competitively for attention and seek to impress the authority (Johnson & Johnson, 1988). Members will be tempted to tell the authority what he or she wants to hear, not what should be said. If the authority encourages genuine disagreement and in no way penalizes members for their honesty, however, he or she can benefit enormously from a dialectical clash of ideas.

Third, in some instances, *executive committees* must be delegated responsibility for making certain decisions because the workload for the group as a whole is overwhelming or the time constraints are prohibitive. The challenge here is to persuade the group to get behind the decision.

Finally, minority rule can take the form of a *forceful faction* making a decision for the group by dominating less forceful members. On rare occasions this may be advisable when the minority faction consists of the most informed, committed members. Too often, however, dominant group members who flex their muscles focus on personal gain more than on what's good for the group (Murnighan, 1978).

Unanimity Rule (Consensus)

The unanimity rule governs some groups. Juries are the most obvious example. Persuading all members of a group to agree on anything can be daunting. The most prevalent form of the unanimity rule is group consensus. Consensus is "a state of mutual agreement among members of a group where all legitimate concerns of individuals have been addressed to the satisfaction of the group" (Saint & Lawson, 1997). Not all unanimous decisions can be considered a true consensus.

<u>True consensus requires agreement, commitment, and satisfaction</u> (DeStephen & Hirokawa, 1988). All members must agree with the group's final decision, but consensus does not require adoption of every member's personal preference. Consensus usually requires some give-and-take. If all members can agree on an acceptable alternative, even if this alternative is not each members' first choice, then you have come close to achieving a true consensus. Once unanimous agreement has been reached, members must be willing to defend the decision to outsiders. This shows commitment. Finally, we rarely commit to a group decision when we have little part in formulating it. True consensus requires the opportunity to influence group discussion and choice. Thus, group members must feel satisfied with the decision-making process. Satisfaction is not derived from bullying members into conformity. Satisfaction comes from a cooperative group climate and reasonable opportunities for all members to participate meaningfully in the decision making.

Groups that use a consensus approach tend to produce better decisions than groups using other decision rules because full discussion of issues is required, every group member must be convinced that the decision is a good one, and minority members will be heard. Members feel more confident about the correctness of their decisions with consensus and they are more satisfied with the group as a whole (Abramson, 1994; Miller, 1989).

Nevertheless, there are two principal limitations to consensus decision making. First, achieving unanimous agreement from group members is very difficult, especially when the issues are emotionally charged. Discussions can become contentious and time consuming. Members who resist siding with the majority lengthen the deliberations and increase the frustration level among those looking for a quick decision. Second, consensus is increasingly unlikely as groups grow larger. Groups of 15 or 20 will find it nearly impossible to achieve a consensus on much of anything. Seeking a consensus, however, even if one is never quite achieved, can produce most of the benefits of true consensus.

FOCUS 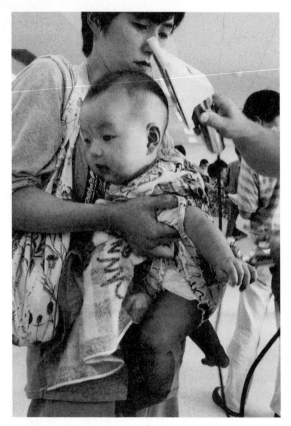 **on Culture**

Japan's Nuclear Emergency and Consensus Decision Making

September 30, 1999 saw Japan's worst ever nuclear accident. A processing plant at Tokaimura, 75 miles northeast of Tokyo, released radiation levels that were 20,000 times the normal rate (Watson et al., 1999). Three workers were severely injured and 69 other people, mostly workers, were exposed to significant doses of radiation ("Uranium Crew," 1999). Potentially catastrophic effects were avoided only because the amount of fissionable material was small and radioactive particles were not released into the air, only radioactive isotopes with a short half-life (Efron, 1999).

What was particularly noteworthy and alarming, however, was the incredibly slow response by nuclear officials and the government to the emergency. Prime Minister Keizo Obuchi wasn't informed about the emergency until an hour and a half after it occurred. Even then, an emergency crisis management team wasn't established for nearly 11 hours (Zielenziger & Lubman, 1999). Citizens living in close proximity to the plant were making calls from pay phones, shopping in a nearby convenience store, or standing in the radioactive drizzle ignorant of the danger.

Why was the response so slow? This is not the first emergency that Japanese officials have been slow to address. "Be it a massive earthquake in Kobe, the surprise launch of a missile by North Korea over Japan's airspace, the breakup of a Russian oil tanker on Japan's northwest coast, or Thursday's nuclear accident, Japanese have grown weary, not to mention wary, of a government unable to respond crisply and decisively to national crises" (Zielenziger & Lubman, 1999, p. 20A). Takao Toshikawa, a political commentator in Japan, notes, "We have a habit of being not very decisive on serious issues involving security, a crisis or even diplomacy" (Zielenziger & Lubman, 1999, p. 20A).

One suggested reason for the slow response is "the cultural preference for the slow process of

A five-month-old is held by her mother as she is checked for radiation following the October, 1999, nuclear accident in Tokaimura, Japan. Slow decision making from government officials exposed Japanese citizens to a potentially serious health hazard.

making decisions by consensus, rather than valuing decisive leadership" (Zielenziger & Lubman, 1999, p. 20A). This highlights an important limitation of consensus decision making. In times of crisis where quick, decisive action must be taken to avert catastrophe, deciding by group consensus is inappropriate. Lives can be lost while groups discuss, debate, and strive for unanimity. Steven Vogel, a political scientist and specialist on Japan at the University of California-Berkeley explains that consensus decision making works well for Japan when long-term policy is devised, but it works poorly in a crisis situation. "When a policy decision is made, everyone is on board and implementation tends to be more effective because all sides know about it and are in agreement," says Vogel. "In that sense, the Japanese system is highly efficient. But when you have a crisis, the same decision procedures that work well for more routine long-term policy changes become totally ineffective" (Lubman, 1999, p. 21A).

Questions for Thought

1. Can you think of any crisis situation where consensus decision making might be appropriate and effective?
2. Has the United States government ever been slow to respond to a crisis situation? If so, what was the reason for the slow response since the United States generally favors majority rule, not consensus?

Achieving consensus in groups is not easy; sometimes it is impossible. Consensus seeking is time-consuming and can be tension-producing. Several guidelines, however, can help a group achieve a consensus (Hall & Watson, 1970; Saint & Lawson, 1997).

1. *Follow the Standard Agenda.* Structured group discussion, not aimless conversation, improves the chances of achieving consensus.
2. *Establish a cooperative group climate.* Supportive patterns of communication encourage consensus; defensive patterns discourage consensus.
3. *Identify the pluses and minuses of potential decisions under consideration.* Write these positives and negatives on a chalkboard, large tablet, or transparency so all group members can easily see them. (Avoid confirmation bias.)
4. *Discuss all concerns of group members and attempt to resolve every one.* Try to find alternatives that will satisfy members' concerns. (Avoid groupthink.)
5. *Avoid adversarial, win–lose arguments.* Don't stubbornly argue for a position to achieve a personal victory. Seek ways to break a stalemate. (Avoid "enemy–friend" competitive false dichotomy.)
6. *Request a "stand aside."* A **stand aside** means a team member continues to have reservations about the group decision but, when confronted, does not wish to block the group choice. (Avoid the blocker role.)
7. *Avoid conflict-suppressing techniques such as coin flipping and swapping* ("I'll support your position this time if you support mine next time"). The primary objective is to make a high-quality decision, not avoid conflict. Seek differences of opinion. Conflict-suppressing techniques also will not usually produce commitment to the group decision. (Resist groupthink.)
8. *If consensus is impossible despite these guidelines, seek a supermajority* (a minimum two-thirds agreement). A supermajority at least captures the spirit of consensus by requiring substantial, if not total, agreement.

Some individuals complain that the Standard Agenda and the consensus method are rational approaches to decision making. Unfortunately, they argue, groups do not act in strictly rational ways (Conrad, 1990; Fisher and Ellis, 1990). This is true. Nevertheless, as Hirokawa (1988) has verified, the

CLOSER LOOK

The People vs. Juan Corona

On May 20, 1971, sheriff's deputies uncovered a body in an orchard near Yuba City, California. In the next two weeks, twenty-five victims were unearthed. All had been savagely mutilated by a knife or meat cleaver-type weapon. On May 26, 1971, before all the bodies were discovered, Juan Corona, a labor contractor, was arrested. He was eventually charged with all twenty-five murders.

Victor Villasenor (1977), in a remarkable book, *Jury: The People vs. Juan Corona*, reconstructed the jury deliberations by painstakingly interviewing all twelve jurors. Since jury deliberations are conducted behind closed doors, how juries arrive at a consensus verdict is difficult to know. Villasenor provides the most thorough account ever attempted of a jury engaged in the often-contentious process of arriving at a unanimous determination of guilt or innocence. Several aspects of effective group decision making are illustrated by the jury in the Juan Corona trial.

A juror named Ernie Phillips, highly talkative and the first to speak, was nominated and appointed foreman almost immediately. Ernie proved to be a capable leader. Information overload was the initial problem facing the jury. The task of sorting through testimony on twenty-five separate murders from 117 witnesses and thousands of pieces of evidence presented over a 5-month period was daunting. To compound the problem, all jurors agreed that the prosecution's case was mistake-ridden, confusing, complex, and totally circumstantial. There were no eyewitnesses and no one had reported any of the murdered persons as missing.

Ernie immediately established rules of discussion so no one would monopolize and dominate conversation. Then the jury brainstormed possible procedures for tackling the voluminous evidence. After a lengthy period of discussion, jurors agreed to organize their deliberations victim by victim.

Criteria for weighing the evidence were established by specific instructions read to the jury by the judge. The criteria for a verdict of guilty was innocent unless proven guilty, beyond a reasonable doubt, and to a moral certainty. The Corona jury continually returned to these criteria throughout their deliberations as Standard Agenda requires. For instance, in the latter stages of the process, a juror named Rick argued forcefully for a guilty verdict on the basis of the reasonable doubt criterion. Here is some of what he said: "What I'm trying to say, simply, is that we have no more doubts that are reasonable. We only have doubts that are possible, or imaginary, or in the realm of speculation, and we're not supposed to go that far . . . because we're supposed to follow the law, the Judge's instructions, and be reasonable" (p. 234).

The jury properly discussed procedures and criteria for decision making before discussing outcomes (a verdict). In fact, the jury resisted taking a vote the first day of deliberations before reviewing the evidence. The judge had warned against premature commitment to a verdict before a fair discussion had taken place. On the second day, the jury took its first vote by secret ballot. There were seven for innocent and five for guilty.

Repeatedly, jurors resisted the temptation to fall victim to collective inferential error. Every time assumptions and speculation occurred, at least one juror would call attention to the unwarranted inferences and the potential for faulty decision making. For instance, Naomi, destined to be a lone holdout, at one point drifted into dangerous inferential territory when she said: "I got one thing to say. If Corona is so guilty, then why didn't the sheriff himself ever testify? Ah, why didn't the sheriff come and tell us that he knows Corona is guilty?" Donald Rogers, another juror, shot back the answer: "Because that's not evidence! That would be hearsay!"(p. 149).

When individual jurors wondered aloud why Corona never took the witness stand, why there was no case presented for the defense, and why Corona looked startled when a witness named Pervis came to testify, at least one juror reminded everyone that this did not constitute evidence in a murder trial. Drawing any conclusions regarding Corona's guilt from these observations would require questionable inferences. The group performed an error-correction function admirably.

Not surprisingly, obtaining a consensus was the most difficult part of the 8 days of deliberations. When the decision is important and the emotions run strong, achieving a consensus can be torturous. Tempers flared. Conversations were not always polite. Sometimes jurors screamed at each other. Rick, toward the end, shouted at Naomi, the lone remaining vote for innocent, "Dammit! It's so simple if you just follow the Judge's definition and don't go daydreaming all over the place" (p. 230). He suddenly realized he had been shaking his fist in Naomi's face. The jurors complained about little things such as someone "always smiling." When Naomi needled Donald for speculating (making questionable inferences), he angrily retorted, "I only speculated after you started speculating" (p. 182).

Despite the dissension, the weariness, and the contentiousness, the jury refused to accept a verdict unless all members were committed to the decision. <u>A true consensus is one in which, not only is there unanimous agreement, but also satisfaction with and commitment to that deci-</u>sion. Naomi seemed adamant in her resolve to acquit Corona. Apart from an occasional outburst by a juror, she was treated well despite her deviance from the group. When she asked a juror named George, "Should I tell them I'll vote their way and do it just to get it over with?" George replied, "No, you can't do that. You got to vote the way you think" (p. 254). When Naomi finally did make the guilty verdict unanimous, two other jurors named Faye and Jim insisted that Naomi's vote not be accepted unless she honestly believed that Corona was guilty. When she stated that her decision was not made because of exhaustion or for the sake of convenience, the deliberations ended.

POSTSCRIPT: On August 1, 1990, Juan Corona was refused parole by the California Board of Prison Terms. When asked if he killed twenty-five people, Corona responded, "I don't remember" (Cox, 1990). He is currently serving twenty-five concurrent life terms in Soledad State Prison in Monterey County, California.

Questions for Thought

1. True consensus requires members' satisfaction with the group process. Do you think the Corona jury was satisfied with the group process? Explain.
2. What do you think might have happened if majority rule, not consensus, had been the requirement for this jury?

---

degree to which groups satisfy the four critical functions of effective decision making in a systematic manner is of central concern. These four functions (problem assessment, criteria, merits and demerits of decisions) can be satisfied without insisting that group members become robots. Clearly, groups can be affected by nonrational influences and still reap the benefits of a systematic, rational approach to decision making, as the jury in the Juan Corona trial demonstrated. Neither the Standard Agenda nor consensus decision making guarantee quality group choices. Both do improve the likelihood of effective decisions, however, compared to groups that exhibit more haphazard, nonrational approaches.

Group Decision-Making Rules

RULES	PROS	CONS
Majority Rule		
	Quick	Minorities vulnerable to tyranny of majority
	Efficient	Quality of decision suspect
		Usually alienates minority
	Expedient in large groups	Underutilization of resources
Minority Rule		
Designated Expert	Saves time	Expertise hard to determine
		No group input
Designated Authority	Clear	Members vie for attention
	Efficient	Members vie to impress authority
Executive Committee	Divides labor	Weak commitment to decision
Forceful Faction	Faction may be informed/committed	Likely Me-not-We oriented
Unanimity Rule (Consensus)		
	Quality decisions	Time consuming
	Commitment	Difficult
	Satisfaction	Tension producing

CRITICAL THINKING AND EFFECTIVE DECISION MAKING

The gathering and evaluation of information play a significant role in small group decision making. Group members must exercise their critical reasoning abilities at every stage of the Standard Agenda in order to maximize the probabilities of effective decisions (Hirokawa, 1992). Consequently, how you go about gathering information and the critical eye you focus on information gathered should be primary concerns.

Gathering Information

The output of groups is likely to be no better than the input available to its members. Faulty or insufficient information easily produces collective inferential error.

Information gathering impinges on all six steps of the Standard Agenda. Gathering information should be a focused effort by all group members. Search for information that shows the significance of the problem, that reveals the causes of the problem, that identifies what steps have already been taken to resolve the problem, that offers suggested solutions, and that determines the advantages and disadvantages of each proposed solution.

With these specific issues in mind, <u>the group should divide the labor</u>. Some members may concentrate on certain issues while other members research different ones. The library is usually the place to start the information search. There are numerous standard references that can be enormously helpful on most topics. Let me list just a sample.

The *Readers' Guide to Periodical Literature* is the research bible for many students. There is a computer version entitled *Reader's Guide Abstracts*. There are additional periodical indexes, such as *InfoTrac Magazine Index* (current affairs, science, education, art), *Public Affairs Information Service* (journal articles and government documents), *Hispanic American Periodicals Index* (Hispanic American interests), *Index to Black Periodicals* (African American issues), and *Women's Resources International* (women's issues). Excellent guides to professional and scholarly articles include *Psychological Abstracts*, *Sociological Abstracts*, and *International Index: Guide to Periodical Literature in the Social Sciences and Humanities*.

Good sources of statistical information on a wide range of topics include the *Statistical Abstract of the United States, Facts on File, Information Please Almanac, Vital Statistics of the United States, World Almanac, Monthly Labor Review, Report of the President's Council of Economic Advisors,* and the *FBI Uniform Crime Report.* For government-related information, consult the *Monthly Catalog of United States Government Publications, The Congressional Index, Congressional Quarterly Weekly Report,* and *The Congressional Record.* For information of general interest, consult encyclopedias such as *Encyclopedia Britannica, World Book Encyclopedia,* and *Collier's Encyclopedia* as well as newspaper indexes such as *New York Times Index* and an index to your local newspaper.

For the most up-to-date information, use the Internet. Learning to use the proper search engines and focusing your search take time to master. Consult your librarian for assistance if you have no experience using the Internet. Some useful research sites on the Internet are:

http://www.trib.com/NEWS/apwire.html (Associated Press news)

http://www.nytimes.com (New York Times)

http://www.abcnews.com (ABC News)

http://www.cnn.com (CNN news, current events)

http://www.healthcentral.com (Dr. Dean Edell)

http://www.cdc.gov/ (health and disease issues)

http://www.quackwatch.com (health fraud issues)

http://www.census.gov/ (U.S. Census Bureau stats)

http://www.ed.gov/NCES/ (National Center for Education Statistics)

http://www.ciesin.org/ (International Earth Science Information Network)

http://sosig.ac.uk/ (Social Science Information)

http://law.house.gov/ (Law Library of U.S. House of Representatives) http://www.public.asu.edu/corman/infosys (International Communication Association)

http://www.apa.org (psychology)

Searching for information can be a tedious process. Remaining focused by following the suggestions I've offered will reduce the tedium and increase group efficiency.

Evaluating Information

Knowing where to find appropriate information is helpful, but group members must also know how to evaluate information. All information is not created equal. There are <u>five criteria for evaluating information</u>.

1. **Credibility.** Is the information believable and reliable? <u>When the source of your information is biased (gains something by taking certain positions)</u>, credibility is low. The Quaker Oats company sponsored studies that reported reduction in cholesterol from eating oat bran contained in its cereals. The reduction was a paltry 3% but manufacturers began adding oat bran to nacho chips, toothpaste, and beer to cash in on the illusory health benefit claimed by a biased source. Then there are the psychic hotline wars on TV. Individuals with dubious credentials battle over whose psychics are legitimate and whose are fakes, begging the credibility question: Are *any* phone psychics legitimate? Cash-conscious, self-proclaimed seers who make vague predictions about people's lives after fleeting interactions over the phone hardly seem credible. In January 2000, Ruth Reinecke, an official of the Human Resources Administration of New York City revealed that the city's welfare department was recruiting welfare recipients to work from home as phone psychics for the Psychic Network. Fifteen recipients had been placed and more would be. Qualifications for the job did not include psychic powers (Bernstein, 2000). And do you ever hear how often these phone psychics make incorrect predictions (re-emphasizing the need to combat confirmation bias)? Credible evidence for the existence of legitimate phone psychics is still lacking—and I predict that this will not change in the foreseeable future.

   <u>Authorities quoted outside of their field of expertise are also not credible</u>. Iben Browning predicted a major earthquake for December 3 and 4, 1990, along the New Madrid Fault located in the Midwest. Schools in several states were dismissed during these two days as a result of his prediction. Was Browning a credible expert on earthquakes? He had a doctorate in physiology and a bachelor's degree in physics and math. He was the chief scientist for Summa Medical Corp. He studied climatology in his spare time. Earthquake experts around the country repudiated Browning's predictions. He was not a credible source since his earthquake predictions were not in his field of expertise. (As you undoubtedly know, his predictions were wrong.)

   Let me also note here that <u>the Internet itself is not a credible source</u>. The Internet is merely a search vehicle for finding information. There is garbage galore on the Internet. As a critical thinker, you must separate the gems from the garbage. Quoting the Internet as your source is tantamount to quoting the radio.

2. **Currency.** <u>Information should be as up-to-date as possible</u>. What used to be taken as fact may be called into question with new information. Only a few years ago cholesterol levels below 300 were thought to pose no significant risk of heart disease. Now, the current advice calls for cholesterol levels below 200, and a 150 level is preferred in order to keep heart disease risk low. Currency is especially important when an event or situation is volatile and likely to change rapidly. Quoting last month's or even last week's stock prices could leave you a pauper if you act on such dated information. Interest rates on home mortgages change daily. You must have current rates before you decide to lock in a fixed-rate mortgage on a house you're purchasing.

3. **Relevance.** <u>Information should actually support claims made</u>. Groups opposed to gun control repeatedly argue that only a tiny fraction of all the guns owned in America are ever used to commit violent crimes. If someone is a gun collector and owns a hundred guns but uses only one to kill you, are you any less dead? Showing the percentage of homicides where a gun was the weapon used is relevant information to make a claim for or against gun control. Citing the percentage of the American arsenal used in homicides is irrelevant.

4. **Representativeness.** A single example or statistic may or may not accurately reflect what is true in a particular instance. If a vivid example (e.g., testimonial from a victim of black lung disease on the health risks of mining coal) illustrates the truth of a claim already supported by solid scientific evidence, then it is representative and provides dramatic impact to the claim. If, however, a claim rests solely on a few or even many examples, then a real question of representativeness exists. Examples to support a claim may be selectively chosen (confirmation bias), so they may not reflect what is true generally.

    There are two principal guidelines for determining whether statistics are representative. First, <u>the sample size (in polls, surveys, and studies) must be adequate</u>. This can be determined most easily by the *margin of error*, which is the degree of sampling error accounted for by imperfections in selecting a sample. As the margin of error increases, the representativeness of the statistic decreases. If the margin of error reaches more than plus or minus 3%, the representativeness of the statistic becomes questionable. A study ("Pre-employment," 1990) of 103 California companies testing job applicants for drug use revealed that 17.8% of the applicants tested positive. The margin of error, however, was 7.8%. Thus, the results are questionable since the true level of drug use among the job applicants may have been 10% (17.8% minus 7.8% margin of error) or 25.6% (17.8% plus 7.8% margin of error) and still fall within the sampling error rate. The drug use problem may be substantially overstated or understated by the 17.8% statistic.

    A second guideline for assuring representative statistics is that <u>the sample must be randomly selected, not self-selected</u>. A *random sample* is a part of the population drawn in such a manner that every member of the entire population has an equal chance of being selected. A *self-selected sample* is one in which the most committed, aroused, or otherwise atypical parts of the population studied are more likely to participate.

    The 1999 Iowa straw poll for the GOP presidential nomination was an unrepresentative self-selected sample. The 25,000 voters who turned up to cast their ballot each had to pay $25 to do so. Candidates literally bought votes by paying individuals' travel costs, providing free entertainment and food, and in some cases paying the $25 entrance fee. Candidate Steve Forbes paid about $400, on average, for each vote he received ("Straw Strategy," 1999). Candidate John McCain refused to participate because the straw poll was "meaningless."

5. **Sufficiency.** When do you have enough information to support your claims? There is no magic formula for sufficiency. Determinations of sufficiency are judgment calls. Nevertheless, there are some guidelines for making such a determination.

First, <u>what type of claim are you making</u>? Causal relations require more evidence than a single study. In January 2000, results of a study showed that men with significant hair loss on the crown of their heads had a higher risk of heart attack than men with hair loss on the front of their heads. One study is insufficient to establish a causal relationship, so no conclusion can be drawn from this study. Claiming that violence depicted on television "may contribute" to antisocial behavior, however, requires less stringent criteria for sufficiency since only a weak connection is claimed.

Second, <u>extraordinary claims require extraordinary proof</u> (Abell, 1981). When a claim contradicts a considerable body of research and knowledge, extraordinary proof must accompany such a claim. A claim that Earth has been visited by extraterrestrials requires much more evidence than a few alleged sightings. Claims of cancer cures must be rigorously tested. The claims are extraordinary, so they require more than ordinary, commonplace evidence. Ordinary claims, however, such as "flu viruses pose a serious health hazard to the elderly" can be demonstrated sufficiently with one authoritative statistic from the Center for Disease Control. (See Appendix B for additional relevant material on critically examining information and claims.)

PARTICIPATION

Does involvement by all members of the group inevitably lead to quality decision making and problem solving? In the next section, I will discuss the pros and cons of participation in the decision-making/problem-solving process.

Focus Questions

1. In what ways is communication competence central to the issue of how much participation in group decision making/problem solving is useful?
2. Which group members should be encouraged to participate and which should not?

Pros and Cons of Participation

<u>Involving group members in the decision-making process, especially when the decisions affect their lives directly, can be very beneficial.</u> Participating in decision making has three advantages (Johnson & Johnson, 1991). First, participation increases members' allegiance to the group because they feel they are active

and valued contributors. Second, participation improves the quality of the decisions because the full resources of the group are utilized. Third, participation increases the commitment of group members to implementing decisions once they have been made because members all had a say in the decision and the result was not imposed on them from the outside.

FOCUS on Culture

Cultural Diversity and Participation in Small Groups

One of the significant challenges facing teachers in an increasingly multicultural educational environment is how to increase the participation level in class of some ethnic minority students. Japanese students, for example, initiate and maintain fewer conversations and are less apt to talk in class discussions than are other students (Ishii et al., 1984). This reticence to participate verbally in class carries over to small-group situations. Contributions to group decision making by ethnic minorities are consistently lower than non-minorities (Kirchmeyer, 1993). In 76% of the small groups in one study (Kirchmeyer & Cohen, 1992), the member who contributed the least was Asian.

Why is there this difference in verbal participation in small-group decision making? First, the value of verbal participation in decision making is perceived differently from culture to culture. As already noted, silent individuals are not seriously considered for the role of leader in American culture. Speaking is highly valued in the United States. Silence is not prized. Americans usually interpret silence in mostly negative ways: as indicating sorrow, critique, obligation, regret, or embarrassment (Wayne, 1974). Talking in an individualist culture is a way of showing one's uniqueness (Samovar & Porter, 1995).

In collectivist cultures and subcultures, by contrast, speaking is not highly prized. Students from collectivist cultural traditions typically see speaking too much in class as a sign of conceit and superficiality (Samovar & Porter, 1995). Among the Japanese, Vietnamese, Cambodians,

and Chinese, emphasis is given to minimal vocal participation. The Chinese have a proverb that states, "Those who know do not speak; those who speak do not know" (Lewis, 1996). Inagaki (1985) surveyed 3,600 Japanese regarding their attitude toward speaking. He found that 82% agreed with the saying, "Out of the mouth comes all evil" (p. 6). For the Japanese "silence is considered a virtue as well as a sign of respectability and trustworthiness" (McDaniel, 1993, p. 19). In business negotiations, Japanese, Chinese, and Koreans are more at ease with long pauses and silences than are Americans. As Andersen (1985) explains, "Cultures reflecting Buddhist tradition hold that knowledge, truth, and wisdom come to those whose quiet silence allows the spirit to enter" (p. 162). Many Native Americans equate silence with a great person (Samovar & Porter, 1995). Johannesen (1974) claims that the Native American "derives from silence the cornerstone of character, the virtues of self-control, courage, patience, and dignity" (p. 27).

Second, a relative disadvantage in ability to communicate effectively in groups limits verbal participation of ethnic minorities. Minorities report considerably less facility for communicating with others in a college setting (Kirchmeyer, 1993). Not only are ethnic minorities at a distinct disadvantage if English is their second language, but they are at a disadvantage during group discussions dominated by members who are more aggressive and less concerned about other group members (Kirchmeyer, 1993, p. 142).

Third, lackluster participation from ethnic minorities in decision making may result from weak commitment to the group. Weak commitment may result from group members' failure to indicate that participation from minorities is valued, or cultural differences with members of the dominant culture may make minorities feel less like they belong in the group (Kirchmeyer & Cohen, 1992).

If tapping the resources of cultural diversity is an important group goal, and this would seem to be significant given the synergistic potential inherent in diversity (McLeod et al., 1996), then finding ways to boost the verbal participation rates of ethnic minorities in an American culture that values speech is a worthy undertaking. The methods outlined in this chapter for encouraging constructive participation from low-contributors in general apply well to ethnic minorities.

Questions for Thought

1. Should nonminority Americans value silence as much as some ethnic minorities do?
2. Should Americans de-emphasize speaking ability?
3. Should you expect ethnic minority group members to become more assertive and outspoken participators in small groups even though this is not highly valued in their communities? Explain.

Participation, as important as it is to produce group synergy, is not the ultimate remedy for bad decision making. Enthusiastic participation by those who have demonstrated their lack of knowledge regarding the task will not improve the quality of decisions. Those who do not possess the requisite knowledge may bog down the group in worthless discussion about pointless issues. Member participation is valuable, but effective group decision making requires competent communication, not merely communication of any sort.

Increasing Constructive Participation

There are several steps that can be taken to promote constructive participation from group members. First, encourage contributions from low-participators. This is especially important for involving those ethnic minorities whose cultural values discourage assertiveness (Tang & Kirkbride, 1986). Solicit input from reticent members by asking open-ended questions of the group (e.g., "What does everyone think?"). When low-participators do offer contributions, indicate that this is valued by actively listening to what that person has to say.

Second, make issues and problems for discussion relevant to the interests of low-participators. When groups work on interesting, involving, or challenging tasks, member contributions increase (Forsyth, 1990).

Third, give low-participators responsibility for certain tasks. When individuals are designated as responsible for certain important tasks, they are less likely to sit back and wait for someone else to assume the responsibility. If low-participators believe that their efforts have an impact on the group's final decision or product, they are less likely to remain uninvolved (Kerr & Bruun, 1983).

Fourth, establish a cooperative group climate. This is particularly important for ethnic minorities from collectivist cultures who are likely to feel more comfortable and committed in such an atmosphere.

Fifth, <u>encourage devil's advocacy and dialectical inquiry</u>. These two methods of combating groupthink also encourage constructive participation from all group members. With their emphasis on stimulating a variety of ideas and opinions, fully sharing information, openly addressing differences of opinion, and carefully evaluating alternatives, devil's advocacy and dialectical inquiry substantially increase the participation of ethnic minorities (Kirchmeyer & Cohen, 1992).

 ## CLOSER LOOK

Conducting Meetings: Standard and Technological Forms of Participation

Humorist Dave Barry (1991), comparing meetings to funerals, seems to prefer funerals. He claims, "The major difference is that most funerals have a definite purpose. Also, nothing is ever really buried in a meeting" (p. 311).

Business consultant Mitchell Nash (Dressler, 1995) lists six common complaints associated with group meetings. These six complaints are as follows: there is an <u>unclear purpose</u> for the meeting, <u>participants are unprepared</u>, <u>key individuals are absent or late</u>, <u>discussion drifts</u> into irrelevant conversation on unrelated topics, <u>some participants dominate the conversation</u> and <u>stifle discussion,</u> and <u>decisions made at meetings are not implemented</u>.

John Kenneth Galbraith viewed meetings as "indispensable when you don't want to do anything." Meetings, however, don't have to be time wasters or sedatives. Whoever chairs a meeting has specific responsibilities. <u>As the chair, there are several ways that you can structure meetings to make them efficient and effective decision-making arenas</u>. First, don't call a meeting unless there is no other good alternative. If an immediate response is required, group participation is essential, participants are prepared to discuss relevant issues, and key players can be present, then hold a meeting. Disseminating information, meeting because you are scheduled to do so every Tuesday afternoon, using the meeting as an opportunity to recruit help in researching a topic, or hoping to try out new ideas on colleagues are not solid reasons to hold meetings. If these objectives can be accomplished without meeting in a group, then don't meet. One of life's little pleasures is the surprise notification, "Meeting has been cancelled."

Second, contact every participant. Indicate in a memo or e-mail what the specific purpose of the meeting is, where, when, and how long it will be held, and what materials, if any, each participant should bring to the meeting.

Third, prepare a clear agenda and distribute it to all participants 3 days or more in advance of the meeting. The agenda should list the topics of discussion (see Appendix C for sample agendas). If reading materials must accompany the agenda, make certain that they are concise and essential to the discussion. Avoid information overload.

Fourth, provide accurate information on issues discussed, clarify complex issues, correct misconceptions, and especially keep the discussion on track and on point. Aimless discussions suck the life out of meetings and cause participants to feel a little like hostages in a hijacking—captive listeners forced to endure tedious, brain-killing chatter. Do not allow any participant to be a stagehog and dominate the discussion.

Fifth, designate a specific time allotment for every discussion item. A timekeeper should be assigned at the start of each meeting. When the time on a discussion item has elapsed, the group may decide to extend the time allotment or move to the next item. Time limits establish a crisp pace for the meeting. Keep meetings as short as possible.

Sixth, reserve a few minutes at the end of the meeting to determine whether the objectives of the meeting were accomplished. If further work and discussion is deemed necessary, schedule discussion for unfinished business for the next meeting. If decisions have been made by the group, implementation of these decisions must be monitored. This is usually the chair's responsibility, but all participants have some responsibility for this.

Seventh, distribute the minutes of the meeting as soon as possible. The minutes should indicate what was discussed, who said what, what action was taken, and what remains to be deliberated and decided.

In-person meetings are what most of us are accustomed to, but there are several electronic alternatives to the standard format. The *teleconference,* commonly referred to as the conference call, is a meeting conducted over the telephone. When face-to-face meetings are expensive to convene because participants are separated by geography, the conference call is a useful option. Teleconferences are easy to set up. Most business and many residential phone services provide conference call capability. Most of the guidelines for conducting efficient and effective meetings already discussed apply to teleconferences. The conference call should be necessary, focused, organized (have an agenda), and short.

Videoconferences are more technologically sophisticated. Meetings are conducted via closed-circuit or satellite-linked television. The videoconference, similar to the teleconference, is a useful option when participants cannot meet easily in person. Videoconferences provide nonverbal cues such as facial expressions, posture, and eye contact unavailable in teleconferencing. Body language cues help participants to assess messages more accurately and they are instrumental in defining relationships between participants. The technology has become so sophisticated that virtual team members meeting by videoconferencing across several time zones begin to feel that they are all in the same room. Members will offer each other sandwiches or snacks, forgetting they're thousands of miles apart (Lipnack & Stamps, 1997). Videoconferences, as with any meeting, should be necessary, focused, organized, and short.

Electronic mail, or *e-mail meetings* are a third technological alternative to the in-person meeting. E-mail discussions take place in written form only. Messages appear on computer screens. This encourages low-status members to participate in discussions and to stand their ground more firmly on controversial or contentious issues (Sproull & Kiesler, 1991). In-person discussions can be intimidating, especially if some participants are dominating and aggressive when expressing their points of view. Typing responses on a computer keyboard can embolden reticent participants to say exactly what they are thinking.

There are also electronic aids for in-person meetings. Group Decision Support Systems (GDSS) are hardware and software options that facilitate in-person meetings. The simplest version permits participants to register votes electronically on issues discussed during meetings. This allows for anonymity. Another version of GDSS is for brainstorming ideas. Other systems can provide structure for group discussions.

<u>Despite the advantages of electronic alternatives to standard meetings, there are some drawbacks</u>. First, electronic alternatives may be cost prohibitive. Computers, satellite hookups, video cameras, hardware, and software can be expensive. There are additional costs associated with using and maintaining these electronic alternatives once they are available.

Second, one can be seduced easily into believing that technology is a quick fix for fruitless meetings. Sophisticated technologies are just complicated toys if they are not matched properly with the purposes and objectives of the group. If participants are unfamiliar with or intimidated by computer alternatives then expensive hardware will gather dust. The surest way to discourage reticent group members from participating is to conduct meetings electronically when members feel intimidated by the hardware and unskilled in the use of software alternatives. Proper training, which can be time-consuming and expensive, is necessary for optimum utilization of electronic meetings.

Third, electronic meetings may produce information overload. E-mail meetings can degenerate easily into message fatigue. Participants can be bombarded with facts, figures, opinions, and the ever-popular "attachments." The easier it is to send large amounts of information, the more information overload becomes a serious roadblock to effective decision making.

Fourth, electronic meetings usually require more planning and organization than simpler in-person meetings. Setting up equipment, having an expert standing by in case of equipment failure or glitches, and making sure that all participants are familiar with the systems they are using can produce a four-aspirin headache.

Fifth, e-mail meetings may encourage *flaming*, the indiscriminate or overzealous expression of anger or disagreement. Participants may not edit their written communication as carefully as they edit their oral communication during in-person confrontations. They may experience *rage regret* (e.g., "Why did I call my boss a lobotomized moron in need of a brain transplant?"). It is also more

difficult for participants to claim that they were misunderstood when a hard copy of their intemperate statement can be printed and disseminated.

Sixth, viewpoints and opinions may become more polarized and extreme, making consensus more difficult. The more removed participants feel from personal contact, the more this is likely to be true. This is generally true of e-mail meetings but not videoconferencing.

Electronically mediated meetings have their place. When issues are complex or ambiguous and emotions are running high, however, in-person meetings are preferred. Both in-person and electronically mediated meetings benefit from following the guidelines for efficient and effective meetings.

Questions for Thought

1. Can you think of additional advantages and disadvantages of electronically mediated meetings?
2. Do you think that we'll ever get to a time when in-person meetings will be replaced entirely with electronic alternatives? Explain.

CREATIVE PROBLEM SOLVING

Years ago, a prisoner escaped from a penitentiary in the western United States. He was recaptured after a few weeks. On his return, prison officials grilled him. "How did you cut through the bars?" they demanded. Finally, he confessed. He said he had taken bits of twine from the machine shop, dipped them in glue, then in emery. He smuggled these makeshift "hacksaws" back to his cell. For three months he laboriously sawed through the one-inch-thick steel bars. Prison officials accepted his story, locked him up, and kept him far away from the machine shop. End of the story? Not quite. Three-and-one-half years later, he escaped again by cutting through the cell bars. He was never recaptured, but how he escaped became a legend in the underworld. It seems that his original story was a phony. He hadn't fashioned a hacksaw from any materials in the machine shop. Instead, he had used woolen strings from his socks, moistened them with spit, and rubbed them in abrasive dirt from the floor of his cell, then painstakingly sawed through the cell bars (Rossman, 1931). The prisoner had fashioned a creative solution to a challenging problem. Creative problem solving is the focus of this section.

Focus Questions
1. How do imagination and knowledge relate to creative problem solving?
2. How do rational and creative problem solving relate to each other?

General Overview

The story of the prisoner's resourceful escape highlights several important points about creativity and problem solving. First, to borrow Thomas Edison's comment on genius, <u>creativity is more perspiration than inspiration</u>. We have to work to find creative solutions to problems. This means devoting time and energy to the task, not hoping for imaginative ideas to fall from the sky and clunk us on the head.

Second, <u>creativity is spurred by challenges</u>. As the old adage says, "Necessity is the mother of invention." We are creative in response to some felt need, to some problem that requires a solution. The bigger the challenge, the more complex the problem, the greater is the need for creativity.

Third, <u>creativity flourishes in cooperative, not competitive environments</u>. In a competitive atmosphere thinking "may be used to plan, strategize, and coerce rather than to problem solve and collaborate" (Carnevale & Probst, 1998, p. 1308).

Fourth, <u>creativity requires sound ideas not just imaginative ones</u>. As Vincent Ruggiero (1988) puts it, creative ideas must be more than uncommon; they "must be *uncommonly good*" (p. 77). Or, as former prime minister of Great Britain, Harold Macmillan, once sarcastically remarked: "As usual the Liberals offer a mixture of sound and original ideas. Unfortunately, none of the sound ideas is original and none of the original ideas is sound" (Metcalf, 1986, p. 148). Creative solutions are original, but they also must work.

I once heard a radio commentator read recipes submitted by children for preparing a Thanksgiving turkey. One child wrote: "Put ten pounds of butter on the turkey and five pounds of salt. Cook it for 20 minutes." M-m-m-m-m good! Some culinary concoctions just don't work. The recipes are imaginative, but repulsive, like spaghetti and liver sauce or a tofu and oyster milkshake. Alfred North Whitehead makes my point succinctly: "Fools act on imagination without knowledge; pedants act on knowledge without imagination." Creative problem solving and decision making require imagination *and* knowledge. Children create foolish things because they don't know any better. Competent communicators create solutions that are workable and effective.

Fifth, <u>creativity requires many ideas</u>. As Linus Pauling once remarked, "The best way to have a good idea is to have a lot of ideas." Although sheer quantity doesn't guarantee great solutions, the fewer the ideas, the less probable is the discovery of at least one good idea—that flower among all the thistles.

Finally, <u>creativity requires breaking mindsets and thinking "outside the box."</u> Unless we try adopting different ways of approaching problems we'll remain stuck in place.

Specific Creative Techniques

As I have emphasized already, group decision making and problem solving are usually more effective when systematic procedures are followed. Systematic procedures apply to group creativity as well (Firestein, 1990). Haphazard, unfocused efforts to induce creativity are often not as productive as more focused efforts.

Brainstorming and Nominal Group Techniques   "Encourage Wild Ideas" appears in large print on the walls of each brainstorming room, sanctuaries of creativity where product design teams composed of engineers, industrial designers, and behavioral psychologists at IDEO Product Development company fling ideas back and forth in a frenzy of mental activity (O'Brien, 1995). Faced with the problem of an electric car that is so quiet that it would likely cause accidents, the brainstormers attack the problem with relish. "How about tire treads that play music?" one team member offers. "How about a little Eric Clapton?" another chimes in, and the ideas begin to fly.

The brainstorming technique was introduced in 1939 by Alex Osborn. **Brainstorming** is a creative problem-solving technique that promotes plentiful, even zany ideas in an atmosphere free from criticism with enthusiastic participation from all group members. Rational approaches to decision making and problem solving run the danger of becoming methodical, stale, and unimaginative. Brainstorming can regenerate a group by opening up a stuffy, plodding, and inhibited group process. There are several guidelines for using this technique:

1. *Don't evaluate ideas while brainstorming.* Critiques will inhibit contributions from group members. Group members need to be self-monitoring. Idea slayers, such as "You can't be serious," "That will never work," and "It's completely impractical," should be squelched by members. Even a positive evaluation, such as "Great idea," is out of order because group members will quickly interpret absence of positive evaluation as a negative assessment of their ideas.
2. *Don't clarify or seek clarification of an idea.* This will slow down the process. Clarification can come later after a list of ideas has been generated.
3. *Encourage zany ideas.* What appears to be a dumb idea initially can provoke a really good solution to a problem. Bolton (1979) cites the example of a brainstorming session by managers of a major airport who were generating ideas regarding ways to remove snow from the runways. One participant offered the idea that snow could be removed by putting a giant frog on the control tower. The frog could push the snow aside with its enormous tongue. This zany idea provoked a practical solution—a revolving cannon that shoots a jet airstream. Even if zany ideas never trigger effective solutions to problems, they at least encourage a freewheeling, fun climate conducive to creativity.
4. *Expand on the ideas of other group members.* Halpern (1984) cites the example of a food manufacturer seeking better ways to bag potato chips. Corporate executives were asked to identify the best packaging solution they had ever seen. One

brainstormer said that bagging leaves wet was the best method. Dry leaves crumble and use up more air space. Wet leaves pack more easily and require fewer bags. Expanding on this idea, the manufacturer tried packing potato chips wet. When the potato chips dried they became tasteless crumbs. Nevertheless, from this initial failure sprang the popular potato chips in a can, in which a potato mixture is cooked in chip-shaped molds and then stacked in the can. From a bad idea came a good one.

5. *Record all ideas without reference to who contributed the idea*. Do not censor any ideas, no matter how silly they may seem as long as they are focused on the problem.

6. *Encourage participation from all group members*. The maximum number of ideas requires the maximum effort from every group member.

<u>Brainstorming normally is instituted during the solutions suggestion step of the Standard Agenda</u>. Determining the quality of the ideas generated from brainstorming comes during the solution evaluation and selection step. Ideas are evaluated in terms of solution criteria established earlier in the Standard Agenda process.

A second creative problem-solving method is **nominal group technique** (Delbecq et al., 1975). Individuals work by themselves generating lists of ideas on a problem, then convene in a group where they merely record the ideas generated (usually on a chart or blackboard for all to see). Interaction occurs only to clarify ideas, not to discuss their merits and demerits. Individuals then select their five favorite ideas, write them on a card, and rank them from most to least favorite. The rankings are averaged and the ideas with the highest averages are the ones selected by the group.

Some research has shown nominal group technique generates more and better ideas than brainstorming (Paulus et al., 1993; Valacich et al., 1994). Mongeau (1993), however, argues that "although considerable research has been performed on brainstorming, little of this research is a valid test of Osborn's ideas" (p. 22). Results have been derived from student groups that have no history together and no future, have no training and experience using the brainstorming technique (aside from a brief explanation of the rules), are provided no opportunity to research the task prior to brainstorming, are given little time to think about the task, are given tasks that are often unrelated to students' interests, and groups never actually make choices regarding which ideas are best (Kramer et al., 1997).

Brainstorming, *if done properly*, should be highly effective. Osborn actually suggested that the <u>proper brainstorming format should involve first an individual, then a group, followed by an individual brainstorming session</u>. Members should be provided with a well-defined problem a few days in advance of the group brainstorming session so members can research it and think of solutions to contribute. Then members meet as a group to share their ideas and generate new ones. After the group session, individuals are given a few days to contemplate further ideas on their own. In addition, members should not be strangers and they should belong to a long-standing (not a zero-history) group. They should also receive training and experience in how to use the brainstorming technique. Research shows that training and experience in brainstorming vastly improves idea generation (Firestein, 1990).

Electronic brainstorming occurs when group members sit at computer terminals and brainstorm ideas using a computer-based file-sharing procedure (e.g., Group Decision Support System). This offers an additional method for improving idea generation and creativity. Group members type their contributions, then send the file to a shared pool. Comments are made, ideas are added and shared with group members. This can be done anonymously if group members fear a critique. Electronic brainstorming has sometimes outperformed nominal groups in idea generation (Valacich et al., 1994).

Despite the effectiveness of electronic brainstorming, it has many of the drawbacks of electronic meetings previously discussed. First, the appropriate technology must be available. This is not always feasible or affordable. Second, electronic brainstorming requires greater, more meticulous planning and organization than does ordinary face-to-face, unmediated brainstorming. Third, some may feel electronic brainstorming is impersonal, lacking the more personal face-to-face interaction of unmediated brainstorming. Finally, electronic brainstorming may intimidate those who view technology with suspicion or even revulsion. Nevertheless, electronic brainstorming certainly offers an interesting, potentially promising method for generating creative ideas and solutions to problems.

Framing/Reframing   Consider the following problem offered by psychologists Tversky and Kahneman (1981):

> Imagine that the government is preparing for an outbreak of a rare disease that is expected to kill 600 people. Two programs are available. If Program A is adopted, then 200 people will be saved. If Program B is adopted, then there is a one-third chance that 600 people will be saved, and a two-thirds chance that nobody will be saved. Which program should be adopted?

When the problem is framed in this way, the vast majority of subjects prefer Program A over Program B. People want to avoid the risk that nobody will be saved. Now consider this statement of the problem:

> Imagine that the government is preparing for an outbreak of a rare disease that is expected to kill 600 people. Two programs are available. If Program X is adopted, then 400 people will die. If Program Y is adopted, then there is a one-third chance that nobody will die, and a two-thirds chance that 600 people will die.

When the problem is framed in this way, the vast majority of subjects choose Program Y over X. Subjects want to avoid the certainty that 400 people will die. Yet, Programs A and X have identical outcomes, as do B and Y. So why did one group predominantly choose Program A while the other group predominantly chose Program Y? The wording of the problem is identical and the outcomes are identical, yet the choices are opposite. The reason for the difference lies in how the problem is framed—the way in which it is presented.

When MBA students and managers were informed that a particular corporate strategy had a 70% chance of success, most favored it. When it was framed as a 30% chance of failure, however, the majority opposed the strategy (Wolkomir & Wolkomir, 1990). When people were presented with two options for treating lung cancer, 84% chose the surgery option when it was framed in terms of living, while 56% chose the surgery option when it was presented in terms of dying (McNeil et al., 1982).

<u>Our frame of reference can lock us into a mindset, making solutions to problems difficult if not impossible to discover</u>. Someone once said that an optimist sees the silver lining in every cloud, but the pessimist sees the cloud around every silver lining. Our frame of reference predisposes us to see the world in certain ways. This mental gridlock can block the free flow of creative ideas. Postman (1976) provides an example.

> You have the number VI. By the addition of a single line, make it into a seven. The answer is simple: VII. Now consider this problem: You have the number IX. By the addition of a single line, make it into a six.

The answer is not so obvious because of your frame of reference, which identifies the number as a Roman numeral and all lines as straight. Not until you break away from this frame of reference by reframing the problem—by no longer assuming that the answer must be in terms of a Roman numeral and that all lines are straight—will you solve the problem. Have you found the answer? How about **S**IX?

Reframing is the creative process of breaking a mindset by placing the problem in a different frame of reference (Watzlawick et al., 1974). In a photograph, the way you frame the shot determines which part of the subject will be your focus and which part will be excluded. If you cut off people's heads or have the main focus of interest off to the side, then the picture will be poor in quality. So it is with framing problems. If you cut off possibilities by framing a problem in only one way, then potentially effective solutions will be excluded from view. Frames determine whether people notice problems, how they understand and remember problems, and how they evaluate and act on them (Fairhurst & Sarr, 1996). You must consider the problem from a different frame of reference, or reframed, in order to see new solutions.

Learning to reframe problems can be a highly useful skill for the competent communicator and it is an essential part of effective leadership in groups (Fairhurst & Sarr, 1996). Reframing a dispute from a competitive exercise to a cooperative one can assist groups in finding mutually satisfactory solutions for both sides (Brett et al., 1990). Breaking through mindsets can generate creative solutions to seemingly intractable problems.

When groups become stumped by narrow or rigid frames of reference, <u>interjecting certain open-ended questions can help reframe the problem and the search for solutions</u>. My personal favorite is "What if . . . ?" The group asks, "What if we don't accept this cutback in resources as inevitable?" "What if employees really want to produce quality work but find the work environment unmotivating?" "What if we tried working together instead of against each other?" Additional reframing questions include: "Why are these the only options?" "What happens if we reject the proposal?" "How could this be turned into a win–win situation for everyone?"

Consider some examples of reframing. A service station proprietor put an out-of-order sign on a soda machine. Customers paid no attention to the sign, lost their money, then complained to the station owner. Frustrated and annoyed, the owner changed the sign to read "$2.00" for a soda. No one made the mistake of putting money in the faulty soda pop dispenser. The problem was reframed. Instead of wondering how to get customers to realize that the machine was on the fritz, the owner changed the frame of reference to one that would make customers not want to put money in the dispenser.

When a 7-Eleven store in British Columbia faced a problem of teenagers loitering in front of the store, instead of framing the problem as an issue of coercion (i.e., how to force the teenagers to stop congregating), the problem was reframed into a question—what would motivate the teenagers to leave of their own volition? Answer: The store piped Muzak into the parking lot. Loitering stopped. Was this cause and effect? It's difficult to know for sure, but as one teen put it when faced with listening to loud Mantovani recordings, "I'm out of here, dude. They want to listen to that stuff, they can have it" ("As they see it," 1990, p. 2C).

If your group is faced with a cut in resources, group members can frame this as a dispiriting event bound to adversely affect the product of members' endeavors. This situation could be reframed, however, by posing the question, "What if we accept this as a challenge to be embraced?" Breaking our mindsets is an important step in the process of creative problem solving.

One of the advantages of reframing is that <u>once a different frame of reference is presented, the mindset often is broken permanently</u>. For instance, what is the correct answer to the following problem?

Radar is to level as pup is to:

a. Mitten
b. Madam
c. Bird
d. Pope

Stuck? If so, then the likely reason is your frame of reference. When faced with questions framed as analogies, we are inclined to look for strictly logical connections. Try looking for a nonlogical relationship. What if you reframed the problem as a search for a common construction of the words? Does this help? The correct response is b. All four words are palindromes—words that read the same forward and backward. Now that you know the frame of reference, you're not likely to be stumped in the future by such an analogy on a standardized test. Likewise, once your group has met a challenge in the past by reframing the problem, it has the experience and know-how to meet similar challenges when they present themselves.

Integrative Problem Solving   Decision making often involves conflicts of interest. Groups, or factions within groups, perceive each other as desiring mutually exclusive goals. Thus, they compete, entering into a power struggle hoping that the other side will capitulate. <u>Integrative problem solving is a creative approach to conflicts of interest that is built on cooperation</u>.

An integrative approach to conflict searches for solutions to problems that benefit everyone. Two of these types—expanding the pie and bridging—are particularly appropriate for this discussion of creative decision making (Pruitt & Rubin, 1986).

Expanding the pie refers to increasing the resources as a solution to a problem. When faced with scarce resources, groups often become competitive and experience serious strife, warring over who gets the biggest or best piece of the limited pie. Groups, however, sometimes accept the inevitability of scarce resources—what Bazerman and Neale (1983) call the "bias of the fixed pie"—without fully exploring options that might expand the resources.

School districts in California, faced with ever-present lean budgets, could issue a collective sigh and proceed to cut programs and teachers. Instead, many districts have found creative ways to increase resources beyond what the state legislature provides. Some districts have established private foundations, raising as much as $435,000 each year in community donations. These foundations throw $125-a-plate dinners, organize black-tie auctions, stage celebrity tennis and golf tournaments, do car washes, and one district foundation purchased a 10-acre vacant school site, developed it, and sold it for a $4 million profit (Le, 1995). These efforts to expand the resource pie save teachers' jobs and maintain important educational programs.

Bridging is the second type of integrative solution to conflicts. **Bridging** offers a new option devised to satisfy all parties on important issues. Bridging was used to solve a conflict of interest over where to eat dinner involving a couple, a friend of the couple's, and her two teenage children. All three adults wished to eat dinner at a moderately priced restaurant specializing in fresh fish entrees served with wine. The teenagers wanted burgers, fries, and colas. After a fair amount of wrangling, the pouting and whining began—from the teenagers, not the adults. Frustrated, the mother of the teenagers declared, "I think we'll just take off and eat at home. This isn't working out." A suggestion was made by one of the other adults: "Why don't we send the kids over to that burger joint up the street, have them bring back their meal, ask the restaurant if they mind having food brought in by the kids, and if not, the adults will order dinners with all the trimmings." The restaurant cooperated and both the adults and the teenagers enjoyed their meals.

Competent communicators vigorously explore possible integrative solutions to problems. In order to do this successfully, <u>there are several steps involved in finding an integrative solution to conflicts of interest</u> (Pruitt & Rubin, 1986). They are:

1. *Integrating requires a clear statement of issues and goals from the conflicting parties*. If all are to benefit from the integrative solution, what the parties want to accomplish must be apparent. Rausch and his colleagues (1974) discovered that 66% of the conflicts they examined were successfully resolved when the issues

were clearly stated; only 18% of the conflicts were effectively resolved when the issues remained vague or unstipulated.

2. *Parties in conflict must determine whether a real conflict of interest exists.* Family members argue over whether to get a dog or not. The two kids say they want a dog very much, the father and mother say they do not. On the surface this looks like a standard conflict of interest. Yet when the issue is discussed, what becomes clear is that the mother doesn't want to take care of the dog and the father dislikes barking. When asked whether a cat would serve as an adequate substitute, the kids enthusiastically agree since they really just want a pet. No conflict really exists since the parents actually like cats, which are low maintenance and mostly quiet, and the kids get their pet.

3. *The parties in disagreement should stick to their goals but remain flexible regarding the means of attaining them.* Both expanding the pie and bridging allow conflicting parties to find flexible, creative means of attaining goals without compromising those goals.

4. *If stalemated, concede on low-priority issues or discard low-priority interests.* The prime goals remain intact. The focus continues to be a solution that satisfies the goals of both parties. You give on minor issues that are relatively unimportant to you but are perhaps more important to the other party.

second look

The Effective Problem-Solving Process

Standard Agenda	Techniques
Problem identification	Framing/reframing
	Formulate question of fact, value, or policy
Problem analysis	Gather/evaluate information
Solution criteria	Consensus
Solution suggestions	Brainstorming/nominal group
	Integrative problem solving
Solution evaluation/selection	Consensus
	Devil's advocacy
	Dialectical inquiry
Solution implementation	PERT

NOTE: Although the consensus technique is used most directly during the solution criteria and solution evaluation/selection steps of Standard Agenda, consensus rules may operate throughout the problem-solving process. Majority or minority rule may also be inserted at various steps if appropriate conditions exist.

In summary, there is no dichotomy between rational and creative decision making and problem solving. The two can be complementary paths to effective decisions in groups. The discussion process, however, should be systematic, not haphazard. Consideration of the problem should come before deliberations on solutions. Standard Agenda is the most common and useful set of procedures for rational decision making. Consensus, when applicable, is an effective process for guiding members toward rational decisions. Brainstorming and nominal group technique, framing/reframing, and integrative problem solving all provide systematic techniques for the discovery of creative solutions to problems.

In the final 3 chapters, I will discuss the interconnected concepts of power and conflict. These concepts have already been addressed superficially in earlier chapters. Those brief references, however, were merely the preliminaries. Power and conflict are integral parts of the small group process that are inescapable in any human system.

Questions for Critical Thinkers

1. Why is majority rule so popular since consensus decision making, by comparison, is more advantageous?
2. Since a true consensus requires agreement, commitment, and satisfaction of group members, do you think groups are likely to achieve a true consensus or is this mostly an ideal?
3. What are some drawbacks to the Standard Agenda approach to decision making? Explain your answer.

Power in Groups:
A Central Dynamic

"Power tends to corrupt, and absolute power corrupts absolutely," Lord Acton reputedly observed. This is a popular view. We are used to thinking of power as illegitimate or unpleasant. The terms *power politics, seizure of power, power struggles, power brokers, power hungry, power mad, power play, high powered,* and *overpowered* reflect just some of the negative ways we associate this central element of human interaction.

Most people are simply uncomfortable with power. For many people "explicit references to power are considered in bad taste" (Kipnis, 1976, p. 2). Naomi Wolf (1994) claims that women in particular harbor "great ambivalence about claiming power" (p. 235), a position supported by others (Haslett et al., 1992). Some individuals find the very thought of power unsavory. Rollo May (1972) terms this denial of one's own power "pseudoinnocence," where we "make a virtue of powerlessness, weakness, and helplessness" (p. 49). <u>There is no virtue in powerlessness</u>. Feelings of powerlessness can induce indifference toward group tasks, diminish task performance, destroy group cohesiveness, strain personal relationships with group members, erode self-esteem, and trigger destructive group conflict (Lee, 1997).

In this chapter, I have four <u>objectives</u>:

1. to explain the significance of power in the small group arena,
2. to define what power is and is not,
3. to delineate the most common sources of power, and
4. to examine the primary indicators of power in small groups.

How we specifically transact power in groups will be discussed in the next chapter.

POWER: AN OVERVIEW

Focus Questions
1. In what ways is power central to small groups?
2. Where does power come from? Do group members possess power or is it conferred on them by the group?

Significance of Power

<u>Power is unavoidable in human transactions</u>. "It permeates human relationships. It exists whether or not it is quested for. It is the glory and the burden of most of humanity" (Burns, 1978, p. 15). Whenever you communicate with another person, power is present. As noted previously, every message has two basic dimensions: content and relationship. The content of a message communicates information regarding people, events, and objects. The relationship dimension communicates information regarding the power distribution between group members.

Abuses have given power a bad reputation. Illegitimate assertions and usurpations of power by scoundrels color our vision. None of you, however, can achieve your individual goals, communicate competently, nor can any group achieve its goals without exercising some power. I am not suggesting that you use power in groups as a Machiavellian manipulation for the achievement of self-centered, dubious goals. Wilmot and Hocker (1998) explain that "one does not have the option of not using power. We only have options about whether to use power destructively or productively" (p. 89).

Power is central to decision making and problem solving in small groups. "It is not possible to discuss group functioning without discussing power" (Johnson & Johnson, 1975, p. 203). Your options lie not in whether to be influential, but in how best to exercise the influence you do have in a group.

Definition of Power

Power *is the ability to influence the attainment of goals sought by yourself or others.* This is a general definition. Let me explain more specifically what power is and conversely what it is not.

The Nature of Power   First and foremost, power is group-centered. The power that you wield is dependent on the relationships you have with group members. Leaders, for instance, require the support of followers to remain in power. As president of the United States, Richard Nixon wielded immense power. When Watergate dethroned our imperial president, he became an easy target for savage ridicule and scorn. Nixon was chastened by his public humiliation brought about by revelations of palpable wrongdoing. Power did not reside in the persona of Richard Nixon. Power came from the relationship Nixon shared with the public. When that relationship turned sour, our 37th president fell from power. Conversely, Bill Clinton weathered the storm of impeachment in 1999 principally because more than 70% of the adult population in the United States approved of the job he was doing as president, even though they overwhelmingly disapproved of his personal behavior with Monica Lewinsky.

We often speak of powerful or powerless individuals as if the power distribution were all one way or the other. This is more the result of our penchant for false dichotomies than it is an accurate assessment of power distribution. No group member is completely powerless. The interconnectedness of components in a system means that all group members have some influence. What one member does or does not do influences other members.

Even marginal members exert influence on a group. I have had numerous groups approach me after class and request permission to dump one of their members for poor attendance and anemic participation at meetings. This is never a casual event. Frustration and anger are evident. As long as a person remains a member of a group, even marginally, he or she influences group decision making. If a marginal member misses several meetings, do you assume he or she no longer wishes to remain a group member? Do you count on this individual to play a part in a group presentation? Intermittent appearances foster ambiguity and can disrupt the group.

If all group members have some degree of power, then a more accurate description of power distribution in a group would be phrased in terms of *degrees* of power. The relevant question then becomes, "How much power does

Person A exert relative to other members in that group?" rather than the false dichotomy, "Is Person A powerful or powerless?"

Forms of Power There are three forms of power (Hollander & Offermann, 1990). The most widely understood form of power is **dominance** or *power over* others. Dominance flows from a hierarchical structure or from structured differences in status among group members. Dominance is competitive. My gain in power is your loss. Your way precludes my way. Thus, a power struggle must ensue to sort out who gets to be the top dog and who plays the junk-yard dog—who is dominant and who is submissive.

A second form of power is called **prevention** or *power from* the influence efforts of others (e.g., followers resist or defy leader dominance). When someone tries to dominate us, psychological reactance occurs. We try to prevent the dominance. Successful efforts to thwart the power plays of others exhibit a different kind of power—the power to prevent. This also is a competitive form of power. Here you're striving not to lose to dominators.

A third form of power is called **empowerment** or *power to* accomplish your own goals or help others achieve theirs (Bate, 1988). Empowerment is cooperative, not competitive. From this vantage point, the group as a whole profits most from all of its members gaining the ability to succeed together. For instance, a football team may have a great quarterback, but if the offensive line performs poorly, the quarterback will get creamed by opposing defensive players bent on knocking the quarterback into the next time zone. Future Hall of Fame quarterback Steve Young of the San Francisco 49ers learned this the hard way during the 1999 season. A poorly performing offensive line allowed Young to be clobbered by opposing teams. In one game he was knocked to the ground 21 times. During the third game of the season, Young was knocked unconscious. He suffered a serious concussion that at this writing threatens to end his football career. Improving the performance of the offensive line gives the quarterback more time to spot open receivers, score points, and remain healthy. The team as a whole improves as each player's performance improves.

One of the positive aspects of the model of effective leadership offered by Hersey and Blanchard (1988), as discussed in chapter 5, is the emphasis on empowerment rather than dominance. In their view, the leader role is not geared toward ordering underlings around and keeping followers in their place. Instead, effective leaders actively seek to increase the readiness levels of followers, thereby empowering them to accomplish tasks without the leader watching their every move.

These three forms of power are substantially different from one another. Those who try to dominate see power as finite, as an *active* effort to advance personal goals at the expense of others. The power pie is only so large and cannot be expanded. The few, not the many, can exercise power. Power, then, is seen as a struggle between the haves and have-nots. Thus, power must be seized actively by controlling access to power resources.

Those who try to prevent domination by others see power as *reactive*. Power is seen in competitive win–lose terms by those who try to dominate and those who try to prevent the domination. Those who try to prevent domination, however, react to the power initiatives of other group members by fighting back.

Those group members who try to empower see the power pie as expandable. As the range of resources and abilities shared by group members grows, so does the group power. Since the power pie can be expanded, all members may exercise power. Therefore, power can be inclusive rather than exclusive, shared rather than fought over. Group members can assist one another in gaining access to rather than hoarding resources. Empowerment is *proactive*, meaning group members take positive action to assist self and others attain goals cooperatively.

second look

Forms of Power

Type	Definition	Description
• Dominance	• Power over	• Active
• Prevention	• Power from	• Reactive
• Empowerment	• Power to	• Proactive

Those who harbor a negative concept of power are usually responding to the dominance form of power and its companion form—prevention. I would be naive to argue, however, that we can replace dominance with empowerment in all cases. Dominance will assuredly remain as the primary form of power in a competitive society. What can be hoped for is that empowerment will gain a wider audience and become more broadly applied.

Additionally, the dominance form of power is the most relevant in some instances. When resources are scarce, the power pie is not always expandable. Sometimes dwindling resources require layoffs and terminations. Learning to cope with a climate of dominance is the task of a competent communicator and a subject for specific analysis in the next chapter.

CLOSER LOOK

Empowerment and Self-Help Groups

Self-help groups have become a national movement. Almost 8 million Americans are members of such groups and the growth rate is accelerating (Kurtz, 1997). The diversity of such groups is astonishing. In California alone there are approximately 4,000 self-help groups (Kurtz, 1997). Imitating the granddaddy of them all, Alcoholics Anonymous, are groups such as Depressives Anonymous, Gamblers Anonymous, Cocaine Anonymous, Batterers Anonymous, Impotents

Anonymous, Prostitutes Anonymous, and Over-eaters Anonymous. There is a self-help group for almost every medical disorder identified by the World Health Organization (Balgopal et al., 1992).

But this is merely the beginning. Consider just a handful of the more offbeat varieties—Hot Flashes (for menopausal women), Trichotillomania Support Network (for people who pull out their hair), Good Tidings (for women who continually fall in love with priests), Crossroads (for male transvestites), The International Intractable Hiccups Organization, Compulsive Shoppers, and an unnamed self-help group organized in 1993 by a hypnotherapist to assist those who claimed to have been abducted by extraterrestrials (the ultimate illegal aliens) and survived to tell about it. There are even self-help groups to provide comfort for distraught fans of recently departed rock stars, such as the group that formed after the Grateful Dead's Jerry Garcia died in 1995.

Most self-help groups are small and local, although there are more than 1,000 self-help groups on-line (Kurtz, 1997). Even larger organizations such as Alcoholics Anonymous operate local chapters composed of small groups of about 8 to 12 members (Kurtz, 1997). Self-help groups usually emerge spontaneously from a condition of relative powerlessness. They generally fall into four helping categories (Leerhsen et al., 1990): (1) addictive behavior, (2) physical and/or mental illness, (3) transitions (e.g., Recently Divorced Catholics), and (4) friends and relatives of those with a problem (e.g., Adult Children of Alcoholics).

The self-help movement got its biggest boost from the women's consciousness-raising groups in the 1960s (Leerhsen et al., 1990). The principal activity of self-help groups is information sharing (Fawcett, 1988), but with a purpose. What self-help groups do best is empower their members. Self-help groups are vehicles for change. Their attraction is not only the sharing of a common bond (similar problems), but the desire to learn how to solve vexing problems and cope with tribulations of life by receiving the support, comfort, and advice of fellow sufferers (Kurtz, 1997).

Self-help groups usually are leaderless. They operate democratically and encourage high participation. New members are usually warmly accepted into the group. Open communication is the norm. The climate is cooperative, and negative advice (e.g., "Tell your boss to shove it") is normally discouraged.

How effective are self-help groups in producing change through empowerment? The research is inconclusive on this question (Jacobs & Goodman, 1989; Kurtz, 1997). Regardless, self-help groups illustrate that viewing power as simply dominance (power over) ignores the vast arena of empowerment (power to).

Questions for Thought

1. Have you ever belonged to a self-help group? If yes, did you feel empowered by it?
2. Can a person become dependent on a self-help group even though the central purpose is to empower individuals?

POWER RESOURCES

As I stated previously, power is the ability to influence the attainment of goals sought by yourself or others. This ability to influence is derived from resources. A **power resource** is "anything that enables individuals to move toward their own goals or interfere with another's actions" (Folger et al., 1993, p. 100). The range of power resources is broad. I will discuss the primary resources from which power is most extensively derived in group situations. There are five primary power resources relevant to group situations. These five resources are information, expertise, punishments and rewards, personal qualities, and legitimate authority. These resources closely parallel French and Raven's (1959) classic types of power in groups.

Focus Questions

1. Information is power, but is all information power?
2. For expertise to serve as a power resource, must the expert always avoid errors?
3. What are the primary drawbacks of punishment and rewards as power resources?
4. Where does an individual acquire charisma?
5. How does authority become legitimate?

Information

Unquestionably, information is power. In an age of information, how could it be otherwise? Information has become a vital resource for the nations of the world. The U.S. economy has become information-dependent. Teachers, lawyers, ministers, accountants, consultants, and therapists all provide information that can be valuable to us in certain circumstances.

Not all information, however, serves as a source of power. I have already explained that if the quantity of information becomes overwhelming, it is difficult to separate useless from useful information. Information must be valuable or useful to the group for it to have power potential.

Information assumes value or usefulness when it is perceived to be unavailable. If information is readily available to everyone, it has no power potential. Consultants can charge thousands of dollars to groups and organizations because they have information not readily available to members of the group. Who would bother to hire a consultant if that individual merely reiterated what everyone in the group already knew?

Information becomes unavailable primarily from restrictions and scarcity (Brock, 1968). In this era of information overload, restricted or scarce information is the exception, not the rule. Thus, when information is restricted or scarce, whatever is available seems terribly important.

In the 1980s, a controversial woman named J. Z. Knight, who portrayed herself as a celestial channeler in contact with a 35,000-year-old Cro-Magnon prophet named Ramtha, ran her School of Enlightenment in rural Washington state (Conway & Siegelman, 1995). The main attraction for small groups of Ramtha devotees was to hear the "wisdom" of this prophet as he spoke to seminar-like gatherings of fascinated followers. Ramtha "spoke" to these groups through Knight, who appeared to be in a trance. Access to Ramtha was restricted by Knight. He spoke only to those who joined Knight's enlightenment school (and presumably paid the fee to join). It's not every day that you bump into a talkative 35,000-year-old guru from another spirit dimension. The scarcity of such elder prophets made what Ramtha had to say more enticing.

What Ramtha had to say was a conglomeration of unsubstantiated advice. Among other things, Ramtha claimed that every orgasm brings you nearer to death (the same could be said, of course, for every breath you take). He also said that when you die, you do not want to seek the light because "light beings" are waiting to suck the experience from your spirit and leave you to reincarnate with no memory of your last life. Instead, Ramtha urged, seek the darkness, the void. If a 35-year-old guy named Fred offered the same "wisdom," do you think anyone would find this very insightful? Well, many people did when it was viewed as scarce and restricted information shared by a "prophet" from another dimension of time and space (Conway & Siegelman, 1995).

Clearly, <u>information that is perceived by the group to be valuable and useful has power potential</u>. In order for information to be perceived as valuable and useful it must be restricted and scarce. <u>The competent communicator can capitalize on information as a power resource as follows:</u>

1. *Provide useful but scarce or restricted information to the group.* Careful, diligent research often produces valuable information relevant to the group task. If this information is not known to other group members, it then assumes a power potential by increasing your prestige and influence in group decision making. I am not suggesting, however, that you act coy about giving the information to your group. There may be an appropriate moment when revealing the scarce information may have more dramatic impact on group members than some other moment, but trying to manipulate the group could easily invite animosity and reprisals. Competent communicators are We-not-Me oriented so withholding information for personal gain is counterproductive.
2. *Be certain information is accurate.* Sharing misinformation could earn you the enmity of group members. Misinformation could easily lead to collective inferential error, a prime cause of faulty decision making.

Expertise

Information and expertise are closely related, but not identical. A group member can possess critical information without being an expert. A group member may even have a valuable technical report, for example, that makes little sense to him or her but might make great sense to other members who want very much to read it. <u>An **expert** not only has valuable and useful information for a group but also understands the information and knows how to use it to help the group.</u> They can give knowledgeable advice.

We have a real love–hate relationship with experts. We often require their skills and advice, but seem to resent their position of power. Arthur Bloch defined an expert as "the one who predicts the job will take the longest and cost the most." Then there is this anonymous definition of an expert, "One who can take something you already know and make it sound confusing" (Brussell, 1988, p. 186). Our favorite experts to pick on are lawyers. Jokes deriding lawyers have become commonplace (e.g., How can you tell the difference between a dead lawyer and a dead snake in the road? Answer: There are skid marks in front of the snake).

Despite our seeming dislike of experts, with the twin problems of information overload and the explosion of change in our global village, no individual nor group could ever hope to function effectively without at some time requiring their services. What academic department is not dependent on the expert who repairs the computers and Xerox machines? What board of directors has never needed the advice of an attorney? Families require plumbers, hair stylists, financial advisors, roofers, exterminators, counselors, mechanics, and those who repair our appliances, phones, televisions, and broken hearts.

In order for expertise to function as a power resource, at minimum, two conditions must be met. First, the group must be convinced that the person has the requisite skills, abilities, knowledge, and background to function as a real expert. Experts must demonstrate a mastery of relevant information and exhibit skill using it. Ronald Reagan, revered by many, diminished his claim of expertise that usually is accorded sitting presidents when he continued his bad habit of inventing facts during speeches and press conferences. Reagan signaled what was in store for the nation during the 1980 presidential campaign when he asserted that trees and other vegetation cause more air pollution than automobiles. This prompted an anonymous wag in California to post a sign on a tree the next day that read: "Chop me down before I kill again."

Expertise is not a property of the person, but a judgment by others. When judging a group member's expertise, men and women are not viewed through the same lense. Men more than women are encouraged by groups to contribute their expertise, partly because group members, both males and females, don't initially think of women as experts (Propp, 1995). As a result, male experts are more influential than female experts (Littlepage & Mueller, 1997). Female experts who talk frequently and knowledgeably, however, are more easily accepted as experts by group members (Littlepage & Mueller, 1997). Once the group accepts the expertise of an individual of either sex, members are strongly influenced by the expert to accept recommendations that even contradict members' initial points of view (Foschi et al., 1985).

Second, the person who has been accorded status as an expert must demonstrate trustworthiness. Power is not derived from expertise if the group suspects that the expert will lie for personal gain or self-protection. People the world over are more influenced by experts who stand to gain nothing personally than by those who would gain substantially by lying or offering poor advice (McGuinnies & Ward, 1980).

In the summer of 1992, the *National Law Journal* and LEXIS, a database service, conducted the most comprehensive national poll of jurors ever undertaken. Of the nearly 800 individuals who had recently sat on a jury, 95% said that they were impressed by expert testimony during a trial and 70% felt that expert testimony influences the outcome of a trial. Nevertheless, 51% of the jurors said that they didn't necessarily trust the testimony of police officers and 70% of African American jurors felt police testimony was suspect ("Jurors' views," 1993). The power potential of expertise is substantially reduced when trustworthiness is questionable.

There are some interesting intercultural differences related to power and expertise. Although expertise is an important consideration for Americans in choosing individuals for negotiating teams, status is more important to French, British, Chinese, Japanese, and Saudi Arabians (Hellweg et al., 1994). How expertise is perceived also varies from culture to culture. In the United States, an individual with exceptional expertise in one field might be perceived

The power of information and expertise is depicted in this doctor–patient conversation.

as irrelevant when the group discusses issues unrelated to that person's specialization. In Africa, however, opinion leaders are respected and valued over a broader range of topics for which they have no special technical knowledge (Dodd, 1995). Expertise is in the eye of the beholder.

Assuming a group member has special knowledge, skills, or abilities useful to the group, <u>he or she functions as a competent communicator while capitalizing on the power potential of expertise as follows:</u>

1. *Maintain skills, abilities, and knowledge currency.* You're only an expert for as long as the group perceives you as such. Let your knowledge grow out-of-date or your skills and abilities diminish and the group will quickly see you as yesteryear's expert—a relic.

2. *Demonstrate trustworthiness and credibility.* You should exhibit a We-not-Me orientation. Your expertise should be used to benefit the group, not merely bring personal advantages to yourself. Even when a group hires an expert from outside, the group expects that the lawyer, accountant, consultant, or whoever will show commitment to helping the group gain its goals, not simply make a buck for himself or herself.

3. *Be certain of your facts before advising the group.* Bad advice is like misinformation. The results can be disastrous for the group. Advice should be based on the best available information. An occasional error may not tarnish your credibility as an expert. Relatively frequent or serious errors will.

4. *Don't assume an air of superiority.* Putting on an air of superiority will trigger defensiveness among group members.

Rewards and Punishments

Parceling out rewards or meting out punishment can be an important source of power. Salaries, bonuses, work schedules, perks, hirings, and firings are typical job-related rewards and punishments. Money, privacy, car keys, and grounding are a few of the rewards and punishments found in family situations. Grades, letters of recommendation, and social approval or disapproval are a few of the rewards and punishments available to teachers when dealing with students.

The greater the certainty that punishments will be administered, the greater is the potential power of punishment. Idle threats have little influence on group behavior. Parents who threaten spankings or denial of privileges but never follow through soon realize that children easily learn to ignore such impotent bluster. If employees are protected from termination by civil service regulations or tenure, threatening to fire them is laughable. Threats of punishment, however, seem to be more effective when we perceive that the chances of punishment are highly probable (Wooton, 1993). Punishment is a source of power if it can be and likely will be exercised.

There are serious drawbacks to using punishment to influence group members, however (Kassin, 1998; Uba & Huang, 1999). First, punishment indicates what you *should not do* but it doesn't indicate what you *should do.* Firing a worker doesn't teach that person how to perform better in the future. Second, targets of punishment can become angry and hostile toward their perceived tormenters. If the punishment is perceived to be unfair or excessive, a backlash can easily occur. Workplace massacres by disgruntled employees who have been fired have become almost commonplace news events in the United States. Third, punishment can produce a negative ripple effect throughout the group. Punishment is coercive. It easily produces psychological reactance. The more the group tries to bludgeon a deviant member into line, the more this person is likely to resist and sometimes do exactly what the group finds unacceptable. If the punishment doesn't achieve the desired effect, this could have systemwide implications. Other group members may be encouraged to engage in similar deviance. Issues of fairness and just cause may surface and escalate into ugly conflicts, spreading tension and creating a competitive group climate. The sign found in workplaces, "The beatings will continue until morale improves" expresses ironically the difficulty of using punishment to produce positive results in groups.

Rewards, viewed as the opposite of punishment, seem as though they would produce only positive results for groups. Everyone likes to be rewarded, so surely this is a powerful resource for influencing group members. A reward can be an effective power resource if used carefully. Indiscriminate use of rewards, however, can also backfire.

Consider the story of an old man who was besieged daily by a group of ten-year-old boys hurling insults at him as they passed his house on their way home from school. One day, after enduring the boys abusive remarks about how stupid, bald, and ugly he was, he decided on a plan to deal with the little trouble-makers. On the following day, he approached the boys and told them that any-one who came the next day and shouted insults at him would receive a dollar. Dumbfounded, the boys left and returned the next afternoon to scream epithets at the old man. He gave each boy a dollar. He then told them that he would pay each boy 50 cents if they returned the next day and repeated their rude behavior. They returned, shouted insults, and were paid. The old man then said that he would pay them only a dime if they returned the next day and repeated their ugly behavior. At this point, the boys said, "Forget it. It isn't worth it." They never returned.

This story illustrates how <u>an extrinsic reward can diminish intrinsic motivation to behave in certain ways</u>. An **extrinsic reward** motivates us to be-have or perform by offering us an external inducement such as money, grades, praise, recognition, or prestige. **Intrinsic motivation** is enjoying what one does for its own sake, not because of some external reward for doing it (Kohn, 1993). The boys initially were intrinsically motivated by perverse pleasure in tor-menting the old man. When paid to continue the torment, it became more like a job. Once the pay became minimal, the job seemed pointless and they quit. "I owe, I owe, it's off to work I go," and "Work sucks, but I need the bucks" are two bumper stickers that express the common effect an extrinsic reward such as money has on our interest in and enjoyment of work.

When team members are intrinsically motivated by commitment to a shared goal, a desire to "change the world," or a keen interest in the task, teams are likely to perform well. Teams that are held together only by the extrinsic re-wards of money, recognition, or prestige are not as likely to be effective.

Does use of extrinsic rewards always produce negative results, as some have argued (Kohn, 1993)? The answer is no. Verbal praise (extrinsic re-ward), as long as it is not offered as an obvious manipulative strategy to control group members' behavior, can actually *increase* intrinsic motivation (Carton, 1996; Eisenberger & Cameron, 1996). Also, it depends on how recipients per-ceive the extrinsic reward. If they perceive it as a treat, it will increase intrinsic motivation to perform, but if they perceive it as pressure to perform and be cre-ative, it will decrease their intrinsic interest and motivation to perform (Eisen-berger & Armeli, 1997).

<u>Competent communicators use punishment and rewards carefully.</u> Here are some guidelines:

1. *Punishment should be a last resort.* Punishment as a power resource must be ex-ercised with caution and discretion. Because it can produce serious negative consequences, it should be employed rarely and then only when efforts to change group members' behavior by noncoercive means have failed.
2. *Punishment should be appropriate to the act.* Anemic punishment for seriously flawed, irresponsible performance or severe punishment for relatively inconse-quential error is out of proportion to the act. In the former instance, group mem-bers will likely ridicule the ineffectual action, and in the latter instance, group members will likely rebel against the severity of the sanction.

3. *Punishment should be swift and certain*. The more disconnected punishment becomes from an objectionable act because of delays or uncertainty that punishment will occur, the more ineffectual it becomes. Idle threats are pointless. Inconsistent punishment will foster inconsistent compliance from members.

4. *Be generous with praise that is warranted*. Praise recognizes accomplishment, nurtures a positive group climate, and increases intrinsic motivation unless it is obviously manipulative.

5. *Determine what rewards are valued by group members before offering any*. Extrinsic rewards diminish intrinsic motivation when group members are already interested in and committed to the task. They do not diminish intrinsic motivation, however, when group members are not initially interested in a task or they feel inadequate (Ubi & Huang, 1999). Thus, money, awards, recognition, and the like may be effective extrinsic rewards in circumstances where group members aren't initially motivated intrinsically to accomplish a task effectively if group members value the rewards. A $1000 bonus may motivate a poor man, but Bill Gates would likely view this as pocket change.

6. *Administer both punishments and rewards equitably and fairly*. Perceived favoritism in receiving rewards creates a competitive group climate. Punishing those who are perceived to have done little or nothing wrong can lead to a group revolt.

Personal Qualities

We all know individuals who exert some influence over us, not because of any of the previous power resources already discussed, but because of attractive personal qualities they seem to possess in abundance. The research on interpersonal attraction presented in chapter 3 applies to this power resource. We are more likely to be influenced by those individuals whom we find attractive than by those we don't.

Communication researchers have known for some time that physical attractiveness, expertise and mastery of certain persuasive skills, dynamism, trustworthiness, reliability, similarity of values and outlook, and identification with the group all contribute to an individual's ability to influence others. Some or all of these qualities contribute to charisma. The term **charisma** loosely refers to a constellation of personal attributes that people find highly attractive in an individual.

Some people have a great deal of charisma and others have less charisma than driftwood. Charisma, however, is not determined objectively. Groups decide what is attractive and what is not. When John and Jacqueline Kennedy visited Paris in 1962 as president and first lady, they made a lasting impression, Jacqueline more than John. Jacqueline, with her combination of beauty, poise, grace, and ability to speak French, charmed President Charles de Gaulle and the people of France. She stole the spotlight away from her normally charismatic husband who, as president, characteristically commanded center stage. Jacqueline's impact on the French was so complete that when the couple departed, John Kennedy held a press conference (a rare moment when he became the center of attention). In typical witty fashion and recognizing the irony of his wife upstaging the president of the United States, he began, "I do not think it is altogether inappropriate to introduce myself to this audience. I am the man who accompanied Jacqueline Kennedy to Paris, and I have enjoyed it" (Fadiman, 1985, p. 328). Jacqueline Kennedy exercised little tangible power, but she displayed a powerful presence.

Charisma and leadership are often connected, especially in the public mind during political elections. Charismatic or **transformational leaders** communicate a vision to followers. Change is the central mission of the charismatic leader—change in followers' values, goals, needs, and behavior (Fiedler & House, 1988). Charismatic leaders induce fierce loyalty, commitment, and devotion from followers. There is a strong identification with the leader, and the followers' goals, self-esteem, and values become entangled with the charismatic leader–follower relationship. The leader's beliefs are thought to be correct, often absolutely correct.

As I indicated in chapter 5, the trait perspective on leadership does not adequately explain how or why leaders emerge, nor their degree of effectiveness. Charisma is a power resource and charismatic leaders are often capable of generating intense reactions, even collective hysteria. There is no one constellation of traits, however, that makes a person charismatic. What makes a person attractive to a group is contingent on members' preferences.

So how does a competent communicator capitalize on personal qualities as a power resource in small groups? To be a competent communicator and increase power through personal qualities, try the following:

1. *Enhance attractiveness*. Dress for context. Dress appropriately for the context, don't assume one style fits all occasions and situations. Sometimes dressing casually is more powerful than donning a power suit, which may look ridiculous at a sorority meeting to plan a charitable event. The same guideline applies to all other steps taken to improve physical appearance (e.g., cosmetics, hair length, and so forth).
2. *Learn effective presentational skills*. Charismatic individuals are often effective public speakers. In a Michigan poll of 500 adults (Ross, 1989), speaking ability was ranked second on a list of factors deemed most influential in choosing a political candidate, behind party affiliation and ahead of appearance or good looks.

Legitimate Authority

We all play roles, but some of us exercise greater influence in groups because of our acknowledged position or title. Power can be derived from the shared belief that some individuals have a legitimate right to influence us and direct our behavior by virtue of the roles that they occupy. Parents occupy a position of legitimate authority. In addition to other power resources they have at their disposal, parents are supposed to be accorded respect and deference simply because they are parents. We believe parents have the right to discipline their children and to expect obedience. Similarly, teachers and supervisors at work occupy an authority position considered legitimate by most groups.

Can you explain in what ways the Pope used information, expertise, legitimate authority, punishment and rewards, and personal qualities to maintain his power as head of the Catholic Church and as a worldwide figure of renown?

Obedience to legitimate authority is intricately woven into the fabric of our society. We learn about the virtues of obedience to authority figures in school, at work, in church, in courtrooms, and in military barracks. The result is a mental set lasered into our brains: OBEY LEGITIMATE AUTHORITY.

Just how strong is our mental set that programs us to obey legitimate authority? Kelman and Lawrence (1972) report the results of an unsettling nationwide study concerning perhaps the most notorious event of the Vietnam War. Lieutenant William Calley ordered a group of soldiers under his command to slaughter all inhabitants (men, women, children, and babies) of a village called My Lai. Of those responding to the Kelman and Lawrence survey, 67% believed most people would follow orders and shoot villagers as soldiers did at My Lai, and 58 percent said they personally would shoot and kill women and children, even babies, if ordered to do so by someone in authority. Kelman and Lawrence conclude that "many Americans feel they have no right to resist authoritative demands. They regard Calley's actions at My Lai as normal, even desirable, because he performed them (they think) in obedience to legitimate authority" (p. 45).

CLOSER LOOK

The Milgram Studies

An amazing series of studies conducted by Stanley Milgram (1974) in the 1960s lends substantial support to the fear that as a society we have absorbed the lesson of obedience to legitimate authority so completely that <u>we are inclined to automatically obey authority figures</u>. We may obey even when it is dangerous or morally questionable to do so.

The basic experimental design of the obedience to authority studies by Milgram consisted of a naive subject who acted as "teacher" and a confederate who acted as "student." The naive subjects were told that the purpose of the experiment was to determine the effects of punishment on memory. Punishment consisted of electric shocks. The electric shocks were administered to the student for every wrong answer on a word-association test. Shocks began at 15 volts and increased by 15-volt increments up to a maximum of 450 volts for each wrong answer from the victim. The experimenter directed the subjects to administer the increasingly intense shocks for every wrong answer even when the subjects objected. The experimenter served as legitimate authority in each of Milgram's experiments.

<u>Almost two-thirds of the subjects progressed to 450 volts</u> and delivered the maximum shock until they were instructed to stop by the experimenter. Subjects continued to administer the shocks even when they could hear the victim's screams of pain and agony. (The victim's anguish was cleverly faked: no electric shocks were actually delivered, but all except an insignificant few of the subjects perceived the punishment to be real.)

In one of the experiments, the victim complained of a heart condition exacerbated by the shocks. Nevertheless, 26 of the 40 subjects administered the maximum shocks at the direction of the experimenter. In all, Milgram conducted 18 variations of the obedience to authority study. More than 1,000 subjects from a wide range of ages and walks of life participated. Others replicated his experiments in America and abroad sometimes gaining as high as 85% compliance (Milgram, 1974).

One of the more dramatic replications was conducted by Sheridan and King (1972). In this experiment, the victim was a cute fluffy puppy dog, not a human confederate. Although the victim in Milgram's studies appeared to be, but was never actually, shocked, Sheridan and King had the subjects actually shock the helpless puppy.

Despite the disbelief commonly manifested by my students that anyone would continue to shock an adorable, helpless puppy held captive in a box whose floor was an electrified grid from which there was no escape, the results of the experiment contradict conventional wisdom. <u>Three-quarters of the subjects, all college students, were obedient to the end</u> (54% of the men and 100% of the women). At the behest of the experimenter, they delivered the maximum intensity shock to the cute puppy dog whose pain they could witness directly. They complained, some female subjects even wept, but they obeyed.

The Milgram studies and replications that followed reveal the awesome power of legitimate authority. Milgram (1974) argues that <u>the "most fundamental lesson" of his studies</u> is that "even when the destructive effects of their work become patently clear, and they are asked to carry out actions incompatible with fundamental standards of morality, relatively few people have the resources to resist authority" (p. 6). Subjects obeyed not because they were evil or sadistic but because they couldn't defy legitimate authority.

Perhaps you still think that these are merely laboratory results unrelated to real life. No such luck. In one field study (Hofling et al., 1966), 21 out of 22 nurses followed orders from an individual posing as a physician over the phone and headed for a patient's room to administer a potentially lethal dose of a drug. They were inter-

Would you administer 450-volt shocks to this help-less dog? In one experiment 100% of the women and 54% of the men did just that to a puppy.

are vigilant and challenge authorities when un-ethical or destructive decisions are ordered, they can withstand the authority's power. One study (Gamson et al., 1982) found that when group members discussed their misgivings about what a legitimate authority told them to do most group defied the authority figure. One advantage of groups is that there is strength in numbers. Group discussion, however, is a critical factor in defiance. Group members must share con-cerns about what authorities tell them to do so individual members realize that they are not alone in their dissension. The process of defi-ance will be discussed in greater detail in the next chapter.

Questions for Thought

1. Are the Milgram studies ethical research? Ex-plain.
2. Do you believe that obedience to authority is as widespread as the Milgram studies in-dicate?
3. Do you think you would have refused to obey the experimenter in these studies? If yes, ex-plain what makes you different from the major-ity who inflicted the maximum intensity shock to the innocent victim.
4. Would the results of the Milgram studies have been the same if he had used a woman as the authority figure? A woman as the victim? A child as the victim? Explain.
5. In Sheridan and King's (puppy dog as victim) replication of the Milgram studies, 100% of the female subjects but 54% of the male subjects obeyed. Why the difference in results? Do you think women are more inclined to obey legiti-mate authority? This study was conducted in 1972. Would similar findings result from repli-cation of this study now? Explain.

cepted by an observer. The September 28, 1986, issue of the *Los Angeles Times* reported an inci-dent in which an AIDS patient was killed when a nurse administered a lethal injection on the or-ders delivered over the phone of someone posing as a physician. The power of legitimate authority is real and requires vigilance if tragedies are to be averted.

Group members do not have to be the pawns of legitimate authority. In fact, if group members

An important point to note here is the power potential of *legitimate* authority. We are not inclined to comply with directives from those individ-uals acting authoritatively but who are not deemed legitimate. Group members must grant legitimacy before authority will have any weight. Those individuals perceived to be authorities without legitimacy will exercise substantially less influence in a group than those perceived to be authorities with legitimacy. A study of groups (Read, 1974) revealed that how the leader becomes an authority figure can be a decisive issue. Leaders who usurp authority are not granted legitimacy by the group. These pretenders to the throne of power have less influence than appointed or elected group leaders. Groups whose leaders have a weak basis of legitimacy (e.g., randomly appointed leaders) exhibit inferior performance compared to groups whose leaders have a strong basis of legitimacy (e.g., leaders appointed for their competence or elected by the membership) (Hollander, 1985).

The sad, sorry lot of inexperienced substitute teachers illustrates the problem of authority without legitimacy. Students frequently subject them to a kind of ritual hazing. I'm reminded of the old westerns on TV where the timid stranger in town is forced to dance to the beat of a six-shooter firing lead at the newcomer's vulnerable tootsies. Students can make an exasperated substitute teacher perform a little dance of sorts by hurling verbal shots of disrespect and insult at the stranger in the schoolroom. Teachers are authority figures in a school environment, but substitute teachers must struggle to establish legitimacy in students' eyes. They must combat the strong impression that as a substitute, they are not "real teachers." This is a perceptual challenge. No individual possesses legitimate authority. This power resource is conferred by the group.

Although the results from the Milgram studies (see Closer Look) and subsequent replications by other researchers are disturbing, defiance of all authority is as empty-headed as consistent compliance. Both are manifestations of communication incompetence. What kind of society would you live in if few people obeyed police, teachers, parents, judges, bosses, or physicians? There are solid reasons why you should obey legitimate authorities in most circumstances. The answer to the excessive influence of legitimate authority rests with your ability to discriminate between appropriate and inappropriate use of authority, the task of a competent communicator, not the exercise of indiscriminate rebellion against all authority.

Those who aspire to be competent communicators while capitalizing on legitimate authority as a power resource should:

1. *Become an authority figure.* There are two principal sources of authority: appointed (designated) leader and emergent leader (Forsyth, 1990). Becoming either grants you authority. Emergent leader has already been discussed in chapter 5. Appointed leader occurs because you gain favor of a powerful person, earn the right to be appointed (e.g., seniority), or are the only group member willing to accept the appointment.

2. *Gain legitimacy.* Legitimacy comes from conforming to accepted principles, rules, and standards of the group. Authority that is imposed on the group (leader appointed from outside the group) usually has problems of legitimacy because the group resents nonparticipation in making the appointment. Authority that springs from the group (e.g., voted by membership to represent the group in bargaining talks or earned by demonstrating competence) has a solid base of legitimacy.

3. *Encourage participative decision making.* Keeping in mind the qualifiers attached to participative decision making discussed in the preceding chapter, if you are in a position of authority, encouraging participative decision making can help maintain the legitimacy of your authority by retaining the goodwill of group members.

4. *Act ethically.* The abuses of legitimate authority are the product of unethical practices. Honesty, respect, fairness, and choice should guide legitimate authorities whenever they use their power in groups.

---

second look

Competent Communicator's Guide

Power Resource	Communication Guidelines
Information Power	• Provide group scarce but useful information • Be certain information is accurate
Expertise	• Maintain knowledge currency • Demonstrate trustworthiness and credibility • Be certain of your facts before advising • Don't assume air of superiority
Rewards/Punishments	• Punishments should be a last resort • Punishment should be appropriate to the act • Punishment should be swift and certain • Be generous with praise that is warranted • Determine what rewards are valued by group members before offering any • Administer both punishment and reward equitably and fairly
Personal Qualities	• Enhance attractiveness • Learn effective presentational skills
Legitimate Authority	• Become an authority figure • Gain legitimacy • Encourage participative decision making • Act ethically

---

Power resources are not properties of individuals. A person does not possess power, but is granted power by the group. Power occurs within a system. As such, the group must endorse the resource for it to be influential (Folger et al., 1993). Group endorsement usually depends on whether the resource meets a need of the group. Will the group find this resource valuable and significant? Will it assist the group in attaining an important goal?

Group endorsement also depends on whether you can deliver the goods. Can you help the group gain access to the resource (empowerment) or can you restrict the availability of the resource for others (dominance)? Group members who promise to provide valuable information necessary for a group project lose power if they cannot deliver the information.

What should be clear by now is that groups determine the power any individual member wields. If the resources that we bring to the group are endorsed by the group, then we will exercise some degree of power with the membership. Power is a transaction among the members of a group.

INDICATORS OF POWER

Wilmot and Hocker (1998) observe, "Since power is a dynamic product of shifting relationships, precise measurement of the amount of power parties have at any one time cannot be measured precisely" (p. 94). Assessing the resources valued by the group is a starting place in ascertaining the power dynamics in a group. Determining the relative degree of power each member wields, however, is more complicated than a resource inventory. If one member has legitimate authority, and another member has valued information, while a third group member has expertise, and a fourth member is charismatic and has rewards to distribute, which member is most powerful? This type of resource inventory merely tells you that all four group members have some degree of power.

Nevertheless, there are many indicators of power present in all group transactions. Without complete precision, you can ascertain in a general way the distribution of power in a group. Determining such a distribution requires an ability to recognize indicators of power.

There are three main categories of power indicators: general, verbal, and nonverbal. Indicators are simply the ways in which relative degrees of power are communicated in groups.

Focus Questions
1. "Those who define, control." What does this mean?
2. In what ways do male and female communication patterns differ in regards to verbal dominance?
3. What are the effects of "powerless" verbal and nonverbal communication patterns?

General Indicators

There are several general indicators of power in groups. First, who defines whom and makes the definition stick? Those who define, control. Ordinarily we define people by attaching a label to them. Teachers define students (e.g., smart), physicians define patients (hypochondriac), psychiatrists define clients (schizophrenic), parents define children (incorrigible), and bosses define employees (good worker).

The relationship between definition and power can be seen clearly by considering just a few of the more embarrassing and controversial mental illness designations of the past from the field of psychiatry. There was the form of "insanity" called *drapetomania,* the mental disease afflicting slaves who continually tried to escape from bondage. Then there was *masturbatory insanity*. An editorial on this "mental illness" appearing in a mid-nineteenth century issue of the *New Orleans Medical and Surgical Journal* (Szasz, 1980) asserted: "Neither plague, nor war, nor smallpox, nor a crowd of similar evils, have resulted more disastrously for humanity than the habit of masturbation: it is the destroying element of civilized society" (p. 18). *Protest psychosis* branded as crazy primarily black militants who reject white culture. Finally, there was *homosexuality,* which the American Psychiatric Association designated a mental illness until 1973. Then APA members in 1974 had a change of heart and instantly transformed a so-called mental illness into an "alternative lifestyle."

The power of definition can be highly consequential. When the APA in May 1993 proposed labeling women who experience severe premenstrual syndrome as having *premenstrual mood disorder,* a firestorm of opposition erupted. The National Organization for Women denounced the idea. Fearful that in child custody, rape, and sexual harassment cases women with severe PMS (broadly defined by the APA) would be branded as mentally ill and thus discredited, NOW organized a street protest outside the APA conference in San Francisco. Deborah Glenn, the vice president of NOW's San Francisco office said, "When women become aware of this, they become outraged" (Alvarado, 1993, p.1A).

The fact that such labeling is taken seriously indicates that psychiatrists, physicians, teachers, parents, bosses, and the like do have influence even if they're pinheads or bigots. If the individual or group, however, discounts the definition, then this indicates relative powerlessness in this situation. If a teacher labels a student a troublemaker but the entire class does not, then the teacher exercises little influence in this regard. In fact, any effort to punish this student may be viewed as unfair and encourage a backlash against the teacher's authority in class.

<u>Whose decisions are followed</u> is a second general indicator of power in a group. In a family, do the kids obey the father but ignore the mother or vice versa? Does it depend on the type of decision being made? Who is accommodated in the group? An alcoholic father may command obedience from his kids only by coercion. He may lose the respect of his children due to his obnoxious drinking and acts of physical violence. If the father loses respect, he erodes his legitimate authority. In this case, the mother may actually exercise greater power because she has the respect and trust of the children. Whenever the hammer of repression is not directly swung, the children will likely follow the mother's directives and ignore the father's whenever possible.

<u>Who opposes significant change</u> is a third general indicator of power. Those who have been accorded power by the group are usually uncomfortable with change that goes much beyond a little fine-tuning. Substantial change may alter the power relationships. The disaffected and relatively powerless individuals and groups clamor for substantial change as a general rule. Adapting to

change in any social system is critically important, yet significant change is normally the product of the disgruntled, not those ensconced in positions of authority.

Verbal Indicators

Power is reflected in the way we speak. Many communication researchers have argued that the language choices and sentence construction of the relatively powerful tend to be distinctly different from the language choices and sentence structure of the less powerful.

The speech of a subordinate is often flooded with self-doubt, hesitancy, approval seeking, overqualification, and self-disparagement. Examples of "powerless" speech patterns include the following (Mulac & Bradac, 1995):

Hedges: *"Perhaps* the best way to proceed is . . ." "I'm a *little* concerned that this *might* cause problems."

Hesitations: *"Well, uhm,* the important thing to remember is . . ." *"Gosh, ah,* shouldn't we, *ah,* delay the decision?"

Tag Questions: "The meeting will be at noon, *okay?"* "This point seems irrelevant, *doesn't it?"*

Disclaimers: *"You may disagree with me,* but . . ." *"This is probably a silly idea,* but . . ."

Excessive Politeness: "I'm *extremely sorry* to barge in like this, but . . ."

Powerless speech suggests uncertainty, indecisiveness, lack of confidence, vacillation, and deference to authority. "Powerful" speech is generally direct, fluent, declarative, commanding, and prone to interrupt or overlap other group members' speech (Pearson et al., 1991).

The consequences of using powerless speech are revealed in a study set in a courtroom arena (Erickson et al., 1978). The researchers constructed two distinctly different versions of a witness's key testimony in a trial. The powerless version included many hedges, hesitations, tag questions, and other variants of verbal submissiveness, while the powerful version included none of these. A male and female were trained to read each version of the testimony to subjects. Both male and female speakers were rated as more credible, competent, likable, strong, and active when they read the powerful version. Power is perceptual. Choosing language that may connote weakness to the group will often produce the perception that you are also weak (Hackman & Johnson, 1996).

Dominance is on the other end of the power spectrum from submissiveness. Power is sometimes indicated by verbal bullying. Competitive interrupting, contradicting, berating, and sheer quantity of speech are examples of **verbal dominance.** Monopolizing a conversation, for example, has obvious power implications. Those who dominate conversations during group meetings are able to get their point presented to members. Those who can't sandwich a word into the conversation are unable to articulate their point of view. More importantly, as previously discussed, those who talk the most are more likely to be perceived as leaders in groups than are quiet members.

Interrupting to seize conversational control clearly reflects the status of individuals in a group. Relatively powerful individuals may interrupt the less powerful, but not vice versa. The peons are expected to defer to the pooh-bahs when interrupted.

FOCUS *on gender/culture*

Powerful Language Differences

Verbal indicators of power in our culture follow a gender pattern in several instances. Men are typically more verbose, more given to long-winded verbal presentations, and more talkative in mixed-sex groups than are women (James & Drakich, 1993). Talkativeness is associated with leader emergence. Men are more verbally aggressive than women (Nicotera & Rancer, 1994; Stewart et al., 1996), meaning men are more inclined to verbally attack the self-concepts of others. Men are also more argumentative than women (Stewart et al., 1996), meaning men are more likely to advocate controversial positions during group discussions or to challenge the positions on issues taken by other group members. Women are inclined to view verbal aggressiveness and argumentativeness as strategies of dominance and control; a hostile, combative act (Nicotera & Rancer, 1994). Since men are more likely to seek status and women are more likely to seek connection in conversations (Tannen, 1990), these gender differences in verbal indicators of power are not surprising.

Tavris (1992) argues, however, that the use of relatively powerless speech by women—the use of hedges, tag questions, disclaimers, qualifiers, and hesitations—can be used to influence men. A study by Carli (1990) supports this interpretation. Carli found that women are more inclined to use powerless speech patterns when conversing with men, but not with other women.

Tag questions, hesitations, and the like seem to reassure men that women are not attempting to enhance their status. Thus, women pose no threat to male status in groups, so men are more likely to listen to nonthreatening women. Does the strategy work? Apparently it does, because, paradoxically, women are more influential with men when using powerless speech. Other women, however, view powerless speech as annoying when it is used to influence them.

The issue of powerless versus powerful speech takes on added complexity when culture is added to the mix. What is viewed as powerful speech is culture-specific. The Japanese, for example, and most Asian cultures would view our version of powerful speech as immature because it indicates insensitivity to others and is likely to make agreement more difficult (Wetzel, 1988). In Malagasy society (Madagascar) "women have lower status than men but they use our stereotypical 'powerful' language; they do the confronting and reprimanding and in so doing . . . their constant violation of societal norms is seen as confirmation of their inferiority" (Smith-Hefner, 1988, p. 536). In Western societies, verbal obscenity and swearing is perceived as powerful language. Neither Japanese men nor women, however, use such language except in rare instances (De Klerk, 1991). In Malagasy and the Bhojpuri community in northeast India, "women are more abusive than men, and this . . . increases as we go down in the caste hierarchy" (Misra, 1980, p. 177).

When cultures clash over issues of significance, these different views of powerful and powerless speech can pose serious problems. When negotiating teams from Japan and the United States meet, misunderstandings easily arise (Hellweg et al., 1994). The language of Japanese negotiators is rife with indirect language viewed as powerless to American negotiators unfamiliar with cultural differences in perception. Japanese negotiators use such expressions as *I think, perhaps, probably*, and *maybe* with great frequency. They will also expect no interruptions while they speak. Americans negotiate in blunt terms, will in-terrupt, and view indirect and qualifying language as signs of weakness and lack of resolve. Misunderstandings of this nature make negotiations difficult and decision making troublesome.

Questions for Thought

1. If the powerless speech used by some women influences men, doesn't that make the language powerful, not powerless?
2. Do you think there is a relationship between powerful-powerless speech patterns in a culture and the individualism-collectivism focus of the culture? Explain.

Powerful speech is not always appropriate. Abusive and obscene language may be perceived in our culture as powerful speech, but it will offend group members and can destroy the cohesiveness of the group. Sometimes deferential language is a sign of respect and not merely powerless speech. Even tag questions can sometimes be used powerfully. If the leader of a small group says, "You'll see that this is done, won't you?" this may be issued more as a directive than a request. Then the tag question is authoritative, not weak.

Nonverbal Indicators

There are many nonverbal indicators of power. Let me provide just a sample of the more important ones.

Space is the prerogative of the powerful. Parents get the master bedroom while children may have to share a bedroom. The best offices with the most space are occupied by those individuals with the greatest power (Durand, 1977). The prime parking spaces are reserved for the higher-status individuals, as students experience on college campuses across the nation. Allocation usually follows a pecking order. Privacy of space is the prerogative of the powerful. Those individuals who are regarded as powerful may violate the space of those less powerful, but not vice versa. You must be granted access to the chambers of the privileged.

Posture and gestural communication are also markedly different for superordinates and subordinates. Generally, the powerful exhibit more relaxed, casual posture (Pavitt & Curtis, 1994). They feel free to slouch in chairs, place feet on tables, spread their arms and legs wide. The less powerful must be more concerned about posture, lest they offend. Their posture tends toward the stiff, tense, erect, and inhibited. Arms are kept close to the body or folded across the chest, and when sitting, knees may appear welded together. Subordinates can be

Space communicates power. Workers with low power are often given cramped offices that look more like rabbit warrens than comfortable places to conduct business. Spacious offices are normally given to the most powerful members of an organization.

directed to "sit up straight" or told to "stop slouching" by superordinates. Parents can tell children how to stand, sit, and move their bodies, but children do not have the same prerogative.

Touch clearly indicates power relationships in groups (Henley, 1995). Superordinates touch subordinates far more frequently than vice versa. The less powerful often feel required to yield to the touch of their superiors even when the touching is unwanted and offensive. Laws prohibiting sexual harassment have been established in the United States to protect the less powerful from the tactile abuse (among other inappropriate acts) of the more powerful. These statutes recognize that uneven power distribution plays a primary role in most cases of sexual harassment. Harassers take advantage of their power position and the vulnerability of those who are their targets.

Eye contact is yet another nonverbal indicator of relative degrees of power (Henley, 1995). Staring is done more freely by the powerful. The less powerful must monitor their eye contact more carefully. If a superordinate is speaking to a group of subordinates during a meeting, eye contact connotes active listening and deference to authority. Superordinates, however, may feel no obligation to exhibit interest or attentiveness to subordinates by maintaining eye contact. Submissiveness is also manifested by lowering your eyes and looking down.

Finally, nonverbal symbols of power include a wide variety of objects and tangible materials. Large desks, plush carpets, office windows, master keys, company cars, computers, the list could go on and on.

The consequences of using powerful versus powerless nonverbal communication can be seen from a study by Lee and Ofshe (1981). Subjects in this study read a summary of a personal-injury lawsuit. They then estimated how much money should be awarded to the injured party. Initially, all subjects favored no less than $10,000. A videotape was shown to the subjects showing a man arguing that the plaintiff should receive only $2,000. Although the man's arguments remained exactly the same, there were three separate nonverbal conditions. As Forsyth (1990) labels them, there was the "deference-demanding condition" (exhibited powerful nonverbal behaviors), the "deferential condition" (exhibited powerless nonverbal behaviors), and the "neutral condition" (moderate mixture of powerful and powerless nonverbal behaviors). The deference-demanding (powerful) speaker on the videotape influenced subjects to reduce the award by an average of $4,273. The neutral speaker influenced the subjects to reduce the award substantially less—an average of $2,426. The deferential (powerless) speaker, however, did not fare so well. Subjects *increased* the award an average of $2,843.

Much more could be added here regarding nonverbal indicators of power, but my point has been made. You can discern the relative distribution of power in a group by observing both verbal and nonverbal indicators and noticing a few general communication patterns.

---

second look

Indicators of Power

General Indicators
- Who defines whom
- Whose decisions are followed
- Who opposes significant change

Verbal Indicators
- Verbal dominance
- Powerless/powerful speech patterns

Nonverbal Indicators
- Space
- Posture and gestural communication
- Touch
- Eye Contact
- Objects and tangible materials

In summary, power is a central dynamic in all groups. Power is the ability to influence the attainment of goals sought by yourself and others. Power is not a property of any individual. Power is the product of transactions between group members. Information, expertise, rewards and punishments, personal qualities, and legitimate authority are primary resources of power. Groups must endorse these resources before they have power potential. The influence that you wield cannot be determined precisely. Nevertheless, you can approximate the distribution of power in groups by observing certain general patterns of communication, plus verbal and nonverbal indicators.

Questions for Critical Thinkers

1. Information is power. Can misinformation also serve as a power resource? Explain your answer.
2. Can a person learn to be charismatic?
3. If punishment has significant drawbacks, why is it typically used more frequently than rewards by those in power positions?

1. id problem

2. set date to talk about

3. describe problems "I" statements

4. paraphrase bACK

5. solicate their needs as well (id I problem will bring up others)
      others

6. you understand other person / paraphrase
      bACK what you hear

7. negotiate solution

CHAPTER 9

Power: An Architect of Conflict

The television remote control was invented for Zenith Corporation by Dr. Robert Adler. It first appeared on June 8, 1956. There are approximately 400 million remote controls in use according to the Consumer Electronics Manufacturers Association, and this simple technological device has contributed to many power struggles (McCall, 1996). Who do you think most often controls the remote during family television viewing: men, women, or children? Sociologist Alexis Walker, president of the National Council of Family Relations, claims on the basis of a study she conducted that men are the predominant channel surfers, much to the exasperation of other family members (McCall, 1996). Numerous studies reveal similar findings (Bellamy & Walker, 1996). One frustrated woman in Walker's study volunteered, "He just flips through the channels. It drives me crazy" (McCall, 1996, p. D1). The hand that holds the remote control dictates the television watching for the entire family. The battle over the remote control exemplifies how a commonplace power imbalance can be consequential in groups.

Power imbalances are a daily occurrence. At work, the shift from job talk to personal chatting is usually initiated by the most powerful person (Tannen, 1994). If the office manager takes a break and starts telling stories, other workers of lesser status and position feel free to join. Similar behavior from underlings, however, may be perceived as loafing if not sanctioned by a more powerful person. This "double standard" can make employees edgy, even resentful.

Apologies for mishaps and misdeeds are expected from the less powerful but rarely from the more powerful who often feel they owe no apology to underlings. Children are expected to apologize to parents if they smash up the family car, but parents don't normally feel compelled to apologize to children for crashing the family car, even though such an occurrence may pose a significant inconvenience to children. Compliments are more often offered by more powerful individuals in a work environment (Tannen, 1994). When less powerful employees offer compliments to supervisors they have to be concerned not to look like a "suck up" to their boss and fellow workers.

Imbalance of power is a key communication issue for groups. The primary focus of this chapter will be on how we transact power in groups, especially when power is unequally distributed. My <u>objectives</u> are:

1. to discuss the relationship between power imbalances and conflict in groups,
2. to explain the five general responses to power differences in groups, and
3. to describe ways that the competent communicator can transact power in small groups.

IMBALANCE OF POWER

<u>When power is inequitably distributed in a group and dominance becomes the focus, systemwide power struggles often ensue</u> (Wilmot & Hocker, 1998). In an atmosphere of dominance and submissiveness, those who exercise the greatest influence are stimulated by their ability to manipulate and control events and people. They usually jealously guard their power. Those who exercise relatively

A courageous, unarmed man stops tanks during the Tiananmen Square upheaval in China in 1989. An imbalance of power, starkly evident here, often leads to conflict and defiance.

little power, however, will often feel angered, frustrated, or disheartened by their impotence (Baumeister et al., 1996). This emotional disparity between the relatively powerful and the relatively powerless can serve as a catalyst for conflict. Ugly instances of violence and aggression may result from a competitive dominance-prevention power imbalance.

Focus Questions

1. How are power imbalances and violence related?
2. "Dominance is an architect of conflict." What does this mean?

Physical Violence and Aggression

<u>Significant power disparities, especially when the more powerful individual acts on his or her advantage, often fosters violent or aggressive transactions.</u> Gelles and Straus (1988) in their extensive study of family violence conclude: "The greater the inequality, the more one person makes all the decisions and has all the power, the greater the risk of violence. Power, power confrontations, and perceived threats to domination, in fact, are underlying issues in almost all acts of family violence" (p. 82). In families and marriages where the husband insists on being the dominant decision maker, breakup of the marriage and family or

persistent unhappiness experienced by all parties is *four times more likely* than in families where the husband shares power (Gottman & Silver, 1999).

Violence easily spills beyond the husband–wife relationship and becomes a systemwide problem. The anger and frustration a victim of violence feels often becomes displaced when the victim attacks innocent, less powerful targets. "It is not unusual to find a pattern of violence in a home where the husband hits his wife, the wife in turn uses violence toward her children, the older children use violence on the younger children, and the youngest child takes out his or her frustration on the family pet . . . At each level the most powerful person is seeking to control the next least powerful person" (Gelles & Straus, 1988, p. 35).

When people exercise power over us, destructive conflict often results. In the workplace, nasty conflicts are a serious problem. The United States has the highest rate of homicide in the workplace of any industrialized nation, averaging more than 1,000 homicides each year ("Survey," 1998). Many of these homicides are the direct result of firings or attempted firings of workers by supervisors or teams. According to a 1998 report by the U.S. Justice Department, almost two million people each year are victims of violence on the job (Lardner, 1998). Too often we "settle" our power struggles at work with aggression. "Workplace bullying" is also an increasing problem. **Workplace bullying** occurs when supervisors scream at subordinates and coworkers and humiliate competent employees by taking away their responsibilities when work is not performed to the exact specifications of the bullying supervisor. An International Labor Organization survey conducted in 1998 in 32 countries found that workplace bullying is one of the fastest-growing areas of workplace aggression in these countries ("Survey," 1998). Although a troublesome problem in the United States, it is even worse in other countries. In Britain, 58% of the workers surveyed reported being victims of workplace bullying. In Japan, the problem is so bad that a "bullying hotline" has been established to assist harassed workers ("Survey," 1998). Dominance is an architect of conflict.

Verbal and Nonverbal Contempt

Power struggles in families and groups do not always end in physical violence. In fact, a more likely initial consequence of power imbalance in groups is verbal and nonverbal expressions of contempt. Coaches of teams, for example, will simply tear apart the self-esteem and self-worth of players. Team leaders in the workplace will berate less powerful team members.

Contempt is the verbal or nonverbal expression of insult that emotionally abuses others. It is a potent form of verbal aggression. Contempt is not merely criticism (Gottman, 1994). It is more destructive than criticism because it seeks to humiliate, even destroy, whoever is targeted. Name-calling ("stupid," "fool," "idiot," "incompetent"), cursing, hostile humor (jokes that hurt and ridicule others), vicious sarcasm, and insulting body language (rolling your eyes, curling your upper lip in a sneer, shaking your head side-to-side while laughing snidely) are types of contempt. A 36-year-old female trucking company executive expresses her contempt for men in power positions this way: They are "a bunch of shallow, bald, middle-aged men with character disorders. They don't have the emotional capacity it takes to qualify as human beings. One good thing about these white, male, almost extinct mammals is that they are growing old. We get to watch them die!" (Gates, 1993, p. 49). Ouch! Contempt is not subtle.

Power imbalances easily create a climate that encourages physical, verbal, and nonverbal aggression. Both aggressors and victims engage in such negative behavior in a dominance-prevention power struggle. A more equitable sharing of power is a primary preventive of such competitive ugliness in groups.

FOCUS on Culture

Power Distance and Cultural Differences

In the United States, power imbalances are often the catalyst for aggressive behavior. The responses to power imbalances in some cultures, however, are strikingly different from the United States. <u>Cultures vary in their attitudes concerning the appropriateness of power imbalances</u>. Hofstede (1991) terms these variations the power distance dimension (herein referred to simply as PD).

Countries that are culturally classified as *low-PD* (<u>relatively weak emphasis on maintaining power differences</u>), such as the United States, Sweden, Denmark, Israel, and Austria, are guided by norms and institutional regulations that minimize power distinctions among group members and between groups. Challenging authority (not easy in any culture, as the Milgram studies demonstrate), flattening organizational hierarchies, and using power legitimately are subscribed to by low-PD cultures. Low-PD cultures do not advocate eliminating power disparities entirely, and in a country such as the United States, power differences obviously exist. The emphasis on maintaining hierarchical boundaries between the relatively powerful and powerless, however, are de-emphasized in low-PD cultures. Workers in low-PD cultures may disagree with their supervisors, in fact, disagreement may be encouraged by bosses. Even socializing outside of the work environment and communication on a first-name basis between workers and bosses is not unusual (Brislin, 1993).

Countries culturally classified as *high-PD* (<u>relatively strong emphasis on maintaining power differences</u>), such as the Philippines, Mexico, India, Singapore, and Hong Kong, are guided by norms and institutional regulations that accept, even cultivate, power distinctions. The actions of authorities are rarely challenged, the powerful are thought to have a legitimate right to use their power, and organizational and social hierarchies are encouraged (Lustig & Koester, 1999). Workers normally do not feel comfortable disagreeing with their bosses, and friendships and socializing between the two groups are rare.

The reactions by members to power imbalances in small groups are likely to reflect where a culture falls on the power distance dimension. One study (Bond et al., 1985) compared people's reactions to insults in a high-PD (Hong Kong) and a low-PD (United States) culture. Subjects from Hong Kong were less upset than those from the United States when they were insulted, as long as the initiator of the insult was a high-status person. As Brislin (1993) explains, "When people accept status distinctions as normal, they accept the fact that the powerful are different than the less powerful. The powerful can engage in behaviors that the less powerful cannot, in this case insult people and have the insult accepted as part of their rights" (p. 255).

Differences in power distance do not mean that high-PD cultures never experience conflict and aggression in small groups emanating from power imbalances. <u>Members of low-PD cultures, however, are more likely to respond with frustration, outrage, and hostility to power imbalances than are members of high-PD cultures</u> because low-PD cultures value power balance even though the experience of everyday life in such cultures may reflect a somewhat different reality. In a low-PD culture, the struggle to achieve the ideal of balanced power in small groups is more compelling and the denial of power is likely to be perceived as more unjust, even intolerable, than in a high-PD culture where power balance is not viewed from the same vantage point.

Questions for Thought

1. Is it merely ethnocentric bias ("My culture is better than your culture") that Americans typically regard power balance as preferable to power imbalance?
2. Which leadership style would likely be preferred in high-PD cultures, directive or participative? How about low-PD cultures? Explain.
3. If you were an exchange student in a high-PD culture, would you have difficulty adjusting to the "Don't challenge your teachers" norm in the high-PD culture?

TRANSACTING POWER

Power is transacted in groups in far more complicated ways than by merely going nitro when there's a power struggle. Transacting power in groups can involve any of five general responses. These responses are Compliance, Alliance, Resistance, Defiance, and Significance (C-A-R-D-S). <u>The last four alternatives are the ways members attempt to balance the power in groups</u>.

Compliance: The Power of Groups

Compliance is the process of consenting to the dictates and desires of others. Compliance involves both obedience to authority and conformity to group norms.

Focus Questions
1. How are obedience and conformity similar to and different from each other?
2. "Expedient conformity can lead to private acceptance." How?
3. How does deindividuation and pressure toward uniformity encourage conformity?

Conformity versus Obedience   When compliance is the result of group influence on the individual, it is usually referred to as conformity, since we are expected to comply with norms established by the group. When compliance is the result of a high-power group member (e.g., leader) influencing lower-power members, it is normally referred to as obedience. <u>Both conformity and obedience are powerful forms of compliance</u>. "Obedience and conformity both refer to the abdication of initiative to an external source" (Milgram, 1974, p. 114).

An interesting variation of the standard Milgram obedience-to-authority studies pitted conformity against obedience. In this modification (Milgram, 1974), there were two confederates and one naive subject. The two confederates administered the test and the naive subject administered the punishment (increasing levels of electric shock) for incorrect answers. At the 150-volt shock level, one of the confederates refused to continue taking part in the experiment despite the experimenter's insistence. At 210 volts, the second confederate bailed out of the experiment.

With two defectors for support, 90% of the naive subjects refused to comply with the experimenter's command to increase the shocks all the way to 450 volts. Most of the 40 naive subjects, 60%, stopped at 210 volts or less. Yet in a comparison study where the naive subject faced the experimenter alone, only 35% refused to comply with the experimenter's command and *refusal never occurred before 300 volts*. <u>Conformity to group norms can sometimes prove to be a more powerful tendency than obeying authority</u>. The defectors created a group norm that opposed shocking a victim against his will. Most subjects complied with the norm instead of following the authority figure's insistent directives.

<u>Compliance in either form (conformity or obedience) seems to be the rule, not the exception</u>. The ease with which individuals can be directed to behave compliantly has been demonstrated countless times by Allen Funt's *Candid Camera*. Consider the person who stopped eating a hamburger whenever the "Don't Eat" sign flashed; the man who turned right, then left, then faced the rear of an elevator whenever a group of fellow travelers led the way; the people who stopped at a red light hanging over a sidewalk; and the drivers who, when presented with a roadblock and a sign reading, "Delaware Is Closed Today," turned around and drove away. One woman asked meekly if New Jersey was open. As a rule, most people are compliant in most situations.

Why we conform to group norms and pressure and under what conditions we are likely to conform was discussed in chapter 3. The process of inducing conformity and its relation to power imbalances, however, has not been discussed.

Two Types of Conformity   There are two types of conformity relevant to group communication: expedient conformity and private acceptance (Smith, 1982). **Expedient conformity** occurs when an individual expresses attitudes and exhibits behaviors acceptable to the group, yet harbors private beliefs at odds with the group. Expedient conformity happens primarily because the conformist wishes to avoid specific punishment for noncompliance or hopes to gain a specific reward for publicly parroting the party line. Expedient conformists remain true to the group only when they are under surveillance.

The aftermath of the Beijing massacre is a stark illustration of expedient conformity. Mandatory "study sessions," indoctrination meetings aimed at intimidating the population into submissiveness and proselytizing the big lie that no one was killed in Tiananmen Square in June 1989, were scheduled at workplaces throughout China after the popular uprising was squashed. Some actually came to believe the Orwellian version of events, but as journalist Lewis Simons (1989) reported, many citizens simply engaged in expedient conformity. As one young Chinese man explained, "No one makes any comments. If it's absolutely unavoidable, we give a very short answer and try to make it seem that our thinking is very close to the mainstream. Not exactly the same, because that looks suspicious, but similar" (p. 2A).

Closer to home, you are often faced with circumstances requiring expedient conformity. The consequences are likely to be far less severe than what the Chinese people experienced. Nevertheless, there will be times when being a team player is expected of you even though you may privately disagree with the group's decision. Your job, even friendships, may depend on following group orthodoxy.

In contrast, **private acceptance** occurs when an individual's public and private attitudes and beliefs are compatible with the group's norms and viewpoint. The individual accepts the norms of the group as his or her own. The individual and the group are congruent in their values and outlook. Close surveillance is unnecessary because the individual has internalized the norms of the group and the values and attitudes that act as the underpinnings of these norms. In some cases, what begins as expedient conformity can develop into private acceptance (see Closer Look: "The Bizarre Case of Patty Hearst").

CLOSER LOOK

The Bizarre Case of Patty Hearst

Expedient conformity can lead to private acceptance. One of the most dramatic and publicized instances of such conversion began on February 3, 1974. Patricia Campbell Hearst, granddaughter of the late newspaper tycoon William Randolph Hearst, was kidnapped from her Berkeley, California, apartment by a small group of self-proclaimed revolutionaries who called themselves the Symbionese Liberation Army. The SLA demanded that the wealthy Hearst family purchase several million dollars' worth of food and distribute it to the poor of California. The SLA threatened to execute Patty Hearst unless this ransom was disseminated to the "people oppressed by capitalism." The de-

mand was met. The nation watched transfixed by this prisoner-of-war melodrama. After 2 months of captivity, 2 weeks of which Patty Hearst spent blindfolded and incarcerated in a closet, the melodrama took a startling twist. The captive became an SLA convert.

Patty Hearst pictured before her kidnapping by the SLA and after her conversion when she became Tania, "urban guerrilla."

Patty Hearst, nineteen-year-old politically naive college student and kidnap victim, announced that she had joined the SLA. She renounced her family, calling them "pig Hearsts," and proclaimed herself Tania, "urban guerrilla." A disbelieving public was further shaken when, on April 15, she participated with the SLA in a bank robbery recorded on camera for all to see. Just in case anyone doubted Patty Hearst's conversion, on May 16, she assisted the escape from arrest of two of her captors, William and Emily Harris, by covering their retreat with a fusillade of bullets from her automatic weapon. The next day, all members of the SLA except the Harrises and Tania were killed in a shootout with police in Los Angeles. Patty Hearst eluded an intensive 20-month search spearheaded by the FBI before she and the Harrises were captured.

So the facts are these: The SLA kidnapped Patty Hearst, brutally beat her boyfriend during the commando-like capture, blindfolded her and threw her in a closet for 2 weeks, abused her, and threatened to execute her if the ransom wasn't paid. Sure sounds like a group I'd want to join. How about you? So why did this heir to the Hearst newspaper empire choose to become an SLA member? How could such a radical transformation have happened to Patty Hearst? How could she have moved from expedient conformity (e.g., doing everything the SLA told her to say and do in order to stay alive) to actual private acceptance, from average college student to defiant revolutionary?

There are several explanations for Patty Hearst's bizarre conversion. First, she fell victim to the **Stockholm Syndrome,** named for a hostage situation that developed during a bank robbery in Sweden's capital city. Galanter (1989) explains why this occurs: "The agent inflicting distress on the dependent person is also perceived as the party who can provide relief. Thus, pressure is exerted on those experiencing distress to accommodate to the party who comes to be seen as the only one able to offer relief" (p. 105).

Patty Hearst feared for her life during the initial stages of her confinement. When the SLA eventually released her from the closet, then treated her well, she was understandably relieved, even grateful to her captors. By communicating her fidelity and compliance SLA members might continue treating her well (Galanter, 1989). She became dependent on her captors. The SLA became her "protector."

Second, the SLA used **boundary control** as a means of inducing internalization of its political views. The only information communicated to Patty Hearst was from her SLA captors. Politically naive and indifferent at the outset, Patty Hearst had no reservoir of knowledge, no means of independently assessing the validity of SLA propaganda. She was unable to communicate with others who could bolster any attempts she might make to resist the SLA persuasion effort.

Third, Patty Hearst gradually came to believe that she had the freedom to walk undeterred out the door and return to her family and friends. She was strongly encouraged, however, to join the SLA. This was an important final step in the conversion of Patty Hearst. The internalization of an attitude or belief as one's own emanates from a **perception of free choice,** not coercion. Expedient conformity is induced by threats of punishment or offers of extrinsic rewards (e.g., payoffs in money or gifts). Private acceptance flows from the perception of unimpeded choice. Patty Hearst came to believe that she had arrived at her new worldview through many hours of thoughtful group discussion with her captors. This group discussion was critical to her transformation. She began to accept "freely" that "U.S. imperialism is the enemy of all oppressed people."

Patty Hearst ultimately survived her harrowing group experience, but not without consequences. She reverted to her more conventional worldview following arrest. A "brainwashing" defense put on by internationally renowned lawyer F. Lee Bailey, however, failed to sway the jury in her trial on bank robbery charges. The jury accepted the less melodramatic explanation for her behavior, namely, that conversion from expedient conformity to private acceptance of the SLA came through some coercion but mostly through standard group conformity techniques and was therefore of her own volition. She served almost 2 years in prison before her sentence was commuted by President Jimmy Carter. After her release, she married her former bodyguard, had two daughters, and in 1996 she published her first novel.

Her saga didn't end there, however. In July, 1999, Kathleen Ann Soliah, who joined the SLA long after Patty Hearst was kidnapped, was nabbed by the FBI on attempted bombing charges, after living a quiet life in Minnesota for almost a quarter of a century as Sara Jane Olson, mother of three. The Patty Hearst case once again was front-page news because of Soliah's SLA association. Soon after, in October 1999, former President Jimmy Carter pressed President Clinton to pardon Patty Hearst. "The fact is she deserves the pardon," claimed Carter. "Her oldest daughter has just entered college. And all this time Patty has not been able to vote; she's not been a full-fledged American citizen. And I think she's a special case" (Nelson, 1999, p. 3B). As of this writing, no decision had been made.

Questions for Thought

1. Can you think of experiences in your own life where expedient conformity to a group has led eventually to private acceptance?
2. Would you have found Patty Hearst guilty if you had been on the jury? Explain.
3. Should she receive a presidential pardon?

Group Influence and Conformity   There is a process called **deindividuation** that liberates group members' inhibitions to behave antisocially. Deindividuation occurs when individuals shed their personal identities and replace them with a group persona (Jessup et al., 1990).

Why does deindividuation occur in groups? *Anonymity* is the principal reason (Wade & Tavris, 1998). As a group increases in size, an individual can meld into the group more easily. An antisocial act becomes a group act, not an individual one. Anonymity provided by the mask of groupness can embolden even normally hesitant individuals. Once the individual assumes a group identity, responsibility becomes diffused among the many. Individual acts appear relatively inconsequential even though the collective result may be serious. After all, screaming at an official, cursing at, taunting, and verbally abusing an opposing team may seem relatively harmless. Collectively, however, it may precipitate an ugly riot.

The term "fan" is short for fanatic, and deindividuated sports fanatics worldwide have produced ugly riots with increasing frequency. Fans enraged by England's loss to Germany in a soccer match in 1990 rioted throughout Great Britain, resulting in three deaths, dozens of injuries, and 600 arrests. Celebration of the Chicago Bulls' third straight NBA championship erupted into a riot that left two dead, 700 arrested, and caused massive property damage. Championship victories led to riots by celebrating fans in Montreal, Dallas, and Chicago in 1993, and Denver in 1999.

In addition to the process of deindividuation, group influence manifests itself in **pressure toward uniformity** among members. Solomon Asch (1952) found that when a group composed of confederates of the experimenter unanimously judged the length of a line *incorrectly,* 35% of the naive subjects unaware of the set-up consistently conformed with the obviously erroneous group judgment. Social psychologist Anthony Pratkanis of the University of California Santa Cruz replicated this study for *Dateline NBC* in August 1997. In his

Riots by deindividuated sports fans are not uncommon even when a sports team is victorious.

study, 9 of 16 college students studied fell in line with the unanimous choice made by 6 other group members, even though the choice was clearly incorrect.

There is an understanding from experience and observation that to go along is to get along. There are rewards for compliance and there are sanctions for noncompliance. <u>Group influence is a significant factor inducing compliance in individuals.</u>

Alliance: Coalition Formation

Subgroups inevitably form in a human system of any size larger than two. These subgroups often develop around some issue or idea that triggers a conflict within the system. **Alliances** are associations in the form of subgroups entered into for mutual benefit or a common objective. Groups normally splinter into subgroups when there is a disagreement concerning how best to achieve a group goal. In most circumstances, alliances in groups are temporary. They are expedient unions between two or more group members primarily to increase the influence of specific individuals in matters of mutual importance. These temporary alliances are called **coalitions.**

Power is central to coalition formation (Grusky et al., 1995). Group members form coalitions to increase their power and thus control decisions made in the group when group members don't agree on issues of significance to the group.

Focus Questions

1. Which theory of coalition formation is stronger: minimum power or minimum resources?
2. From your experience and observations, do coalitions form primarily from attitude similarity, identification with group members, or determinations of power distribution and potential rewards?

Minimum Power versus Minimum Resources

Weaker members of groups increase their power primarily by forming coalitions (Folger et al., 1993). Weaker members acting alone pose no threat to stronger members unless weaker members organize and form coalitions. The less powerful seek coalitions to balance power in groups more evenly.

Because coalitions can change the distribution of power in a group, coalition formation is adversarial, competitive, and contentious. Coalition formation may occur when your group works on a project for class. Coalitions are formed not simply to advance the goals of the allied members (e.g., choosing the preferred topic or option for a group project), but also to prevent the attainment of noncoalition members' goals (e.g., choosing an objectionable topic or option for a group topic). Consequently, powerful members often move to stymie formation of coalitions among weaker members. This can be accomplished by forming their own coalitions with weaker parties or by confusing issues and arousing discontent in the ranks of the weak, thus splintering potential allies.

There are two classic theories of coalition formation. The first is Caplow's (1968) **minimum power theory** or the "weakness is strength" perspective. In a triad (group of three), the weakest member will be the only one who will always be included in a coalition. Coalitions form on the basis of the minimum power necessary to overcome an opponent. Group members are guided by a desire to maximize their control over others and to minimize the control others exercise over them.

Gamson's (1961) **minimum resources theory** rests on a "strength is weakness" point of view. Group members with the most power are included in coalitions less often than are weaker members (Murnighan, 1978). This is true because more powerful members would lay claim to a larger share of the rewards for joining a successful coalition than weaker members, leaving less for other members. Also, sometimes powerful members are unaware of the necessity to protect their power position by forming alliances (Komorita & Ellis, 1988).

Research shows that minimum power theory accurately predicts likely coalitions when the group members are highly sophisticated strategic players. Minimum resource theory accurately predicts likely coalitions when group members are inexperienced and naive about coalition formation (Komorita & Kravitz, 1983). Neither theory offers a complete explanation for how coalitions form in groups.

Additional Perspectives

Some coalitions obviously form not on the basis of minimum power or resources, but on the basis of identification with another member (personal qualities as a power resource). Adcock and Yang (1984) argue that in a family, children are more likely to ally with the same sex parent because they can identify more closely with that parent. Thus, the odds of coalition formation with *either* parent would not be 50–50 as predicted in the minimum power or minimum resources theories.

Personal observation also reveals that despite the predictions, coalition formation doesn't always follow probabilities. Parents do form alliances in order to present a united front against their children, especially on matters of potential disagreement, such as discipline, curfews, drug use, or dating. One study (Grusky et al., 1995) found that 41% of the coalitions that formed in four-person families were parental coalitions that reinforce the status differences between parents and their children. <u>Coalitions that split parents risk eroding family solidarity and may threaten the survival of the family system</u>. Coalitions involving the father were the strongest whereas coalitions involving the youngest child were the weakest.

As useful as these explanations of coalition formation are, there is one crucial element missing from all of the theories discussed. <u>Coalitions do not form in the absence of communication</u>. Human beings don't always choose what is in their best self-interest. Sometimes we make choices based more on interpersonal attraction or revulsion than we do on more objective determinations of rewards, attitudinal similarity, or power potential.

It's plausible that you might form a coalition with other group members in order to command a larger share of the rewards or because of similarity of worldviews and goals. But as sure as mildew finds a home in Seattle, incompetent communication can dampen enthusiasm for the development of such an alliance. Skillful, competent communication, however, can enhance the probabilities that a coalition will form even in unlikely circumstances.

---

second look

Theories of Coalition Formation

Theory	Explanation
• Minimum Power	• Weakness is strength
• Minimum Resources	• Strength is weakness
• Identification	• Affiliation with/attraction to group members
• Attitude Similarity	• Commonality of goals—expedience

Resistance: Covert Noncompliance

<u>Resistance is normally the choice of the less powerful</u>. **Resistance** is a covert form of communicating noncompliance, and it is often duplicitous and manipulative. Resisters are subtle saboteurs. When faced with a dominant individual (supervisor, parent, or group leader) it is often safer to employ indirect means of noncompliance than direct confrontation or open defiance. Nevertheless, even high-power individuals on occasion will use resistance strategies. If

undercurrents of dissatisfaction are apparent, openly defying the wishes of group members may provoke outright rebellion.

Resistance is the prevention form of power (power from). Done craftily, resistance can be difficult to identify unequivocally for those who are its targets because the sabotage is ambiguous, often communicating a seemingly sincere effort to comply. The target is often left mostly convinced that resistance is taking place, but is unable to make this apparent to the group due to the mixed messages being sent.

In this section I will discuss specific communication strategies of resistance, or what Bach and Goldberg (1972) term "passive aggression." I have combined their list of strategies with my own.

Focus Questions

1. Since resistance strategies rely on deceit and mixed messages, should competent communicators always avoid them?
2. How should a competent communicator deal with resistance strategies?

Strategic Stupidity   Your group is working on an important class presentation. Each member has been assigned a topic area to research. At one of your meetings, an inventory is taken regarding information collected up to this point on relevant topic areas. When asked for a status report, one of the members of your group whines, "I couldn't find anything on world hunger." Are you faced with a drooling dolt or is this person covertly resisting active involvement in the group project? Bet your money on the latter.

When you do not want to expend energy on a project, especially if the project was not of your choosing, you may feel hesitant directly complaining to the group about your dissension. If you have been outvoted in the group when the proposal for the project was decided, you may resent having little influence on the group decision. You may feign stupidity in order to penalize the group and to exercise influence, at least in a negative way. When the success of the group presentation depends on all members pulling a load, one resistant member can create systemwide problems.

Strategic stupidity can effectively thwart compliance attempts by more powerful group members because in most instances the strategy is part of a recurring pattern. If used only once, it becomes an isolated incident. If used repeatedly as is often the case, strategic stupidity can frustrate the dominant party to the point of capitulation. If group members must spoon-feed their strategically stupid member on where to look on the Internet or in the library for information on world hunger, they may decide that this takes too much effort, surrender in exasperation, and do the research themselves.

Strategic stupidity works exceedingly well when the low-power person claims stupidity, is forced to attempt the task anyway, then purposely performs the task ineptly. Doing a half-baked job of a simple task can exasperate even the most patient person. If criticized for doing a poor job, the low-power person can always retort, "How was I supposed to know?" or "I told you I didn't know how to do it." The pathetic performance becomes proof that the stupidity was "real." To expect any better performance in the absence of careful and persistent tutelage would be an injustice.

Loss of Motor Function   This resistance strategy is an effective companion to strategic stupidity. Here the low-power person doesn't pretend to be stupid. The resister just acts incredibly clumsy, often resulting in costly damage. There is a mixed message here. <u>The nonverbal behavior displays resistance but the verbal statement that often accompanies it feigns a genuine attempt to comply</u>.

      I still remember an incident that happened to me years ago when as a college student I worked summers at a can factory. I was a worker in quality control. In a less-than-admirable effort to avoid the horrid press department, I kept ducking out of sight at the start of the morning shift in order to avoid the supervisor, who had a habit of selecting some poor college student employee to replace a worker who had quit the press department. The press department was where can lids were stamped out and sent through a machine, coated, and packed in boxes or paper sleeves stacked onto wood pallets.

      One day the supervisor spotted me and sent me to the press department to replace someone who had quit. I went reluctantly. The job I was given pitted me against a machine that pumped out can lids in rapid fashion. I had to stack the lids without spilling them onto the floor. I purposely adopted the loss of motor function strategy in order to get out of the job. By the end of my shift, I had spilled thousands of lids onto the factory floor, shut the machine down four times, incensed the machinist who had to spend 20 minutes starting up the machine each time it was shut down, and forced my supervisor to call in two workers to clean up my mess. I was making the system adapt to my act of sabotage. All the while I insisted in bellicose tones to my upset supervisor that I was trying hard but that the job was impossible to do. The next day I returned to my previous job (half-expecting to be fired), hid out, watched my supervisor pick another college student to take my press job, and I spent the rest of the summer free from press department duties. I even received a promotion. Ironically, I ended up in the press department the next summer and, with a change of attitude, managed to master the job with little difficulty.

      <u>It is the apparent effort exerted that makes this strategy so effective</u>. In my can factory incident I had sweat rolling down my face. I seemed to be making every effort possible to keep up with the diabolical machine. I just couldn't quite stay with it. If the high-power person alleges deliberate sabotage, the low-power person can always become incensed, even incredulous that anyone would even suggest such a thing. It's an awkward position for a high-power person. How does one conclusively prove willfulness? You don't want to look like you're beating up on a less-powerful group member. If you make an accusation of willfulness but fail to convince the group, then you may lose power by diminishing your credibility (personal qualities as a power base).

The Misunderstanding Mirage   This is the "I thought you meant" or the "I could have sworn you said" strategy. The resistance is "expressed behind a cloak of great sincerity" (Bach & Goldberg, 1972, p. 110).

I have observed numerous instances of this strategy in my group communication classes. Typically, a student will deliberately miss an important meeting with his or her group then claim, "Oh, I thought we were going to meet on *Thursday*. Sorry. I just got confused." I have lost count of the number of times students have used this strategy to excuse their late assignments. "You said it was due Friday, not today, didn't you?" they'll say hopefully. If I respond, "No, your paper is due today," my resistant student often replies, "Well, I thought you said Friday so can I turn my assignment in then without a penalty?" The implied message attached to this ploy is clear: "Since this is a simple misunderstanding, penalizing me for a late assignment would be unfair."

Again, the high-power person is placed in a seemingly awkward position. The teacher may lose some power (legitimate authority) if the class sees his or her behavior as capricious and unfair.

<u>High-power persons sometimes use this strategy of misunderstanding in order to avoid felt obligations.</u> Teachers may purposely miss appointments with students or committee meetings on campus because they'd prefer to leave town before the rush-hour traffic. Pretending to have misunderstood when the meeting was scheduled relieves them of having to confront directly their own irresponsibility.

Selective Amnesia   Have you ever noticed that some people are very forgetful? This seems especially true regarding those things that these same individuals find distasteful. This temporary amnesia is highly selective when used as a resistance strategy. We rarely forget what is important to us and what we like doing.

<u>The message is again mixed.</u> You manifest no outright signs of noncompliance. You outwardly agree to perform the distasteful task. Appointments, promises, and agreements just slip your mind. If your group insists that you assume a larger share of unpleasant tasks, you can always agree, then forget to do them.

A more sophisticated version of this strategy, however, is truly selective. Take an errand such as purchasing office supplies for your department. Remember to buy all the items except one or two important ones. Hey, you did pretty well, didn't you? So you forgot the disks for the computers and now the entire office staff is affected. No one's perfect. If your selective amnesia proves to be a recurring problem, that errand gig may shift to someone else.

Tactical Tardiness   When you really don't want to go to a meeting, a class, a lecture, or whatever, you can show your contempt by arriving late. If you don't arrive too late, you can still claim that you attended the event, so you're protected from punishment for being absent. Showing up late irritates, frustrates, and even humiliates those who take the meeting seriously. Tactical tardiness is intended to produce these very feelings in those requiring attendance.

Tactical tardiness asserts power in disguised form. The group is faced with a dilemma. The group may wait for your arrival, but this holds the entire group hostage until you arrive. Members' plans for the day may be trashed by the delay. The other alternative is to commence without you. This also may prove to be problematic, however. Once you saunter in you'll naturally expect an update on the meeting. If you offer reasonable sounding excuses for your late arrival, the group will feel bound to clue you in on what has already transpired, thereby halting progress until you have been informed.

All instances of tardiness are not necessarily tactical. Occasionally, getting to meetings on time is not possible through no fault of our own. Tactical tardiness is a recurrent pattern of resistance, not a rare occurrence.

Tactical tardiness is not the sole province of the less powerful. High-power persons may also use this strategy to reinforce their dominance. Self-important celebrities with egos swelled like puffer fish often arrive late to functions. They hope to underscore their perceived superiority over the peons who admire them by making them wait.

Purposeful Procrastination   Most people put off doing that which they dislike. There is nothing purposeful about this. There is no strategy involved. Procrastinators just tend to be hedonistic: they pursue pleasure and avoid pain. Procrastination, or what someone once called the "hardening of the oughteries," can become a resistance strategy when it is purposefully aimed at a target.

Purposeful procrastinators pretend that they will pursue a task "soon." While promising imminent results, they deliberately refuse to commit to a specific time or date for task accomplishment. Trying to pin down a purposeful procrastinator is like taking a knife and stabbing Jell-O to a wall—it won't stick. They'll make vague promises. When you become exasperated by the ambiguity and noncommittal attitude, the purposeful procrastinator will try to make you the problem. "Relax! You'll stroke out if you're not careful. I said I'd get to it, didn't I?" The implication is clear. You're impatient and unreasonable. The job will get done—not without delay after delay, however. If the task doesn't get accomplished, it is because "something came up unexpectedly." If you express irritation at the delays, you're a nag.

---

second look

Resistance Strategies

Strategic Stupidity—smart people acting dumb on purpose; feigned stupidity
Loss of Motor Function—sudden attack of the clumsies
The Misunderstanding Mirage—illusory mistakes
Selective Amnesia—no fear of Alzheimer's; forgetting only the distasteful
Tactical Tardiness—late for reasons within your control
Purposeful Procrastination—promising to do that which you have no intention of doing anytime soon, if ever

---

All six resistance strategies I have discussed result from a dominance form of power. When power is imbalanced, low-power group members will often fight a covert battle of resistance to domination.

Resistance strategies are generally viewed as negative and unproductive (Bach & Goldberg, 1972). This is true in an ideal sense. Resistance strategies are underhanded, deceitful, and rest on mixed messages. This doesn't make for terribly competent communication, nor do such strategies make conflict management easy. Resistance strategies are not the type of skills a competent communicator needs to learn. Nevertheless, I am not willing to rule them out unequivocally. Low-power members may have no better tools to resist dominant group members. The essence of the problem doesn't lie in the resistance strategies. The dominance form of power creates a competitive group atmosphere where resistance strategies are nurtured and encouraged.

From the standpoint of competent communication, however, my emphasis must be on how to deal effectively with resistance, since the resistance may not always be noble. <u>There are three principal ways for the competent communicator to deal with resistance strategies in groups</u>:

1. *Confront the strategy directly*. Identify the communication pattern and ferret out the hidden hostility. Once this has been accomplished, efforts must be made to discover alternatives to dominance–submissiveness power patterns. Care should be taken to use the descriptive pattern of communication discussed in chapter 4 on group climate.

2. *Thwart the enabling process*. We become enablers when we allow ourselves to become ensnared in the resister's net of duplicity. When we continue to wait for the chronically late, we encourage tactical tardiness. If we perform the tasks for those who use loss of motor function to resist, we reward their behavior and guarantee that the behavior will persist. Group members thwart the enabling process by their own acts of noncooperation. <u>You have to refuse to be a party to the resistance</u>. If a staff member "forgets" an item at the supplies store, guess who gets to make a return visit? If you hear the old refrain, "I can't be expected to remember everything," tell him or her to make a list. If someone is continually late for appointments, inform them that you will leave after 10 minutes if it happens in the future, then follow through with your threat if tardiness actually recurs. If the person is repeatedly late for committee meetings, refuse to fill them in on what they missed and encourage them to come on time. Continued tardiness may necessitate expulsion from the group.

3. *Give clear directions regarding specific tasks*. You want no possibility that confusion or honest misunderstanding can be used to excuse the poor behavior. Have the group members repeat the directions if resistance is suspected.

Again, I must emphasize that <u>the appropriate focus should not be on how to combat resistance, but instead on why the resistance occurs in the first place</u>. If the main cause of resistance resides in the dominance form of power, then the focus of attention should be on how to reduce the power disparity, or at least its perception.

Defiance: Overt Noncompliance

Defiance stands in bold contrast to resistance. It is an overt form of communicating noncompliance. It is unmitigated, audacious rebellion against attempts to induce compliance. Defiance, like resistance, is a prevention form of power, but unlike resistance there is no ambiguity in defiance. There is no subtlety. No one is left guessing whether an individual supports a specific norm or goal of the group. <u>Those who are defiant dig in their heels, while those who merely resist drag their feet</u>.

When individuals exhibit behaviors that do not conform to group norms, they are called deviants. <u>When this deviance is a purposeful, conscious, overtly rebellious act, it becomes defiance</u>. Group members typically turn to defiance when they perceive little or no chance of enhancing their power position through formation of an alliance, resistance strategies seem either inappropriate or ineffective, or they feel like exhibiting independence from group conformity.

Focus Questions

1. Why are defiant members a threat to the group?
2. What is the best strategy for a defiant member to take when trying to convert the rest of the group to his or her viewpoint?
3. What strategies are typically used by a group to command compliance from a defiant member?

Threat of Contagion   Defiance can be contagious. Someone who refuses to conform to group norms—who defies conventions—can be a threat to the group. If a group tolerates even a single defiant group member, the degree of uniformity in decision making and behavior will be significantly affected.

In the Asch (1952) study, previously discussed, an interesting wrinkle was added. When one of the confederates deviated from the group judgment regarding the correct length of a line, naive subjects' conformity dropped precipitously from 35% to 8%. A single deviant encourages independent decision making, even outright rebellion. In another study, even when the deviant was wearing glasses with "Coke bottle" lenses and the task required visual discrimination, the influence of the deviant was so strong that the support of an obviously visually impaired person was sufficient to induce naive subjects to defy the collective misperception of the group (Allen & Levine, 1971).

Variable Group Reaction   All defiance is not created equal. Some instances of noncompliance will produce nary a ripple of concern in the group. Other instances will be perceived as intolerable. Whether a group takes steps to squash noncompliance, adopts a calculated indifference to the defiance, or explores ways to adapt to the challenge posed by the deviant depends in large part on three factors.

First, <u>some norms are not as important to a group as others</u>, so the reaction to defiance will vary. For a basketball team, curfews and eating meals together before a game may be considered terribly important, but socializing with team members outside of the basketball environment may be perceived as relatively unimportant.

Second, the <u>degree of deviation from the norm</u> also affects whether a group discourages nonconformity and, if so, to what extent. A group may have a norm requiring punctuality. If a member is a few minutes late to a meeting, this deviance is usually ignored. If a member arrives two-thirds of the way through a meeting, however, group members may not look so kindly on this degree of noncompliance.

Third, the <u>deviation from the norm has to be a matter of obvious defiance, not inadvertent noncompliance</u>. Showing up for a new job dressed inappropriately is rarely an act of defiance. Normally, this show of deviance will be interpreted as a clueless blunder, not an act of rebellion. *Not all deviance is defiance*. Deviance must be overt, conscious, and clearly intended to flout group norms before it becomes defiance. The group reaction to inadvertent deviance will likely be mild compared to unmistakable defiance. We smile indulgently when a small child bangs on the bathroom door and inquires, "Whatdya doin' in there?"

Extinguishing Defiance   Defiance is the exception, compliance is the rule. Small wonder. Groups often apply intense pressure on defiant members to get them back in line. A defiant individual threatens the power of a group to command compliance from its members. Leavitt (1964) identifies <u>four communication strategies groups typically use to command compliance from defiant members</u>. These strategies tend to follow a sequential order, although there may be variation in some circumstances.

First, group members attempt to *reason* with the deviant. The quantity of talk aimed at the deviant increases substantially when nonconformity is first recognized (Schachter, 1951). Groups show an intense interest in convincing defiant members of their folly. Clearly, groups expect deviants to change their point of view and behavior.

If reason fails to sway a defiant member into compliance, a group will often try *seduction*. This is usually a ploy to make the deviant feel guilty or uncomfortable because the group is made to look bad in the eyes of outsiders. Telling the defiant member that his or her efforts are wasted and will accomplish nothing is another form of the seduction strategy. "You won't get anywhere anyway so why cause such turmoil?" is the seduction strategy at work.

A classic seduction strategy is called **co-optation.** Here you offer the rebellious individual a piece of the power pie, thus, effectively buying their support instead of their defiance. Offers of promotions, perquisites, monetary incentives, and the like in exchange for compliance are examples of attempts to co-opt defiant individuals.

The third line of defense against deviants is *coercion*. This is where groups begin to get rough. Communication turns abusive and threatening. Groups attempt to force compliance by using nasty and unpleasant tactics; what Zimbardo (1988) refers to as the "three deadly R's: ridicule, repression, and rejection" (p. 631).

As the disparity in power between conflicting parties increases, the temptation to use coercive tactics also increases. As Shaw (1981) concludes on the basis of several studies, "In general, the more power a person has, the greater the probability that he or she will use it" (p. 301).

Glazer and Glazer (1986) studied 55 whistleblowers over a period of several years. Whistleblowers are individuals who expose to the light of public scrutiny such abuses as waste, fraud, corruption, and dangerous practices in corporations and organizations. Coercive tactics against these whistleblowers included threats of firing and sometimes actual terminations. In addition, some were transferred to undesirable jobs and locations, demoted, harassed, and intimidated by supervisors and peers. On December 10, 1993, CNN, reporting on a study of whistleblowers, noted that 88% of whistleblowers had suffered personal reprisals for their defiance. Workers file, on average, more than 2,000 complaints each year charging that they were fired, demoted, or penalized for reporting health and safety violations to employers or to the government (Pear, 1999).

The final stage of group pressure to induce compliance from a deviant is *isolation*. There are situations (e.g., tenure or civil service protections) where the group cannot eliminate the deviant from the group, at least not immediately. In such an instance, the group can physically and psychologically isolate the deviant. Here the offending member remains part of the group only artificially. If the isolation is prolonged, the deviant may eventually submit to the pressure and become compliant. If not, the deviant is at least contained.

Isolation is a primary tactic used to contain whistleblowers if coercion fails to force compliance. Coworkers often disassociate themselves from whistleblowers to protect their own jobs. Friends and family become impatient with the battle and may come to view the effort as a tedious, even destructive, waste of time. Donald Soeken, formerly a psychiatric social worker for the U.S. Public Health Service and a one-time whistleblower, turned a farm in West Virginia into a haven for whistleblowers he calls The Whistlestop. Soeken says, "Blowing the whistle is not easy. And it's almost insurmountably lonely" (Anderson, 1991, p. 17). The 1999 movie *The Insider*, dramatically depicts the true story of the personal hell whistleblowers often must endure.

Shannon Faulkner's effort to become the first female cadet at the Citadel, a military academy in Charleston, South Carolina, was met with open hostility. She became the campus leper. Forced by the courts to accept her first as a student, then later as a cadet, the students hit Faulkner with derision, isolation, and ostracism. She was "booed, mooed, hissed at and scorned as 'Shrew Shannon' and 'Mrs. Doubtgender'" (Goldstein, 1994, p. 13A). Bumper stickers advocating "Save the Males" and "Shave Shannon's Head" appeared. One teacher observed that Faulkner was wise to sit in the front of her class so she couldn't see the looks from boys sitting behind her.

Those who defended Faulkner's attempt to crack the all-male brotherhood at the Citadel received similar treatment. Faulkner's mother, Sandra, a social studies teacher, was ostracized by some of her colleagues. Faulkner's father, Ed, saw his fence company business suffer. A black student, Von Mickle, defended Faulkner because it reminded him that African Americans were not welcome at the Citadel until 1966. He was "spoken to" by other students and was ridiculed in the student newspaper.

Faulkner's attempt to become the first female graduate from the Citadel ultimately failed. She left the Citadel in her first week as a cadet. Other women, however, followed her lead and were successful.

Defiant Member's Influence   Given the tremendous pressure to conform exerted on those who defy, how do we explain the individual who converts the group to his or her way of thinking, as dramatized in *Twelve Angry Men*? Admittedly not a frequent occurrence, defiant members do influence groups.

If the immediate group cannot reject you (e.g., jury or elected official), then the deviant's best chance of converting the group is to remain unalterably and confidently defiant throughout discussions—in other words, defy without cracking (Gebhardt & Meyers, 1995). If, however, the group has the power to exclude the deviant from the group or the deliberations, then the deviant stands a better chance if he or she remains uncompromisingly defiant until the group seems about fed up. At this point the deviant should indicate a willingness to make some degree of compromise (Wolf, 1979). The group is more likely to modify its position if it sees the deviant as coming around and being more reasonable. Remaining intransigent when the group can reject you is a losing battle. Your consistent defiance will be taken as legitimate justification for your ostracism.

I should note that remaining unalterably defiant will win you no friends. As Moscovici and Mugny (1983) indicate, unwavering deviants are seen as less reasonable, fair, warm, cooperative, liked, admired, and perceptive than other group members. This is not surprising since the deviant creates secondary tension in the group. Although the consistent deviant is not viewed as competent by the group, deviants are perceived to be confident and self-assured, independent, active, even original.

Consistency may increase the influence of defiant members in groups, especially when there is some ambiguity and indecision among majority members, but it does not necessarily improve group decision making (Gebhardt & Meyers, 1995). Flexibility is a key to communication competence in groups. Intransigence aimed at winning over the group will likely produce counter-rigidity from the majority of group members. When both the defiant individual and the group members remain rigidly consistent, the majority prevails (Gebhardt & Meyers, 1995).

second look

Defiance by Group Member

Factors Affecting Group Reaction
- Significance of norm to group
- Degree of deviation from the norm
- Obvious defiance or inadvertent noncompliance

Extinguishing Defiance
- Reason—convincing with logic
- Seduction—deviant made to feel ineffectual; co-opt him or her
- Coercion—ridicule, repression, and rejection
- Isolation—psychological/physical ostracism; group member in name only

Influence Strategies of Defiant Members
- Group cannot ostracize—deviant remains consistent throughout discussion
- Group can exclude—remain consistent until group is about fed up, then indicate willingness to compromise

Significance: Self-Empowerment

When group members grow tired of being dominated by more powerful individuals, they can do more than merely resist or defy demands for compliance. Less powerful members can enhance their relative influence or they can balance the power in the group more evenly by increasing their value to the group. Becoming more significant to the group can occur in two primary ways: by developing communication assertiveness and by increasing personal power resources.

Focus Questions
1. In what ways do aggressiveness and assertiveness differ?
2. Why should group members learn to be assertive?
3. How do mentoring and networking enhance personal power resources?

Assertiveness   The image many people have of an assertive person is that of an obnoxious, overbearing, argumentative, self-centered individual bent on dominating others. This hardly qualifies as a description of a competent communicator, and yet assertiveness is an important skill for the competent communicator to acquire.

I continue to hear the terms assertive and aggressive used synonymously, even in scholarly circles (see especially Infante et al., 1997). Distinguishing assertiveness and aggressiveness conceptually does seem important. This is especially true in light of research on family violence that shows a clear connection between verbal aggression and physical attacks (Straus & Sweet, 1992). If assertiveness is associated with verbal aggression, then ethically I could not encourage anyone to learn and use such incompetent communication.

Adler (1977) defines **assertiveness** as the "ability to communicate the full range of your thoughts and emotions with confidence and skill" (p. 6). Assertiveness falls in between the extremes of passivity and aggressiveness and is distinctly different from either. Aggressiveness puts one's own needs first, while passivity underemphasizes one's needs (Lulofs, 1994). Assertiveness takes into account both your needs and the needs of others.

Adler is very careful to emphasize the "ability" and "skill" aspects of his definition, thus emphasizing communication competence. Assertiveness is perceived by many people to be merely communicating the full range of thoughts and emotions—period. The ability and skill part of the equation is overlooked. So group members sound like arrogant little Nazis in the process of telling the group what they think or feel. Assertiveness is not a "looking out for number one" competitive communication strategy. To be assertive is to be sensitive to others while also looking out and standing up for yourself. You can stand up for yourself without trampling others in the process. Defining assertiveness in terms of empowerment makes this point obvious.

Assertiveness is not a strategy of resistance. As I already explained, resistance tactics are acts of passive aggression. Assertive communication can be employed to defy a group. I have not included assertiveness in the section on defiance, however, because I view it as a *primarily empowering form of communication*. We most often use assertive communication not to defy the group, but instead to assure that our individual needs, rights, and responsibilities are not submerged or ignored by the group. When a formerly passive member is assertive, the group may view this as a highly constructive change, wholly consistent with the norms of the group, and worthy of encouragement, not ostracism.

There are distinct <u>advantages to learning assertiveness</u>. The most obvious advantage is that you won't need to have someone do your asserting for you. More importantly, self-assertion makes you a more significant person in a group. Your potential influence in group decision making will be enhanced. Passive members become isolates and are easily ignored by the group. Assertive members make their presence felt and express their ideas and feelings to the group for consideration. This increases the group's resources and helps promote group synergy.

CLOSER LOOK

Conspicuously Unassertive

Are we generally an assertive bunch? Not really. <u>Assertiveness is often conspicuous by its absence</u>. Several studies by Moriarty (1975) demonstrate how difficult it is for most people to assert themselves. In the first experiment, he had male college students, two at a time, take a difficult 20-minute test. One of the two test-takers was a confederate. Shortly after the test commenced, the confederate turned on a boom box at high volume. Unless their fellow test-taker complained, a 17-minute rock music concert ensued. Some subjects exhibited nonverbal signs of displeasure, but 80% made no verbal objection. Fifteen percent made mild requests of the confederate, who was instructed to continue the rock concert until subjects asked the accomplice 3 times to turn off the music. One subject acted aggressively by leaping up and demanding that the confederate snap off the music. This so startled and intimidated the confederate that he complied.

Moriarty followed this experiment with several interesting field studies on the same question of nonassertiveness. He subjected 40 people reading in a library to loud 7-minute conversations. Only one of the 40 subjects asked the noisy conversationalists to quiet down, while nine left. The remaining 30 subjects endured the disruption. In a similar study in a movie theater, only 35% of the subjects verbally complained when confederates conversed loudly during the movie.

Moriarty had his confederates act even more outrageously in yet another experiment conducted in Grand Central Station in New York City. This time the subjects were 20 men dressed in business suits using the pay phone. As each man finished his call, he was approached by the experimenter who asked the subject if he had seen a ring left in the booth. All subjects answered "No" since no ring was actually left. Then the experimenter said, "Are you sure you didn't see it? Sometimes people pick up things without thinking about it." Another denial followed, whereupon the experimenter asked each subject to empty his pockets as if to verify the subject's truthfulness. Remember, this is New York City, a place renowned for its aggressive citizens. Did the subjects tell the experimenter to take a hike? Did they verbally assault the experimenter for having the audacity to imply that subjects were being less than honest? You might expect such a response, but actually only four of the 20 subjects refused to comply. The rest, 16 subjects (80%), emptied their pockets.

Recently, a group of students in my small group communication class did a similar field study as a "Candid Camera" project. Three group members formed a line in front of two side-by-side ATMs. Neither cash machine was in use and no "Out of Order" sign was posted. Within minutes a long line of people wanting to use the ATM formed behind my students. Some individuals seemed agitated at having to wait in line without anyone using the cash machine, but most never said a word. Several people waited 10 to 15 minutes before giving up and leaving in disgust. One woman did ask my students at the head of the line, "Is there something wrong with the ATM?" My students replied, "I don't know." The woman inquired further, "Why are you standing in line?" My students responded again, "I don't know." Did this inspire the woman to move out of line and use the ATM? No it didn't. She rejoined the line, waited a few more minutes, then left. No one used the ATM the entire time my students stood in line.

Considering previous evidence on compliance rates already cited, these results are not that surprising. We find it difficult to stand up for ourselves, so much so that some individuals have advertised their willingness to act as paid surrogate asserters. That's right! In Chicago, a woman named Marti Hough started her "Speak Up Service" from her home. For a small fee, she delivered messages for her reticent clients because they feared doing it themselves.

Questions for Thought

1. Does the pervasiveness of passivity derive mostly from shyness or does the fact that we live in a violent society, where volatile strangers may do harm to us if we are assertive, play a part?
2. How would you rate your own level of assertiveness? Are there some situations where you are assertive and others where you are either aggressive or passive? If so, which conditions produce aggressiveness and which passivity?

Assertiveness may also prove to be life-saving. Following an airline crash in 1978, the National Transportation and Safety Board recommended that training for cockpit crews include assertiveness, implying that the lack of assertiveness was a causal factor in the crash (Foushee, 1984). In another incident, a jet slid off the runway because of excessive speed. Although the captain was apparently unaware of the excessive speed, the first officer knew but could only manage a sheepish comment about a possible tailwind.

The competent communicator, however, cannot assume that assertiveness is always appropriate. Cultural differences, for example, must be taken into account. Assertiveness is not valued in Japan and many Asian cultures (Samovar & Porter, 1995). Standing up for yourself and speaking your mind are seen as disruptive and provocative acts likely to create disharmony. North American Native Indians "have developed a distaste for Western assertiveness and tend to avoid those who interact in assertive ways" (Moghaddam et al., 1993, p. 124).

Schmidt and Kipnis (1987) also discovered that you can be overly persistent in asserting yourself. They found that excessive assertiveness can result in less favorable evaluations from supervisors, lower salaries, greater job tension, and greater personal stress than a less-vigorous assertion of one's needs and desires.

These results underline how important it is that you not assume that assertiveness is always preferable to passivity or aggressiveness in every circumstance. The advantages and disadvantages must be weighed within each context. As a general rule, however, assertiveness is empowering, especially in American culture, and more advantageous with far fewer and less severe disadvantages than aggressiveness or passivity.

So how do you become more assertive? Bower and Bower (1980) provide a useful framework for learning assertiveness. They call it **DESC** Scripting. The **D** is for *describe;* **E** is for *express;* **S** is for *specify;* and **C** is for *consequences.*

Describe: When there is a conflict between you and group members, you initiate resolution of the conflict by first describing the behavior that is troublesome. My previous discussion of descriptiveness as a supportive alternative to evaluation that produces defensiveness applies here. To recapitulate, descriptiveness requires first person singular language, specificity, and elimination of editorial comments. Thus, description does not involve denouncement of the offending party. For example, instead of attacking the offender (e.g., "That does it! You're not going to get away with stealing any more of my ideas."), you describe as precisely as possible what behavior irks you (e.g., "Last week I suggested we reorganize the program. Now I see my idea attributed to you. I think I deserve an explanation.").

Express: Here you express how you think and feel about the offending behavior. Again, this is not a verbal assault on the offender. All an attack will do is precipitate defensiveness and counterattack. Instead, you formulate a statement from your perspective (e.g., "I believe," "I feel," "I disagree"). The express step is not an opportunity for finger pointing and accusation (e.g., "You made me feel . . ."). This step requires a statement of personal reaction from you to the offensive behavior from another group member.

Specify: This step identifies the behavior you would like to see substituted for the bothersome behavior. Once more, the request needs to be concrete and spelled out, not vague or merely suggestive. "I think it is only fair that I receive sole credit for this proposal, and in the future I expect to receive credit for my ideas" is better than "I want you to stop plagiarizing my ideas immediately."

Consequences: The consequences of changing behavior or continuing the same behavior patterns should be articulated to the offending party. The emphasis, if possible, should be on rewards, not punishments. "I like working here and expect to continue as long as I'm treated fairly" is better than "If you continue to steal my ideas I'll be forced to quit."

The DESC guidelines for assertiveness will prove to be nothing more than an idealized fantasy cooked up by academic types unless "powerless" language and anemic nonverbal behavior are eliminated from the process. Description should not include requests for permission to speak, think, or disagree. Scrap the "Do you mind if I" or the "If it's okay with you, may I please speak with you" forms of passivity. Replace permission requests with direct declarative statements, such as, "I'd like to discuss this matter with you," or "I need to schedule a meeting with you." You can still remain polite without becoming passive.

Expressing your thoughts and feelings must be accomplished with confidence and skill. This requires direct eye contact, not looks cast downward or side-to-side. Posture should be erect, not slouched in a cowering whipped puppy stance. Tone of voice should be modulated so aggression doesn't spill out or passivity creep in. Tag questions, hedges, hesitations, disclaimers, and overly polite references should be minimized or eliminated if possible. If you are interrupted, calmly indicate, "I'm not finished with my thought."

Everything I've suggested regarding how to be assertive requires practice. To become a competent communicator you must be willing to expend some energy honing your skills. You will find that assertiveness is far easier in some circumstances than in others. Assertiveness is an important empowering communication skill.

Increasing Personal Power Resources

Since the group confers power on the individual, a person can enhance his or her power by increasing personal resources valued by the group. There are a number of avenues available for personal power enhancement.

Husbands who assume a greater portion of the domestic chores may increase their value in the family. Children whose parents are unemployed or underemployed can exercise greater power if they find a part-time job to supplement family income. Learning certain skills valued by the group can enhance your power position. If you master the skills required to use computers and no one in your group is computer proficient, then your power increases when the group requires such technical expertise.

Finally, the mentoring and networking processes can enhance personal power resources. **Mentors** are knowledgeable individuals who have achieved some success in their profession or jobs and who assist individuals trying to get started in a line of work. Mentors can provide information to the newcomer that prevents mistakes by trial and error. Mentoring seems to have been especially useful for women in their rise to upper echelons of organizations (Noe, 1988). One study showed that women who have mentors move up the corporate ladder much faster than women without mentors. Women also receive promotions more quickly when they are helped by mentors (Kleiman, 1991). Mentors are essential for women trying to advance to the highest levels of corporate leadership (Hackman & Johnson, 1996).

Networking is a form of group empowerment. Individuals with similar backgrounds, skills, and goals come together on a fairly regular basis and share information that will assist members in pursuing goals. Networks also provide emotional support for members, especially in women's networks (Stewart et al., 1996).

second look

Significance (Empowerment)

Assertiveness
- *Describe* the behavior that is troublesome
- *Express* how you think and feel about the offending behavior
- *Specify* behavior preferred as a substitute for bothersome behavior
- *Consequences* of changing behavior or continuing without change should be articulated

Increasing Personal Power Resources
- Personal improvement
- Learn valued skills
- Mentoring and networking

In summary, an imbalance of power in groups promotes conflict and power struggles, and in some instances can lead to violence. The five ways we transact power in groups, especially when power is unequally distributed, are compliance, alliance, resistance, defiance, and significance. Compliance primarily aims to bring the less powerful in line with the dictates of the more powerful and to discourage deviance, which can be contagious. Alliance, resistance, defiance, and significance are all means used by members to balance the power more equitably in small groups.

Questions for Critical Thinkers

1. Have you ever used resistance strategies? Did they work? Were they used against dominant individuals?
2. Can you think of instances in your own experience where assertiveness was inappropriate?

CHAPTER

10

Conflict Management in Groups

A. DEFINITION OF TERMS
1. Definition of conflict
   a. General definition
   b. Destructive versus constructive conflict
2. Conflict resolution versus management

B. STYLES OF CONFLICT MANAGEMENT
1. Collaborating (Problem solving)
2. Accommodating (Yielding)
3. Compromising
   Closer Look: The Case of the Effective Compromise
4. Avoiding (Withdrawing)
5. Competing (Power/Forcing)
   Focus on Culture: Culture and Conflict Styles

C. TRANSACTING CONFLICT
1. Primary situational variables
   a. Nature of the conflict
   b. Nature of the relationship
   c. Timing
2. Conflict spirals
   Closer Look: KILL Radio Conflict Case Study
3. Negotiating strategies
   a. Tit for tat
   b. Reformed sinner
   c. Positional bargaining
   d. Principled negotiation

D. ANGER MANAGEMENT
1. Constructive and destructive anger
2. Managing your own anger
3. Managing the anger of others

Look up the word *conflict* in a thesaurus and you'll see synonyms such as "clash," "discord," "disharmony," "fight," "friction," "hostility," and "strife." Finding any positive meaning associated with conflict can be difficult, and no wonder. There's tension, unpleasantness, and vulnerability in most conflict transactions. Addressing conflict takes time. Almost 30% of all meetings in the corporate arena are scheduled just to manage a conflict (Drew, 1994).

Despite its potential for negative consequences, conflict can be a constructive force in groups *if managed competently*. John Dewey observed many years ago that conflict "stirs us to observation and memory. It instigates invention. It shocks us out of sheep-like passivity, and sets us at noting and contriving." Brent Rubin (1978) argues that "conflict is not only essential to the growth, change, and evolution of living systems, but it is, as well, a system's primary defense against stagnation, detachment, entropy, and even extinction" (p. 202).

I'm convinced that it is the uncertainty inherent in conflict that produces the greatest unease. What will happen if I do X? Our imaginations can easily shift us into disaster mode. Most people feel ill-prepared and ill-equipped to deal effectively with life's disputes. Disaster can seem to be ever-lurking in the dark shadows when our alternatives are unclear and our confidence in our own abilities to handle conflict constructively is shaky.

My purpose here is to show you ways to manage conflict constructively in groups. Unquestionably, if conflict is handled ineffectually, group productivity, cohesiveness, and satisfaction will be threatened. Conflict, managed poorly, can tear a group asunder. Incapacitation and serious disruption of the group can be prevented, however, if you learn to manage conflict adroitly.

In previous chapters, I have already discussed at length several sources of conflict and their corresponding antidotes. Briefly, these are:

Sources	Solutions
Competitive group climate	Structure cooperative group climate
Defensive communication patterns	Structure supportive communication
Self-centered disruptive roles	Adopt strategies for dealing with difficult group members
Imbalance of power	Balance power among group members
Conflicts of interest	Use integrative problem solving

I wish to build on this foundation of previous discussion by accomplishing these three <u>objectives</u>:

1. to define conflict, identifying the difference between its constructive and destructive form,
2. to explain the communication styles available for dealing with conflict, and,
3. to discuss how to transact conflict effectively in small groups.

DEFINITION OF TERMS

Consider the following events (based on a real situation) as a case study illustrating conflict:

VILLAGE HAVEN TOWNHOMES CASE STUDY

Once upon a time there was a quiet little condominium complex composed of 18 units beside a meandering creek in a forest setting. The residents enjoyed seeing the deer wander down in the evening from their habitat above the complex. Wildlife was abundant. A climate of tranquillity enveloped this special place.

Then one day, bulldozers and earth movers of every variety rumbled in unannounced. Peace and quiet were abruptly replaced by ear-splitting noise, incessant vibration from the heavy equipment thundering back and forth across the once-emerald terrain. Families residing in Village Haven were understandably shaken by the realization that 32 additional units were about to be squeezed onto every speck of available space a mere 30-feet across from the original 18 residences.

The situation, however, did not improve once construction of the condos began. Residents were awakened regularly at 6:30 a.m. on weekdays and sometimes on weekends to the sounds of hammering, sawing, and shouting from workers. Cars previously parked along the curb of the one-way road into and out of the complex had to be moved to a small paved area in the center of the development where bulldozers and forklifts whizzed by, showering the autos with dirt and debris. Tires were regularly punctured by nails strewn across the road by careless workers. Huge trucks and construction equipment frequently blocked the single-lane road into and out of the complex, stranding residents in their cars, sometimes for 10 to 15 minutes. Residents occasionally found pathways to their homes dangerous to traverse.

At one point, a signed message from the developer and contractor was taped to the doors of the condos. Residents were instructed to remove their cars from the street so "demolition and reconstruction" could take place. Residents were now ordered to park their cars on a street overlooking the complex about two blocks up a very steep, poorly lighted hill. During the demolition, two residents had stereos stolen out of their cars while parked on this street. The homeowners as a group were not happy!

The inhabitants of Village Haven, working under the auspices of the complex's Homeowners Association, considered legal action, but ran into numerous technical and political roadblocks. The developer and the contractor were asked to begin construction at 8 a.m. instead of 6:30 a.m. Residents were informed that early starts were "the nature of construction" and couldn't be changed. When representatives of the association raised objections to the edict requiring removal of all cars to the street above, they were told that this was an unavoidable inconvenience. Several residents got into shouting matches with the developer and the contractor.

Vandalism started to crop up here and there. The professionally painted sign at the entrance to the complex that read, "Village Haven Forest Townhomes," was painted over to read, "Village of the Damned." Another sign that read, "Welcome to Village Haven" was changed to read, "Welcome to Hell." Windows freshly installed in new units were sporadically smashed. Security patrols were increased to thwart the vandals, with little apparent success.

A few days after the message ordering the removal of all cars from paved areas was attached to residents' doors, a tongue-in-cheek message appeared on everyone's doorstep. Attributed to the contractor and developer (real author unknown), but obviously intended as an underground satirical jibe at these two individuals, the message was addressed to Village Haven Residents and purported to answer complaints from homeowners. The bogus message was signed under the names of the contractor and developer, with the appellation "The Village Idiots" added.

Frustrated and weary, residents began listing their units for sale. The project was finally completed, some of the original residents left, but the animosities lingered.

Definition of Conflict

The Village Haven Townhomes battle provides us with a means of explaining the definition of conflict in a group context.

General Definition   I define **conflict** as the expressed struggle of interconnected parties who perceive incompatible goals and interference from each other in attaining those goals (Donohue & Kolt, 1992; Wilmot & Hocker, 1998). Let me explain each element of my definition in terms of the Village Haven fracas.

First, conflict is an *expressed struggle* between parties. If the homeowners of Village Haven had merely sat and stewed over perceived outrages, then no conflict would have existed because the developer and contractor wouldn't have known there was a problem. Often the expression of a struggle is manifested in shouting matches, such as occurred between the residents of Village Haven and the developer and contractor. Sometimes it is expressed more indirectly, such as the exchange of written messages placed on residents' doorsteps. Occasionally, the expression is of a nonverbal nature. Vandalism and the reaction to it (beefed-up security) are examples from the Village Haven conflict.

Second, conflict occurs between *interconnected parties* in a group system. (Some experts prefer the term "interdependent," but dependence denotes submission, thus suggesting that interdependence is mutual submission. I prefer interconnected because it strikes me as a more neutral term.) Interconnected parties means that for a conflict to exist, the behavior of one or more parties must produce consequences for the other party or parties. The invasion of the bulldozers significantly affected the residents of Village Haven. Likewise, the developer and contractor could not completely ignore residents' reactions. People shouting at them, needling them in a bogus message, and vandalizing property (although it is unclear whether residents were actually the vandals) are acts difficult to ignore.

Third, conflict involves *perceived incompatible goals*. Sometimes we perceive incompatible goals where none exist. This perception, however, is reality until both parties are convinced that they are not working toward mutually exclusive goals. In other cases, the goals are incompatible. The residents of Village Haven would have preferred an 18-unit complex to a 50-unit complex. The developer and contractor couldn't make any money that way. The goal of the builders to erect 32 additional units collided squarely with the desire of the residents for peace and quiet. Construction is obtrusive and disruptive. Other goals were perceived at least by one party to be incompatible, but probably didn't need to be. A plan to begin construction later than 6:30 in the morning and reduce some of the frustrating side effects of living in the middle of a construction zone (e.g., nails in the road, or equipment blocking access to residents' units) should have been achievable.

Finally, conflict involves *interference from each other* in attaining desired goals. Unless one party attempts to block the attainment of another party's goal, there is no conflict. You and I may express a disagreement, be interconnected parties, and we may even perceive our goals to be incompatible, yet conflict may not exist even then. You may, in an act of pure selflessness, assist me in the attainment of my goal at the expense of attaining your own goal. There must be an attempt to interfere with another's goal attainment for conflict to exist.

In Village Haven, interference abounded. Builders interfered with residents' tranquillity and convenience and transformed the environment from a low-density to a high-density development. None of the original occupants wanted this change. Residents' reaction to this interference was interference of their own in the form of verbal abuse and vandalism (again assuming the culprits were residents).

Destructive versus Constructive Conflict   Most conflict probably seems destructive given how poorly conflict is typically managed in groups. Nevertheless, destructive and constructive conflict are distinctly different. **Destructive conflict** is characterized by domination, escalation, retaliation, competition, and inflexibility (Lulofs, 1994; Wilmot & Hocker, 1998). When conflict spirals out of control it is destructive. Participants lose sight of their initial goals and focus on hurting their adversary.

On February 6, 1999, the Allied Pilots Association, which represented American Airlines' 9,200 pilots, began a sickout (pilots called in claiming to be sick when they weren't) in response to a dispute over pay. The sickout lasted 10 days, caused 6,600 airline flights to be cancelled, inconvenienced and outraged 600,000 passengers, and cost American Airlines $225 million ("American Air Union," 1999). U.S. District Court Judge Joe Kendall of Dallas ordered the pilots union to end the sickout. When the union was slow to respond to the judge's order, Kendall found the union in contempt and fined it $46 million, one of the largest fines ever imposed against a labor union. In Judge Kendall's words, "The Allied Pilots Association seems determined to fly American Airlines into the side of the mountain, taking themselves, the company, their co-workers and their customers with them" (Swoboda, 1999, p. 1A). The pilots union action was a heavy-handed, competitive, illegal action that backfired, leaving no winners and many losers—typical of a destructive conflict.

The Village Haven conflict was essentially a destructive conflict. There was escalation, vandalism, threats, shouting, inflexibility on both sides, and expressions of contempt and ridicule. Neither side seemed able to work together to find a mutually satisfactory solution to the conflict.

Donohue and Kolt (1992) identify how to recognize quickly destructive conflict as it is happening. <u>When it becomes obvious to you that, "Gee, I'm getting stupid," you're engaged in destructive conflict</u>. When you see yourself engaging in petty, even infantile tactics to win an argument, you're getting stupid. Becoming physically and verbally aggressive moves the conflict into destructive territory. This doesn't mean that you can never raise your voice, express frustration, or disagree with other group members. Conflict can remain constructive even when discussion becomes somewhat contentious. When conflict becomes more emotional than reasonable, however, when you can't think straight because you are too consumed by anger, then conflict has become destructive (Gottman, 1994).

Constructive conflict is characterized by a We-orientation, cooperation, and flexibility (Lulofs, 1994; Wilmot & Hocker, 1998). It is competent communication in action. The principal focus is on trying to achieve a solution between struggling parties that is mutually satisfactory to everyone.

Conflict Resolution versus Management

The two terms used most frequently to describe the process for dealing with conflict are *resolution* and *management*. I have chosen the term management because it is more appropriate for a systems perspective of small group communication. Resolution suggests settling conflict or terminating the struggle, as if ending conflict by any means is always desirable. Since conflict can be an essential catalyst for growth in a system, resolving conflict is not necessarily desirable. In some instances, increasing conflict may be required to evoke change. Civil rights demonstrators purposely provoked conflict to challenge racist laws in the South. Women who file sexual harassment lawsuits provoke conflict in order to end an evil.

Managing conflict implies no end to the struggle. Although some conflict episodes do end within a group and are therefore resolved, conflict overall in a system is a continuous phenomenon varying only in intensity. Management of conflict also implies no judgment on the goodness or badness of struggles in general.

STYLES OF CONFLICT MANAGEMENT

Communication is central to conflict in groups. Our communication can signal that conflict exists, it can create conflict, and it can be the means for managing conflict constructively or destructively (Wilmot & Hocker, 1998). Consequently, communication styles have been the center of much research and discussion. A communication style is an orientation toward conflict. <u>Styles exhibit predispositions or tendencies regarding the way conflict is managed in groups</u>.

Blake and Mouton (1964) initiated the styles approach to conflict management. Kilmann and Thomas (1977) elaborated and modified the styles approach. There are five communication styles of conflict management articulated by these theorists. I will explain each of the five styles adding some modifications of my own.

Focus Questions

1. How do communication styles of conflict management differ on task and social dimensions of small groups?
2. Should group members always use the collaborating style and avoid the competing (forcing) style?

Collaborating (Problem Solving)

The most complex and potentially productive conflict style is collaborating, or what some refer to as problem solving. Someone employing this style has a high concern for both task and social relationships in groups. The **collaborating** style recognizes the interconnection between the task and social components of groups and deals directly with both requirements. This is a win–win, cooperative approach to conflict. The collaborating style attempts to satisfy all parties.

A collaborating style has three key components. The first is *confrontation*. When you confront, you bring conflict out into the open for examination. There is a recognition that conflict exists and must be faced directly or the clash will become dysfunctional for the group. Problems between parties in a dispute cannot be solved and the dispute resolved unless grievances and differences are discussed openly.

Although the news media are fond of using the term confrontation in a negative sense, as in "There was a violent confrontation between protesters and police," this is not the meaning relevant to this discussion. Confrontation as a conflict style incorporates all the elements already discussed at length regarding assertiveness (describe, express, specify, and consequences), supportive communication patterns (description, problem orientation, etc.), and consensus decision making. The purpose of confrontation is to manage conflict in a productive way for all parties involved.

Not all issues are worth confronting. Members who confront even trivial differences of opinion or can't let a momentary flash of pique go unattended can be quite tiresome. Groups have to decide which issues and concerns are priorities and which are tangential. You can overuse confrontation and make yourself a nuisance. *offer solutions*

The second component of collaboration is *integration.* Since I have already discussed how to find integrative solutions to problems in chapter 7, I will not belabor the point. Integration as a collaborative technique, however, has not been given the attention that it deserves. Brett and her associates (1990) argue that negotiators in organizations are better at maximizing their own gains (competitive) than they are at maximizing joint gains (integrative). Pruitt (1981) also notes that negotiators tend to reach agreement on the first satisfactory proposal that comes along rather than looking for a better solution. Training through lecture, reading, and exercises, however, has excellent success in improving integrative skills of group members (Neale et al., 1988).

*tend to
others
Needs*

A third component of collaboration is *smoothing.* Group members who feel slighted or picked on during conflict interactions may need to have their ruffled feathers smoothed out. "Let's all calm down. Attacking each other won't help us find a solution everyone can accept" is an example of smoothing. Tending to the concerns and needs of others, rather than merely looking out for number one, can be a constructive way of dealing with conflict and an indication of communication competence. Supportive, confirming remarks bolstering the image of group members who disagree with you can rejuvenate their interest in finding a viable solution to a problem. The remarks, of course, must seem genuine or they will exacerbate the tension and strife.

*best
way
usually
hardest
away.*

Since collaborating is such an effective communication technique for solving conflicts of interest, why isn't it always used in these situations? There are several reasons. Collaborating usually requires a significant investment of time and effort along with greater-than-ordinary communication skills. Even if you are willing to employ the collaborating techniques of confrontation, integration, and smoothing, collaborating requires mutually agreeable parties. I have witnessed several instances where an integrative solution was constructed, yet the group rejected it because the members disliked the person who originated the proposal. Collaboration is built on trust. If parties are suspicious of each other and worry that one will betray the other by not honoring agreements, then even an integrative solution may be rejected. Also, parties in a conflict sometimes do not share the same psychological investment in finding an agreeable solution for all involved. *long term solution
supportive comm.
I statements Not You*

Accommodating (Yielding)

*1) issues not of
great
importance
to you*

A second communication style of conflict management is **accommodating.** This style yields to the concerns and desires of others. Someone using this style shows a high concern for social relationships but low concern for task accomplishment. This style may camouflage deep divisions among group members in order to maintain the appearance of harmony. If the task can be accomplished without social disruption, fine. If accomplishing the task threatens to jeopardize the harmonious relationships within the group, however, a person using this style will opt for appeasing members, even though this may sacrifice productivity. Generally, group members with less power are expected to accommodate more often and to a greater degree than more powerful members (Lulofs, 1994).

*2) temporary to
get to a point
to better deal
with issues.*

Although we tend to view accommodating in a negative light, as appeasement with all its negative connotations, this style can be quite positive. A group that has experienced protracted strife may rejoice when one side accommodates even on an issue of only minor importance. Yielding on issues of incidental concern to you but of major concern to other parties can serve as a cooperative gesture. *NONassertive*

Compromising

When we compromise, we lower our expectations and goals. We give up something in order to get something. Some have referred to this as a lose–lose style of conflict management because neither party is ever fully satisfied with the solution. **Compromise** is a middle ground. Someone using this style shows a moderate concern for both task and social relationships in groups. The emphasis is on workable but not necessarily optimal solutions. Someone using this style shows moderate concern for group harmony but takes the attitude that a solution the group can live with should be satisfactory, if not exactly cause for celebration.

Compromise evokes ambivalence—both negative and positive reactions. We speak disparagingly of those who would "compromise their integrity." On some issues, usually moral or ethical conflicts such as abortion or capital punishment, compromise is thought to be intolerable. Pruitt and Rubin (1986) argue that compromise arises "from one of two sources—either lazy problem solving involving a half-hearted attempt to satisfy the two parties' interests, or simply yielding by both parties" (p. 29). Yet despite this negative view of compromise, negotiations of labor-management contracts and political agreements are expected, even encouraged, to end in compromise. Members of task forces, ad hoc groups, and committees of many shapes and sizes often seek a compromise as an admirable goal.

Half a loaf is better than starvation—not in all circumstances, but certainly in some. When an integrative solution cannot be achieved, when a temporary settlement is the only feasible alternative, or when the issues involved are not considered critical to the group, compromise can be a useful conflict style.

CLOSER LOOK

The Case of the Effective Compromise

Compromise can be effective when used as a fall-back approach after other styles have proved to be relatively unproductive. I was once a member of an academic search and selection task force composed of 15 members and charged with writing specific procedures for hiring new faculty. One of the contentious issues that incited the most divisiveness concerned the presence of deans on hiring committees. This issue was debated at length with little progress. Virtually all faculty representatives on the task force wanted deans off the hiring committees. The faculty felt that having deans on such committees made candidate interviews and meetings for final selection difficult to schedule. In addition, choosing a colleague was thought to be outside the responsibilities of a dean, who usually had little or no knowledge of the relevant discipline. Also, their presence was thought to be intimidating because their power position could influence deliberations and even the final selection.

Management was adamant that deans remain because some overview of the process was essential if for no other reason than to protect the college from potential lawsuits on issues of Affirmative Action or committee bias. Management also felt an overall responsibility for ensuring that the college select the highest-quality candidates.

At one point in the deliberations, a proposal that deans remain on committees but have no voting power nor say in the final selection was offered. Initially, the proposal was virtually ignored. When it became apparent that stalemate was looming on the horizon, the same proposal was introduced a second time. Faculty were mostly opposed to it. Management seemed marginally satisfied with the compromise since they still had oversight of the committee process. In private, hesitant faculty members were encouraged to accept the compromise as a step toward the eventual elimination of deans from selection committees. The argument that the faculty could expect no better agreement at the moment was advanced vigorously by several committee members. Under this agreement, the deans may prove themselves irrelevant, making their elimination easier to argue in the future, so went the reasoning. The faculty accepted the proposal with resignation if not enthusiasm. Stalemate would have accomplished nothing after many hours of negotiations.

Questions for Thought

1. If none of the parties in conflict are actually happy with a compromise, how can it be viewed as effective?
2. How would you determine whether a compromise is acceptable or not?

Avoiding (Withdrawing)

Avoiding is a strategy of withdrawing from potentially contentious and unpleasant struggles. Gouran and Baird (1972) found that groups typically change the subject under discussion soon after a period of disagreement among members. *Flights from fights* may seem constructive at the time because they circumvent unpleasantness. In the long run, however, facing problems proves to be more effective than running from them. Someone using the avoiding conflict style shows little concern for both task and social relationships in groups. Avoiders shrink from conflict, even fear it. By avoiding conflict they hope it will disappear. Group tasks are sacrificed to a preoccupation with avoiding trouble. Social relationships within the group have scant possibility of improving when the conflict distorts the behavior of those doing the avoiding.

Avoiding, nevertheless, is sometimes appropriate. If you are a low-power person in a group and the consequences of confrontation are potentially hazardous to you, avoiding might be a reasonable strategy until other alternatives present themselves. Standing up to a bully at school may work out well in movies, but confronting antisocial types who look like they eat raw meat for breakfast and might eat you for lunch may not be a very bright choice. Staying out of a bully's way, although not ego-boosting, may be the best *temporary option* in a bad situation.

The study of family violence by Gelles and Straus (1988), based on interviews of more than 6,000 individuals, found avoiding to be a sometimes effective strategy for dealing with spousal violence. Avoiding was the most common method women used for dealing with physical abuse. Sixty-eight percent of women whose husbands had pushed, slapped, shoved, or thrown things at them said that simply keeping out of their husband's way and trying to anticipate what they should avoid saying or doing that might anger their husbands proved to be an effective strategy for preventing further physical abuse. *Fewer than a third* of those women, however, whose husbands had choked, beaten, punched, or kicked them found that avoiding was an effective approach to prevention of further violence against them.

By inference, children in a family dominated by an abuser would also find avoiding a sometimes necessary strategy for dealing with an ugly situation. Children learn avoiding as a strategy of survival when one or both parents are abusers.

Preventing violence in this manner, of course, can take its toll on the victims' self-esteem and sense of personal power. This style of conflict management is hard to recommend except in the most dire situations where <u>avoiding may be a temporary expedient necessary for self-protection</u>. Avoiding to prevent being pulverized promotes a dominance power perspective. Living in fear of triggering a spouse's or parent's violent rages through even the most innocent comment or innocuous behavior puts the abuser in charge of the lives of the less powerful family members.

<u>If the advantages of confrontation do not outweigh the disadvantages, avoiding the conflict might be a desirable course of action</u>. In some cases, tempers need to cool. Avoiding contentious issues for a time may prove to be constructive. When passions run high, reason usually trails far behind. We often make foolish, irrational choices when we are stressed out.

<u>In most cases, however, avoiding rather than confronting is highly counterproductive</u>. From their research, Gelles and Straus (1988) conclude: "Delaying until the violence escalates to a frequency or severity that would generally be considered abusive is too late. A firm, emphatic, and rational approach appears to be the most effective personal strategy a woman can use to prevent future violence" (p. 159). They suggest *confronting the very first incident of even minor violence,* not waiting to see if it happens again before firmly communicating to the perpetrator of the violence that such behavior is unacceptable and must stop.

Competing (Power/Forcing)

[handwritten: directly aggressive) last resort]

The **competing** or power/forcing style flows from the dominance perspective on power. Competing and forcing your will on others is a win–lose style. Someone using a competing or forcing style shows high concern for task but low concern for relationships in groups. Task comes first. If accomplishing the group task requires a few wounded egos, that is the price of productivity. Someone using the competing/forcing style sees task accomplishment as a means of furthering personal more than group goals (Me-not-We orientation). Making friends and developing a positive social climate is secondary and expendable.

One notable aspect of the competing style is the tendency to ascribe blame when groups don't function perfectly. *Blame* "produces disagreement, denial, and little learning. It evokes fears of punishment . . . Nobody wants to be blamed, especially unfairly, so our energy goes into defending ourselves" (Stone et al., 1999, pp. 11–12). Blame is about looking backward to judge a group member. "You blew it" is blame aimed at assigning responsibility, not on solving the problem.

Since I have already discussed at length the consequences of competitiveness, communication patterns that aim to control others, and power imbalances, I will not repeat the problems associated with a competing-power/forcing style. As with all other styles, however, this style also has its constructive side. If a troublemaker in the group shows no signs of ending disruptions and the seriousness of the situation is clear, then forcing out this difficult member may be the correct choice. As I have noted, one person can affect the entire group because in a system all components are interconnected. Eliminating a troublemaker can revitalize the remaining members and allow progress on the task to proceed unimpeded.

Competing-power/forcing is a style of last resort, except in times of emergencies in which quick, decisive action must be taken and discussion has no place. If all other approaches to conflict produce little result, then competing may be a necessary means of managing the dispute.

[handwritten margin notes: communication!; nonassertive; go along w/ group; directly aggressive; passive aggressive; sound like U R cooperating w/ you aren't; indirect; Western not desired; Eastern desired; assertive; most desired]

---

second look

Communication Styles of Conflict Management

Style	Task-Social Dimension
Collaborating (Problem Solving)	High task, high social *successful*
Accommodating (Yielding)	Low task, high social
Compromising	Moderate task, moderate social *neutral*
Avoiding (Withdrawing)	Low task, low social
Competing (Power/Forcing)	High task, low social

[handwritten: assertive (above Collaborating)]

All five styles of conflict management exhibit predispositions or tendencies. These predispositions, however, are not 100% predictable. Someone using the competing-power/forcing style may, in some circumstances, manifest genuine concern for social climate. Low concern doesn't mean no concern. An accommodator on occasion may regard the task accomplishment as vital. All of these styles represent standard operating procedures, not unalterably fixed ways of managing conflict.

As a general rule, research clearly favors some conflict styles over others, even though many styles may be used over the coarse of a conflict. Burke (1970) reported several studies comparing the five principal conflict styles. Collaborating and accommodating were more successful methods for managing conflict than were competing and avoiding. Phillips and Cheston (1979) compared collaborative problem solving and power-forcing styles in 52 conflict cases. Forcing was used twice as often as problem solving, yet in about half the situations where forcing was used the outcomes were bad, whereas in all instances where problem solving was used the outcomes were good. More recently, a scant 5% of first-line supervisors, middle managers, and top managers and administrators admitted to actually using the collaborating style in specific conflict situations while 41% selected competing and 26% chose avoiding styles

(Gayle, 1991). Both male and female supervisors and managers, according to this study, typically select the least effective styles of conflict management.

The competent communicator tends to use the collaborating/problem-solving conflict style, whereas the less-competent communicator opts most often for competing-power/forcing (Canary & Spitzberg, 1987; Gottman & Silver, 1994, 1999). Overall, the collaborating style in a variety of contexts produces better decisions and greater satisfaction from parties in conflict (Gayle-Hackett, 1989; Tutzauer & Roloff, 1988). Competing tends to promote destructive conflict. Collaborating encourages constructive conflict.

The results of research comparing the effectiveness of conflict styles are not surprising. I've already discussed at length the negative aspects of competing. Psychological reactance is the likely response to power/forcing. The collaborative/problem solving style is a win–win cooperative approach to conflict. Since the goal is to satisfy all parties, collaboration by its very nature should prove to be a more effective style in a greater number and variety of instances than competing/forcing.

FOCUS on Culture

Culture and Conflict Styles

Individualist and collectivist cultures exhibit a specific difference in communication styles. Individualist cultures such as the United States and most Western European countries typically employ what Hall (1981) calls a low-context communication style while collectivist countries such as most Latin American and Asian countries use a high-context communication style (Griffin, 1994). A **low-context style** has a message-*content* orientation and a **high-context style** has a message-*context* orientation. "In low-context communication, the listener knows very little and must be told practically everything. In high-context communication, the listener is already 'contexted' and does not need to be given much background information" (Hall & Hall, 1987, p. 183).

The primary difference between the two styles is exhibited in verbal expression. A low-context style is verbally precise, direct, literal, and explicit. A legal contract is an example of low-context communication. Instructions given to computers and e-mail addresses are also examples of low-context communication. Computer instructions must be exact for the computer to function as you desire and e-mail addresses must have every space, number, period, and letter typed exactly.

High-context communication uses indirect verbal expression, such as "I'll think about it" as a face-saving means of saying no in Japan, or it is assumed that no verbal expression is required to state what should be obvious from the nonverbal context. You are expected to "read between the lines" by recognizing hints and knowing the cultural context and unspoken rules, rituals, and norms. During the Tiananmen Square protest in China in the summer of 1989, there was much confusion concerning who was in control of the government and what position would be taken regarding political and economic reform in the country. Rumors abounded that Chinese leader Deng Xiaoping was dead and civil war was imminent. No statement was released by the government to clarify the situation, as would certainly occur in a low-context culture such as the United States under similar circumstances. Instead, Chinese Premier Li Peng, a hardline conservative, appeared on Chinese national television. He made no effort to clarify the situation verbally, but he wore a "Chairman Mao uniform" instead of the more usual western business suit. Viewers could easily interpret what this meant within the context of Chinese culture and history. Li Peng's clothing was a throwback to the uniform commonly worn by Chinese citizens during the conservative, hard-line era of Mao Tse Tung. Li Peng was signaling that he was in charge and a conservative position on political and economic reform prevailed in the government (Muir, 1992).

Individualist, low-context cultures favor direct competitive or compromising styles of conflict management. Communication during conflict is explicit and direct. Americans are inclined to become impatient when members of collectivist cultures "beat around the bush." Allowing a conflict to go unresolved makes most Americans uncomfortable, even agitated. Collectivist, high-context cultures favor avoiding or accommodating styles of conflict management (Chen & Starosta, 1998). Assertive confrontation is considered rude and offensive. It is too direct, explicit, and unsettling. The Chinese culture, for example, considers "har-

mony as the universal path which we all should pursue" (Chen & Starosta, 1997, p. 6). This philosophy translates into avoiding conflicts that might stir up trouble and disharmony. Conflicts handled ineptly might bring shame on the individual and the entire group.

Managing intercultural conflicts where expectations on the appropriateness of different communication styles differ is challenging. Remaining flexible, employing a style that is well suited to cultural expectations, is a key to effective conflict management in such situations.

Questions for Thought

1. In a culturally diverse group with members from both individualist, low-context cultures and collectivist, high-context cultures, which communication styles should be used? How would this be determined?
2. Is there ever a time or situation where the typical American approach to managing conflict should be imposed on a culturally diverse group or should you always remain sensitive to differences in expectations?

Overall, the probabilities of successfully managing conflict are higher with collaborating/problem solving than with competing/forcing. Probabilities, however, do not mean certainties. Thus, the danger of overemphasizing the superior probabilities of one style over another can produce rigidity, making adaptation to change in the system difficult. Flexibility is a key ingredient of communication competence. Individuals can become locked into a ritualistic, inflexible pattern of conflict management where every time a conflict arises, the same conflict styles are employed, regardless of the circumstances. Some people with tripwire tempers escalate conflicts into pyrotechnic events with annoying regularity no matter how minor the provocation. Others avoid conflicts or accommodate antagonists, never attempting to confront or find an integrative solution.

Within systems, inflexible patterns of managing conflict can lead to interlocking behavior whose rigidity stymies effective management of disputes. Parents may use competing/forcing styles to deal with all clashes with their children. "Do what I say and don't ask questions." The children reluctantly may, in turn, accommodate the parents because they fear the consequences, but resentment and hostility build with each act of yielding, and the family unit experiences recurrent tensions and strife. Group leaders may try to confront every difference of opinion among members, producing frustration and annoyance because the leader seems incapable of discriminating between important and trivial differences. Effective conflict management is adaptive, not rigid.

TRANSACTING CONFLICT

Conflict is a transactional process. To understand how to transact conflict effectively in a small-group context, I will discuss three areas: primary situational variables, the problem of escalating spirals of conflict, and negotiating strategies.

Focus Questions
1. How do group members short-circuit conflict spirals?
2. Why is principled negotiation superior to other negotiating strategies?

Primary Situational Variables

Conflict styles function within a system, so they must be adapted to the changing dynamics of the group. Although some conflict styles have a higher probability of effectiveness than do others, the choice of styles always operates within a context. Effective conflict management is not a matter of deciding out of context what styles will be employed. "I think I'll use mostly collaborating/problem solving today and maybe round that out with a bit of accommodating/smoothing, but tomorrow I'm all competing/forcing, so look out" would be the strategy of the lame communicator.

Nature of the Conflict   The first situational variable that should be considered when deciding how to transact conflict in groups is the nature of the conflict. For instance, is the struggle primarily a *content or relationship issue*? At a college where I was employed, the faculty union and management engaged in bitter negotiations for 2 years. Resources were tight. The union's opening position called for a salary increase of 4% the first year of the new contract and 5% the next. Management countered with opening offers of 1% and 0% salary increases respectively. Management apparently hoped to send a message to the union that tough bargaining was ahead. The message that was received was quite different. Faculty members felt unvalued and were incensed by what they perceived to be an insulting and contemptible initial offer.

Management miscalculated. A tense, combative climate permeated the bargaining. Even though management eventually accepted the initial salary increase the union proposed, which should have been viewed as an achievement by the union, a residue of hard feelings remained. The nature of the conflict was relational rather than content-based. The dollars and cents proved to be less important than the attitude management communicated to the faculty. If you damage the relationship between disputing parties, even concessions or an integrative solution may not wash away the stains of ill feelings. The conflict may take on a different dimension of a more personal nature.

The following year, management shifted to a collaborative style of bargaining, made a reasonable opening offer, and negotiations were completed in record time without the bitter recriminations. If you focus on content issues when the conflict is primarily relational, you're headed for disaster.

A second aspect of the nature of the conflict is *how deeply held are the beliefs and values* that are at the source of the dispute among members (Borisoff & Victor, 1989). The most difficult disputes to manage are value conflicts. We may clash over ideas and still walk away friends, especially if the ideas do not touch on deeply held values. Beliefs such as, "Republicans favor big business," or "Alcoholism is not a disease" may provoke animated dissent among group members, but civility is usually maintained. When disputes over ideas and beliefs spill over into value clashes, however, especially when the values are held passionately, then you have a conflict of a different ilk. Battles over abortion, pornography, creationism versus evolution, flag-burning, hate speech, and the like leave little if any room for compromise. When dichotomous battle lines are drawn—friends versus enemies, saviors versus sinners—forcing is often the style required for conflict management. The courts have had to settle these issues by declaring what is permissible, even essential, and what is prohibited.

Values conflicts are especially difficult to manage when members of different cultures clash over divergent worldviews. Rubenstein (1975) presented a hypothetical situation to Arabs and Americans. Suppose that a small boat is occupied by a man and his wife, mother, and child when it capsizes. The man is the only one of the occupants who can swim. The man can save only one of the three nonswimmers. Which person should he save? All of the Arabs asked by Rubenstein would save the mother because a wife and child can be replaced, but not a mother. Sixty of 100 American college freshmen, however, would save the wife and 40 would save the child. Saving the mother while sacrificing the wife and child was thought to be laughable. Intercultural value conflicts are probably the most difficult to manage.

When the nature of the conflict is *a power struggle,* the choice of styles will depend on the relative power relationships between the parties involved. A conflict between relative equals sets the stage for a collaborative effort or, at the very least, compromise. Conflicts between relative unequals, however, may require more accommodating and avoiding on the part of the lower-power parties in the group than would be necessary if the power was more balanced.

Conflict is transactional. You choose your styles of conflict management within the context of communication choices made by all parties in the conflict. What one person does affects other group members. Lower-power group members may want to collaborate. Dominating high-power group members, however, may see little need to collaborate since they can impose their will on you. Granted, competing/forcing may be an unwise choice for the powerful parties in the long run, but it may be an unavoidable reality you have to face. Until you can balance the power more equitably by employing strategies of alliance, resistance, defiance, or significance, collaborating with unwilling, dominating group members is wishful thinking.

Years ago a friend of mine worked as a temporary employee in the company headquarters for a large retail firm. The firm had a system of rules that seemed to have little purpose except to control employees. Office workers were required to punch in and out for their 15-minute breaks. Managers, without consulting anyone, assigned specific times for subordinates to take their breaks. No personal possessions were permitted on subordinates' desks (managers had no such restriction). This meant employees were not allowed to display family photos, keepsakes, or any items that might reflect an individual's personality. Subordinates were written up by managers for every three instances of tardiness (even if one minute late). Two write-ups in one year meant termination. One woman, a 10-year employee and revered by all the nonmanagement workers, was "written up" twice. This occurred even though she called the office to report each time she was delayed by personal problems such as a sick child and a car wreck. She was terminated despite an exemplary record of service.

The workers erupted. Formerly docile employees became activists. Workers began demanding that the union show some teeth. Long-standing grievances were formally filed. Management was confronted about its heavy-handed forcing style. The response? "If you don't like the way we run things—leave." Many employees followed the advice. The result was predictable. The company began to fail, in no small part because of the incompetent communication patterns of management. The parent corporation stepped in. There was a major shakeup in management and the company was renamed. If the relatively powerful refuse to collaborate, then different conflict styles and strategies are required.

Nature of the Relationship   The nature of the relationships among group members is a second situational factor that should be considered when transacting conflict. In actual practice, we do make style choices in terms of our relationships with the other parties. Power-forcing is the most common style managers use in handling differences with subordinates (Phillips & Cheston, 1979). Managers typically handle conflict with superiors and peers differently (Rahim, 1985). They are primarily accommodating with superiors and compromising with peers.

These style choices revealed in the research do not represent ideal choices. As previously indicated, the Phillips and Cheston (1979) study found power-forcing to be an ineffective style about half the time. Nevertheless, we **style shift,** flexibly adapting our communication to the changes in the system, depending on the nature of relationships between ourselves and others.

If our relationship is one of trust and cooperation, regardless of the power disparities, then collaborating has real potential. As Tjosvold (1985) discovered, high-power supervisors in cooperative environments actually used their power to assist subordinates in solving problems. This was not so true in environments characterized by a competitive or individualistic climate. If our relationship is one of mistrust and suspicion, then collaborating will be difficult. Riccillo and Trenholm (1983) found that power-forcing is the style of choice among supervisors dealing with subordinates they do not trust.

In relationships poisoned by mistrust, a collaborative attempt by one party may be seen as a ploy to gain some unforeseen advantage. Accommodating by one party, even as a gesture to change the negative dynamics of the parties in conflict, may be viewed as weakness and a sign that capitulation is likely to occur after a period of waiting.

Timing   A third situational factor that should be considered by group members when transacting conflict is timing. Confrontation can be a highly effective style but not when used as a hit-and-run tactic (Johnson & Johnson, 1987). Confronting contentious issues 5 minutes before the group is due to adjourn or just before you leave for a luncheon date provides no time for the other person to respond constructively. **Hit-and-run confrontations** look like guerrilla tactics, not attempts to communicate competently and work out disputes.

I have a friend who is fond of the hit-and-run confrontation. As the other person starts to respond to his revelation, he abruptly excuses himself, pleading an "urgent" appointment that can't be missed or a "Sorry, I'm late for work" apology. This timing is strategic. If you hit, then run, you don't take the risk of getting hit back, at least not right away. The target of the hit-and-run gets to stew over your revelation and fume over your perceived insensitivity. The perpetrator, however, likely feels relieved that a great weight has been lifted by his or her self-disclosure. If you're going to confront, make time for it.

Power-forcing may be required at some point in the conflict, but as a first choice during the initial struggle, forcing is almost always an unwise decision. Power-forcing typically produces psychological reactance. If you try to force, are met with resistance, then attempt to collaborate or accommodate, you may find that this sequence of styles suffers from poor timing. Trying to collaborate after unsuccessfully forcing will be seen as the disingenuous act of a person whose bluff and bluster were challenged. On the other hand, temporarily withdrawing after a protracted feud has stalemated might allow heads to clear and passions to cool. Sometimes we just need a break from the struggle, a chance to think calmly and dispassionately.

Conflict Spirals

Minor conflicts can easily escalate into major destructive conflicts spiraling out of control when groups are faced with failure, poor working conditions, intense competition, stress, or a defensive climate. Managing conflict in challenging circumstances can be difficult. French (1941), in an early study of escalating aggression as an outgrowth of conflict in groups, documented how quickly conflict can spiral out of control. Offensive remarks flew back and forth among group members so rapidly that observers could only estimate the total number. In a 45-minute period while group members worked on an insoluble and frustrating task, observers estimated that more than 600 offensive remarks were made.

As already noted, the principle of reciprocation operates universally in all societies. When someone assists us we feel obligated to return the favor. The principle of reciprocation can be exploited as a powerful compliance-gaining strategy or inducement for cooperation in small groups. There is another side to the strategy, however, called **negative reciprocation.** Here those who do harm to us or threaten our well-being are thought to deserve harm or threats in

Minor conflicts can easily escalate into major conflict spirals if handled poorly. This labor–management dispute in Minnesota was a power-forcing debacle.

return, and as Carroll (1987) found, <u>negative reciprocation tends to be stronger than its positive form</u>.

Group members often overreact to perceived threats or offenses especially from more-powerful members, setting in motion a destructive conflict spiral (Youngs, 1986). This overreaction has a chain reaction or ripple effect on the whole system. Disputing group members often do more than merely reciprocate each other's negative behavior in exact proportion. They usually ratchet up the level of negativity. A mildly abusive remark from one member may invite a more aggressive remark from a second member that may in turn incite a highly abusive and threatening remark from a third member, and so forth.

CLOSER LOOK

KILL Radio Conflict Case Study

The Situation (based on a real event): Open warfare has been raging for almost a year at public radio station K-I-L-L (slogan: "Live radio that'll knock you dead"). The station operates from facilities on the campus of Bayview Community College in Tsunami, California. KILL radio has 1,000 watts of power, enough to reach into the local Tsunami community (population 42,000).

The program director quit after a feud with the general manager (GM). The GM resigned soon after. His reasons for leaving, stated in his letter of resignation, were as follows:

1. The volunteer staff (community members who were not students) inappropriately editorialized while reading news on the air and presented only one side on controversial issues, both violations of Federal Communications Commission (FCC) regulations for public radio stations.
2. The volunteers were "insubordinate" when they refused to obey his directives concerning substitution of other programs for previously scheduled regular shows.
3. They threatened him with bodily injury when he ordered the volunteers either to implement his directives or terminate their association with the station.

The volunteer staff countered these allegations with its own accusations: the GM showed them little respect and treated them abusively; they were overworked and underappreciated; and the GM never sought their input on programming and scheduling concerns.

The volunteers issued the following demands:

1. Programming should not be determined by one person, but by a consensus of the staff.
2. Program substitution should be made only when prior notice (at least 2 weeks in advance) has been given so staff members will not prepare material destined to be preempted at the last minute.
3. Volunteers should run the station since they do the lion's share of the work and are the only ones with the necessary technical expertise.

The college supports the station with $85,000 annually, but is seriously considering a drastic cut in the station's budget due to the persistent conflict and because students are not actively involved in the station. The administration wants the station to be a learning laboratory for stu-

dents interested in pursuing careers in broadcasting.

The volunteer staff has threatened to quit en masse unless their demands are met. The school's board of trustees is getting twitchy because of all the commotion; the faculty in the Department of Mass Communication are in a dither about the conflict because it is disruptive. The local community highly values the station and is upset by the dispute. The college administration named the chair of the mass communication department at Bayview College as the new general manager and temporary program director of the station.

Before reading further, analyze this dispute. How would you manage this conflict if you were the new GM? Which conflict styles would you employ? When? How?

The Analysis: The KILL radio dispute is a power struggle. Competing/forcing has become the primary style of managing the conflict. The previous GM threatened the staff with termination and the staff threatened the GM with bodily injury. So far, the forcing style has produced two resignations, the threat of a mass exodus by the staff, several demands from the staff, and a reservoir of ill feeling and disruption. If you, as the new GM, were to continue in this vein by terminating the volunteer staff, you might ignite a conflict spiral. Disgruntled volunteers might vandalize the station in retaliation, and relations between the college and the community would be strained further. The station would have to shut down until qualified staff could be found to replace those individuals terminated. In such an atmosphere, the board and administration just might decide to close the station permanently and cut their losses.

Since the staff has not been actively consulted in the past regarding programming (at least that's the allegation, and perception is the reality you must confront), the climate is one of control, not problem orientation. The staff feels disconfirmed and defensive. The perception exists among them that the previous GM treated them as expendable technicians, not talented employees worthy of respect.

This situation cries out for collaboration. The first step is confrontation. The new GM should immediately meet with the volunteers, probably individually first, to gather information from their perspective. This is a relational issue as well as a content issue. Staff members feel unappreciated and undervalued. Supportive, confirming statements concerning the essential role volunteers play in the functioning of the station should be made to all involved. Smoothing statements (e.g., "We're starting fresh. I want us to work together") should be delivered to the staff. You're seeking a cooperative working relationship with the volunteers.

In keeping with the desire for cooperation, an appeal to the superordinate goal of keeping the station on the air should be delivered. The new GM must impress on the staff that violations of FCC regulations could result in the revocation of the station's operating license. This is not a matter of personal preference but of law. The GM could further state, "Unless we handle our differences constructively, out of exasperation, the college may shut the station down. None of us wants this to happen." There should be no threats about firing anyone. The tone and climate should be positive and focused on the central goal all can agree to, namely, maintaining the station.

Although final say on the programming issue is the GM's responsibility, input from the staff should be sought actively and given serious consideration. After all, the staff has to make the programming work on the air. That's difficult to accomplish if you'd like to play rhythm-and-blues but are ordered to play country-western. The staff could conduct a survey of the community (this is a public radio station) to determine the programming preferences of the station's audience. The GM could then make programming decisions based on data from the survey and not on personal tastes of a single individual or the (possibly narrow) preferences of the staff. One or two experimental programs could be tried as a compromise if community preferences do not match staff preferences in programming. Some compromise may be possible on program substitution (perhaps 1 week prior notice, not 2 as demanded).

Integrating the radio station into the college curriculum should be a fairly simple process. Involving students in the actual operation of the station, perhaps as supervised interns earning class credit, would satisfy a primary concern of the administration and board. This would also expand the resources of the station by training additional individuals to help staff members who already feel overworked.

Finally, the demand that the volunteers run the station would have to be denied. More than likely, however, this demand was made without any expectation that it would be accepted. Avoid this issue unless a staff member raises it. Forcing would be required if this issue came to a showdown. Handling other issues effectively may reduce this issue to irrelevance. If disruptions or violations of FCC regulations recur, then those responsible should be terminated.

The key to the management of this conflict by a competent communicator is the flexible use of several conflict styles. No single style alone could effectively manage this complex dispute. The overriding conflict style, however, is collaboration. You begin by confronting central concerns of disputing parties, not competing/forcing. You find integrative solutions where possible. Termination is a last resort, not a first choice. You compromise only when a better solution cannot be found. You smooth hurt feelings because a supportive environment is essential to the management of conflict. You avoid emotional issues that seem tangential to the real sources of the conflict and are likely to provoke a power struggle.

None of these styles of conflict management, of course, will work unless you think through each step before you take it (*act, don't just react*). The competent communicator must have knowledge of different conflict styles, the skill to use all the styles, a sensitivity for the requirements of the specific situation and the likely outcomes of each choice made, and a commitment to resolving the dispute as equitably as possible. Complex conflicts require sufficient time to be resolved. This means patience.

1. Before you read the analysis of this case study, what action would you have proposed to resolve the conflict? In what ways were your proposals different from the ones suggested in the analysis?

2. Do you disagree with any suggestions provided in the analysis? Explain.

How do groups short-circuit conflict spirals? The basic role of the competent communicator is to avoid negative reciprocation. <u>You must not match the abusive, insulting, or threatening behavior of other group members</u>. This can be best explained by examining negotiating strategies, a final aspect of transacting conflict in small groups.

Negotiating Strategies

Fisher and Ury (1981), in their excellent book on negotiation, *Getting to Yes*, state: "More and more occasions require negotiation; conflict is a growth industry. . . . Whether in business, government, or the family, people reach most decisions through negotiation" (p. xi). **Negotiation** is defined as "a process by which a joint decision is made by two or more parties" (Pruitt, 1981, p. 1). In this section, I will discuss commonly used strategies of negotiating conflict.

Tit for Tat   A first strategy of negotiating is called tit for tat. This is an "eye for an eye, smooch for a smooch" approach to negotiating. Tit for tat reciprocates or matches the behavior of the other party or parties after an initial effort is made to cooperate. You do to them what they did to you in the previous move. You begin by cooperating, but if they compete, then you compete. <u>Since negative reciprocation is more likely than positive reciprocation, a spiral of competitive tit for tat is the usual pattern among group members</u>.

Fisher and Brown (1988) question the advisability of using the tit for tat strategy. They conclude that "as a strategy for building a working relationship—for improving the way we deal with differences—tit for tat would be a mistake" (p. 200). They argue that "the best guideline for building and maintaining a good working relationship is to act in various ways that are unconditional—ways that do not reciprocate what another does . . ." (p. 197).

Those who tout tit for tat (Axelrod, 1984) can make a case for the utility of the strategy when cooperation does occur. Tit for tat will maintain cooperation once it has been initiated because you reciprocate an act of cooperation, thereby encouraging further cooperation from the other party. <u>Tit for tat, however, is an incompetent strategy when you look at its negative sequences of potential moves and countermoves</u>. For example, if someone threatens you in a conflict, should you automatically threaten them back? If your antagonist demands outrageous concessions from you, should you mindlessly match the demands? If someone tries to cheat, blackmail, or exploit you in a dispute, should you reciprocate in kind? If another party has a snit fit, should you likewise throw a temper tantrum? Does any of this sound to you like competent communication? As Fisher and Brown (1988) explain, "If you are acting in ways that injure your own competence, there is no reason for me to do the same. Two heads are better than one, but one is better than none" (p. 202). Tit for tat predisposes us to stoop to whatever level the other party is willing to sink.

The most serious objection to tit for tat, identified by Fisher and Brown, is the likelihood of an endless "malignant spiral" of escalating competitive behavior. In a group, if even one member competes, tit for tat requires that all members compete. Thus, one competitive individual can make the entire group competitive. Since negative reciprocation is more likely than positive reciprocation, a cooperative gesture by one member is less likely to transform competitive members into cooperative ones than vice versa.

Tit for tat offers no way to break the competitive spiral once it has been set in motion, except maybe through outright exhaustion of the combatants or by taking disputants to the brink of catastrophe. Let's assume that every member of your group adopts a tit for tat strategy and sticks to it unswervingly. How do you ever short-circuit a destructive cycle of antagonism when everyone is waiting for someone else to make the first cooperative move? Tit for tat as a negotiating strategy seems extremely limited and mostly counterproductive.

Reformed Sinner A second strategy of negotiating is called reformed sinner (Pruitt & Kimmel, 1977). Someone using this strategy initially competes or acts tough, then cooperates and relaxes demands. The inducement to cooperate is the demonstrated willingness to compete if necessary. Unlike tit for tat, you try to break a conflict spiral by making the first move toward cooperation.

A rather interesting version of the reformed sinner strategy is Osgood's (1959; 1966) GRIT proposal. **GRIT** stands for **G**raduated and **R**eciprocated **I**nitiatives in **T**ension reduction. Originally offered as a means to de-escalate the international arms race, the strategy has been employed in less-global conflicts. Lindskild (1978) summarizes game theory research supporting the effectiveness of the principal steps in the proposal.

GRIT tries to break the malignant spiral of escalating competitive conflict by initiating a cycle of de-escalation using the following sequence of steps (see Folger et al., 1993, for greater detail):

1. Issue a sincere public statement expressing a desire to de-escalate the conflict.
2. Specify the concession to be made, clarifying what, when, and how the action will be undertaken.
3. Follow through and complete the concession, but do not make this contingent on reciprocation by the other parties.
4. Encourage, but do not demand, reciprocation from the other parties.
5. Make no high-risk concessions that leave you vulnerable or in an indefensible position. Don't give away the store.

Someone using this method of promoting cooperation in a competitive conflict situation should consider following the first concession with another concession if no progress is made after a time. Don't pile concession on concession, however, with nothing offered in return. This strategy may take patience and persistence. Offering a minor concession and then withdrawing it when no immediate reciprocation is forthcoming from the other party is not a true GRIT.

Positional Bargaining   In positional bargaining, parties take positions on contested issues, then haggle back and forth until concessions are made and an agreement is reached. There are two styles of positional bargaining—hard and soft. *Hard bargainers* (sometimes called tough bargainers) see negotiation as a contest of wills. Hard bargaining is the "negotiate from strength" approach to conflicts of interest heard so often in foreign affairs deliberations. The focus is on conveying strength and resilience so the other party or parties will yield.

Hard bargaining is a competing/forcing strategy. Hard bargainers can be abusive or sarcastic in an attempt to gain an advantage over the other party. When both sides adopt a hard bargaining style, the battle is joined. Both sides attempt to cut the best deal for themselves (Me-not-We-orientation), not find the most equitable and constructive solution to the conflicts of interest. Opening positions typically are extreme and unreasonable. The more hard bargainers publicly defend these positions, the more hardened the positions tend to become. Egos become identified with positions. Concessions easily take on the appearance of "selling out." Walking out on the negotiations in a huff, refusing to budge even on trivial issues, and issuing ultimatums are commonplace tactics in hard positional bargaining.

Consider this example of hard positional bargaining among house-mates:

GROUP MEMBER A: I want to have a party here at the house on Saturday.

GROUP MEMBER B: Hey, that's a great idea.

GROUP MEMBER C: Sorry, no can do. I have to study for my law exam and I sure can't do that with a couple of dozen Neanderthals belching, retching, and cranking the music beyond 125 decibels. I'd have to lug a truckload of books and notes to the library or anywhere else I might choose to study.

GROUP MEMBER A: Who appointed you king? This is our house too. Since when do you dictate what can and can't happen around here?

GROUP MEMBER C: Since I pay a third of the rent and am not about to sacrifice my standing in law school so you twits can get drunk with your brain-dead friends and act like imbeciles. I'm vetoing your little beer bash.

GROUP MEMBER B: I don't even know why we're bothering to ask for your permission to hold this party. There's no way you can stop us anyway. I say we just go ahead and do it. If you don't like it, sue us, Perry Mason.

GROUP MEMBER A: Yeah! Get used to the idea because we're going to have this party and there isn't anything you can do about it.

GROUP MEMBER C: On the contrary, there is a great deal I can do about it. Suing you is actually an option that appeals to me. I could sue you for damages especially if I do poorly on the exam. I could also argue in small claims court that you violated a verbal contract not to have parties without the consent of all housemates—I have witnesses affirming that you both agreed to such an arrangement. So don't start issuing ultimatums unless you want this party to cost a lot more than the price of beer.

And on and on it goes, a contest of wills complete with recriminations, threats, name-calling, and anger.

Hard bargaining doesn't have to mean ruthless bargaining and obstinacy. Chertkoff and Esser (1976) found that a party can achieve positive results by acting tough. Bartos (1970) revealed that hard bargaining achieved excellent results when both parties were tough. Eventually, though, there has to be some give and take in order for a stalemate to be avoided if all parties assume a hard bargaining strategy. The main difficulty with this strategy is how tough should you be without seeming pig-headed? As with any competitive strategy, when hard bargainers face off against one another, their moves and countermoves can easily produce an impasse. Hard bargainers lower the odds of reaching an agreement (Pavitt & Curtis, 1994). If other parties perceive your opening position as unreasonable, even outrageous, negotiations get off to a rocky start. Hard bargaining that produces yielding by the other parties is also likely to foster bitterness and anger. The key to making this a constructive conflict strategy is to appear tough but fair. When I hear an opening position that is clearly extreme, I have doubts about that party's commitment to a fair settlement. Hard bargainers can slip easily into tough battlers, and that usually spells W-A-R-F-A-R-E.

Warfare is what resulted from hard bargaining that led to the baseball strike of 1994–95. Owners and players both ended up losers. Owners lost $800 million in revenue during the strike and additional millions from lower attendance resulting from fan disgruntlement once the 8-month strike ended a few days into the 1995 season. Players lost $350 million in salaries (Blum, 1995). This doesn't include the vendors who generated no revenue from canceled ballgames and the fans who felt betrayed. This strike can be summarized easily: greed times greed equals greed squared. Hard bargaining can produce nothing but losers.

Soft bargainers, recognizing the high costs of hard bargaining on relationships with people you may have to interact with once the negotiations are concluded, yield to pressure. To soft bargainers, making an agreement and remaining friends is more important than winning a victory. The major drawback to soft bargaining is that you may give away too much in order to maintain harmonious relationships during negotiations. Soft bargainers are reticent to offend housemates by refusing to allow a party. Hard bargainers eat soft bargainers for hors d'oeuvres.

Principled Negotiation   Fisher and Ury (1981) offer a third choice besides hard and soft positional bargaining—**principled negotiation** or interest-based bargaining. Principled negotiation embodies the essential elements of competent communication. All negotiations are conducted according to rules. Principled negotiation changes the rules from competitive (hard bargaining) to cooperative. The four basic elements to this approach with corresponding principles for each element are:

People: Separate the people from the problem.

Interests: Focus on interests, not positions.

Options: Generate a variety of possibilities before deciding what to do.

Criteria: Insist that the result be based on some objective standard. (Fisher & Ury, 1981, p. 11)

Separating the people from the problem reaffirms the importance of supportive climates (e.g., description, problem orientation, equality, or provisionalism) and the inappropriateness of defensive communication patterns (e.g., evaluation, control, superiority, or certainty) during negotiations. Principled negotiation also focuses on content conflicts and strives to reduce relationship conflicts during negotiations.

When Frank Lorenzo became president of Eastern Airlines in 1986, relations between management and labor immediately became tense and personal, and after a year of fruitless negotiations, Eastern's machinists and pilots went on strike. The machinist union targeted Lorenzo as the issue in negotiations, painting him as an unscrupulous takeover artist. The Airline Pilots Association characterized Lorenzo as a Machiavellian sleazeball whose middle name was Greed. Lorenzo fired back, calling the pilots' role in the strike "suicidal" and akin to the Jonestown tragedy. Eastern filed for bankruptcy, and thousands lost their jobs because the parties in conflict could not separate the people from the problem.

Negotiating interests first, not arguing positions, is critical. Positions differ from interests. For instance, a group in my class working on a symposium presentation got into a dispute over topic choice. Two members wanted the group to choose "The Greenhouse Effect." Two other members pushed for "Capital Punishment." The three remaining group members advocated "Animal Rights." Bickering broke out as each faction chose a hard bargaining approach. Nobody was willing to budge. The focus of the bargaining became the weaknesses of each topic advocated by one faction or the other. Putdowns, snide comments, and abusive remarks were flung back and forth.

When instructed to explore their interests, not the positions of each faction, the group found a mutually satisfactory solution. The capital punishment faction had already done a great deal of research on the topic for other classes. Their primary interest was time management since they had families who wanted them home. They wanted to "double dip" by using research for two classes instead of just one. The greenhouse effect faction turned out to have a similar interest. They had done some research on environmental issues. The animal rights faction simply wanted to do a presentation that dealt with an issue of values, not some "dry, scientific report of facts and figures on the environment."

Once the interests of each faction were identified and discussed, the greenhouse effect faction realized that the capital punishment faction had already done most of the necessary research for the entire group presentation. This was far more extensive than the research already completed by those urging the environmental topic. The animal rights group agreed that capital punishment was an issue of values as well as "facts and figures" so they settled on capital punishment as the group topic.

Positions are the concrete things one party wants. Interests are the intangible motivations—needs, desires, concerns, fears, aspirations—that lead a party in the conflict to take a position (Ury, 1993). The struggle over which topic best fulfills the assignment is a position, but time management is the interest behind the position. Interest answers the question why a party takes a position. Focusing on interests instead of positions underlines the importance of structuring cooperation into the deliberations. Positional bargaining structures negotiations as a win–lose game. Negotiating interests structures cooperation into the deliberations because the focus is on the problem and a mutually satisfactory solution, not on the position or the people advocating the position. Focusing on interests, not on positions, is the basis of integrative conflict management.

Generating a <u>variety of options</u> is another aspect of principled negotiation. This involves brainstorming, as already explained in my discussion of problem solving. Integration by expanding the pie or bridging may be discovered in a brainstorming session. The nominal group technique may also prove to be useful here.

Finally, principled negotiation rests on <u>objective standards</u> for weighing the merits and demerits of any proposal. In the conflict over topic choice just discussed, one primary objective standard that was agreed to was "the least number of hours doing research in the library." An objective standard for "fairness" might be that both parties share equally all risks and financial costs.

<u>A specific comparison between hard and soft positional bargaining and principled negotiation is presented in the table constructed by Fisher and Ury</u> (1981).

Positional Bargaining and Principled Negotiation Compared

PROBLEM		SOLUTION
Positional Bargaining: Which Game Should You Play?		Change the Game—Negotiate on the Merits

SOFT	HARD	PRINCIPLED
Participants are friends.	Participants are adversaries.	Participants are problem-solvers.
The goal is agreement.	The goal is victory.	The goal is a wise outcome reached efficiently and amicably.
Make concessions to cultivate the relationship.	Demand concessions as a condition of the relationship.	**Separate the people from the problem.**
Be soft on the people and the problem.	Be hard on the problem and the people.	Be soft on the people, hard on the problem.
Trust others.	Distrust others.	Proceed independent of trust.
Change your position easily.	Dig in to your position.	**Focus on interests, not positions.**
Make offers.	Make threats.	Explore interests.

continued

Disclose your bottom line.	Mislead as to your bottom line.	Avoid having a bottom line.
Accept one-sided losses to reach agreement.	Demand one-sided gains as the price of agreement.	**Invent options for mutual gain.**
Search for the single answer: the one *they will* accept.	Search for the single answer: the one *you will* accept.	Develop multiple options to choose from; decide later.
Insist on agreement.	Insist on your position.	**Insist on using objective criteria.**
Try to avoid a contest of will.	Try to win a contest of will.	Try to reach a result based on standards independent of will.
Yield to pressure.	Apply pressure.	Reason and be open to reason; yield to principle, not pressure.

SOURCE: From *Getting to Yes* by Roger Fisher and William Ury. Copyright 1981 by Roger Fisher and William Ury. Reprinted by permission of Houghton Mifflin Co.

The principled negotiation approach to conflicts of interest must include two additional elements. You must be unconditionally constructive (Fisher & Brown, 1988) and you must develop a **BATNA** (**B**est **A**lternative **T**o a **N**egotiated **A**greement).

Being unconditionally constructive means you make choices and take only those actions that benefit both you and the other parties in the dispute regardless of whether the other parties reciprocate. Remaining unconditionally constructive during negotiations short-circuits conflict spirals. If they become abusive, you remain civil. If they purposely misunderstand or confuse issues, you clarify. If they try to bully, you neither yield nor bully back. You try to persuade them on the merits of your proposal. If they try to deceive you, neither trust nor deceive them. You remain trustworthy throughout the negotiations. If they do not listen carefully, you nevertheless listen to them carefully and empathically. This is not a guide to earning your way into heaven. This is a realistic, eyes-wide-open guide to *effective* negotiations. You remain unconditionally constructive because it serves your own best interests to do so.

A story told (Fadiman, 1985) about Gautama Buddha, an Indian prince who lived in the sixth century B.C. and whose teachings formed the basis of Buddhism, exemplifies the unconditionally constructive attitude necessary for principled negotiations. A man interrupted Buddha's preaching with a torrent of abuse. Buddha waited for the man to finish. He then asked his detractor, "If a man offered a gift to another but the gift was declined, to whom would the gift belong?" The man responded, "To the one who offered it." "Then," said Buddha, "I decline to accept your abuse and request you to keep it for yourself" (p. 84). Reciprocating abuse with abuse only sidetracks negotiations onto unproductive avenues of mutual disparagement. Abuse needs to be short-circuited, not encouraged.

You also need to develop a BATNA as a standard against which any proposal can be measured. Your BATNA tells you what the best you can do is if negotiations fail to produce an agreement. Most importantly, your BATNA keeps you from accepting an agreement worse than what you could have done without negotiations.

For instance, if you have ever visited towns on the Mexican side of the border with the United States, you have undoubtedly engaged in street negotiations with local merchants on items such as hand-crafted rugs, sunglasses, pottery, and other items. Not having a BATNA before entering into negotiations with merchants can lead you to overpay for merchandise. If you have no idea how much comparable items would cost in the United States, then you are likely to make a charitable contribution to the Mexican economy when negotiating with a savvy merchant on what you think is a hot deal. Your BATNA in this instance is a comparable item that sells at a slightly higher price in the United States, a similar item of better quality for more money, or a similar item of lesser quality for less money. You know when you've negotiated a real value if you have such a BATNA. Information is power. A BATNA can save you from making a serious mistake (Fisher & Ury, 1981).

What do you do if the other parties insist on hard bargaining, not principled negotiations? You remain unconditionally constructive. If one of your interests is fairness, ask the other parties to explain how their position is fair. Don't assert that the other side offers an unfair proposal. Asking the hard bargainers to justify their position translates positions (e.g., no parties on weekends) into interests (e.g., peace and quiet in order to study). Personal attacks, threats, and bullying tactics can be handled by confronting them openly and immediately. For example, "Threats are not constructive. I negotiate only on merit. Can we return to the substantive issues?" Openly confront any dirty tactics. If necessary, short-circuit the hard bargainers' game plan by forthrightly asking for the rules of the game. For instance, "Before we go any further, I need to know what rules we are following during this bargaining. Does everyone here want to achieve a fair settlement in the quickest amount of time, or are we going to play the hard bargaining game where blind stubbornness wins out?" Make them convince you that their intentions are honorable. In the process they may convince themselves that hard bargaining isn't appropriate. You want to bring hard bargainers to their senses, not to their knees (Ury, 1993).

ANGER MANAGEMENT

Conflict in most situations produces anger. Thus, managing anger is an important aspect of constructive conflict management in groups.

Constructive and Destructive Anger

There are numerous ways group members express anger. One study (Domagalski, 1998) reported that women more commonly than men use avoiding, crying, and holding back tears as expressions of anger. Men are more likely than

Hard bargaining often leads to destructive anger.

women to express anger outwardly toward others rather than camouflage or hold in the anger. "Domineering, uncivil behavior by others" is the most common trigger of anger in work situations.

The difference between constructive and destructive anger depends on two conditions: the intensity and the duration of the anger expression (Adler & Towne, 1996). The *intensity* of anger can vary from mild irritation to outright rage. Mild to moderate expressions of anger can signal problems that must be addressed in groups. In such circumstances the anger can be constructive. Rage, however, is destructive. It is the antithesis of competent communication because the group member expressing the rage is out of control. In the workplace, rage is not appropriate because it "shows you've lost control—not to mention that it's tough to be articulate if you're having a conniption" (Black, 1990, p. 88). Temper tantrums, ranting, and screaming fits make you look like a lunatic. When used as a power-forcing strategy during conflict, it will likely provoke counter rage.

The *duration*, or how long the anger lasts, also determines whether anger is constructive or destructive. The length of an anger episode can vary from momentary to prolonged. Quick flashes of anger may hardly cause group members to notice. Even intense anger, if brief, can underline that you are very upset without causing irreparable damage. Prolonged expressions of anger, even if mild, can cause group members to tune out and ignore you. Highly intense anger that is long-lasting is a combustible combination. Venting our anger, despite popular notions to the contrary, merely rehearses our anger and can *increase it* (Tavris, 1989). "Blowing off steam" awakens our anger. It doesn't put it to bed.

Managing Your Own Anger

There are several steps you can take to diffuse your own anger when you sense that it is approaching the destructive stage of intensity and duration.

1. *Reframe self-talk*. Thoughts trigger anger. If you think a group member intentionally sabotaged your work, you feel righteously angry, even vengeful. If you believe that no sabotage was intended, however, there was merely a misunderstanding, then anger usually doesn't ignite. As a first step in managing your own anger, try assuming group members did not intend to harm you. View harm as accidental or simply the result of clumsiness unless there is clear evidence to the contrary. Reframing the way we think about events can deflate our anger before it escalates (Baron, 1990).

2. *Listen nondefensively*. When group members criticize, blame, or ridicule you, refuse to be defensive. Reframe the criticism or blame as a challenge or problem, not an opportunity for retaliation. Counter defensive communication from others with supportive communication.

3. *Deliberately calm yourself*. Exercise discipline and refuse to vent your anger. When you sense anger boiling to the surface, deliberately slow your breathing. Count to 10 before responding to give yourself an opportunity to collect yourself. A cooling-off period may be necessary. Typically, it takes about 20 minutes to recover from a surge of adrenalin that accompanies anger. This cooling-off period can work effectively to calm your anger (Goleman, 1995).

4. *Find distractions*. Don't rehearse your anger by constantly revisiting past injustices or slights instigated by fellow group members. Distract yourself when old wounds resurface. Read a newspaper, watch television, play with the dog, take a walk with someone and discuss subjects unrelated to the anger-inducing subject.

Don't attempt to employ all four of these steps at once. Pick one and work on making it an automatic response when your anger wells up. Then try a second step and so on.

Managing the Anger of Others

Managing conflict constructively means defusing and de-escalating the anger of other group members so you can confront issues without eruptions of verbal even physical aggression. It is usually best to address a group member's anger first before dealing with the substance of the dispute that triggers the anger (Donohue & Kolt, 1992). Try these suggestions for defusing the anger of others:

1. *Be asymmetrical*. When a group member is expressing anger, especially if it turns to rage, it is critical that you not strike back in kind. Be asymmetrical, which means do the opposite. Counter rage with absolute calm. Stay composed. Hostage negotiators are trained to defuse highly volatile individuals by remaining absolutely calm throughout the interaction. Use smoothing techniques to quiet the enraged group member.

Moody (1996) reports an incident involving Microsoft CEO Bill Gates. During a meeting with 20 young Microsoft programmers, Gates explodes into rage. "His eyes are bulging and his oversized glasses are askew. His face is flushed and spit is flying from his mouth. . . . Most [of the programmers] look at their chairman with outright fear, if they look at him at all. The sour smell of sweaty terror fills the room" (Moody, 1996, p. 12). Gates continues his tirade. The anxious programmers seated around a table try to reason with him, but to no avail. They seem unable to calm their boss—except for a diminutive, soft-spoken Chinese American woman. She maintains eye contact with Gates as everyone else looks away. Twice she short-circuits his outburst by addressing him in a calm, even voice. Gates is momentarily calmed by the woman's first attempt before revving up another outburst. Her second attempt makes him pause. He listens to her, thoughtfully considers what she has said, then responds, "Okay, this looks good. Go ahead." Crisis past, the meeting adjourns. What this woman said to Gates was only slightly different from what several people in the room had attempted to say throughout Gate's tirade. What she said, however, was not nearly as important as how she said it. She responded asymmetrically to Gates's angry eruption. Gates was "acting stupid." She was calm, the antithesis of an angry person. Her tranquil demeanor broke through and quelled his outburst. It signaled that the intense anger was unnecessary. Blazing anger was extinguished by asymmetrical calm.

2. *Validate the other person.* _{that they are angry} Validation is a form of the smoothing technique of collaborating. Let the person know that his or her point of view and anger has some validity, even though you may not agree. You can validate another person in several ways. You can take responsibility for the other person's anger. "I made you angry, didn't I?" acknowledges your role in provoking anger. You can apologize. "I'm sorry. You have a right to be angry" can be a very powerful validation of the other person. Apologies, of course, should be offered only when truly warranted. Actively listening and acknowledging what the other person has said can also be very validating. "I know it upsets you when I don't come to meetings on time" makes the other person feel heard, even if conflict remains.

3. *Probe.* Seek information from an angry group member so you can understand his or her anger (McKay et al., 1989). When you ask a question of an angry group member, it forces the person to shift from emotional outburst to rational response. Simply asking, "Can we sit down and discuss this calmly so I can understand your point of view?" can momentarily defuse a group member's anger.

4. *Assume a problem orientation.* This is supportive communication. This step should occur once you have calmed the angry group member by using previous steps. Approach the anger display as a problem to be solved, not a reason to retaliate. The question "What would you like to see occur?" invites problem solving.

5. *Refuse to be abused.* Even if you are wrong, feel guilty, or deserve another person's anger, do not permit yourself to be verbally battered (McKay et al., 1989). Verbal aggression is unproductive no matter who is at fault in a conflict. "I cannot discuss this with you if you insist on being abusive. I can see you're upset, but verbally assaulting me won't lead to a solution" sets a ground rule on how anger can be expressed.

6. *Disengage.* This is the final step when all else fails to defuse a group member's anger. This step is especially important if the person continues to be enraged and abusive despite your best, most constructive efforts to calm the emotional

storm. Firmly state, "This meeting is over. I'm leaving. We'll discuss this another time."

Keeping track of all six steps to quell the anger of group members, particularly when faced with an enraged person, is too much to expect. Concentrate on one or two steps until they become almost a reflex reaction, a habit. Being asymmetrical is the crucial first step, with validation a close second. The remaining steps can become part of your anger defusing skill package gradually.

Anger is a common companion of group conflict. The constructive management of conflict can occur only when anger is kept under control. This does not mean squelching anger. A group member can feel angry for good reasons. Anger acts as a signal that changes need to occur. Anger should not be used as a weapon, however, to abuse others. We want to learn ways to cope with and express anger constructively, not be devoured by it.

In summary, conflict is a reality of group life. Although most people would prefer that conflict didn't exist, there are both positive and negative aspects to conflict. Constructive management of conflict can turn conflict into a positive experience for the group. The five primary communication styles of conflict management—collaborating, accommodating, compromising, avoiding, and competing—all have pros and cons depending on the situation. Nevertheless, collaborating has a higher probability of producing constructive outcomes than does competing. Negotiation is a universal process used to manage conflicts of interests. Principled negotiation is the most productive means of resolving conflicts of interests.

This concludes my discussion of communication competence in small groups. One of the central points that I hope has come through loudly and clearly is that one person can make an enormous difference in the quality of the group experience. What you individually do or don't do may be the difference between a successful and a less-than-successful group. Competent communication begins with you. The We-orientation is the core of group effectiveness. Don't look to others to make groups work. Take the knowledge you've garnered from this textbook and the skills that you will develop as you put this knowledge into practice and focus them on improving the group experience.

Questions for Critical Thinkers

1. If competition has so many disadvantages, why would the competing/forcing style ever be appropriate for a competent communicator?
2. If principled negotiating is so effective, why isn't it used more often?

① IF used correctly competition
can be useful. (must not
be above cooperation)

② We-orientation means
primary focuse NOT exclusive
(We-not-me) care for individual Needs

Group Oral Presentations

Groups sometimes have public-speaking responsibilities. In some cases the group has been formed in order to present information orally before an audience of interested people. In order to assist those with little or no training or experience in public speaking, I am including this brief appendix, which will cover some of the basics of oral presentation. This will not be a comprehensive nor in-depth treatment of public speaking, but knowing a bit more about this typically fear-inducing activity can be of some solace to the novice. I will discuss types of group oral presentations, speech anxiety, attention strategies, organization, and use of visual aids.

TYPICAL TYPES OF GROUP ORAL PRESENTATIONS

There are three main types of oral group presentations: panel discussions, symposiums, and forums. **Panel discussions** assemble a small group of participants to engage in an exchange of information and ideas on a specific issue or problem before an audience. Purposes of a panel discussion include solving a difficult problem, informing an audience on an issue or topic of interest, or stimulating audience members to think about the pros and cons of a controversial issue.

Panel discussions require a moderator. The moderator usually organizes the group presentation by soliciting panel members who represent different points of view on the topic or issue. Panel members should be informed in advance of the topic to be discussed and major issues that should be addressed by panelists. The moderator should follow several steps to make the panel discussion successful.

1. Suitable physical arrangements for the panel discussion should be organized in advance. Usually, the number of panelists should be no fewer than three and no more than seven. Panelists should be seated at a long table in front of the audience, normally on a stage overlooking audience members. When group discussions involve more than four or five participants, seating panelists at two tables formed in a slight V-shape to the audience helps panelists address each other during discussions without closing off the audience. Name cards placed on the table in front of each speaker will help the audience become familiar with each panelist. If the room where the panel discussion takes place is relatively large, a

microphone at the table should be available for each speaker. If panelists request a VCR and monitor, easel, chalkboard, or other means of presenting visual aids, provide these and place them in a location where access to them is easy and will not block the audience's view.

2. The moderator usually begins by welcoming the audience, by providing brief background on the topic or issue to be discussed, and by introducing each panel member, citing specific background and qualifications of each speaker.

3. Panelists should be encouraged to bring notes, but discouraged from reading a prepared manuscript.

4. Begin the discussion with a question posed to the panel (e.g., What is the extent of the problem of binge drinking on college campuses?). The opening question can be posed to the entire panel or a specific panelist can be asked to begin the discussion. The moderator identifies who has the floor during the discussion.

5. The moderator acts as a discussion guide. If a panelist has been left out of the discussion, the moderator may direct a question to him or her. If a panelist begins to dominate discussion, the moderator should step in and request participation from other panelists. Controversy should be encouraged, but polite conversation should be the norm. It is the responsibility of the moderator to keep the conversation civil. If it begins to turn ugly, the moderator should remind panelists to disagree without being disagreeable. Move the discussion along so all major issues are discussed in the allotted time (usually about 45 minutes to an hour).

6. The moderator closes discussion by summarizing main points made by panelists and identifying new issues raised during the discussion to be further explored.

A second type of oral group presentation is a symposium. A **symposium** is a relatively structured group presentation to an audience composed of several individuals presenting uninterrupted speeches with contrasting points of view on a central topic. A symposium is similar to a panel discussion except that speakers do not engage in a discussion with each other. They present relatively short speeches (usually 4–6 minutes apiece) addressing the pros and cons of a controversial issue or problem. Often an open forum with the audience occurs once all speeches have been presented. The primary purpose of a symposium is to enlighten an audience on a controversial issue or to inform audience members on a subject of interest.

A symposium also benefits from having a moderator. <u>The moderator should follow a few important steps to ensure a successful symposium.</u>

1. Physical arrangements made for a panel discussion just discussed should also be used for a symposium.

2. The moderator should provide brief background on the subject, introduce the speakers, then identify the speakers' order of presentation.

3. The moderator should choose speakers who have different points of view and will not present redundant information.

The final type of oral group presentation is the forum discussion. A **forum discussion** allows members of an audience listening to a public speech, panel discussion, symposium, or debate to participate in a discussion of ideas presented.

The primary purpose of a forum is to engage the audience in the discussion of issues raised. The moderator's role is critical to the success of a forum discussion. Some suggestions for the moderator who directs the forum include:

1. Announce to the audience that an open forum will occur after a panel discussion or symposium has concluded. Audience members can prepare questions or short remarks as they listen to speakers.
2. Rules for forum participation should be clearly articulated before any discussion occurs. Rules may include: raise your hand to be recognized or stand in a line where a microphone has been placed and wait your turn; keep remarks and questions very brief (about 30 seconds); only one follow-up question for each person.
3. Set a time limit for the forum (usually about 30 minutes). Indicate when there is time for only one or two more questions. Accept questions until the deadline has been reached, then conclude the forum by thanking the audience for its participation.
4. Encourage diverse points of view from the audience. A pro and con line might be established. The moderator could move back and forth recognizing audience members on both sides so a balanced series of questions and comments will be presented.
5. If a question cannot be heard by all members of the audience, the moderator should repeat the question. If a question is confusing, the moderator may ask for a restatement or try to paraphrase the question so panelists or forum speakers can answer.

SPEECH ANXIETY

Virtually everyone experiences some anxiety from having to make a public presentation. In one survey, 85% of the respondents reported that speech anxiety (also referred to by some as stage fright or performance anxiety) was a major and serious fear in their lives (Motley, 1995). My own surveys of college students in speech classes indicate that the vast majority of students experience at least some nervousness about presenting a speech in front of a class. A few students are terrified by the very thought of public speaking. Take any four individuals and odds are that two of the four will feel at least an occasional butterfly in the stomach before giving a speech. The third person will suffer nervousness that can be bothersome, but not incapacitating. The fourth person will be so anxiety-ridden that he or she will avoid classes that require oral presentations, skip meetings, refuse job promotions, or even change jobs or occupations in order to escape public speaking.

Even college instructors experience speech anxiety. In one study, 87% of psychology instructors confessed that they had experienced speech anxiety associated with some aspect of teaching (Gardner & Leak, 1994). Sixty-five percent of these same subjects rated their most extreme case of speech anxiety between "definitely unpleasant" and "severe or extreme." You're not alone if you are anxious about having to make an oral presentation in your class.

If I could offer you a cure for speech anxiety, would you take it? Your answer is probably yes. Actually, there is a cure, of sorts, for speech anxiety. Sedation induced by heavy doses of Valium, Librium, or Xanax will do the trick for even the most terror-stricken speaker. Aside from the physiological dangers associated with these tranquilizers (they're habit-forming and can kill you if used incautiously), these drugs, and others like them, will make you appear witless in front of an audience because they deaden mental acuity. So unless you don't mind appearing lobotomized in front of groups, avoid such a cure.

Curing speech anxiety, however, is not necessarily a very desirable goal. Managing speech anxiety is the appropriate goal. If you are one of those individuals who considers a bad case of the flu on the day of your assigned speech to be a stroke of unparalleled good fortune, you may find it difficult to accept that speech anxiety isn't always an evil to be eradicated. <u>The degree of anxiety, not the anxiety itself, requires attention</u>. A moderate amount of anxiety can enhance performance. When kept under control, speech anxiety can be facilitative. Moderate anxiety can energize a speaker. You can present a more dynamic, forceful presentation when energized than when you feel so comfortable that you become almost listless and unchallenged by the speaking experience.

When the intensity of your fear about speaking in front of people gets out of control, however, it then becomes debilitative and detracts from your performance. Intense anxiety can be cause for real concern if ignored. It will congest your thought pathways, thereby clogging your free flow of ideas. In such a condition, every speaker's nightmare—going blank—will likely occur. Also, a terror-stricken speaker feels an urge to escape. Consequently, a 7-minute speech is compressed into 3 minutes by a staccato, hyperspeed delivery. The quicker the speech, the quicker the escape.

The causes of speech anxiety are complex and varied. Space does not permit a thorough discussion of these causes. Generally speaking, the causes of speech anxiety are self-defeating thoughts and situational factors.

Negative thoughts about your speaking performance are self-defeating. The tendency of many beginning speakers is to predict disaster. Those who think irrationally about their public-speaking performance wildly exaggerate potential problems and thus stoke the furnace of their fears. They predict not just momentary lapses of memory, but a complete meltdown of mental functions ("I know I'll forget my entire speech and I'll just stand there like a nitwit"). Minor problems of organization are magnified into graphic episodes of total incoherence and nonstop babbling. Perfectionists also anguish over every flaw in their speech and overgeneralize the significance of even minor defects. Flawless public-speaking performance is a desirable goal but why beat up on yourself when it doesn't happen? Perfectionists make self-defeating statements to themselves such as "I feel like an idiot. I mispronounced the name of one of the experts I quoted"; "I must have said 'Uhm' at least a dozen times. I sounded like a moron"; and "My knees were shaking. The audience must have thought I was out of control." Ironically, the imperfections so glaringly noticeable to perfectionists usually go unnoticed by most people in the audience. Even the most talented and experienced public speakers make occasional errors in otherwise riveting performances.

Another self-defeating thought that triggers speech anxiety is the desire for complete approval from your audience, especially from those whose opinion we value (such as the teacher). It is irrational thinking, however, to accept nothing less than complete approval from an audience. You cannot please everyone, especially if you take a stand on a controversial issue. If you fear failure, then making complete approval from your audience a vital concern merely sets you up for inevitable failure. When you set standards for success at unreachable heights, you are bound to take a tumble.

The fact that you are evaluated by an audience every time you give a speech, even if no one is formally grading your performance, will usually trigger your anxiety. Human beings are social creatures who dislike, even fear, disapproval from others. Even if you aren't seeking complete approval or adulation from your listeners, you would be a rare individual if you were completely immune to the judgments of others hearing you speak. Public speaking becomes doubly intense when formal grades are given for each speech performance.

There are many situational causes of speech anxiety. Novel situations—ones that are new to you—create uncertainty, and uncertainty can easily make you tense. For most students, public speaking is a novel situation. Few students have given many speeches in their lifetime, and some have never given a formal public address. Fortunately, as you gain experience speaking in front of audiences, the novelty wears off and your anxiety will diminish.

I have polled more than a thousand students in public-speaking classes over the years. When asked what causes their speech anxiety, many students will include "being on stage" or "being in the spotlight." The conspicuousness of the public-speaking situation increases most people's anxiety. Most students tell me that speaking to one or two persons is usually not very difficult, but speaking in front of an entire class or an auditorium filled with a thousand people really gives them the shakes. Here the interaction of conspicuousness and approval can be easily seen. Standing alone before a few people and possibly failing is not nearly as big a deal as possibly failing in front of a huge crowd. In the former situation, your potential failure would likely remain an isolated event, but in the latter situation the entire school might be in on your humiliation—so goes the logic. Substantially reducing the possibility of a poor performance by adequate preparation will certainly help counteract stage fright stimulated by conspicuousness.

So how do you manage your speech anxiety, given the variety of causes that induce it? Weatherman Willard Scott of the *Today* show has tried sticking a pin in his rump hoping to startle himself out of his stage fright. He has also tried screaming off camera (not a very practical solution for a classroom setting). Famous actor Laurence Olivier sometimes swore at his audience backstage hoping to replace anxiety with anger (also not subject to wide application). Numerous individuals have suggested to me that picturing your audience nude, or clothed only in underwear or in diapers, can be helpful (assuming you can stifle your laughter when the image pops into your mind). Breathing deeply is also a favorite tidbit of wisdom offered by many as a quick-fix coping strategy for stage fright, although if done too vigorously, this remedy can cause you to hyperventilate and fall flat on your face from light-headedness.

All of these remedies have some merit, especially if they work for you. None of them, however, offers a reliable solution to speech anxiety. There are many more effective methods for dealing with speech anxiety.

First, there is no substitute for *adequate preparation*. Conducting proper research on your speech topic, organizing your speech clearly and carefully, and practicing it several times are all essential if you hope to manage your anxiety effectively. Adequate preparation must include physiological preparation as well. This means proper nutrition just prior to the speech event. Ignoring your physiological preparation for a speech may cancel out the benefits of other methods used to manage your speech anxiety. Consequently, do not deliver a speech on an empty stomach, but do not fill your stomach with empty calories. You need quality fuel such as complex carbohydrates to sustain you while you're speaking. Simple sugars (doughnuts, Twinkies), caffeine (coffee, colas, chocolate), and nicotine (cigarettes) should be avoided or ingested in very small quantities. Adequate preparation of your speech and yourself will reduce uncertainty and the fear of failure. When you practice, practice until you reduce the novelty of the situation.

Second, use *positive imaging*. Counter negative, self-defeating thoughts with positive thoughts of success. Visualize in what ways your speech will be successful and occupy your mind with those thoughts, screening out thoughts of failure. Make affirmation statements to yourself when negative thoughts creep into your mind. "My speech will be a success" and "I know I can do this speech well" are examples of affirmations to use when self-doubt emerges.

Third, *gather perspective* on your speech situation. Consider the difference between rational and irrational speech anxiety. A colleague of mine, Darrell Beck, worked out a simple formula for determining the difference between the two. The severity of the feared occurrence times the probability of the feared occurrence provides a rough approximation of how much anxiety is rational and when you have crossed the line into irrational anxiety. Severity is approximated by imagining what would happen to you if your worst fears came true—you bombed the speech. Would you leave the state? Would you drop out of school? Probably not, since even dreadful speaking performances do not warrant such drastic steps. You might consider dropping the class, but even this is unlikely since fellow students are very understanding when a classmate delivers a poor speech. So even a poor speech does not rationally warrant significant life changes. The probability that your worst nightmare will come true and you will give a horrible speech, however, is extremely unlikely if you have adequately prepared. Thus, working yourself into a lather over an impending speech lacks proper perspective if you follow the advice given here.

Fourth, *refocus your attention* on your message and your audience and away from yourself (Motley, 1995). You cannot concentrate on two things at the same time. If you dwell on your nervousness, you will be distracted from presenting your message effectively. Focus on presenting your message clearly and enthusiastically. View the speaking experience as a challenge to keep your audience interested, maybe even an opportunity to change their minds on an issue.

Fifth, *make coping statements* to yourself as you give your speech, especially when you momentarily stumble. When inexperienced speakers make mistakes during a speech, they tend to make negative statements to themselves. You forget a point, momentarily lose your train of thought, or stammer. Immediately, the tendency is for you to say to yourself "I knew I would mess up this speech" or "I told everybody I couldn't give a decent speech." Instead, try making coping statements while you're delivering the speech. When problems arise say "I can do better" or "I'm getting to the good part of my speech." Talk to yourself during your speech in positive ways to counteract self-talk that defeats you. When parts of your speech go well, compliment yourself on a job well done. This sustains and energizes you as you proceed through the speech.

GAINING AND MAINTAINING ATTENTION

Renowned author G. K. Chesterton once remarked, "There is no such thing as an uninteresting subject, there are only uninteresting people." We've all suffered through conversations with the dreadfully dull individual whose idea of sparkling dialogue would make cartoon character Homer Simpson sound like Albert Einstein by comparison. You may, however, find Chesterton's view on subject matter difficult to accept. Nevertheless, his viewpoint that no topic is inherently uninteresting has a strong ring of truth to it.

Topics may be poorly chosen for a specific audience, but dull speeches are usually a problem of how the information contained in the speech is presented. Audience interest doesn't just happen magically. Interest is garnered by carefully planning and utilizing strategies of attention.

Although gaining and maintaining attention throughout your speech is an important goal for any speaker, attention strategies should enhance a speech, not detract from it. A disorganized speech gains attention but in a negative way. Frequent verbal and vocal fillers such as "you know," "uhm," and "ah" draw attention to inarticulateness.

Some attributes of stimuli, by their very nature, attract attention. Consider just a few of these attributes and how they can become attention strategies.

First, *intensity* is concentrated stimuli that draw attention. Intensity is an extreme degree of emotion, thought, or activity. Relating a story of a woman fleeing for her life from a stalker can be intense, especially for those who fear such an occurrence. Don't be too graphic when describing emotionally charged events, however, or you may offend and alienate your audience.

Intensity, however, is created in ways other than by using fear- or anxiety-producing stories. There are several basic stylistic techniques that promote intensity and rivet an audience's attention. Direct, penetrating eye contact is a useful technique for producing intensity. Focusing your eye contact on an individual for a prolonged period of time during your speech can snap that person out of his or her daydreaming. How does an inattentive person continue to ignore you when you are zeroing in on the daydreamer with eye contact? <u>The lack of eye contact so typical of manuscript speeches, where every word of your speech is written on the paper in front of you, underlines the importance of not reading a speech to an audience because you break connection with your</u>

listeners. Direct eye contact is an attention builder, but lack of eye contact is an attention destroyer.

Variation in vocal volume is a second technique for provoking intensity. A raised voice can be quite intense. It punctuates portions of your speech much as an exclamation point punctuates a written sentence. The use of a raised voice, however, can be a rather shattering experience for an audience. Incessant, unrelenting, bombastic delivery of a message irritates and alienates an audience. Punctuate with raised voice only those points that are especially significant and deserve closer attention.

Silence can also be intense. Silence as a technique for provoking attention can be used to punctuate important points in your speech in the same way that raising your voice can. A pregnant pause—silence held a bit longer than usual if you were merely taking a breath—interjects drama into your speech and spotlights significant points.

A second stimulus attribute that induces attention is called *the startling*. You try to stun, surprise, and shake up your audience. You want to blast them out of their complacency. A startling statement, fact, or statistic can do this quite effectively. Startling statements such as, "AIDS clearly has the potential to decimate the human population"; "Calories can kill you"; and "Did you know that all those fillings in your teeth may give you mercury poisoning?" can make an audience sit up and take notice. You, of course, do not want to make startling statements that can't be supported with evidence.

That it costs more to feed and house a criminal in prison than it does to send him or her to the most expensive university in the country is a startling fact. There are more homicides in the United States each month than in some war zones is another startling fact. According to the A. C. Nielsen Co., American television sets are turned on an average of more than 7 hours each day, and that is a startling statistic.

Every startling stimulus, however, does not produce constructive attention from an audience. Speakers can startle and offend at the same time. A few examples from my own experience and those of my colleagues make this point. One student (during a speech on food poisoning) gained attention by vomiting scrambled eggs into his handkerchief, raising serious doubts about the speaker's good taste. Another student punched himself so hard in the face that he momentarily staggered himself (the speech was on violence in America). Yet another student fired a pistol at his audience (blanks only). After classmates dusted themselves off and reduced their heart rates, they showed no inclination to listen to the rest of his speech on gun control.

All of these examples have one thing in common. The speakers startled their audience but lost credibility in the process. Tasteless jokes, ethnic slurs, and offensive language will also startle an audience and gain attention, but at a substantial cost to the speaker. The general rule applies—attention strategies should enhance the effectiveness of your speech, not detract from it.

Making a problem or issue appear *vital* to an audience is a third attention strategy. There are two principal ways to make your topic seem vital to an audience. First, the problem must be made vital not in some abstract or general sense, but in a specific, immediate, and meaningful sense. An audience's primary question when told that a problem exists is "How does if affect me?" The problem becomes vital and therefore meaningful when the audience can see how the consequences of inaction directly affect its interests and well-being. "One out of every 10 women in this audience will contract breast cancer and a similar number of men listening to me will contract prostate cancer. Those of you who escape the disease will likely know one or more friends or relatives who will die from these forms of cancer" is an example of how to personalize a problem and make it seem vital to an audience.

A second way that you can make your topic seem vital is to dramatize it. In April 1983, the National Commission on Excellence in Education issued its report called "A Nation at Risk." Not content to describe the problem of a failing educational system in the usual bland, technical language of most other reports on the subject, the authors of the Commission's report exhibited a flair for the dramatic. On the opening page, they woke up the nation to a crisis with these rhetorical flourishes:

> Our nation is at risk. . . . The educational foundations of our society are presently eroded by a rising tide of mediocrity that threatens our very future as a Nation and a people . . . If an unfriendly foreign power had attempted to impose on America the mediocre educational performance that exists today, we might well have viewed it as an act of war. . . . We have, in effect, been committing an act of unthinking, unilateral educational disarmament. ("National Commission," 1983, p. 5)

The nation and the media took notice. The report secured attention from a complacent public and it set an agenda for discussion.

Although characterizing problems and solutions as vital draws attention to urgent concerns, you must be careful not to overstate your case. Depicting even relatively trivial concerns as vital may brand you as simply overwrought or melodramatic. For an issue to be accepted as vital, it must have the ring of truth. Credible evidence must substantiate your claim that the problem is vital and so is its solution.

Using *novelty* is a fourth attention strategy. Audiences are naturally drawn to the new and different. Unusual examples, clever quotations, uncommon stories all attract attention because they are new and different.

Beginning your speech with a novel introduction is especially important. <u>Do not begin by telling the audience what your topic is</u>. That is very unoriginal and boring. Create interest in your topic with a novel opening—an unusual news event, story, or human interest example related to your subject. For instance, notice how the following introduction grabs attention by using novelty:

> Acting as his own attorney, an Oklahoma City robbery suspect became agitated when a witness identified him in court as the guilty party. I should have blown your head off, he screamed, adding on quick reflection, if I'd been the one that was there. The verdict? Guilty. Lesson to be learned? Acting as your own attorney is a foolish idea.

Listing several novel examples related directly to your topic is another effective way to open your speech. For example:

> "The check is in the mail" used to be the standard ploy to ward off bill collectors. Not so anymore. Delinquent customers have adopted more original stalling tactics. Collection agencies have received excuses from the bizarre to the ridiculous. One woman claimed that she had run over her husband with a car, breaking both of his arms thereby making it impossible for him to write checks. Another woman living in Fargo, North Dakota, claimed that she slipped on her way to the post office, lost her checks in the snow and was forced to wait until the spring thaw before retrieving them. Then there was the businessman who placed his own obituary in the local newspaper and promptly sent the clippings to his creditors.

Novelty can be a very effective attention strategy, especially for the introduction to your speech, but also throughout your presentation.

Everyone seems to enjoy a good laugh. Using *humor* is a superior attention strategy if used adroitly. You should be able to incorporate humorous anecdotes, quotations, and personal stories throughout your speech.

There are several important guidelines, however, for using humor effectively as an attention strategy. First, don't force humor. If you aren't a particularly funny person and have never told a joke without omitting crucial details or flubbing the punchline, then don't try to be a comedian in front of your audience. Humorous quotations, funny stories, and amusing occurrences can be used without setting them up as jokes. Simply offer them as illustrations of key points and if the audience is amused then they will laugh.

Second, use only relevant humor. Unrelated stories and jokes may be suitable for a comic whose principal purpose is to make an audience laugh, but a formal speech requires you to make important points. Your use of humor needs to make a relevant contribution to the advancement of the speech's purpose.

Third, use good taste. Coarse vulgarities, obscenities, and sick jokes invite anger and hostility. Humor that rests on stereotypes and putdowns may alienate vast sections of your audience. Sexist, racist, and homophobic jokes that denigrate groups exhibit bad taste and poor judgment.

Fourth, don't overuse humor. Don't become enamored with your own wittiness. Telling joke after joke or telling one amusing story after another will likely produce laughter, but the audience will also be dissatisfied if you substitute humor for substance.

Humor can be risky but very satisfying when it works. Using humor is probably the most effective attention strategy when used appropriately and skillfully.

ORGANIZATION AND OUTLINING

Presenting a well-organized speech is critical to your success as a speaker. This section, by necessity, will be a cursory treatment of organization and outlining.

Perhaps the easiest way of developing the organization of your speech is to think of your speech as an inverted pyramid. The base of your upside-down pyramid represents the most general part of your speech, namely, the topic. Moving down toward the tip of the pyramid, you fill in the purpose statement, then the main points that flow from the purpose statement, then each main point is elaborated with subpoints, and subpoints are divided into sub-subpoints and so forth. You begin with the abstract and work toward the concrete and specific.

Let's say that your group has chosen for its symposium topic the problem of violence in America. First, your group must divide this general topic into manageable subtopics so each group member will have about a 5- to 7-minute speech. Subtopics might include violence on television, violence in the movies, guns and violence, gang violence, social and economic causes of violence, and potential solutions to violence (which could be divided even further into specific proposals such as "three strikes and you're out," outlawing handguns, prison reform, social programs). Each group member would then be given his or her subtopic.

Once you have your subtopic for the symposium, each group member must construct a specific purpose statement. A purpose statement is a concise, precise declarative statement phrased in simple, clear language that provides both the general purpose (to inform or to persuade) and the specific purpose (exactly what you want the audience to understand, believe, feel, or do).

TOPIC: Violence on television
PURPOSE STATEMENT: To inform you that excessive violence on television
    can lead to acts of violence in society.
TOPIC: Guns and violence
PURPOSE STATEMENT: To inform you that handgun violence is a serious
    problem in America.

Your purpose statement becomes the blueprint for your entire speech. <u>You determine your main points from your purpose statement</u>.

PURPOSE STATEMENT: To inform you that handgun violence is a serious
    problem in America.
MAIN POINT **I:** Death from handguns is a serious problem.
MAIN POINT **II:** Serious injury from handguns also poses a serious problem
    for America.

Each main point is then divided into subpoints, sub-subpoints, and so on.

MAIN POINT **I:** Death from handguns is a serious problem.
    SUBPOINT **A:** There are more than 16,000 murders from handguns every
        year in America; Japan has fewer than 100.
    SUBPOINT **B:** More than 1,400 American youths between the ages of 10
        and 19 commit suicide with a handgun each year.

<u>Each subpoint is then broken down further with more detail, examples, and supporting evidence</u>.

SUBPOINT **A:** There are more than 16,000 murders from handguns every year in America; Japan has fewer than 100.

SUB-SUBPOINT **1:** Teenage homicide from handguns has almost doubled in the last decade to more than 5,000 annually.

SUB-SUBPOINT **2:** The teenage handgun death rate now exceeds the mortality rate for young people from all natural causes combined.

SUB-SUBPOINT **3:** Three times more American young men are killed by handguns every 100 hours than were killed during the 100-hour Persian Gulf War.

SUB-SUBPOINT **4:** Provide examples of teenagers gunned down in street violence.

SUBPOINT **B:** More than 1,400 American youths between the ages of 10 and 19 commit suicide with a handgun each year.

SUB-SUBPOINT **1:** Most suicides are from handguns.

SUB-SUBPOINT **2:** Handguns put at risk large numbers of young people who consider suicide.

SUB-SUB-SUBPOINT **a:** More than one in four high school students seriously contemplate suicide.

SUB-SUB-SUBPOINT **b:** Sixteen percent of high schoolers make a specific plan to commit suicide, and half of these actually try to kill themselves.

SUB-SUB-SUBPOINT **c:** Ready availability of handguns makes teen suicide more likely.

SUB-SUB-SUBPOINT **d:** Tell the story of 14-year-old Paul Hoffman.

The resulting outline for your first main point would look as follows:

PURPOSE STATEMENT: To inform you that handgun violence is a serious problem in America.

I. **Death from handguns is a serious problem.**

  A. **There are more than 16,000 murders from handguns every year in America; Japan has fewer than 100.**

    1. Teenage homicide from handguns has almost doubled in the last decade to more than 5,000 annually.

    2. The teenage handgun death rate now exceeds the mortality rate for young people from all natural causes combined.

    3. Three times more American young men are killed by handguns in 100 hours than were killed during the 100-hour Persian Gulf War.

    4. Provide examples of specific teenagers gunned down in street violence.

  B. **More than 1,400 American youths between the ages of 10 and 19 commit suicide with a handgun each year.**

    1. Nearly two-thirds of suicides are from handguns.

    2. Handguns put at risk large numbers of young people who consider suicide.

      a. More than one in four high school students seriously contemplate suicide.

    b.   Sixteen percent of high schoolers make a specific plan to commit suicide, and half of these actually try to kill themselves.
    c.   Ready availability of handguns makes teen suicide more likely.
    d.   Tell the story of 14-year-old Paul Hoffman.

You follow the same procedure for outlining your second main point. Note that every subpoint must relate specifically to the main point and likewise every sub-subpoint must relate specifically to the subpoint above it.

    The form used in the sample outline (and in the outlines preceding each chapter in this text) follows a standard set of symbols composed of Roman numerals, capital letters, and Arabic numbers. Indent all subdivisions of a more general point. This will help you follow the development of your points as you speak. Every point that is subdivided has at least two subpoints.

    Preparing the body of your speech is your most difficult and primary organizational task. The introduction, however, creates the all-important first impression with an audience. <u>Your introduction should satisfy the following objectives, usually in this order</u>:

1.   Gain the attention of the audience.
2.   Provide your purpose statement.
3.   Relate the topic and purpose statement to the needs and interests of the audience (answering the question "Why should the audience care about your topic and purpose?")
4.   Preview the main points of your speech (state them exactly as they appear in your outline.

    <u>The conclusion of your speech should strive to accomplish two objectives</u>:

1.   Wrap up the speech with a brief summary of your main points.
2.   End the speech with an effective attention strategy that brings closure to the speech.

    Once you have prepared your speech outline composed of your introduction, body, and conclusion, practice your speech several times. Speaking from an outline instead of a written manuscript is called the *extemporaneous style* of speaking (extemp for short). When you have prepared your full-sentence outline as already explained, you may want to condense full sentences into terse words or phrases for your actual speaking outline. Under pressure of performing before an audience, it is usually easier to speak extemporaneously when you do not have to read whole sentences. Glancing at a few words or a phrase to remind you of the point you wish to explain to your audience allows you to maintain strong eye contact with your listeners without losing your train of thought.

    Finally, as you present your speech, signpost your primary points. Signposts indicate exactly where you are in your speech so the audience can follow along easily. Restating your main points as you get to each one is an example of signposting. If you had "three causes of gun violence in America" you would signpost each one as you addressed them in turn, such as "the first cause of gun violence is poverty"; "the second cause of gun violence is the ready availability of guns"; and "the third cause of gun violence is the breakdown of the criminal justice system." In this way, signposting underscores your important points as you present your speech.

USING VISUAL AIDS

Visual aids can add interest, clarify complex material, make points memorable, and enhance the credibility of the speaker. There are many types of visual aids and with the advent of computer graphics, laser disks, and technologies still being developed, the possibilities are almost limitless. For inexperienced speakers, however, it is best to keep visual aids simple. Photographs, diagrams, charts, graphs, physical models, video clips, and slides are the standard types of visual aids.

Poorly designed and clumsily used visual aids will detract from your speech. The following guidelines will assist you in preparing and displaying visual aids effectively:

1. *Keep visual aids simple.* Visual aids that work well in books, magazines, or newspapers rarely work well in a speech. In printed material a visual aid can be studied carefully. A complicated visual aid used in a speech will distract audience members from listening to the speaker while they try to figure out the complex graph, chart, or diagram.

2. *Visual aids should be large enough to be seen easily.* The general rule of thumb here is that a person in the back of the room should be able to see the visual aid easily.

3. *Visual aids should be neat and attractive.* Sloppy, hastily constructed visual aids are worse than no visual aids at all.

4. *Display the visual aid where it can be seen easily by all members of the audience.* Audience members should not have to stand up or elongate their necks to see the visual aid.

5. *Practice with the visual aids.* Remember Murphy's Law: Whatever can go wrong likely will go wrong. Slide projector bulbs burn out and poster boards can fall over even if placed on an easel. Check any equipment used before beginning your presentation. You look like an amateur when slides are upside down, VCRs aren't tracking properly, or charts won't stand up in the easel or chalk tray.

6. *Talk to the audience, not the visual aid.* Don't turn your back on your audience while explaining your visual aid. Stand facing your audience, point the toes of your feet straight ahead, and imagine that your feet have been nailed to the floor. You can't turn your body toward the visual aid and screen out your audience when your feet are pointing straight ahead. Stand beside the visual aid when referring to it and use your finger or a pointer to guide the audience.

7. *Keep the visual aid covered when it is not in use.* Audience members may be distracted by the visual aid when you are talking about a point unrelated to the chart or graph.

8. *Do not circulate a visual aid among the audience members.* Passing around pictures or other visual aids while you're still speaking will distract listeners.

APPENDIX B

Critical Thinking Revisited: Fallacies

Chapters 6 and 7 have already delved substantially into the process of critical thinking in small group decision making and problem solving. A critically thinking group member must be able to recognize and deal effectively with problems of information overload and underload, confirmation bias, false dichotomies, collective inferential error, and groupthink. In addition, critical thinking is involved in every step of the Standard Agenda, especially when information is gathered and evaluated, criteria for decision making are developed and applied, and final decisions are made by the group.

This bonus appendix is included because in classrooms in some parts of the country, heavier emphasis is placed on reasoning and use of evidence in the small group context than is true of other parts of the country. The list of fallacies below is not exhaustive. I have chosen only those specific fallacies that seem to occur frequently and that students are likely to encounter almost daily.

In order to understand fallacies clearly, let me first discuss <u>the structure of arguments</u> (Toulmin et al., 1979). An argument or "train of reasoning" is composed of several constituent parts. These parts are:

1. **Claim**—that which is asserted and remains to be proven.
2. **Data**—the grounds (support/evidence) for the claim. Statistical evidence; expert, authoritative testimony; documents; objects; exhibits; conclusions from test results; verifiable facts; and conclusions previously established constitute data.
3. **Warrant**—the reasoning used to link the data to the claim; usually assumed (implied), not stated directly. There are several types of warrants. For example:
   a. *Authority warrants*—data and claim are linked by the credibility of the authority used to support the claim.
      CLAIM: Infants can think conceptually.
      DATA: Professor Johnson claims that this is so.
      WARRANT: Professor Johnson is a highly acclaimed expert on this subject.
   b. *Generalization warrants*—data and claim are linked by the asserted generalizability of one or more specific examples or sets of examples.
      CLAIM: America supports the Republican agenda.
      DATA: Polls in most major cities show strong support for the agenda.

WARRANT: Examples of support in large cities are representative of the entire country.

c. *Analogical warrants* (comparisons)—data and claim are linked by the literal similarity of two things compared.

CLAIM: The decline of moral values in the United States will destroy our country.

DATA: The Roman Empire crumbled from within because of moral decay.

WARRANT: The United States and the Roman Empire are very similar.

4. **Backing**—additional evidence and reasoning used to support the inference made in the warrant.

CLAIM: Poverty is the primary cause of America's social ills.

DATA: Studies show that poverty causes crime, drug abuse, divorce, and spousal abuse.

WARRANT: These are highly reliable studies conducted by experts.

BACKING: These studies were conducted by the New School for Social Science Research, the Camden Foundation, and the American Federation of Social Sciences, all highly respected, nonprofit think tanks.

5. **Reservations**—exceptions or rebuttals that diminish the force of the claim.

CLAIM: Jim Davis should be given antibiotics.

DATA: Davis suffered severe cuts and injuries on his arms and legs in an auto accident.

WARRANT: There is a risk of infection in such injuries.

BACKING: Hospital reports and studies indicate that risk of infection is serious and that antibiotics can prevent infection from occurring.

RESERVATION: Overuse of antibiotics can produce super bugs. Antibiotics should be used only when absolutely necessary or they will eventually prove to be useless to fight disease.

6. **Qualifier**—degree of truth of the claim (i.e., highly probable, plausible, possible, etc.); depends on the degree to which you are confident that the claim is proven. The stronger the truth claim, the greater is the burden of proof.

Understanding fallacies will help you determine the validity of your claim, the strength of your data, and the solidity of your warrant and backing. The arguments I used above to illustrate the elements of an argument are not necessarily good trains of reasoning. Study the fallacies listed below, then review these arguments and determine if they have any weaknesses.

I am dividing this list of fallacies into three types:

I. **Material Fallacies:** errors in the process of using supporting materials as proof.
II. **Logical Fallacies:** errors in the process of reasoning.
III. **Psychological Fallacies:** claims that rest on emotional appeal rather than logic and evidence.

I. **Material Fallacies**

A. **Misuse of Statistics**

1. **Manufactured or Questionable Statistics**—statistics that have been fabricated, or statistics whose validity is highly questionable because there is

no reasonable method for compiling such statistics, or that which is quantified is too trivial to warrant the time, effort, and resources necessary to compile accurate statistics.

    a. Raymond Brown, in his *A Book of Superstitions*, claims that about $275 million in business is lost on Friday the 13th because people are afraid of the danger so they stay home.

    b. Researchers say anywhere from 1 in 10 and 1 in 100 Americans have genital herpes. (Difference between 1% and 10% of American population is enormous—statistics are imprecise, untrustworthy estimates.)

2. **Irrelevant Statistics**—statistics that do not directly prove the implied or stated claim yet they are offered as evidence supporting the claim.

    a. Hot dogs are a nutritionally worthless food. They're 60% water. (So what? Fruit is 90% water. Statistic isn't relevant to claim.)

    b. The United States spends a trilion dollars a year, more than any other nation. Clearly, our health care system is the world's best. (Amount of money spent doesn't prove money was spent wisely, efficiently, or effectively.)

3. **Sample Size Inadequate or Unspecified**—sample size is very small, resulting in a margin of error in excess of plus or minus 3%, or you are left guessing what the sample size might have been.

    a. Eighty percent of those surveyed support the cable TV legislation. (How many surveyed? Ten people, eight of whom favored the legislation?)

    b. Four out of five doctors recommend aspirin for aches associated with flu.

[NOTE: What makes an adequate sample size?

    c. Sample of 1,000 is usually sufficient whether survey is national, state, or local.

    d. Sample must be randomly selected (typically from a table of random numbers).

    e. Margin of error should be no more than plus or minus 3% to be very representative.]

4. **Self-selected Sample**—you choose to participate in a survey; you are not selected as part of a random, representative sample.

    a. Local TV station conducts a call-in poll on some controversial issue. Viewers choose to participate usually if they have a strong motivation, such as anger or a vested interest in the results turning out favorably for their point of view.

    b. Surveys or questionnaires printed in magazines asking readers to respond and mail in their answers are self-selected samples.

5. **Dated Statistics**—statistics that are not current. Statistics should be as up-to-date as possible, especially if the event, phenomenon, or situation is volatile and likely to change quickly (e.g., number of unemployed, long-term interest rates on mortgages, murder rates in various cities, international monetary exchange rates).

NOTE: Some phenomena change very slowly, if at all, over time (e.g., rates of blind obedience to authority figures, deterrent effects of punishment on crime, percentage of U.S. population who call themselves Catholics, Protestants, etc.) requiring less attention to recency of statistics.

a. According to a 1985 United Nations Report, the number of AIDS cases is doubling every 3 years. (Too old to be valuable data. Substantial efforts have been made since 1985 to combat the spread of AIDS.)

b. According to the Department of Housing and Urban Development in a 1991 report to Congress, the median price of a new home in the United States dropped 12%. (A big economic boom in the housing market began after 1991, so statistic is dated and in this case useless except for historical comparison.)

B. **Misuse of Authority**

NOTE: Testimony of experts and authorities is useful as supporting material for claims because experts draw on a larger data and knowledge base than do nonexperts. Experts are not always correct (economists being a notable example), but they are more reliable than someone who is uninformed or only marginally knowledgeable, especially about a highly technical subject.

1. **Incomplete Citation**—reference to the authority is neither specific nor complete. Minimum requirements for a complete citation include qualification of authority if not obvious, place of publication, and date of reference.

a. COMPLETE CITATION SAMPLE #1: The President's Commission on Mental Health, in its January 2000 report entitled Mental Health, Mental Illness, concludes, "The biggest stigma in America is the mental illness label."

b. COMPLETE CITATION SAMPLE #2: The latest report from the U.S. Census Bureau, last July, notes that 19.4% of children in the United States live in poverty.

c. "Research indicates" (unless offered by an expert interpreting the latest results in his or her field), "studies show," and the like are incomplete citations.

2. **Biased Source**—special interest groups or individuals who stand to gain money, prestige, power, or influence simply by taking a certain position on an issue or crusaders for a cause are all biased even though they may have expertise.

a. Quoting AT&T on the advantages of its phone company compared to other phone companies.

b. Quoting the National Rifle Association on gun control.

c. Quoting R. J. Reynolds Tobacco Company on the safety of cigarette smoking.

3. **Authority Quoted Out of His/Her Field**—expertise is not generic. Quote experts in their area of specialization.

a. Professor of Biology, Dr. Ernhard Bousterhaus, claims that electric cars are impractical and will remain so for at least the next 50 years. (What expertise does a biologist have in regard to electric cars?)

b. Dr. Julia Esterhand, Professor of Anthropology at Moreland State University, claims that vitamin supplements are dangerous to your health.

II. Logical Fallacies

A. **Hasty Generalization** (overgeneralizing)—drawing conclusions (generalizations) from too few or atypical examples.

1. German shepherds are mean, vicious dogs. I saw three different German shepherds on three separate occasions attack small children without provocation. (The vividness effect can lead to overgeneralization from a few isolated examples.)

2. Testimonials exalting cancer cures, faith healings, and so on are generalizations based on too few and probably atypical experiences of individuals.

3. The Talk Show Syndrome—audience members stand up and generalize on the basis of their individual experiences.

B. **False Analogy**—two items, events, or phenomena with similarities are viewed as identical. What is true of one is or should be true for the other, so goes the claim, even when a significant point or points of difference exist between the two things compared.

1. Thousands of people are killed annually in automobile accidents but few if any have been killed in the United States by an accident at a nuclear power plant. Yet, we ban nuclear power plants in many parts of the United States, while licensing drivers and automobiles. This makes little sense. (Banning cars would devastate the U.S. economy and create transportation havoc. Banning nuclear power plants has no such significant effects. Also, one major auto accident can kill dozens of people. One major nuclear power plant accident can wipe out an entire state and have international environmental effects for decades.).

2. In Turkey, farmers grow poppies (source of heroin) as a cash crop. In the United States, farmers grow corn and soybeans for cash crops. Why outlaw poppies when we don't outlaw corn and soybeans? (Poppy crop is not

a critical food crop capable of feeding the hungry of the world. Corn and soybeans are critical food crops.)

C. **False Dichotomies** (either-or thinking)—false choice between only two opposites when other choices that fall between the extremes exist.

1. You either support the National Health Care proposal of the Administration or America will go broke from spiraling health-care costs. So make your choice. (Other proposals besides this one exist that may be better options to the health-care problems in America.)

2. Responding to an Ann Landers column, 72% of 64,800 women said they would forego sexual intercourse with their partner if they could be held closely by their partner instead. (Only two choices provided when clearly a third exists, namely, the preference to be held closely and to have sexual intercourse.)

D. **Mistakes in Causation**

1. **Correlation Mistaken for Causation (post hoc ergo propter hoc)**—when two phenomena vary simultaneously or one follows the other, a causal linkage is asserted based solely on the covariation of the two phenomena.

   a. Since minority groups have been given more educational opportunities, we have had an increase in the crime rate in the United States. Educating minorities will simply increase crime.

   b. I ate a lot of chocolate this week and now my face has acne. I guess I'll have to stop eating chocolate so I can get rid of these blasted pimples.

2. **Single Cause**—attributing only one cause to a complex phenomenon with many causes.

   a. Increasing interest rates is the cause of high inflation. (A cause but not necessarily the most important nor the only cause.)

   b. Poor communication is the reason for the alarming increase in the divorce rate. (A cause but not necessarily the most important nor the only cause.)

E. **Criterion Fallacies**

1. **Missing Criterion**—claim requires definition of key term establishing standard for evaluating validity of claim, but no definition is offered.

   a. *Hustler* magazine is an obscene magazine. (Term obscene must be defined before claim can be evaluated.)

   b. The trouble with America is the failure to promote family values. (Must define family values.)

2. **Questionable Criterion**—unreasonably broad or narrow definition of key term on which claim is based.

    a. Those paintings are pornographic. They show naked men and women. (Overly broad definition of pornographic.)

    b. Intelligence is whatever the IQ tests measure. (Overly narrow view of intelligence.)

III. Psychological Fallacies

A. **Personal Attack (ad hominem)**—attacking the messenger in order to divert attention away from the message.

NOTE: Not all attacks on a person's credibility, character, qualifications, and so on are fallacious. If character or credibility is the real issue, then it is relevant argumentation (e.g., attacking Richard Nixon's integrity during Watergate or Bill Clinton's during the impeachment proceedings was not a fallacious personal attack).

1. Why are you always on my back for not studying? Last semester your GPA fell nearly a full point.

2. Why should we listen to his charges of corruption in city government? He's nothing but a rabble-rousing troublemaker.

B. **Popular Opinion (ad populum)**—claim based on popular opinion rather than reasoning and evidence.

1. Go ahead and smoke marijuana. More than a third of all college students do.

2. Eighty-five percent of those polled believe fluoride in the water causes cancer. We should therefore ban fluoride from our water system.

C. **Loaded Language**—claim based on the emotional connotations of words rather than evidence and reasoning. The connotations may be negative or positive.

1. This fanciful and ludicrous proposal for the establishment of a free campus bus system should be rejected.

2. We engage in peaceful propaganda for the advancement of democratic ideals.

D. **Appeal to Tradition**—claim is made that what has always been done should continue to be done just because it has always been done that way.

1. We've never used cooperative learning in the classroom so we don't plan to start now.

2. I've always used a typewriter so I don't expect I'll be using a computer anytime soon.

Sample Agendas for Group Meetings

Agenda for a Business Meeting

Meeting of the Student Senate
Date
Boardroom
2:00–3:30 P.M.

Purpose: Biweekly meeting

    I. Call meeting to order

   II. Approval of the minutes of last meeting (5 minutes)

  III. Additions to the agenda (2 minutes)

  IV. Committee reports

      A. Student fee committee (5 minutes)

      B. Student activity committee (5 minutes)

      C. Student union committee (5 minutes)

   V. Officers' reports

      A. Treasurer's report (5 minutes)

      B. President's report (10 minutes)

  VI. Old business

      A. Textbook prices (10 minutes)

      B. Campus parking problems (10 minutes)

      C. Pub on campus (5 minutes)

 VII. New business

      A. Computer access on campus (5 minutes)

  B. Safety on campus (20 minutes)

 VIII. Building agenda for next meeting (5 minutes)

  IX. Adjournment

Agenda for a Discussion Meeting

Curriculum Task Force
Date
Boardroom
3:00–5:00 P.M.

Purpose: To improve the curriculum change and approval process

  I. How does the current curriculum process work?

  II. What are the primary problems with the present curriculum process?

  III. What causes the problems?

  IV. What criteria determine an ideal curriculum process?

  V. What are some possible improvements in the curriculum process?

  VI. Which suggested improvements are the most promising? Why?

  VII. Are their any drawbacks to these suggested improvements?

 VIII. What needs to occur to implement the most promising suggested improvements?

GLOSSARY

In this text, I have attempted to keep jargon to a minimum. I am not fascinated with jargon, but it does facilitate communication by providing a verbal short-hand for complex concepts and ideas. Nevertheless, a glossary of terms does not substitute for clear understanding of the concepts represented. You can memorize a definition without knowing what it means. Clear understanding requires a context for the jargon. By reading the following terms in the context of this book, you will see the interconnections between and among the terms. All terms included in the glossary appear in **boldfaced** type in the body of the text.

Accommodating Style of conflict management characterized by yielding to the concerns and desires of others.

Adaptability to change The modification of the structure and/or function of the group in response to changing conditions.

Alliance An association, in the form of subgroups, entered into for mutual benefit or the achievement of a common objective.

Ambushing A competitive listener bias exhibited by attacking a speaker verbally, not trying to understand the speaker's point of view.

Analysis paralysis Process whereby a group overanalyzes a problem, preventing it from making a decision.

Appropriateness Complying with rules, norms, and expectations that accompany a specific context.

Assertiveness The ability to communicate the full range of your thoughts and emotions with confidence and skill.

Avoiding Style of conflict management characterized by withdrawing from potentially contentious and unpleasant struggles.

BATNA (Best Alternative To a Negotiated Agreement) A fallback position if a negotiated settlement fails to occur.

Boundary control Setting boundaries that determine the amount of access a group has to input.

Brainstorming A creative problem-solving technique that promotes plentiful, even zany ideas in an atmosphere free from criticism, and energetic participation of all group members in generating new ideas.

Bridging A method of integrative problem solving whereby a new option is offered that satisfies the interests of all parties in a conflict.

Charisma A constellation of personal attributes that people find highly attractive about an individual.

Chunking   Process of recoding information into larger, more meaningful units.

Cliques   Small, narrowly focused subgroups that create a competitive atmosphere.

Cohesiveness   The degree to which members feel a part of the group, wish to stay in the group, and are committed to each other and to the group's work.

Collaborating   Cooperative style of conflict management characterized by confrontation, integration, and smoothing techniques.

Collective inferential error   Assuming as a group that certain inferences are facts without critically analyzing them, then based on these faulty inferences, making further inferences usually resulting in bad decision making.

Commitment   The conscious decision to invest time, energy, thought, and feeling to improve oneself or one's relationships with others.

Communication   A transactional process of sharing meaning with others.

Communication climate   The group atmosphere that varies according to how group members conduct transactions.

Communication competence   The ability to communicate in a personally effective and socially appropriate manner.

Communication skill   The successful performance of a communication behavior and the ability to repeat such a behavior (Spitzberg & Hecht).

Competing   A win–lose style of conflict management whereby one party in a conflict tries to force compliance from another party.

Competition   Mutually exclusive goal attainment (MEGA).

Compliance   The process of acquiescing to the dictates and desires of others.

Compromising   Style of conflict management characterized by giving up something in order to get something in return.

Confirmation bias   Tendency to seek information that confirms predispositions and to ignore or distort information that contradicts currently held beliefs and attitudes.

Conflict   The expressed struggle of interconnected parties who perceive incompatible goals and interference from each other in attaining those goals.

Conformity   Adherence to group norms.

Consensus   Group decision-making process characterized by unanimous agreement, commitment to the decision, and satisfaction with the process and decision.

Constructive conflict   Conflict that is characterized by a We-orientation, cooperation, and flexibility.

Contempt   The verbal or nonverbal expression of insult that emotionally abuses others.

Context   An environment that permeates the communicative act consisting of who, what, to whom, why, where, when, and how the communicative act is done.

Cooperation   Mutually inclusive goal attainment (MIGA).

Co-optation   Seduction strategy that tries to buy off a defiant group member with promises of promotions, perquisites, money, and the like.

Correlation   A consistent relationship between two or more variables.

Credibility   Criterion used to evaluate information on the basis of its believability and reliability.

Critical thinking   The process of analyzing, criticizing, and evaluating ideas and information in order to reach sound judgments and conclusions.

Cult A group that forms around a person who claims he or she has a special mission or knowledge, which will be shared with those who turn over most of their decision making to that self-appointed leader.

Currency Criterion used to evaluate information on the basis of how up to date it is.

Defensive communication Competitive patterns of communication behavior that provoke the perception that one's self-esteem and identity as a person are being threatened.

Defensiveness A reaction to a perceived attack on one's self-esteem and self-concept.

Defiance Purposeful, conscious, overtly rebellious form of communicating noncompliance.

Deindividuation Psychological process that occurs when individuals shed their personal identities and replace them with a group persona.

Delegating style Style of leadership that allows the group to be self-directed.

Denotative meaning Relatively stable, neutral, shared meanings of a group.

Description A first-person report of how one feels, what the individual perceives to be true, and what behaviors have been observed in a specific context.

Destructive conflict Conflict that is characterized by domination, escalation, retaliation, competition, and inflexibility.

Devil's advocacy A role played by one or more group members to prevent groupthink, in which the devil's advocate critiques the group's proposal and arguments supporting the proposal.

Dialectical inquiry A procedure for preventing groupthink in which a subgroup develops a counterproposal and defends it side-by-side with the group's initial proposal.

Disruptive roles Informal roles that serve individual needs or goals while impeding attainment of group goals.

Dogmatism A belief in the self-evident truth of one's opinion, warranting no debate nor disagreement from others.

Dominance A competitive form of power that emphasizes who is on top of the power hierarchy and in control and who is on the bottom and thus subservient.

Effectiveness How well one has progressed toward the achievement of goals.

Electronic brainstorming Group members sit at computer terminals and brainstorm ideas using a computer-based file-sharing procedure.

Empathy Thinking and feeling what you perceive another to be thinking and feeling.

Empowerment The power to accomplish one's own goals or help others achieve theirs.

Equifinality Groups with a similar or identical final goal may reach that end in highly diverse ways; there's more than one way to achieve a goal.

Ethics A set of standards for judging the moral correctness of our behavior.

Expanding the pie An method of integrative problem solving whereby resources are increased as a solution to a problem or conflict.

Expedient conformity Acquiescing to the dictates or desires of a group by expressing attitudes and exhibiting behaviors acceptable to the group while harboring private beliefs at odds with the group.

Expert   An individual who not only has valuable and useful information for a group but also understands the information and knows how to use it to help the group.

Extrinsic reward   Any external inducement such as money, grades, praise, recognition, or prestige that motivates an individual to behave or perform.

False dichotomies   (pronounced DIE-COT-OH-MEES) Either–or thinking; the propensity to view the world in terms of only two opposing possibilities when other possibilities are available, and to describe this dichotomy in the language of extremes.

Formal roles   Explicitly designated roles that exist within the structure of a group or organization.

Forum discussion   Allows members of an audience listening to a public spearker, panel discussion, or debate to participate in a discussion of ideas presented.

Glass ceiling   An invisible barrier of subtle discrimination that excludes women from top jobs in corporate and professional America.

GRIT   (Graduated and Reciprocated Initiatives in Tension reduction) A technique of de-escalating cycles of conflict.

Group   A human communication system composed of three or more individuals, interacting for the achievement of some common purpose(s), who influence and are influenced by one another.

Group endorsement   Approval by group members of an individual's bid to play a particular informal role.

Grouphate   The hostility people harbor from having to work in groups.

Group polarization   The group tendency to make a decision that is more extreme, either riskier or more cautious, after discussion has occurred than the initial preferences of group members.

Groupspeak   Cult jargon that shuts down cult members' critical thinking.

Groupthink   A mode of thinking that people engage in when they are deeply involved in a cohesive in-group, when the members' strivings for unanimity override their motivation to appraise realistically alternative courses of action.

Hidden agendas   Personal goals of group members that are not revealed openly to the group and that can interfere with a group accomplishing its goals.

High-context style   Cultural tendency to emphasize the cultural context of a message when determining meaning.

Hindsight bias   Overestimating or overstating our prior knowledge once we have been told the correct answers.

Hit-and-run confrontations   Confronting another group member with a conflict of interest without giving that individual an adequate opportunity to respond.

Impervious response   A defensive communication pattern that is characterized by a failure to acknowledge another person's communication effort either verbally or nonverbally.

Individual achievement   Improving one's performance without having to defeat another person.

Individualism–collectivism continuum   Cultural variation in the degree to which people explore their uniqueness and independence versus their conformity and interdependence.

Inferences   Conclusions about the unknown based on the known.

Influence of size   The effect variation in size has on systems.

Informal roles   Roles that emerge from communication transactions within a group.

Information bulimia   A binge-and-purge process whereby information is crammed into one's head then quickly regurgitated without serious consideration of the impact of that information on decision making and problem solving.

Information overload   Condition where informational input into a system exceeds a system's capacity to process input effectively.

Information underload   Insufficient informational input available to a group for decision-making purposes.

Input   Access to information, energy, people, ideas, and experiences from the environment outside of the group or from other group members.

Interconnectedness of parts   All parts of a system work together and affect each other and the system as a whole.

Intrinsic motivation   Enjoying what one does for its own sake, not because of some external reward for doing it.

Irrelevant response   A defensive communication pattern manifested by questions or statements having nothing to do with the sender's message that indicates an indifference to the sender's needs.

Knowledge   Understanding the rules, norms, and expectations required to be appropriate and effective in a particular communication context.

Leader as completer   Functional leadership perspective that holds that leaders perform those essential functions within a group that other members have failed to perform.

Leadership   A two-way influence process that is directed toward group goal achievement.

Limiting the search   A method for coping with information overload whereby the search for information is stopped after a certain point in order for decision making to take place.

Linguistic barriers   Language restrictions, such as jargon, erected by a group to create an in-group/out-group division.

Low-context style   Cultural tendency to emphasize the explicit content of a message when determining meaning.

Maintenance roles   Informal roles that focus on the social dimension of the group, especially the nurturance of group cohesiveness.

Mentor   Knowledgeable individuals who have achieved some success in their profession or jobs and who assist other individuals trying to get started in a line of work.

Mindset Psychological or cognitive predisposition to see the world in a particular way.

Minimum power theory States that the weakest member of a triad will be the only member always included in a coalition.

Minimum resources theory States that group members with the most power are included in a coalition less often than are weaker members because more powerful members are entitled to a larger share of the rewards than weaker members.

Mixed messages When verbal messages seem to contradict nonverbal messages and vice versa.

Negative reciprocation Desire to do harm to another because he or she has done harm to you.

Negative synergy When the joint action of group members produces a worse result than expected based on perceived individual abilities and skills of members; the whole is worse than the sum of its parts.

Negotiation A process by which a joint decision is made by two or more parties (Pruitt).

Network A structured pattern of information flow and personal contact.

Networking Individuals with similar backgrounds, skills, and goals come together on a fairly regular basis and share information that will assist members in pursuing goals.

Nominal group technique A creative problem-solving procedure characterized by group members working alone to generate lists of ideas on a problem, convening the group and recording ideas generated, selecting the five favorite ideas, and ranking these five ideas on the basis of the group average.

Norms Rules in a group that stipulate what a person must do, ought to do, or must not do in order to achieve certain goals (Smith).

Openness Continuous interaction with the environment outside of the immediate system.

Output The results of a group's interactions such as productivity (task dimension) and cohesiveness (social dimension).

Panel discussion A small group of speakers who engage in an exchange of information and ideas on a specific issue or problem in front of an audience.

Paraphrasing A concise response to the speaker which states the essence of the other's content in the listener's words.

Participating style Nondirective style of leadership that encourages shared decision making with special emphasis on developing relationships in the group.

Pattern recognition Potentially the most effective method for coping with information overload, whereby patterns are discerned from information in order to utilize information effectively.

Perception of free choice Private acceptance of a belief or attitude flowing from the perception of unimpeded choice.

PERT (Program Evaluation Review Technique) A decision-making procedure for implementing group decisions.

Physical barriers   A type of boundary control using such things as walls, partitions, or other material means of dividing space and segmenting territory.

Power   The ability to influence the attainment of goals sought by yourself and others.

Power distance dimension   Cultural variations in attitudes concerning the appropriateness of power imbalances.

Power resource   Anything that enables individuals to move toward their own goals or interfere with another's actions.

Pressure toward uniformity   Influence applied to group members to comply with the prevailing attitude or viewpoint of the group as a whole, sometimes leading to groupthink.

Prevention   A competitive form of power that tries to thwart domination.

Primary tension   The normal jitters and feelings of unease group members experience when first congregating in a group.

Principled negotiation   A collaborative process of negotiating conflicts of interests on the merits, not on hard bargaining strategies.

Private acceptance   A type of compliance that occurs when an individual's public and private attitudes and beliefs are compatible with the group's norms and viewpoint.

Probing   Seeking additional information from a speaker by asking questions.

Process   Events and relationships are dynamic, continuous, and ever-changing.

Productivity   The output or result of the efficient and effective accomplishment of a group task.

Provisionalism   A flexible attitude; individuals remain open to possibilities and options that may not have been explored.

Pseudo-member   A group member in name only; pursuing individual goals unrelated to and sometimes at the expense of group goals.

Psychological barriers   A type of boundary control where an individual experiences feelings of not belonging in the group.

Psychological reactance   Theory claiming that the more someone tries to control an individual, the more that individual is inclined to resist such efforts, even do the opposite of what someone orders that person to do.

Question of fact   Problem for group discussion formulated as a question that asks whether something is true and to what extent.

Question of policy   Problem for group discussion formulated as a question that asks whether a specific course of action should be undertaken in order to solve a problem.

Question of value   Problem for group discussion formulated as a question that asks for a judgment—to what extent is something good or bad, right or wrong, and so forth.

Readiness   A key aspect of situational leadership; the degree of ability and willingness to perform a particular task in a group.

Reciprocal patterns   A tit-for-tat, spiraling pattern of mutuality; giving what you get and vice versa.

Referent   The object, concept, or event referred to by a word.

Reframing The creative process of breaking a mindset by placing a problem in a different frame of reference.

Relevance Criterion used to evaluate information on the basis of whether or not the information relates directly to claims made.

Reminder role A formally designated role in groups where the member playing this role raises questions in a nonaggressive manner regarding collective inferential error, false dichotomies, confirmation bias, and other potential group errors that might give rise to groupthink.

Representativeness Criterion used to evaluate information on the basis of whether or not the specific example, statistic, or instance accurately reflects what is generally true.

Resistance The prevention form of power; covert form of communicating noncompliance.

Ripple effect Chain reaction of one system part on the whole system.

Role conflict Playing two roles that contradict each other.

Role fixation Acting out a specific informal role, and that role alone, no matter what the situation might require.

Role reversal Stepping into a role that is distinctly different from or even opposite a role we usually play, such as student instead of teacher, employee instead of boss.

Roles Expected patterns of behavior for group members.

Role specialization The primary informal role played by a group member.

Role status The relative importance, prestige, or power accorded a particular role by group members or society.

Rules Regulations that define appropriate behaviors in specified social situations.

Secondary tension The stress and strain that occurs within a group (later in its development) manifested by disagreements and conflict.

Selectivity A method for coping with information overload whereby an individual chooses on the basis of group priorities and goals what information to pay attention to and what to ignore.

Self-confirmation Extreme form of confirmation bias whereby all evidence and reasoning, no matter how apparently contradictory, is distorted to confirm a belief or point of view.

Selling style A directive style of leadership characterized by high emphasis on task accomplishment and high interest in social relationships among group members.

Sensitivity The ability to pick up signals from a group that indicate such things as disharmony, conflict, anger, and frustration and also showing concern for others.

Shift response A competitive listening pattern whereby listeners attempt to shift the focus of attention from others to themselves by changing the topic of discussion.

Social dimension The relationships of members in groups and their impact on the group as a whole.

Social loafing The tendency of individual group members to reduce their work effort as groups increase in size; the inclination to goof off in groups.

Social tension   Anxiety felt when interacting with other group members.

Specialization   A method for coping with information overload whereby an individual will know a lot about a little.

Stand aside   This occurs when a team member continues to have reservations about the group decision but, when confronted, does not wish to block the group choice

Stockholm Syndrome   Psychological process whereby victims come to identify with their aggressors.

Structure   The systematic interrelation of all parts to the whole, providing form and shape.

Style shift   Using several styles of conflict management flexibly depending on the circumstances.

Sufficiency   Criterion used to evaluate information on the basis of whether or not there is enough information to support claims made.

Superordinate goals   Goals that are compelling for all parties in a conflict, the attainment of which are beyond reach without the cooperation of all parties.

Supportive communication   Cooperative patterns of communication behavior that bolster a person's self-image and self-esteem.

Support response   An attention-giving, cooperative effort by a listener to focus attention on the other person, not on oneself.

Symbol   That which represents something other than itself but bears no natural relationship to that which it represents.

Symposium   A relatively stuctured group presentation composed of several individuals presenting uninterrupted speeches with contrasting points of view on a central topic of interest to an audience.

Synergy   When the joint action of group members produces performance that exceeds expectations based on perceived abilities and skills of individual members; the whole becomes greater than the sum of its individual parts.

System   A set of interconnected parts working together to form a whole in the context of a changing environment.

Tangential response   A defensive communication pattern that minimally acknowledges what a speaker had to say, then steers the conversation in another direction.

Task dimension   The work performed by the group and its impact on the group.

Task roles   Informal roles that move the group toward the attainment of its goals.

Telling style   Directive style of leadership characterized by high emphasis on task accomplishment and low interest in social relationships among group members.

Transaction   Each person communicating is both sender and receiver simultaneously and all parties communicating have an impact on each other.

Transactional communication   Group members are both senders and receivers simultaneously and each influences the definition of the other and the relationship continuously.

Transformational leader   Charismatic leader who communicates a vision of change to followers.

Twenty Percent Rule   The minimum standard to combat gender and ethnic bias in groups; when no less than 20% of group membership is composed of women or minorities discrimination against these groups drops substantially.

Verbal dominance   Verbal bullying characterized by such communication behaviors as interrupting, contradicting, berating, and monopolizing the conversation.

Virtual team   A small group whose members interact by means of electronic technologies, not face-to-face, oftentimes across vast distances.

Vital functions   Functional leadership perspective that sees leaders performing a number of essential group functions different in kind and degree from other members.

Vividness effect   Graphic, outrageous, shocking, controversial, dramatic events that draw our attention and stick in our minds.

Workplace bullying   Supervisors scream at subordinates and coworkers and humiliate employees by taking away their responsibilities when work is not performed to the exact specifications of the bullying supervisor.

Work teams   Small groups of interdependent individuals who share responsibility for outcomes for their organization.

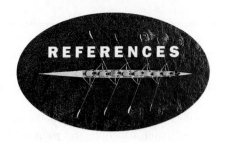

REFERENCES

Abell, G. (1981). Astrology. In G. Abell and B. Singer (Eds.), *Science and the paranormal*. New York: Charles Scribner's Sons.

Abramson, J. (1994). *We, the jury*. New York: Basic Books.

Acker, J. (1990). Hierarchies and jobs: Notes for a theory of gendered organizations. *Gender and Society*, 4, 139–158.

Adcock, A., & Yang, W. (1984). Parental power and adolescents' parental identification. *Journal of Marriage and the Family*, 46, 487–494.

Adler, J., & Springen, K. (1999, May 3). How to fight back. *Newsweek*, 36–38.

Adler, R. (1977). *Confidence in communication: A guide to assertive and social skills*. New York: Holt, Rinehart & Winston.

Adler, R., Rosenfeld, L., & Towne, N. (1989). *Interplay: The process of interpersonal communication*. New York: Holt, Rinehart & Winston.

Adler, R., & Towne, N. (1999, 1996) *Looking out, looking in*. New York: Holt, Rinehart & Winston.

Advertising is hazardous to your health. (1986, July). *University of California, Berkeley Wellness Letter*, 1–2.

Aguayo, R. (1990). *Dr. Deming: The American who taught the Japanese about quality*. New York: Simon & Schuster.

Alexander, N. (1989, September 17). How to stop wasting time at meetings. *San Jose Mercury News*, p.1PC.

Allen, C., & Straus, M. (1980). Resources, power, and husband-wife violence. In M. Straus & G. Hotaling (Eds.), *The social causes of husband-wife violence*. Minneapolis: University of Minnesota Press.

Allen, V., & Levine, J. (1971). Social support and conformity: The role of independent assessment of reality. *Journal of Experimental Social Psychology*, 7, 48–58.

Alvarado, D. (1993, May 22). Furor over new diagnosis for PMS. *San Jose Mercury News*, p.1A.

American Air union socked with huge fine. (1999, April 16). *San Jose Mercury News*, pp. 1C, 7C.

Amparano, J. (1997, January 23). Taking good care of workers pays off. *The Arizona Republic*, pp. E1, E3.

Anatomy of a massacre. (1999, May 3). *Newsweek*, 25–31.

Andersen, J. (1985). Educational assumptions highlighted from a crosscultural comparison. In L. Samovar & R. Porter (Eds.), *Intercultural Communication: A reader*. Belmont, CA: Wadsworth.

Andersen, J. (1988). Communication competency in the small group. In R. Cathcart & L. Samovar (Eds.), *Small group communication: A reader*. Dubuque, IA: Wm. Brown & Company.

Anderson, J. (1991, August 18). A haven for whistleblowers. *Parade*, pp.16–17.

Andersen, P. (1999). *Nonverbal communication: Forms and functions*. Mountain View, CA: Mayfield.

Appel, W. (1983). *Cults in America: Programmed for paradise*. New York: Holt, Rinehart & Winston.

Aratoni, L. (1999, January 12). Teachers shoulder blame. *San Jose Mercury News*, p. 3B.

Aronson, E. (1999). *The social animal*. New York: Worth.

As they see it. (1990, August 26). *San Jose Mercury News*, p. 2C.

Asch, S. (1952). *Social Psychology*. New York: Prentice-Hall.

Axelrod, R. (1984). *The evolution of cooperation*. New York: Basic Books.

Bach, G., & Goldberg, H. (1974). *Creative aggression*. New York: Avon.

Baker, R. (1996, May/June). The silencing of the persecuting prosecutors. *Skeptical Inquirer*, 42–45.

Balgopal, P., Ephross, & Vassil, T (1992). Self-help groups and professional helpers. In R. Cathcart & L. Samovar (Eds.), *Small group communication: A reader*. Dubuque, IA: Wm. C. Brown.

Baran, S. (1999). *Introduction to mass communication: Media literacy and culture*. Mountain View, CA: Mayfield.

Barge, J., & Hirokawa, R. (1989). Toward a communication competency model of group leadership. *Small Group Behavior*, 20, 167–189.

Barker, L., et al. (1981). An investigation of proportional time spent in various communication activities by college students. *Journal of Applied Communication Research*, 101–109.

BarNir, A. (1998). Can group- and issue-related factors predict choice shift? *Small Group Research*, 29, 308–338.

Baron, R. (1988). Negative effects of destructive criticism: Impact on conflict self-efficacy and task performance. *Journal of Applied Psychology*, 73, 199–207.

Baron, R. (1990). Countering the effects of destructive criticism: The relative efficacy of four interventions. *Journal of Applied Psychology*, 75, 235–243.

Barry, D. (1986). *Claw your way to the top*. Emmaus, PA: Rodale Press.

Barry, D. (1991). *Dave Barry's guide to life*. New York: Wings Books.

Bartos, O. (1970). Determinants and consequences of toughness. In P. Swingle (Ed.), *The structure of conflict*. New York: Academic Press.

Bass, M. (1960). *Leadership, psychology and organizational behavior*. West Port, CT: Greenwood Press.

Bate, B. (1988). *Communication and the sexes*. New York: Harper & Row, 1988.

Baumeister, R., Smart, L., & Boden, J. (1996). Relation of threatened egotism to violence and aggression: The dark side of high self-esteem. *Psychological Review*, 103, 5–33.

Baxter, T. (1996, September 13). Dole's attack is puzzling. *San Jose Mercury News*, p. 11B.

Bazerman, M., & Neale, M. (1983). Heuristics in negotiation: Limitations to dispute resolution effectiveness. In M. Bazerman & R. Lewicki (Eds.), *Negotiating in organizations*. Beverly Hills, CA: Sage.

Bechler, C., & Johnson, S. (1995). Leadership and listening: A study of member perceptions. *Small Group Research*, 26, 77–85.

Belbin, R. (1996). *Team roles at work*. London: Butterworth-Heinemann.

Bell, M. (1974). The effects of substantive and affective conflict in problem-solving discussions. *Speech Monographs*, 41, 19–23.

Bellamy, R., & Walker, J. (1996). *Television and the remote control*. New York: Guilford Press.

Benne, K., & Sheats, P. (1948). Functional roles of group members. *Journal of Social Issues*, 4, 41–49.

Bennis, W., & Biederman, P. (1997). *Organizing genius: The secrets of creative collaboration*. New York: Addison-Wesley.

Berg, D. (1967). A descriptive analysis of the distribution and duration of themes discussed by task-oriented small groups. *Speech Monographs*, 34, 172–175.

Berge, Z. (1994). Electronic discussion groups. *Communication Education*, 43, 102–111.

Berko, R., & Brooks, M. (1994). *Rationale kit: Information supporting the speech communication discipline and its programs*. Annandale, VA: Speech Communication Association.

Bernstein, N. (2000, January 28). N.Y. recruiting telephone psychics. *San Jose Mercury News*, p. 16A.

Bettinghaus, E., & Cody, M. (1987). *Persuasive communication*. New York: Holt, Rinehart & Winston.

Black, K. (1990, March). Can getting mad get the job done? *Working Woman*, 86–90.

Blake, R., & Mouton, J. (1964). *The managerial grid*. Houston: Gulf Publishing.

Blum, R. (1995, March 3). Lawyers only winners. *Santa Cruz Sentinel*, p. B3.

Blumner, R. (1999, August 15). "Voyeur" case bears watching. *San Jose Mercury News*, p. 3C.

Bok, S. (1978). *Lying: Moral choice in public and private life*. New York: Random House.

Bolton, R. (1979). *People skills: How to assert yourself, listen to others and resolve conflicts*. New York: Simon & Schuster.

Bond, M., Wang, K., Leung, K., & Giacalone, R. (1985). How are responses to verbal insults related to cultural collectivism and power distances? *Journal of Cross-cultural Psychology*, 16, 111–127.

Bordevich, F. (1995, February). The country that works perfectly. *Reader's Digest*, pp. 101–106.

Borisoff, D., & Victor, D. (1989). *Conflict management: A communication skills approach*. Englewood Cliffs, NJ: Prentice-Hall.

Bormann, E. (1990). *Small group communication: Theory and practice*. New York: Harper & Row.

Bormann, E., & Bormann, N. (1988). *Effective small group communication*. Edina, MN: Burgess Publishing.

Bostrom, R. (1970). Patterns of communicative interaction in small groups. *Speech Monographs*, 37, 257–263.

Bower, S., & Bower, G. (1976). *Asserting yourself*. Reading, MA: Addison-Wesley.

Boyd, R. (1996, June 9). Survival of the most cooperative? New insights into Darwin's theory. *San Jose Mercury News*, p. 1C.

Brannigan, M. (1997, May 30). Why Delta Air Lines decided it was time for CEO to take off. *The Wall Street Journal*, pp. A1, A8.

Brecher, E. (1989, December 15). Furor over Florida rape case clouds disturbing facts. *The Seattle Times*, p. B1.

Brehm, J. (1972). *Responses to loss of freedom: A theory of psychological resistance*. Morristown, NJ: General Learning Press.

Brett, J. et al. (1990, February). Designing systems for resolving disputes in organizations. *American Psychologist*, pp. 162–170.

Brewer, M. (1979). In-group bias in the minimal intergroup situation: A cognitive-motivational analysis. *Psychological Bulletin*, 86, 307–324.

Brewer, M., & Miller, N. (1984). Beyond the contact hypothesis: Theoretical perspectives on desegregation. In N. Miller & M. Brewer (Eds.), *Groups in contact*. Orlando, FL: Academic Press.

Brilhart, J., & Galanes, G. (1998). *Effective group discussion*. Dubuque, IA: Wm. C. Brown.

Brislin, R. (1993). *Understanding culture's influence on behavior*. Fort Worth, TX: Harcourt Brace Jovanovich.

Brock, T. (1968). Implications of commodity theory for value change. In A. Greenwald, T. Brock, and T. Ostrom (Eds.), *Psychological foundations of attitudes*. New York: Academic Press.

Broeder, D. (1959). The University of Chicago jury project. *Nebraska Law Review*, 38, 760–774.

Bronner, E. (1999, June 13). Colleges are getting more competitive, students find. *San Jose Mercury News*, p. 13A.

Broome, B., & Fulbright, L. (1995). A multistage influence model of barriers to group problem solving: A participant-generated agenda for small group research. *Small Group Research*, 26, 25–35.

Brownell, J. (1990). Perceptions of listening behavior: A management study. *Journal of Business Communication*, 27, 401–416.

Brue, M. (1989, June 29). Youths deciding to quit sports. *San Jose Mercury News*, p. 7G.

Brumley, A. et al. (1995, November 19). You say you want a revolution. *San Jose Mercury News*, p. 3A.

Brussell, E. (Ed.). (1988). *Webster's new world dictionary of quotable definitions*. Englewood Cliffs, NJ: Prentice-Hall.

Bryson, B. (1990). *The mother tongue*. New York: Avon Books.

Building on faith. (1999, August/September). *Habitat World*, p. 14.

Burggraf, C., & Sillars, A. (1987) A critical examination of sex differences in marital communication. *Communication Monographs*, 54, 276–294.

Burke, R. (1970). Methods of resolving superior-subordinate conflict: The constructive use of subordinate differences and disagreements. *Organizational Behavior and Human Performance*, 5, 393–411.

Burns, J. (1978). *Leadership*. New York: Harper and Row.

Burrows, W. (1982, November). *Psychology Today*, 43.

Businesspeople suffering information indigestion. (1996, October 25). *San Jose Mercury News*, p. IC.

Butt, D. (1976). *Psychology of sport: The behavior motivation, personality, and performance of athletes*. New York: Van Nostrand Reinhold.

Buzaglio, G., & Weelan, S. (1999). Facilitating work team effectiveness: Case studies from Central America. *Small Group Research*, 30, 108–129.

Byrne, J. (1999). *Chainsaw: The notorious career of Al Dunlap in the era of profit-at-any-price*. New York: HarperBusiness.

Campbell, A. (1993). *Men, women, and aggression*. New York: Basic Books.

Canary, D., & Spitzberg, B. (1987). Appropriateness and effectiveness perceptions of conflict strategies. *Human Communication Research*, 14, 93–118.

Caplow, T. (1968). *Two against one: Coalitions in triads*. Englewood Cliffs, NJ: Prentice-Hall.

Carletta, J., Garrod, S., & Fraser-Krauss, H. (1998). Placement of authority and communication patterns in workplace groups: The consequences for innovation. *Small Group Research*, 29, 531–559.

Carli, L. (1990). Gender, language, and influence. *Journal of Personality and Social Psychology*, 59, 941–951.

Carnevale, P., & Probst. (1998). Social values and social conflict in creative problem solving. *Journal of Personality and Social Psychology*, 74, 1300–1309.

Carroll, J. (1987). Indefinite terminating points and the iterated Prisoner's Dilemma. *Theory and Decision*, 22, 247–256.

Carron, A., & Spink, K. (1995). The group size-cohesion relationship in minimal groups. *Small Group Research*, 26, 86–105.

Carter, S., & West, M. (1998). Reflexivity, effectiveness, and mental health in BBC-TV production teams. *Small Group Research*, 29, 583–601.

Carton, J. (1996). The differential effects of tangible rewards and praise on intrinsic motivation: A comparison of cognitive evaluation theory and operant theory. *Behavior Analyst*, 19, 237–255.

Cathcart, R., & Samovar, L. (1996). *Small group communication: A reader*. Dubuque, IA: Wm. C. Brown.

Charnofsky, H., Cherny, R., DuFault, D., Kegley, J., & Whitney, D. (1998, December 16). Final report of Merit Pay Task Force, CSU Academic Senate [on-line]. Available: www.academicsenate.cc.ca.us.

Chatman, J., & Barsade, S. (1995). Personality, organizational culture, and cooperation: Evidence from a business simulation. *Administrative Science Quarterly*, 40, 423–443.

Cheating at work blamed on squeeze of job pressures. (1997, April 5). *San Jose Mercury News*, pp. 1C, 10C.

Chen, G., & Starosta, W. (1997). Chinese conflict management and resolution. Overview and implications. *Intercultural Communication Studies*, 7,1–16.

Chen, G., & Starosta, W. (1998). *Foundations of intercultural communication*. Boston: Allyn & Bacon.

Chertkoff, J., & Esser, J. (1976). A review of experiments in explicit bargaining. *Journal of Experimental Social Psychology*, 12, 464–486.

Chin, P. (2000, January 24). The buddy system. *People*, 98–105.

Christensen, D. et al. (1980). Sensitivity to nonverbal cues as a function of social competence. *Journal of Nonverbal Behavior*, 1980, 4, 145–156.

Cialdini, R. (1993). *Influence: The new psychology of modern persuasion*. Glenview, IL: Scott, Foresman.

Clanton, J. (1988). The Challenger disaster that didn't happen. In L. Schnoor (Ed.),*Winning Orations*. Northfield, MN: Interstate Oratorical Association.

Clark, N., & Stephenson, G. (1989). Group remembering. In P. Paulus (Ed.), *Psychology of group influence*. Hillsdale, NJ: Lawrence Erlbaum.

Claymon, D. (1999, October 6). Color Apple giddy as it updates iMac. *San Jose Mercury News*, pp. 1C, 12C.

Clemetson, L. (1999, June 7). Trying to close the achievement gap. *Newsweek*, 36–37.

Coates, J. (1993). *Women, men, and language*. New York: Longman.

Cohen, M., & Davis, N. (1981). *Medication errors: Causes and prevention*. Philadelphia: G. F. Stickley.

Cole, D. (1989, May). Meetings that make sense. *Psychology Today*, 14–15.

Coleman, D., & Straus, M. (1986). Marital power, conflict, and violence in a nationally representative sample of American couples. *Violence and Victims*, 1, 141–157.

Collingwood, H. (1997, January). Forget the Fortune 500: For big bucks, think smaller and smarter. *Working Woman*, 24–25.

Conboy, W. (1976). *Working together: Communication in a healthy organization*. Columbus, OH: Charles Merrill.

Conrad, C. (1990). *Strategic organizational communication: An integrated perspective*. New York: Holt, Rinehart & Winston.

Conway, F., & Siegelman, J. (1995). *Snapping: America's epidemic of sudden personality change*. New York: Stillpoint Press.

Cookson, P., & Persell, C. (1983, March). The price of privilege. *Psychology Today*, 31–35.

Cooper, V. (1997). Homophily or the Queen Bee Syndrome: Female evaluation of female leadership. *Small Group Research*, 28, 483–499.

Corcoran, K. (1993, May 30). Society's violence mirrored on ball field. *San Jose Mercury News*, p. 1A, 10A.

Cose, E. (1999, June 7). The good news about black America. *Newsweek*, 29–32.

Cox, J. (1990, August 2). Corona is silent. *The Sacramento Bee*, p. B1.

Cox, T., Lobel, S., & McLeod, P. (1991). Effects of ethnic groups' cultural differences on cooperative and competitive behavior on a group task. *Academy of Management Journal*, 34, 827–847.

Crandall, C. (1988). Social contagion of binge eating. *Journal of Personality and Social Psychology*, 55, 588–598.

Crowe, B. et al., (1972). The effects of subordinates' behavior on managerial style. *Human Relations*, 25, 215–37.

Cult compound grew on rules, isolation. (1993, March 3). *San Jose Mercury News*, p. 8A.

Davidson, J. (1996). The shortcomings of the information age. *Vital Speeches*, 495–503.

De Klerk, V. (1991). Expletives: Men only? *Communication Monographs*, 58, 156–169.

De Souza, G., & Kline, H. (1995). Emergent leadership in the group goal-setting process. *Small Group Research*, 26, 475–496.

Delbecq, A. et al. (1975). *Group techniques for program planning*. Glenview, IL: Scott, Foresman.

Denison, D., & Sutton, R. (1990). Operating room nurses. In J. Hackman (Ed.), *Groups that work (and those that don't)*. San Francisco: Jossey-Bass.

Derber, C. (1979). *The pursuit of attention: Power and individualism in everyday life*. New York: Oxford University Press.

DeStephen, R., & Hirokawa, R. (1988). Small group consensus: Stability of group support of the decision, task process, and group relationships. *Small Group Behavior, 19*, 227–239.

Deutsch, M. (1979). Education and distributive justice: Some reflections on grading systems. *American Psychologist, 34*, 391–401.

Deutsch, M. (1985). *Distributive justice: A social-psychological perspective*. New Haven: Yale University Press.

DeVito, J. (1989). *The interpersonal communication book*. New York: Harper & Row.

DeVito, J. (1990). *Messages: Building interpersonal communication skills*. New York: Harper & Row.

Dewey, J. (1910). *How we think*. Lexington, MA: D. C. Heath.

Diamond, R. (1997, August 1). Designing and assessing course and curricula. *Chronicle of Higher Education*, p. B7.

Didsbury, H. (Ed.). (1982). *Communications and the future*. Bethesda, MD: World Future Society.

Ditch hubby, keep pal, 2610 in Germany say. (1988, February 25). *San Jose Mercury News*, p. 6F.

Dodd, C. (1995). *Dynamics of intercultural communication*. Dubuque, IA: Wm. C. Brown.

Domagalski, T. (1998). *Experienced and expressed anger in the workplace*. Unpublished doctoral dissertation, University of South Florida.

Donohue, W., & Kolt, R. (1992). *Managing interpersonal conflict*. Newbury Park, CA: Sage.

Dorsey, A., Miller, K., & Scherer, C. (1999). Communication, risk behavior, and perceptions of threat and efficacy: A test of a reciprocal model. *Journal of Applied Communication Research, 27*, 377–395.

Drecksel, G. (1984). *Interaction characteristics of emergent leadership*. Unpublished doctoral dissertation, University of Utah.

Dressler, C. (1995, December 31). Please! End this meeting madness! *Santa Cruz Sentinel*, p. ID.

Drew, J. (1994). *Mastering meetings: Discovering the hidden potential of effective business meetings*. New York: McGraw-Hill.

Dreyfuss, I. (1999, August 30). Sports parents need to keep cool. *Santa Cruz Sentinel*, p. A9.

Drucker, P. (1988, July 6). Leadership: More doing than dash. *The Wall Street Journal*, p. 1.

Dunlap, A. (1997). *Mean business: How I save bad companies and make good companies great*. New York: Simon & Schuster.

Durand, D. (1977). Power as a function of office space and physiognomy: Two studies of influence. *Psychological Reports, 40*, 755–760.

Eagly, A., Karau, S., & Makhijiani, M. (1995). Gender and the effectiveness of leaders: A meta-analysis. *Journal of Personality and Social Psychology, 117*, 125–145.

Eagly, A., Makhijiani, M., & Klonsky, B. (1992). Gender and the evaluation of leaders: A meta-analysis. *Psychological Bulletin, 111*, 3–22.

Early, C. (1989). Social loafing and collectivism: A comparison of the United States and the People's Republic of China. *Administrative Science Quarterly, 34*, 555–581.

Ebbeck, V., & Gibbons, S. (1998). The effect of a team building program on the self-conceptions of grade 6 & 7 physical education students. *Journal of Sport and Exercise Psychology, 20*, 300–310.

Efron, S. (1999, October 8). Samples point to wider radioactive impact. *San Jose Mercury News*, p. 6A.

Eisenberger, R., & Armeli, S. (1997). Can salient reward increase creative performance without reducing intrinsic creative interest? *Journal of Personality and Social Psychology, 72*, 652–663.

Eisenberger, R., & Cameron, J. (1996). Detrimental effects of reward: Reality or myth? *American Psychologist, 51*, 1153–1166.

Elliott, J. (1977). The power and pathology of prejudice. In P. Zimbardo and F. Ruch, *Psychology and life*. Glenview, IL: Scott, Foresman.

Epstein, A. (1996, January 8). Legal profession still makes it tough for aspiring women. *San Jose Mercury News*, p. 10A.

Equality still eludes female lawyers, experts say. (1996, August 18). *San Jose Mercury News*, p. 7A.

Erickson, B., Lind, A., Johnson, B., & O'Barr, W. (1978). Speech style and impression formation in a court setting: The effects of "powerful" and "powerless" speech. *Journal of Experimental Social Psychology, 14*, 266–279.

Evans, C., & Dion, K. (1991). Group cohesion and performance: A meta-analysis. *Small Group Research, 22*, 175–186.

Face it: Looks pay. (1989, August 13). *San Jose Mercury News*, p. 2PC.

Fadiman, C. (Ed.). (1985). *The Little, Brown book of anecdotes*. Boston: Little, Brown & Company.

Fairhurst, G., & Sarr, R. (1996). *The art of framing: Managing the language of leadership*. San Francisco: Jossey-Bass.

Fandt, P. (1991). The relationship of accountability and interdependent behavior to enhancing team consequences. *Group and Organization Studies*, 16, 300–312.

Farace, R. (1977). *Communicating and organizing*. Reading, MA: Addison-Wesley.

Fausto-Sterling, A. (1993, April). Is nature really red in tooth and claw? *Discover*, 24–27.

Fearing heckling, CHP officer let King bleed. (1993, March 30). *San Jose Mercury News*, p. 3B.

Feder, B. (1999, October 6). Web site gets colleges bidding for students. *San Jose Mercury News*, pp. 1A, 16A.

Fernald, L. (1987). Of windmills and rope dancing: The instructional value of narrative structures. *Teaching Psychology*, 14, 214–16.

Fiedler, F. (1967). *A theory of leadership effectiveness*. New York: McGraw-Hill.

Fiedler, F. (1970). *Leadership*. Morristown, NJ: General Learning Press.

Fiedler, F., & House, R. (1988). Leadership theory and research: A report of progress. In C. Cooper and I. Robertson (Eds.), *International review of industrial and organizational psychology*. New York: John Wiley & Sons.

Filley, A. (1975). *Interpersonal conflict resolution*. Glenview, IL: Scott, Foresman.

Firestein, R. (1990). Effects of creative problem solving training on communication behaviors in small groups. *Small Group Research*, 21, 507–521.

Firestone, I. et al. (1973). Anxiety, fear and affiliation with similar-state versus dissimilar-state others: Misery loves miserable company. *Journal of Personality and Social Psychology*, 26, 409–414.

Fisher, B. A. (1986). Leadership: When does the difference make a difference. In R. Hirokawa & M. S. Poole (Eds.), *Communication and group decision-making*. Beverly Hills, CA: Sage.

Fisher, B., & Ellis, D. (1990). *Small group decision making: Communication and the group process*. New York: McGraw-Hill.

Fisher, C., & Gitelson, R. (1983). A meta-analysis of the correlates of role conflict and ambiguity. *Journal of Applied Psychology*, 68, 320–333.

Fisher, R., & Brown, S. (1988). *Getting together: Building a relationship that gets to yes*. Boston: Houghton Mifflin.

Fisher, R., & Ury, W. (1981). *Getting to yes: Negotiating agreement without giving in*. New York: Penguin Books.

Fitzhenry, R. (Ed.). (1993). *The Harper book of quotations*. New York: HarperPerennial.

Flippen, A. (1999). Understanding groupthink from a self-regulatory perspective. *Small Group Research*, 30, 139–165.

Folger, J., Poole, M., & Stutman, R. (1993). *Working through conflict: A communication perspective*. Glenview, IL: Scott, Foresman.

Forsyth, D. (1990). *Group dynamics*. Pacific Grove, CA: Brooks/Cole Publishing Co.

Forsyth, D., Heiney, M., & Wright, S. (1997). Biases in appraisals of women leaders. *Group Dynamics: Theory, Research, and Practice*, 1, 98–103.

Foschi, M. et al. (1985). Standards, expectations, and interpersonal influence. *Social Psychology Quarterly*, 48, 108–117.

Foushee, H., & Manos, K. (1981). Information transfer within the cockpit: Problems in intracockpit communications. In C. Billings and E. Cheaney (Eds.), *Information transfer problems in the aviation system (NASA Report No. TP-1875)*. Moffett Field, CA: NASA-Ames Research Center.

Foushee, M. (1984). Dyads and triads at 35,000 feet: Factors affecting group process and aircraft performance. *American Psychologist*, 39, 885–893.

Freed, A. (1992). We understand perfectly: A critique of Tannen's view. In K. Hall, M. Bucholtz, & B. Moonwomon (Eds.), *Locating power*, Berkeley, CA: Berkeley Women and Language Group, University of California Berkeley.

Freeman, K. (1996). Attitudes toward work in project groups as predictors of academic performance. *Small Group Research*, 27, 265–282.

French, J. (1941). The disruption and cohesion of groups. *Journal of Abnormal and Social Psychology*, 36, 361–377.

French, J., & Raven, B. (1959). The bases of social power. In D. Cartwright (Ed.), *Studies in social power*. Ann Arbor, MI: Institute for Social Research, 150–167.

Frey, L. (1994). *Group communication in context: Studies of natural groups*. Hillsdale, NJ: Lawrence Erlbaum Associates.

Fuller, M. (1995). *A simple, decent place to live*. Dallas, TX: Word Publishing.

Gabrenya, W., Wang, Y., & Latane, B. (1985). Social loafing on an optimizing task: Cross-cultural differences among Chinese and Americans. *Journal of Cross-cultural Psychology*, 16, 223–242.

Gaillard, F. (1996). *If I were a carpenter: Twenty years of Habitat for Humanity*. Winston-Salem, NC: John F. Blair Publisher.

Galanter, M. (1989). *Cults: Faith, healing, and coercion*. New York: Oxford University Press.

Gamson, W. (1961). An experimental test of a theory of coalition formation. *American Sociological Review*, 26, 565–573.

Gamson, W., Fireman, B., & Rytia, S. (1982). *Encounters with unjust authority*. Homewood, IL: Dorsey.

Gardner, L. & Leak, G. (1994). Charactristics and correlates of teacher anxiety among college psychology teachers. *Teaching of Psychology*, 21, 28–32.

Garrett, L. (1994). *The coming plague: Newly emerging diseases in a world out of balance*. New York: Penguin Books.

Garrity, J. (1989, November 20). A clash of cultures on the Hopi reservation. *Sports Illustrated*, 10–16.

Gastil, J. (1994). A meta-analytic review of the productivity and satisfaction of democratic and autocratic leadership. *Small Group Research*, 25, 384–410.

Gates, D. (1993, March 29). White male paranoia. *Newsweek*, 48–53.

Gayle, B. (1991). Sex equity in workplace conflict management. *Journal of Applied Communication Research*, 19, 152–169.

Gayle-Hackett, B. (1989, February 17–21). *Do females and males differ in the selection of conflict management strategies: A meta-analytic review*. Paper presented at the Western Speech Communication Convention, Spokane, WA.

Gebhardt, L., & Meyers, R. (1995). Subgroup influence in decision-making groups: Examining consistency from a communication perspective. *Small Group Research*, 26, 147–168.

Geier, J. (1967). A trait approach in the study of leadership in small groups. *Journal of Communication*, 17, 316–123.

Geis, F. et al. (1984). Sex vs. status in sex-associated stereotypes. *Sex Roles*, 11, 771–786.

Gelles, R., & Straus, M. (1988). *Intimate violence: The causes and consequences of abuse in the American family*. New York: Simon and Schuster.

Gelman, D., & Rogers, P. (1993, March 12). Mixed messages. *Newsweek*, 28.

Gerow, J. (1995). *Psychology: An introduction*. New York: HarperCollins.

Getter, H., & Nowinski, J. (1981). A free response test of interpersonal effectiveness. *Journal of Personality Assessment*, 45, 301–308.

Gibb, C. Leadership. (1969). In G. Lindzey & E. Aronson (Eds.), *The handbook of social psychology* (Vol. 4). Reading, MA: Addison-Wesley, 205–282.

Gibb, J. Defensive communication. (1961). *The Journal of Communication*, 11, 141–148.

Gilovich, T. (1991). *How we know what isn't so: The fallibility of human reason in everyday life*. New York: The Free Press.

Glass ceiling intact, statistics show at hearing. (1994, September 27). *San Jose Mercury News*, 1E.

Glassman, J. K. (1998, May 29). Put shootings in proper perspective. *San Jose Mercury News*, p. B7.

Glazer, M., & Glazer, P. (1986, August). Whistleblowing. *Psychology Today*, 37–43.

Gleick, J. (1999). *Faster: The acceleration of just about everything*. New York: Pantheon Books.

Goethals, G., & Darley, J. (1987). Social comparison theory: Self-evaluation and group life. In B. Mullen & G. Goethals (Eds.), *Theories of group behavior*. New York: Springer-Verlag.

Goktepe, J., & Schneier, C. (1989). Role of sex and gender roles, and attraction in predicting emergent leaders. *Journal of Applied Psychology*, 74, 165–167.

Goldhaber, G. (1990). *Organizational communication*. Dubuque, IA: Wm. C. Brown.

Goldman, A. (1988). *The lives of John Lennon*. New York: William Morrow & Co.

Goldstein, S. (1994, April 11). Citadel's lone woman ostracized. *San Jose Mercury News*, p. 13A.

Goldston, L. (1995, November 19). Women make a big impact. *San Jose Mercury News*, p. 2A.

Goldston, L., & Torriero, E. (1990, January 8). McMartin sex case hinges on health of 12 weary jurors. *San Jose Mercury News*, 1A.

Goleman, D. (1995). *Emotional intelligence: Why it can matter more than I.Q.* New York: Bantam.

Goleman, D. (1998). *Working with emotional intelligence*. New York: Bantam Books.

Gomes, L. (1995, March 3). Intuit fesses up again. *San Jose Mercury News*, p. 1C.

Goodstein, L. (1997, March 30). Heaven's Gate had all the classic cult traits, experts say. *The Washington Post*, p. A1.

Gottman, J., & Silver, N. (1994). *Why marriages succeed or fail*. New York: Simon & Schuster.

Gottman, J., & Silver, N. (1999). *The seven principles for making marriage work*. New York: Crown.

Gould, S. (1981). *The mismeasure of man*. New York: W. W. Norton.

Gouran, D. (1981). Cognitive sources of inferential error and the contributing influence of interaction characteristics in decision-making groups. In G. Ziegelmueller and J. Rhodes (Eds.), *Dimensions of argument: Proceedings of the Second Annual Summer Conference on Argumentation*. Annandale, VA: Speech Communication Association.

Gouran, D. (1982). *Making decisions in groups: Choices and consequences*. Glenview, IL: Scott, Foresman.

Gouran, D. (1982, April). *A theoretical foundation for the study of inferential error in decision-making groups*. Paper presented at the Conference on Small Group Research, Pennsylvania State University.

Gouran, D. (1983). Communicative influences on inferential judgments in decision-making groups: A descriptive analysis. In D. Zarefsky et al. (Eds.), *Argument in transition: Proceedings of the Third Summer Conference on Argumentation*. Annandale, VA: Speech Communication Association.

Gouran, D. (1986). Inferential errors, interaction, and group decision-making. In R. Hirokawa and M. Poole (Eds.), *Communication and group decision-making*. Beverly Hills, CA: Sage.

Gouran, D. (1988). Principles of counteractive influence in decision-making and problem-solving groups. In R. Cathcart and L. Samovar (Eds.), *Small group communication: A reader*. Dubuque, IA: Wm. C. Brown.

Gouran, D., & Baird, J. (1972). An analysis of distributional and sequential structure in problem-solving and informal group discussions, *Speech Monographs*, 39, 16–22.

Griffin, E. (1994). *A first look at communication theory*. New York: McGraw-Hill.

Grogan, B. et al. (1993, May). Their brothers' keepers? *People*, 45.

Grusky, O., Bonacich, P., & Webster, C. (1995). The coalition structure of the four-person family. *Current Research in Social Psychology*, 2, 16–28.

Gudykunst, W. (1991). *Bridging differences: Effective intergroup communication*. Newbury Park, CA: Sage.

Gully, S., Devine, D., & Whitney, D. (1995). A meta-analysis of cohesion and performance: Effects of level of analysis and task interdependence. *Small Group Research*, 26, 497–520.

Gumpert, R., & Hambleton, R. (1979, December). Situational leadership: How Xerox managers fine-tune managerial styles to employee maturity and tasks needs. *Management Review*, 9.

Hackman, J. (1987). The design of work teams. In J. Lorsch (Ed.), *Handbook of organizational behavior*. Englewood Cliffs, NJ: Prentice-Hall, 315–342.

Hackman, M., & Johnson, C. (1996). *Leadership: A communication perspective*. Prospect Heights, IL: Waveland Press.

Hall, E. (1981). *Beyond culture*. New York: Doubleday.

Hall, E., & Hall, M. (1987). *Understanding cultural difference*. Yarmouth, ME: Intercultural Press.

Hall, J., & Donnell, S. (1979). Managerial achievement: The personal side of behavioral theory. *Human Relations*, 32, 77–101.

Hall, J., & Watson, W. (1970). The effects of a normative intervention on group decision-making. *Human Relations*, 23, 299–317.

Halpern, D. (1984). *Thought and knowledge: An introduction to critical thinking*. Hillsdale, NJ: Lawrence Erlbaum.

Hamill, R. et al. (1979). Ignoring sample bias: Inferences about collectivities from atypical cases. Unpublished manuscript, University of Michigan.

Haney, W. (1967). *Communication and organizational behavior*. Homewood, IL: Richard D. Irwin.

Hare, A. (1994). Types of roles in small groups: A bit of history and a current perspective. *Small Group Research*, 25, 433–448.

Haslett, B. et al. (1992). *The organizational woman: Power and paradox*. Norwood, NJ: Ablex Publishing.

Hassan, S. (1988). *Combatting cult mind control*. Rochester, VT: Part Street Press.

Hastie, R., Penrod, S., & Pennington, N. (1983). *Inside the jury*. Cambridge, MA: Harvard University Press.

Hawkins, K. (1995). Effects of gender and communication content on leadership emergence in small task-oriented groups. *Small Group Research*, 26, 234–249.

Heat's on to close wage gap. (1999, January 30). *San Jose Mercury News*, pp. 1A, 10A.

Hellweg, S., Samovar, L., & Skow, L. (1994). Cultural variations in negotiation styles. In L. Samovar & R. Porter (Eds.), *Intercultural communication: A reader*. Belmont, CA: Wadsworth.

Hendra, T. (Ed.). (1982). *Meet Mr. bomb*. New London, NH: High Meadow Publishing.

Henley, N. (1995). Body politics revisited: What do we know today? In P. Kalbfleisch & M. Cody (Eds.), *Gender, power, and communication in human relationships*. Hillsdale, NJ: Lawrence Erlbaum.

Henry, J. (1963). *Culture against man*. New York: Random House.

Hensley, T., & Griffin, G. (1986). Victims of groupthink: The Kent State University Board of Trustees and the 1977 gymnasium controversy. *Journal of Conflict Resolution*, 30, 497–531.

Herbold, S. (1998, May 3). Venture capitalists' slang puts the "go" into "argot." *San Jose Mercury News*, pp. 1A, 26A.

Herek, G. et al. (1987). Decision making during international crises: Is quality of process related to outcome? *Journal of Conflict Resolution*, 31, 203–226.

Hersey, P., & Blanchard, K. (1988). *Management organizational behavior: Utilizing human resources.* Englewood Cliffs, NJ: Prentice-Hall.

Hickson, M., & Stacks, D. (1989). *Nonverbal communication: Studies and applications.* Dubuque, IA: Wm. C. Brown.

Hillary: It will happen again. (1996, August). *Life*, 41.

Hirokawa, R. (1983). Group communication and problem-solving effectiveness: An investigation of group phases. *Human Communication Research*, 9, 291–305.

Hirokawa, R. (1985). Discussion procedures and decision-making performance: A test of a functional perspective. *Human Communication Research*, 12, 203–224.

Hirokawa, R. (1987). Why informed groups make faulty decisions: An investigation of possible interaction-based explanations. *Small Group Behavior*,18, 3–29.

Hirokawa, R. (1992). Communication and group decision-making efficacy. In R. Cathcart and L. Samovar (Eds.), *Small group communication: A reader.* Dubuque, IA: Wm. C. Brown.

Hirokawa, R., & Pace, R. (1983). A descriptive investigation of the possible communication-based reasons for effective and ineffective group decision-making. *Communication Monographs*, 50, 363–379.

Hirokawa, R., & Scheerhorn, D. (1986). Communication in faulty group decision-making. In R. Hirokawa & M. Poole (Eds.), *Communication and group decision-making.* Beverly Hills, CA: Sage.

Hite, S. (1987). *Women and love: A cultural revolution in progress.* New York: Alfred A. Knopf.

Hoffman, C., & Hurst, N. (1990). Gender stereotypes: Perception or rationalization? *Journal of Personality and Social Psychology*, 58, 197–208.

Hofling, C., Brotman, E., Dalrymple, S., Graves, N., & Pierce, C. (1966). An experimental study in nurse-physician relationships. *Journal of Nervous and Mental Disease*, 143, 171–180.

Hofstede, G. (1991). *Cultures and Organizations: Software of the mind.* New York: McGraw-Hill.

Holguin, R. (1985, September 1). Stalker suspect caught. *Santa Cruz Sentinel*, p. A1.

Hollander, E. (1978). *Leadership dynamics.* New York: Free Press.

Hollander, E. (1985). Leadership and power. In G. Lindzey & E. Aronson (Eds.), *Handbook of Social Psychology.* New York: Random House, 485–537.

Hollander, E., & Offerman, L. (1990, February). Power and leadership in organizations. *American Psychologist*, 179–189.

Hollingshead, A. (1998). Group and individual training: The impact of practice on performance. *Small Group Research*, 29, 254–280.

Home chores still a battle of the sexes. (1993, February 16). *San Jose Mercury News*, p. 5A.

Hong, L. (1978). Risky shift and cautious shift: Same direct evidence on the cultural-value theory. *Social Psychology*, 41, 342–346.

Hotz, R. (1999, October 1). 'Dumb' math error blamed for death of Martian probe. *San Jose Mercury News*, p. 1A.

How America measures up. (1999, August 2). *Newsweek*, 50–53.

Howell, J. (1985). *A laboratory study of charismatic leadership.* Working paper, University of Western Ontario.

Huckshorn, K. (1996, March 4). Human rights in Asia: Society comes first. *San Jose Mercury News*, pp. 1A, 15A.

Hughes, R., Ginnett, R., & Curphy, G. (1996). *Leadership: Enhancing the lessons of experience.* New York: McGraw-Hill.

Hunt, M. (1982). *The universe within: A new science explores the human mind.* New York: Simon & Schuster.

Husband, R. (1992). Leading in organizational groups. In R. Cathcart and L. Samovar (Eds.), *Small group communication*, Dubuque, IA: Wm. C. Brown, 464–476.

Inagaki, Y. (1985). *Jiko hyogen no gijutsu (Skills in self-expression).* Tokyo: PHP Institute.

Infante, D., Rancer, A., & Womack, D. (1997). *Building communication theory.* Prospect Heights, IL: Waveland Press.

Irons, E., & Moore, G. (1985). *Black managers: The case of the banking industry.* New York: Praeger.

Ishii, S., Klopf, D., & Cambra, R. (1984). The typical Japanese student as an oral communicator: A preliminary profile. *Otsuma Review*, 17, 39–63.

Ivins, M. (1992, August). The billionaire boy scout. *Time*, 38–39.

Jacobs, J. (1989, October 2). Designs for better education elude summiteers. *San Jose Mercury News*, p. 5B.

Jacobs, J. (1996, January 4). Who will raise the children? *San Jose Mercury News*, p. 7B.

Jacobs, J. (1999a, February 18). The proof is in the winning. *San Jose Mercury News*, p. 11B.

Jacobs, J. (1999b, April 12). Women deserve equity, not advantage. *San Jose Mercury News*, p. 7B.

Jacobs, M., & Goodman, G. (1989, March). Psychology and self-help groups. *American Psychologist*, 536–545.

Jaksa, J., & Pritchard, M. (1994). *Communication ethics: Methods of analysis*. Belmont, CA: Wadsworth.

James, D., & Clarke, S. (1993). Women, men, and interruptions: A critical review. In D. Tannen (Ed.), *Gender and conversational interaction*. New York: Oxford University Press.

James, D., & Drakich, J. (1993). Understanding gender differences in amount of talk: A critical review of research. In D. Tannen (Ed.), *Gender and conversational interaction*. New York: Oxford University Press.

Janis, I. (1983). *Groupthink: Psychological studies of policy decisions and fiascoes*. Boston: Houghton Mifflin.

Jessup, L., Connolly, T., & Tansik, D. (1990). Toward a theory of automated group work. *Small Group Research*, 21, 333–348.

Johannesen, R. (1974). The functions of silence: A plea for communication research. *Western Speech*, 38, 20–35.

Johnson, D., & Johnson, F. (1991, 1975). *Joining together: Group theory and group skills*. Englewood Cliffs, NJ: Prentice-Hall.

Johnson, D., & Johnson, R. (1987). *Learning together and alone: Cooperative, competitive, and individualistic learning*. Englewood Cliffs, NJ: Prentice-Hall.

Johnson, D., & Johnson, R. (1989). *Cooperation and competition: Theory and research*. Edina, MN: Interaction Book Co.

Johnson, D., & Johnson, R. (1998). Cooperative learning and social interdependence theory. In R. Tinsdale et al. (Eds.), *Theory and research on small groups*. New York: Plenum Press.

Johnson, D., & Johnson, R. (1987). *Cooperation and competition*. Hillsdale, NJ: Lawrence Erlbaum.

Johnson, D., Johnson, R., & Holubec, E. (1986). *Circles of Learning: Cooperation in the classroom*. Edina, MN: Interaction Book Company.

Johnson, D., Maruyama, G., Johnson, R., Nelson, D., & Skon, L. (1981). Effects of cooperative, competitive, and individualistic goal structures on achievement: A meta-analysis. *Psychological Bulletin*, 89, 47–62.

Johnson, S., & Bechler, C. (1998). Examining the relationship between listening effectiveness and leadership emergence: Perceptions, behaviors, and recall. *Small Group Research*, 29, 452–471.

Ju, L., & Cushman, D. (1995). *Organizational teamwork in high-speed management*. Albany, NY: SUNY.

Judge, C. (1998, July 31). Rookie's father would be proud. *San Jose Mercury News*, p. D8.

Jurors' views differ on King beating trial. *San Jose Mercury News*, February 15, 1993, 3B.

Kantrowitz, B., & Wingert, P. (1990, Winter/Spring). Step by step. *Newsweek Special Issue*, 24–34.

Kassin, S. (1998). *Psychology*. Upper Saddle River, NJ: Prentice-Hall.

Katz, D. (1982). The effects of group longevity on project communication. *Administrative Science*, 27, 81–104.

Kelman, H., & Hamilton, V. (1989). Crimes of obedience: Toward a social psychology of authority and responsibility. New Haven, CT: Yale University Press.

Kelman, H., & Lawrence, L. (1972). American response to the trial of Lt. William L. Calley. *Psychology Today*, 41–45.

Kerr, N., & Bruun, S. (1983). Dispensability of member effort and group motivation losses: Free-rider effects. *Journal of Personality and Social Psychology*, 44, 78–94.

Kessler, J. (1973). An empirical study of six- and twelve-member jury decision-making processes. *University of Michigan Journal of Law Reform*, 6, 712–734.

Killian, A. (1996, August 5). VanDerveer ordeal proves worth it for well-drilled team. *San Jose Mercury News*, p. 1D.

Killian, L. (1952). The significance of multiple-group membership in disaster. *American Journal of Sociology*, 57, 309–314.

Kilmann, R., & Thomas, K. (1977). Developing a force-choice measure of conflict-handling behavior: The MODE instrument. Educational and Psychological Measurement, 37, 309–325.

Kipnis, D. (1976). *The powerholders*. Chicago: University of Chicago Press.

Kirchmeyer, C. & Cohen, A. (1992). Multicultural groups: Their performance and reactions with constructive conflict. *Group and Organization Management*, 17, 153–170.

Kirchmeyer, C. (1993). Multicultural task groups: An account of the low contribution level of minorities. *Small Group Research, 24,* 127–148.

Klapp, O. (1978). *Opening and closing: Strategies of information adaptation in society.* New York: Cambridge University Press.

Kleiman, C. (1991, July 28). A boost up the corporate ladder. *San Jose Mercury News,* p. 1PC.

Kleiman, C. (1998, June 21). Underpaid women should not go quietly. *San Jose Mercury News,* p. 1PC.

Klein, S. (1996). Work pressure as a determinant of work group behavior. *Small Group Research, 27,* 299–315.

Kohn, A. (1987, October). It's hard to get left out of a pair. *Psychology Today* 53–57.

Kohn, A. (1992). *No contest: The case against competition.* Boston: Houghton Mifflin.

Kohn, A. (1993). *Punished by rewards.* New York: Houghton Mifflin.

Kolb, J. (1997). Are we still stereotyping leadership? *Small Group Research, 28,* 370–393.

Komorita, S., & Ellis, A. (1988). Level of aspiration in coalition bargaining. *Journal of Personality and Social Psychology, 54,* 421–431.

Komorita, S., & Kravitz, D. (1983). Coalition formation: A social psychological approach. In P. Paulus (Ed.), *Basic group processes.* New York: Springer-Verlag.

Koury, Renee. (1996, July 7). UC spends millions on sex-bias cases. *San Jose Mercury News,* p. 1A.

Kramer, M., Kuo, C., & Dailey, J. (1997). The impact of brainstorming techniques on subsequent group processes: Beyond generating ideas. *Small Group Research, 28,* 218–242.

Kruglanski, A. (1986, August). Freeze-think and the Challenger. *Psychology Today,* 48–49.

Kukla, R., & Kessler, J. (1978). Is justice really blind? The effect of litigant physical attractiveness on judicial judgment. *Journal of Applied Social Psychology, 4,* 336–381.

Kurtz, L. (1997). *Self-help and support groups: A handbook for practitioners.* Thousand Oaks, CA: Sage.

Kutner, L. (1994, February 20). Winning isn't only thing that counts. *Santa Cruz Sentinel,* p. D2.

Lancashire, D. (1970, April 13). When Yoko walked in, McCartney said 'O No!' *New York Post,* p. 1.

Landers, A. (1995, February 25). Low income families need fire protection too. *Santa Cruz Sentinel,* p. D5.

Landy, D., & Sigall, H. (1974). Beauty is talent: Task evaluation as a function of the performer's physical attractiveness. *Journal of Personality and Social Psychology, 29,* 299–304.

Langfred, C. (1998). Is group cohesiveness a double-edged sword? *Small Group Research, 29,* 124–143.

Larson, C., & LaFasto, M. (1989). *Teamwork: What must go right, what can go wrong.* Newbury Park, CA: Sage.

Laughlin, P., & Adamopoulos, J. (1980). Social combination processes and individual learning for six-person cooperative groups on an intellectual task. *Journal of Personality and Social Psychology, 38,* 941–947.

Le, P. (1995, October 23). Foundations give schools a growing shot in the arm. *San Jose Mercury News,* p. 1A.

Leak, G. K., & Gardner, L. E. (1992, January). *Teaching anxiety among college psychology teachers.* Paper presented at the Fourteenth Annual National Institute on the Teaching of Psychology, St. Petersburg, Florida.

Leana, C. (1985). A partial test of Janis's groupthink model: Effects of group cohesiveness and leader behavior on defective decision making. *Journal of Management, 11,* 5–17.

Leary, M. (1983). *Understanding social anxiety.* Newbury Park, CA: Sage.

Leathers, D. (1970). The process effects of trust-destroying behaviors in the small group. *Speech Monographs, 37,* 180–187.

Leathers, D. (1979). The impact of multichannel message inconsistency on verbal and nonverbal decoding behaviors. *Communication Monographs, 46,* 88–100.

Leathers, D. (1986). *Successful nonverbal communication: Principles and applications.* New York: Macmillan.

Leavitt, H. (1964). *Managerial psychology.* Chicago: University of Chicago Press.

Lee, B. (1997). *The power principle: Influence with honor.* New York: Simon & Schuster.

Leerhsen, C. et al. (1990, February 5). Unite and conquer. *Newsweek,* 50–55.

Levine, J., & Moreland, R. (1990). Progress in small group research. *Annual Review of Psychology, 41,* 585–634.

Levine, S. (1984, August). Radical departures. *Psychology Today,* August 20–27.

Levy, S. (1995, November 27). Bill's new vision. *Newsweek,* 54–57.

Lewallen, J. (1972, April). Ecocide: Clawmarks on the yellow face. *Earth,* 36–43.

Lewin, K. (1953). Studies in group decision. In D. Cartwright and A. Zander (Eds.), *Group dynamics.* Evanston, IL: Row, Peterson.

Lewin, K., Lippitt, R., & White, R. (1939). Patterns of aggressive behavior in experimentally created social climates. *Journal of Social Psychology*, 10, 271–99.

Lewis, R. (1996). *When cultures collide: Managing successfully across cultures*. London: Nicholas Brealey.

Li, C. (1975). *Path analysis: A primer*. Pacific Grove, CA: Boxwood Press.

Lindskold, S. (1978). Trust development, the GRIT proposal, and the effects of conciliatory acts on conflict and cooperation. *Psychological Bulletin*, 85, 772–793.

Lipnack, J., & Stamp, J. (1997). *Virtual teams: Reaching across space, time, and organizations with technology*. New York: John Wiley & Sons.

Littlejohn, S. (1999). *Theories of human communication*. Belmont, CA: Wadsworth.

Littlejohn, S., & Jabusch, D. (1982). Communication competence: Model and application. *Journal of Applied Communication Research*, 10, 29–37.

Littlepage, G., & Mueller, A. (1997). Recognition and utilization of expertise in problem-solving groups: Expert characterizations and behavior. *Group Dynamics: Theory, Research, and Practice*, 1, 324–328.

Lorant, R. (1996, December 11). Rebuilding corporate compassion. [on-line]. Available: www.new@seatimes.com.

Lubman, S. (1996, September 15). Volunteers bring schools more than they bargained for. *San Jose Mercury News*, p. 1A.

Lubman, S. (1999, October 13). Nation's response to crisis belies its devotion to detail. *San Jose Mercury News*, p. 21A.

Lulofs, R. (1994). *Conflict: From theory to action*. Scottsdale, AR: Gorsuch Scarisbrick.

Lumsden, G., & Lumsden, D. (1993). *Communicating in groups and teams: Sharing leadership*. Belmont, CA: Wadsworth.

Lustig, M., & Koester, J. (1999). *Intercultural competence: Interpersonal communication across cultures*. New York: Longman.

Luthans, L. et al. (1988). *Real managers*. Cambridge, MA: Ballinger Press.

MacNeil, M., & Sherif, M. (1976). Norm change over subject generations as a function of arbitrariness of prescribed norm. *Journal of Personality and Social Psychology*, 34, 762–73.

Man survives stupid arrow stunt. (1993, May 6). *San Jose Mercury News*, p. 9A.

Marak, S. (1964). The evolution of leadership structure. *Sociometry*, 27, 174–82.

Mathison, D. (1987). Sex differences in the perception of assertiveness among female managers. *Journal of Social Psychology*, 126, 599–606.

May, R. (1972). *Power and innocence: A search for the sources of violence*. New York: W. W. Norton.

McCall, W. (1996, June 25). The hand that holds the remote rules the most. *San Jose Mercury News*, p. D1.

McCauley, C., & Segal, M. (1987). Social psychology of terrorist groups. In C. Hendrick (Ed.), *Review of personality and social psychology: Group process and intergroup relations*. Beverly Hills, CA: Sage, 9.

McDaniel, E. (1993, November). *Japanese nonverbal communication: A review and critique of literature*. Paper presented at the Annual Convention of the Speech Communication Association, Miami Beach, FL.

McGregor, D. (1960). *The human side of enterprise*. New York: McGraw-Hill.

McGuinnies, E., & Ward, C. (1980). Better liked than right: Trustworthiness and expertise as factors in credibility. *Personality and Social Psychology Bulletin*, 6, 467–472.

McKay, M., Rogers, P., & McKay, J. (1989). *When anger hurts: Quieting the storm within*. Oakland, CA: New Harbinger.

McLeod, H., & Cooper, J. (1996, July 31). Politically unplugged. *San Jose Mercury News*, p. 7B.

McLeod, P., Lobel, S., & Cox, T. (1996). Ethnic diversity and creativity in small groups. *Small Group Research*, 27, 248–264.

McNeil, B. J., Pauker, S.G., Sox, H.C., & Tversky, A. (1982). On the elicitation of preferences for alternative therapies. *New England Journal of Medicine*, 306, 1259–1262.

McNutt, P. (1997, October/November). When strategic decisions are ignored. *Fast Company*.

Meacham, J. (1996, July 27). Revenge of the nerd. *San Jose Mercury News*, p. 1DD.

Mead, M. (1961). *Cooperation and competition among primitive peoples*. Boston: Beacon.

Men more willingly accept women leaders. (1988, March 4). *The Wall Street Journal*, p. 31.

Metcalf, F. (1987). *The Penguin dictionary of modern humorous quotations*. New York: Penguin Books.

Michaelson, L. et al. (1989). A realistic test of individual versus group consensus decision making. *Journal of Applied Psychology*, 74, 834–839.

Michener, J. (1971). *Kent State: What happened and why*. New York: Random House.

Milgram, S. (1974). *Obedience to authority*. New York: Harper and Row.

Miller, C. (1989). The social psychological effects of group decision rules. In P. Paulus (Ed.), *Psychology of group influence*. Hillsdale, NJ: Lawrence Erlbaum.

Miller, K., & Monge, P. (1986). Participation, satisfaction, and productivity: A meta-analytic review. *Academy of Management Journal*, 29, 727–753.

Miranda, S. (1994). Avoidance of groupthink: Meeting management using Group Support Systems. *Small Groups Research*, 25, 105–36.

Misra, R. (1980). *The social stratification and linguistic diversity of the Bhojpuri speech community*. Unpublished doctoral dissertation. University of Poona.

Moghaddam, F. et al. (1993). *Social psychology in cross-cultural perspective*. New York: W. H. Freeman.

Mongeau, P. (1993, February 15). *The brainstorming myth*. Paper presented at the Western States Communication Association Conference, Albuquerque, NM.

Moody, F. (1996, June/July). Wonder woman in the rude boys' paradise. *Fast Company*, 12–14.

Moorhead, G., & Montanari, J. (1986). An empirical investigation of the groupthink phenomenon. *Human Relations*, 39, 399–410.

Moreland, R., & Levine, J. (1987). Group dynamics over time: Development and socialization in small groups. In J. McGrath (Ed.), *The social psychology of time*. Beverly Hills, CA: Sage.

Moriarty, T. (1975, April). A nation of willing victims. *Psychology Today*, 43–50.

Morreale, S. (1999, March). Ability to communicate ranked no. 1 by employers. *Spectra*, 35, p. 10.

Morrison, A., & Von Glinow, M. (1990, February). Women and minorities in management. *American Psychologist*, 200–208.

Moscovici, S., & Mugny, G. (1983). Minority influence. In P. Paulus (Ed.), *Basic group processes*. New York: Springer-Verlag.

Motley, M. (1995). *Overcoming your fear of public speaking: A proven method*. New York: McGraw-Hill.

Moving forward, but still behind. (1999, June 7). *Newsweek*, 32–33.

Mudrack, P., & Farrell, G. (1995). An examination of functional role behavior and its consequences for individuals in group settings. *Small Group Research*, 26, 542–571.

Muir, J. (1992). *C-Span in the communication classroom*. Annandale, VA: Speech Communication Association.

Mulac, A., & Bradac, J. (1995). Women's style in problem solving interaction: Powerless, or simply feminine? In P. Kalbfleisch & M. Cody (Eds.), *Gender, power, and communication in human relationships*, Hillsdale, NJ: Lawrence Erlbaum.

Mullen, B. (1994). Group cohesiveness and quality of decision making. *Small Group Research*, 25, 189–204.

Murnighan, J. (1978). Models of coalition formation: Game theoretic, social psychological, and political perspectives. *Psychological Bulletin*, 85, 1130–1153.

Narcisco, J., & Burkett, T. (1975). *Declare yourself*. Englewood Cliffs, NJ: Prentice-Hall.

Neale, M. et al. (1988). *Joint effects of goal setting and expertise on negotiator behavior*. Unpublished manuscript, Northwestern University, Evanston, IL.

Nelson, J. (1999, October 6). Carter seeks pardon for newspaper heiress. *San Jose Mercury News*, p. 3B.

Nelson, M. (1998). *Embracing victory: Life lessons in competition and compassion*. New York: William Morrow & Company.

New rulers aren't sure what's next. (1988, December 12). *San Jose Mercury News*, p. 1A.

Nicotera, A., & Rancer, A. (1994). The influence of sex on self-perception and social stereotyping of aggressive communication predispositions. *Western Journal of Communication*, 58, 283–307.

Nisbett, R., & Ross, L. (1980). *Human inference: Strategies and shortcomings of social judgment*. Englewood Cliffs, NJ: Prentice-Hall.

Noe, R. (1988). Women and mentoring. *Academy of Management Review*, 13, 65–78.

Northouse, P. (1997). *Leadership: Theory and practice*. Thousand Oaks, CA: Sage.

O'Brien, T. (1995, November 5). No jerks allowed. *West*, 8–26.

O'Leary, K., Curley, A., & Clark, C. (1985). Assertion training for abused wives: A potentially hazardous treatment. *Journal of Marital and Family Therapy*, 11, 319–322.

Ogilvie, B., & Tutko, T. (1971, October). Sport: If you want to build character, try something else. *Psychology Today*, 61–63.

Orlick, T. (1978). *Winning through cooperation: Competitive insanity, cooperative alternatives*. Washington, DC: Acropolis Books.

Osgood, C. (1959). Suggestions for winning the real war with communism. *Journal of Conflict Resolution*, 3, 295–325.

Osgood, C. (1966). *Perspective in foreign policy*. Palo Alto, CA: Pacific Books.

Parks, C., & Vu, A. (1994). Social dilemma of individuals from highly individualist and collectivist cultures. *Journal of Conflict Resolution*, 3, 708–718.

Paulus, P., Dzindolet, M., Poletes, G., & Camacho, M.L. (1993). Perceptions of performance in group brainstorming: The illusion of group productivity. *Personality and Social Psychology Bulletin*, 19, 78–89.

Pavitt, C., & Curtis, E. (1994). *Small group discussion*. Scottsdale, AZ: Gorsuch Scarisbrick.

Pear, R. (1999, March 15). Clinton seeks to protect whistle-blowers better. *San Jose Mercury News*, p. 4A.

Pearson, J., West, R., Turner, L. (1995). *Gender & communication*. Dubuque, IA: Wm. C. Brown.

Peterson, M. (1997). Personnel interviewers' perception of the importance and adequacy of applicants' communication skills. *Communication Education*, 46, 287–291.

Pettigrew, T., & Martin, J. (1987). Shaping the organizational context for black American inclusion. *Journal of Social Issues*, 43, 41–78.

Phillips, E., & Cheston, R. (1979). Conflict resolution: What works? *California Management Review*, 21, 76–83.

Philp, T. (1990, April 21). CSU leader resigns amid public furor. *San Jose Mercury News*, p. 1A.

Playing havoc with hormones. (1996, June 7). *San Jose Mercury News*, p. 14A

Plotz, D. (1997, August 30). Al Dunlap: The chainsaw capitalist. [On-line] Available: www.slate.com/Assessment/97–08–30/Assessment.asp.

Poll: More women than men say wives should stay home. (1993, September 20). *San Jose Mercury News*, p. 3A.

Poole, M. (1983). Decision development in small groups III: A multiple sequence model of group decision making. *Communication Monographs*, 50, 321–341.

Poole, M., & Roth, J. (1989a). Decision development in small groups IV: A typology of group decision paths. *Human Communication Research*, 15, 323–356.

Poole, M., & Roth, J. (1989b). Decision development in small groups V: Test of a contingency model. *Human Communication Research*, 15, 549–589.

Postman, N. (1976). *Crazy talk, stupid talk*. New York: Dell.

Praise thy employee, survey says. (1994, September 13). *San Jose Mercury News*, p. 1E.

Pratkanis, A., & Aronson, E. (1992). *The age of propaganda*. New York: W. H. Freeman & Company.

Pre-employment drug tests ground almost 20% in state. (1990, May 24). *San Jose Mercury News*, p. 1A.

Propp, K. (1995). An experimental examination of biological sex as a status cue in decision-making groups and its influence on information use. *Small Group Research*, 26, 451–474.

Prothrow-Stith, D. (1991). *Deadly consequences*. New York: HarperCollins.

Pruitt, D. (1981). *Negotiation behavior*. New York: Academic Press.

Pruitt, D., & Kimmel, M. (1977). Twenty years of experimental gaming: Critique, synthesis, and suggestions for the future. *Annual Review of Psychology*, 28, 363–392.

Pruitt, D., & Rubin, J. (1986). *Social conflict: Escalation, stalemate, and settlement*. New York: Random House.

Purdy, M. (1996, August 1). Don't bow to King Carl. *San Jose Mercury News*, p. 1D.

Put enjoyment ahead of achievement. (1994, February 20). *Santa Cruz Sentinel*, p. D2.

Putnam, L. (1986). Conflict in group decision-making. In R. Hirokawa, and M. Poole (Eds.), *Communication and group decision-making*, Beverly Hills, CA: Sage.

Quattrone, G., & Jones, E. (1980). The perception of variability within in-groups and out-groups: Implications for the law of small numbers. *Journal of Personality and Social Psychology*, 38, 141–152.

Rabbie, J. (1993). Determinants of ingroup cohesion and outgroup hostility. *International Journal of Group Tensions*, 23, 309–328.

Rahim, M. (1985). Referent role and styles of handling interpersonal conflict. *The Journal of Social Psychology*.

Ramirez, L. (1999, August 11). Report: Fewer students take firearms to school. *San Jose Mercury News*, p. 10A.

Raush, H. et al. (1974). *Communication, conflict, and marriage*. San Francisco: Jossey-Bass.

Read, P. (1974). Source of authority and the legitimation of leadership in small groups. *Sociometry*, 37, 189–204.

Reckman, R., & Goethals, G. (1973). Deviancy and group orientation as determinants of group composition preferences. *Sociometry, 36*, 419–423.

Report of the Commission on the space shuttle Challenger disaster. (1986). Washington, DC: Government Printing Office.

Riccillo, S., & Trenholm, S. (1983). Predicting managers' choice of influence mode: The effects of interpersonal trust and worker attributions on managerial tactics in a simulated organizational setting. *Western Journal of Speech, 47*, 323–339.

Ries, P., & Stone, A. (Eds.). (1992). *The American woman 1992–93: A status report*. New York: W. W. Norton.

Ritter, M. (1996, August 12). Sometimes nice guys really do get the girl. *San Jose Mercury News*, p. 1A.

Rogelberg, S., & Rumery, S. (1996). Gender diversity, team decision quality, time on task, and interpersonal cohesion. *Small Group Research, 27*, 79–90.

Rohlen, T. (1973). Spiritual education in a Japanese bank. *American Anthropologist, 75*, 1542–1562.

Rohrlich, T. (1993, April 23). On King jury: Bickering, tears and catharsis. *Seattle Times*, p. A1.

Rosenfeld, L. (1983). Communication climate and coping mechanisms in the college classroom. *Communication Education, 32*, 169–174.

Ross, H. (1984). Social control through deterrence: Drinking-and-driving laws. *Annual Review of Sociology, 10*, 21–35.

Ross, L., Amabile, T. M., & Steinmetz, J. L. (1977). Social roles, social control and biases in the social perception process. *Journal of Personality and Social Psychology, 35*, 485–494.

Ross, R. (1989). *Speech communication: The speechmaking system*. Englewood Cliffs, NJ: Prentice-Hall.

Rossman, J. (1931). *The psychology of the inventor*. Washington, DC: Inventors' Publishing Company.

Ruben, B. (1978). Communication and conflict: A system theoretic perspective. *The Quarterly Journal of Speech, 64*, 202–210.

Ruben, B. (1984). *Communication and human behavior*. New York: Macmillan.

Rubenstein, M. (1975). *Patterns of problem solving*. Englewood Cliffs, NJ: Prentice-Hall.

Ruggiero, V. R. (1988). *The art of thinking: A guide to critical and creative thought*. New York: Harper & Row.

Salazar, A. (1995). Understanding the synergistic effects of communication in small groups. *Small Group Research, 26*, 169–199.

Samovar, L., & Porter, R. (1995). *Communication between cultures*. Belmont, CA: Wadsworth.

Samuelson, R. (1999, March 22). Why I am not a manager. *Newsweek*, 47.

Sandoval, R. (1998, July 7). Misery knows no borders. *San Jose Mercury News*, pp. 1C, 4C.

Sao Paulo tries to stop police from killing suspects, civilians. (1996, August 1). *Santa Cruz Sentinel*, p. A10.

Schachter, S. (1951). Deviation, rejection, and communication. *Journal of Abnormal and Social Psychology, 46*, 190–207.

Schachter, S. (1959). *The psychology of affiliation*. Stanford, CA: Stanford University Press.

Scheer, R. (1983). *With enough shovels: Reagan, Bush and nuclear war*. New York: Vintage Books.

Schindehette, S., & Kelley, J. (1990, February 5). After the verdict, solace for none. *People*, 70–80.

Schittekatte, M., & Van Hiel, A. (1996). Effects of partially shared information and awareness of unshared information on information sampling. *Small Group Research, 27*, 431–449.

Schmidt, S., & Kipnis, D. (1987, November). The perils of persistence. *Psychology Today*, 32–34.

Schultz, B., Ketrow, S., & Urban, D. (1995). Improving decision quality in the small group: The reminder role. *Small Group Research, 26*, 521–541.

Schuster, M. (1984). The scanlon plan: A longitudinal analysis. *Journal of Applied Behavioral Science, 20*, 23–28.

Schwartz, S. (1990). Individualism-collectivism: Critique and proposed refinements. *Journal of Cross-cultural Psychology, 21*, 139–157.

Seligman, J., & Murr, A. (1993, April 12). A town's divided loyalties. *Newsweek*, 29.

Sexism prevails in law schools, bar study finds. (1996, February 4). *Santa Cruz Sentinel*, p. A7.

Shaw, M. (1981). *Group dynamics: The psychology of small group behavior*. New York: McGraw-Hill.

Shenk, D. (1997). *Data smog: Surviving the information glut*. New York: HarperCollins.

Sheridan, C., & King, R. (1972). Obedience to authority with an authentic victim. *Proceedings of the 80th Annual Convention, American Psychological Association, 7*, 165–166.

Sherif, M. (1966). *In common predicament*. New York: Houghton Mifflin.

Sherif, M. et al. (1988). *The Robbers Cave Experiment*. Middletown, CT: Wesleyan University Press.

Shimanoff, S. (1992). Group interaction via communication rules. In R. Cathcart & L. Samovar (Eds.), *Small group communication: A reader*. Dubuque, IA: Wm. C. Brown.

Shimanoff, S., & Jenkins, M. (1996). Leadership and gender: Challenging assumptions and recognizing resources. In R. Cathcart, L. Samovar, & L. Henman (Eds.), *Small group communication: Theory and practice*. Dubuque, IA: Brown & Benchmark.

Shirley, D. (1997). Managing creativity: Inventing, developing, and producing innovative products. [On-line]. Available: http://www.managingcreativity.com.

Sieburg, E., & Larson, C. (1971). Dimensions of interpersonal response. Paper presented to the International Communication Association, Phoenix, AZ.

Sigall, H., & Ostrove, N. (1975). Beautiful but dangerous: Effects of offender attractiveness and the nature of the crime on juridical judgment. *Journal of Personality and Social Psychology*, 31, 410–414.

Simons, L. (1989, June 19). China's effort to control minds. *San Jose Mercury News*, p. 1A.

Simons, L., & Zielenziger, M. (1996, March 3). Culture clash dims U.S. future in Asia. *San Jose Mercury News*, p. 1A.

Sims, R. (1992). Linking groupthink to unethical behavior in organizations. *Journal of Business Ethics*, 11, 651–662.

Singer, M. (1995). *Cults in our midst: The hidden menace in our everyday lives*. San Francisco: Jossey-Bass.

Smith, M. (1982). *Persuasion and human interaction: A review and critique of social influence theories*. Belmont, CA: Wadsworth.

Smith, P. (1990). *Killing the spirit: Higher education in America*. New York: Viking.

Smith-Hefner, N. (1988). Women and politeness: the Javanese example. *Language in Society*, 17, 535–554.

Sorensen, S. (1981, May). *Grouphate*. Paper presented at the International Communication Association, Minneapolis, MN.

Spitzberg, B., & Cupach, W. (1989). *Handbook of interpersonal competence research*. New York: Springer-Verlag.

Spitzberg, B., & Hecht, M. (1984). A component model of relational competence. *Human Communication Research*, 10, 575–599.

Sproull, L., & Kiesler, S. (1991). *Connections: New ways of working in the networked organization*. Cambridge, MA: MIT Press.

Stahelski, A., & Tsukada, R. (1990). Predictors of cooperation in health care teams. *Small Group Research*, 21, 220–233.

Stanovich, K. (1992). *How to think straight about psychology*. New York: HarperCollins.

Starr, M., & Brant, M. (1999, July 19). It went down to the wire . . . and thrilled us all. *Newsweek*, 46–54.

Stasser, G., & Titus, W. (1987). Effects of information load and percentage of shared information during group discussion. *Journal of Personality and Social Psychology*, 53, 81–93.

Stasson, M., & Bradshaw, S. (1995). Explanations of individual-group performance differences: What sort of bonus can be gained through group interaction? *Small Group Research*, 26, 296–308.

Stern, A. (1992, May). Why good managers approve bad ideas. *Working Women*, 104.

Stewart, J. (Ed.). (1986). *Bridges not walls*. New York: Random House.

Stewart, L., Cooper, P. J., Stewart, A. D., & Friedley, S. (1996). *Communication and gender*. Scottsdale, AR: Gorsuch Scarisbrick.

Stockman, D. (1986). *The triumph of politics: The inside story of the Reagan revolution*. New York: Avon.

Stogdill, R. (1972). Group productivity, drive, and cohesiveness. *Organizational Behavior and Human Performance*, 8, 26–43.

Stone, D., Patton, B., & Heen, S. (1999). *Difficult conversations: How to discuss what matters most*. New York: Viking Press.

Straus, M., & Sweet, S. (1992). Verbal/symbolic aggression in couples: Incidence rates and relationship to personal characteristics. *Journal of Marriage and the Family*, 54, 346–357.

Straw strategy. (1999, August 17). *San Jose Mercury News*, p. 6B.

Street, M. (1997). Groupthink: An examination of theoretical issues, implications, and future research suggestions. *Small Group Research*, 28, 72–93.

Study finds fewer female lawmakers. (1995, February 12). *San Jose Mercury News*, p. 10A.

Study shows women are gaining parity with men at work. (1997, January 3). *The Maui News*, p. B8.

Study's verdict: Law schools still sexist. (1996, February 3). *San Jose Mercury News*, p. 9A.

Sundell, W. (1972). *The operation of confirming and disconfirming verbal behavior in selected teacher-student interactions*. Doctoral dissertation, University of Denver.

Sundstrom, E. et al. (1990, February). Work teams: Applications and effectiveness. *American Psychologist*, 120–133.

Sutton, C., & Moore, K. (1985). Executive women—20 years later. *Harvard Business Review*, 63, 43–66.

Swoboda, F. (1999, February 14). Judge fines pilots union. *San Jose Mercury News*, pp. 1A, 28A.

Sykes, C. (1988). *Profscam: Professors and the demise of higher education*. Washington, DC: Regnery.

Szasz, T. (1980). *Sex by prescription*. New York: Penguin Books.

Tang, S., & Kirkbride, P. (1986). Developing conflict management skills in Hong Kong: An analysis of some cross-cultural implications. *Management Education and Development*, 17, 287–301.

Tannen, D. (1990). *You just don't understand: Women and men in conversation*. New York: Ballantine Books.

Tannen, D. (1994). *Talking from 9 to 5: Women and men in the workplace: language, sex, and power*. New York: Avon Books.

Taps, J., & Martin, P. (1990). Gender composition, attributional accounts, and women's influence and likability in task groups. *Small Group Research*, 21, 471–491.

Tavris, C. (1989). *Anger: The misunderstood emotion*. New York: Simon & Schuster.

Tavris, C. (1992). *The mismeasure of women*. New York: Simon & Schuster.

Teal, T. (1996, November 11). Not a fool, not a saint. *Fortune*.

The criticism that hurts. (1989, March). *Psychology Today*, 16.

They're still on top. (1995, November 25). *San Jose Mercury News*, p. 4A.

Tjosvold, D. (1986). *Working together to get things done*. Lexington, MA: Lexington Books.

Toulmin, S., Rieker, R., & Janik, A. (1979). *An introduction to reasoning*. New York: Macmillan.

Townsend, P. (1999, April 18). Dealing with difficult people. *Santa Cruz Sentinel*, pp. 1C, 2C.

Townsend, P. (1999, May 23). Some students watch the "in crowd" from afar. *Santa Cruz Sentinel*, pp. A1, A8–9.

Trenholm, S., & Jensen, A. (1988). *Interpersonal communication*. Belmont, CA: Wadsworth.

Triandis, H. (1990). Cross-cultural studies of individualism and collectivism. In J. Berman (Ed.), *Cross-cultural perspectives*. Lincoln, NE: University of Nebraska Press, 41–133.

Tubbs, S. (1984). *A systems approach to small group interaction*. Reading, MA: Addison-Wesley.

Tubbs, S., & Carter, R. (1977). *Shared experiences in human communication*. Rochelle Park, NJ: Hayden.

Tuckman, B. (1965). Developmental sequences in small groups. *Psychological Bulletin*, 63, 384–399.

Tutzauer, F., & Roloff, M. (1988). Communication processes leading to integrative agreements: Three paths to joint benefits. *Communication Research*, 5, 360–380.

TV or not TV. (1993, April 19). *San Jose Mercury News*, p. 5E.

Tversky, A., & Kahneman, D. (1981, June 30). The framing of decisions and the psychology of choice. *Science*, 453–458.

U.S. Department of Labor. (1991). *Skills and the new economy*. Washington, DC: U.S. Government Printing Office.

Uba, L., & Huang, K. (1999). *Psychology*. New York: Longman.

Unsafe sex in gang rites alleged. (1993, April 27). *San Jose Mercury News*, p. 4A

Uranium crew was unaware of atomic risks. (1999, October 23). *San Jose Mercury News*, p. 15A.

Ury, W. (1993). *Getting past no: Negotiating your way from confrontation to cooperation*. New York: Bantam Books.

Valacich, J., Dennis, A. R., & Connolly, T. (1994). Idea generation in computer-based groups: A new ending to an old story. *Organizational Behavior and Human Decisions Processes*, 57, 448–467.

Valdez, C. (1983, November 1). Cults focus on identity search. *Western Front*, p. 7.

Van Oostrum, J., & Rabbie, J. (1995). Intergroup competition and cooperation within autocratic and democratic management regimes. *Small Group Research*, 26, 269–295.

Vangelisti, A., Knapp, M., & Daly, J. (1990). Conversational narcissism. *Communication Mongraphs*, 57, 251–274.

Veitch, M. (1997, December 8). Data overload causing addiction—Reuters. [On-line] Available: www.zdnet.co.uk/news/news1/ns-3381.html.

Ventura: Keillor book "cheating." (1999, February 6). *San Jose Mercury News*, p. A2.

Villasenor, V. (1977). *Jury: The people vs. Juan Corona*. Boston: Little, Brown & Company.

Wachtel, P. (1983). *The poverty of affluence: A psychological portrait of the American way of life*. New York: Free Press.

Wacky life forms are pursuing E. T. exile. (1996, June 21). *San Jose Mercury News*, p. 4A.

Wade, C., & Tavris, C. (1998). *Psychology*. New York: HarperCollins.

Wanous, J. (1980). *Organizational entry: Recruitment, selection, and socialization of newcomers*. Reading, MA: Addison-Wesley.

Ward, E. et al. (1986). *Rock of ages: The Rolling Stone history of rock and roll*. New York: Rolling Stone Press.

Warnemunde, D. (1986). The status of the introductory small group communication course. *Communication Education*, 10, 389–396.

Wasserman, E. (1996, July 28). Out from under the glass ceiling. *San Jose Mercury News*, p. 1A.

Waters, H. (1990, March 26). If it ain't broke, break it. *Newsweek*, 58–59.

Watson, C. (1988). When a woman is the boss: Dilemmas in taking charge. *Group and Organizational Studies*, 13, 163–181.

Watson, R., Wehrfritz, G., & Hayden, T. (1999, October 11). Can it happen here? *Newsweek*, 44–47.

Watzlawick, P. et al. (1967). *Pragmatics of human communication*. New York: W. W. Norton.

Watzlawick, P. et al. (1974). *Change: Principles of problem formation and problem resolution*. New York: W. W. Norton.

Wayne, M. S. (1974). The meaning of silence in conversations in three cultures. In International Christian University Communication Student Group (Ed.), *Patterns of communication in and out of Japan*. Tokyo: ICU Communication Department.

Wech, B., Mossholder, K., Streel, R., & Bennett, N. (1998). Does work group cohesiveness afflict individuals' performance and organizational commitment? *Small Group Research*, 29, 472–494.

Weick, K. (1990). The vulnerable system: An analysis of the Tenerife air disaster. *Journal of Management*, 16, 571–593.

Weiner, M., & Wright, F. (1973). Effects of undergoing arbitrary discrimination upon subsequent attitudes towards a minority group. *Journal of Applied Social Psychology*, 3, 94–102.

Wen, P. (1999, July 8). Search is on for low-tech refuge from high-tech life. *Santa Cruz Sentinel*, p. D1.

Wetzel, P. (1988). Are powerless communication strategies the Japanese norm? *Language in Society*, 17, 555–564.

Whistle-blowers claim humiliating retaliation. (1989, August 6). *San Jose Mercury News*, p. 11A.

Whitchurch, G., & Pace, J. (1993). Communication skills training and interspousal violence. *Journal of Applied Communication*, 21, 96–102.

Whitkin, R. (1987, September 19). FAA says Delta had poor policies on crew training. *New York Times*, p. 1.

Who's keeping score? (1999, September 13). *Newsweek*, 56.

Who's the hot group in '96? The Beatles. (1996, October 23). *San Jose Mercury News*, p. 4A.

Wilmot, W., & Hocker, J. (1998). *Interpersonal conflict*. New York: McGraw-Hill.

Wilson, G., and Hanna, M. (1990). *Groups in context*. New York: Random House.

Wolf, N. (1994). *Fire with fire: The new female power and how to use it*. New York: Fawcett Columbine.

Wolf, S. (1979). Behavioral style and group cohesiveness as sources of minority influence. *European Journal of Social Psychology*, 9, 381–95.

Wolkomir, R., & Wolkomir, J. (1990, February). How to make smart choices. *Reader's Digest*, pp. 27–32.

Wood, J. (1997). *Gendered lives: Communication, gender, and cultures*. Belmont, CA: Wadsworth.

Wood, J. et al. (1986). *Group discussion: A practical guide to participation and leadership*. New York: Harper & Row.

Woodward, B., & Armstrong, S. (1979). *The brethren: Inside the Supreme Court*. New York: Simon & Schuster.

Wooley, S., Switzer, T. G., Foster, G. C., Landes, N. M., & Robertson, W. C. (1990, April). BSCS cooperative learning and science program. *Cooperative Learning*, 32–33.

Wooton, J. (1993, September 13). Lessons of Pop Jordan's death. *Newsweek*, 12.

Wright, R. (1993, July 1). Women are taking center stage in the worldwide political arena. *San Jose Mercury News*, p. 10A.

Wurman, R. (1989). *Information anxiety*. New York: Doubleday.

Yoshitake, D. (1996, August 5). Even hackers try support groups. *San Jose Mercury News*, p. A7.

Young, F. (1965). *Initiation ceremonies*. New York: Bobbs-Merrill.

Youngs, G. (1986). Patterns of threat and punishment reciprocity in a conflict setting. *Journal of Personality and Social Psychology*, 51, 541–546.

Yu, X. (1998). The Chinese "native" perspective on Mao-dun (conflict) and Mao-dun resolution strategies: A qualitative investigation. *Intercultural Communication Studies*, 7, 63–82.

Zander, A. (1982). The psychology of removing group members and recruiting new ones. *Human Relations*, 29, 1–8.

Zielenziger, M., & Lubman, S. (1999, October 3). Japan's dislike of quick action proves costly. *San Jose Mercury News*, pp. 1A, 20A.

Zimbardo, P. (1992, 1988). *Psychology and life*. Glenview, IL: Scott, Foresman.

Literary Credits

Brecher, Elinor. "Furor Over Florida Rape Case Clouds Disturbing Faces," *Seattle Times*, December 15, 1989, pp. B1–B2. Copyright © 1989 by Elinor Brecher. Reprinted with permission of the Miami Herald.

Fisher, B. and Ellis, D. *Small Group Decision Making*, 3rd edition by B. Fisher and D. Ellis. Copyright © 1990. Reprinted by permission of the McGraw-Hill Companies.

Fisher, R., Ury, W., and Patton, B. Excerpts from *Getting to Yes*, 2nd edition by Roger Fisher, William Ury, and Bruce Patton. Copyright © 1981, 1991 by Roger Fisher and William Ury. Reprinted by permission of Houghton Mifflin Company. All rights reserved.

Gibb, Jack "Defensive Communication," *Journal of Communication*, Vol. 11, 141–148, 1961. Copyright © 1961 by *Journal of Communication*. Reprinted by permission of Oxford University Press.

Hersey, Paul and Blanchard, Kenneth H. *Management of Organizational Behavior*, 5th edition, © 1988, pp. 287 & 175. Reprinted by permission of Center for Leadership Studies, Inc., Escondido, CA. Situational Leadership® is a registered trademark for the Center for Leadership Studies, Inc. All rights reserved.

Hirokawa, R. "Why Informed Groups Make Faulty Decisions," *Small Group Behavior*, February 1987, Vol.18, No. 1, pp. 17–18, 22. Copyright © 1987 by R. Hirokawa. Reprinted by permission of Sage Publications, Inc.

Janis, Irving L. *Groupthink*, pp. 9, 142, 175, © 1982 by Houghton Mifflin Company.

Villasenor, Victor. From *Jury: The People vs. Juan Corona* by Victor Villasenor. Copyright © 1977 by Victor Edmundo Villasenor. By permission of Little, Brown and Company.

Photo Credits

Chapter 1: p. 12, © AP/Wide World Photos; p. 13, © Reuters/Rick Wilking/Archive Photos; p. 20, © Michael Newman/PhotoEdit. **Chapter 2:** p. 27, © Kent Reno/Jeoboam, Inc.; p. 28, Courtesy, The History Museums of San Jose; p. 30, © Associated Press/AP/Wide World Photos; p. 36, © John Berry/The Gamma Liaison Network; p. 36, © Woodstock/Gamma Liaison; p. 39, © Associated Press/AP/Wide World Photos; p. 46, The Everett Collection, New York. **Chapter 3:** p. 54, © MTV Networks/The Everett Collection, New York; p. 57, © Archive Photos; p. 66, © AP/Wide World Photos; p. 66, © AP/Wide World Photos; p. 75, © Jeff Greenberg/PhotoEdit. **Chapter 4:** p. 85, © Steve Takatsuijo/Jeroboam, Inc.; p. 85, © 1985 Bob Clay/Jeroboam, Inc.; p. 86, © Robert Maass/Sipa Press; p. 87, © Steve Malone/Jeroboam, Inc.; p. 90, © Alan Berliner/Liaison Agency; p. 90, © Amy Sancetta/Associated Press/AP/Wide World Photos; p. 100, © Julie Lopez/Habitat for Humanity International. **Chapter 5:** p. 121, © Philip G. Zimbardo; p. 134, © Associated Press/Ken Levine/AP/Wide World Photos; p. 138, © Laura Ranch/AP/Wide World Photos; p. 138, © Corbis/Bettmann; p. 138, © Brad Market/The Gamma Liaison Network; p. 138, © Corbis - Bettmann; p. 140, © UPI/Corbis-Bettmann; p. 140, © AP/Wide World Photos; p. 140, © Channel 9 Australia/Gamma Liaison; p. 140, © AP Photo/APTV/AP/Wide World Photos. **Chapter 6:** p. 155, © Amy C. Etra/PhotoEdit; p. 162, © Corbis-Bettmann; p. 170, © Dan Coyro/Santa Cruz Sentinel; p. 176, © George Kochaniec/Denver Rocky Mountain News; p. 176, © AP Photo/Gary Tramontina/AP/Wide World Photos; p. 180, © Archive Photos. **Chapter 7:** p. 198, © ATC Productions/The Stock Market; p. 199, © 1995 Danny Lyon/Magnum Photos, Inc.; p. 202, © Reuters/Eriko Sugaita/Archive Photos. **Chapter 8:** p. 234, © Joseph Schuyler/Stock Boston; p. 239, © Vittoriano Rastelli/Corbis-Bettmann; p. 241, © Kay Lawson/Jeroboam, Inc.; p. 249, © Amy Etra/PhotoEdit. **Chapter 9:** p. 255, © Associated Press/Jeff Widener/AP/Wide World Photos; p. 260, © AP/Wide World Photos; p. 260, © AP/Wide World Photos; p. 263, © AFP/Corbis-Bettmann; p. 271, © The Boston Globe. **Chapter 10:** p. 301, © Bruce Ayres/Tony Stone Images; p. 312, The Everett Collection, New York.

Author Index

Subject Index